ARTIFICIAL INTELLIGENCE IN
ECONOMICS AND MANAGEMENT

ARTIFICIAL INTELLIGENCE IN ECONOMICS AND MANAGEMENT

edited by

L. F. PAU
Battelle Memorial Institute
Carouge
Switzerland

NORTH-HOLLAND
AMSTERDAM • NEW YORK • OXFORD • TOKYO

ISBN: 0 444 87961 7

First edition: 1986
Second edition: 1987

Publishers:
ELSEVIER SCIENCE PUBLISHERS B.V.
P.O. Box 1991
1000 BZ Amsterdam
The Netherlands

Sole distributors for the U.S.A. and Canada:
ELSEVIER SCIENCE PUBLISHING COMPANY, INC.
52 Vanderbilt Avenue
New York, N.Y. 10017
U.S.A.

Library of Congress Cataloging-in-Publication Data
Main entry under title:

Artificial intelligence in economics and management.

A collection of some of the papers written after the International Workshop on Artificial Intelligence in Econmics and Management, held Mar. 12-14, 1985 in Zurich, Switzerland, whose main sponsor was IFAC.
Includes bibliographies and index.
1. Economics--Data processing--Congresses. 2. Management--Data processing--Congresses. 3. Artificial intelligence--Congresses. 4. Expert systems (Computer science)--Congresses. I. Pau, L.-F. (Louis-François), 1948- . II. International Workshop on Artificial Intelligence in Economics and Management (1985 : Zurich, Switzerland) III. International Federation of Automatic Control.
HB143.5.A78 1986 330'.028'563 85-31139
ISBN 0-444-87961-7

PRINTED IN THE NETHERLANDS

PREFACE
ARTIFICIAL INTELLIGENCE IN ECONOMICS AND MANAGEMENT: WHY ?

L.F. PAU

Battelle Institute
7, route de Drize
CH - 1227 Carouge
Switzerland

1. GENERAL INTRODUCTION

Artificial intelligence (AI), that is:

- knowledge based/expert systems (KBS)
- natural language analysis
- search, inference and planning procedures

has recently experienced significant progress in research and implementation. Economists, banks, financial services, as well as management departments, are paying increase attention to this surge of activity; they realize that the AI field can have far-reaching consequences for their own activities (see below). As a result, questions are being asked and issues raised, such as:

- how will AI developments affect currently used methods or procedures ?
- do these developments represent real breakthroughs and hence significant opportunities ?
- which are the limitations and areas for further research ?
- what applications are possible in economic analysis, finance, banking and management ?

At the same time, very few AI researchers have sofar ventured into economic or management problems, and even fewer economists have received training to start investigating the potential of AI techniques. All felt isolated from other researchers with similar interests.

This is the justification for the initiative taken to organize the International Workshop on artificial intelligence in economics and management, with the International Federation of Automatic control (IFAC) as main sponsor. The workshop was held March 12 - 14, 1985 in Zürich, Switzerland, and attended by more than 140 persons. Especially the authors enjoyed this first opportunity to meet.

This volume is a collection of some of the papers written by the workshop authors after the event.

2. ARTIFICIAL INTELLIGENCE AND KNOWLEDGE-BASED SYSTEMS

Artificial Intelligence is the branch of computer science that focuses on developing computer programs that can perform tasks normally associated with intelligent human behavior.

A knowledge-based system is a computer program that uses knowledge and problem-solving techniques on a skill level comparable to those of human experts. These systems consist of a knowledge base containing facts, rules, heuristics, and situation patterns, and an inference system that makes decisions within a domain. Recent applications of KBS have demonstrated potential to achieve a high level of human performance, while preserving knowledge that otherwise could be lost by attrition, retirement, or death.

The essential components of such systems can be depicted by the following diagram.

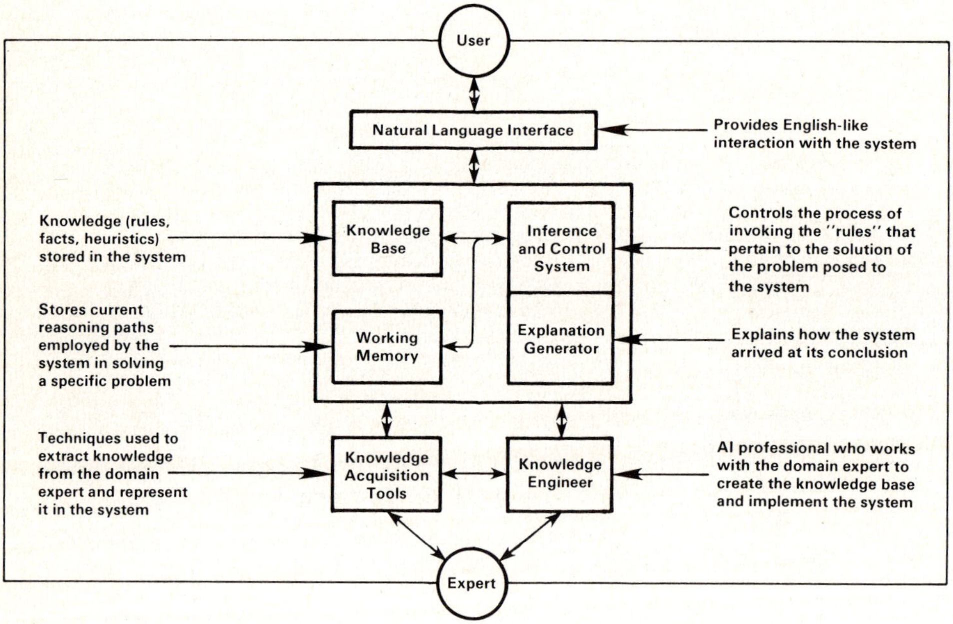

KBS differ from conventional software systems, such as decision support packages, in that they use symbolic manipulations rather than numeric calculations in carrying out their tasks. More important, they can handle uncertainty or other situations where a strictly numerical solution would be difficult or impossible to achieve.

Because the performance of KBS is based on symbol manipulation, these systems are generally programmed in a symbol-processing language such as LISP or PROLOG. These languages are usually embedded in a powerful development environment that allows for easy debugging and rapid prototyping of new systems. These programming tools provide for a high level of productivity during software development. The increase in the availability of such tools, including powerful LISP processors and AI software development tools, is one of the fundamental reasons for the surge in AI activity.

The growing interest in KBS is attributable to the many potential benefits they can provide, including:

. The ability to codify human expertise permanently

. Wider accessibility to that precious expertise

. A second opinion to that of a practicing expert

. The opportunity to explore "what if..." situations with different types of inputs

. The ability to handle uncertainty when data are incomplete

. The ability to solve problems that have extremely large sets of possible solutions to explore.

Further, KBS have several significant capabilities that most computer programs lack, including explanation of reasoning, handling information at a conceptual level, use of sophisticated search strategies.

Because conventional computer programs use algorithms (step-by-step plans), a KBS can help when a problem does not fit into an algorithmic solution strategy. Knowledge-based systems also allow us to separate knowledge from the procedures for using it. Thus, enhancing a KBS is easier than modifying a conventional system.

The main drawbacks of KBS include the shortage of qualified AI practitioners needed to build them, the potential complexity and hence magnitude of the development effort, and the relative cost of specialized AI hardware and software tools required.

Despite these drawbacks, the advantages and benefits of KBS will sometimes outweigh any disadvantages. In addition, as major vendors enter the specialty AI hardware market, the cost of development equipment will fall rapidly. Knowledge-based systems will move within the reach of a much larger community of users. The banking, management, financial services industry is an especially fertile market for applying this technology. Indeed, a number of large firms are already taking decisive steps in exploring how KBS can be utilized in their businesses. Strategies for seeking ways to exploit KBS deserve high priority.

3. POTENTIAL APPLICATIONS

There is a broad range of possible applications for AI based systems, many of them being at this stage only untested ideas or concepts.

Many of these were put forward during the panel sessions held during the above mentioned workshop:

Panel A: AI in decision support systems

Panel B: AI education for economists and managers

Panel C: AI in public services

Panel D: Methodology and basic research on AI, pattern recognition, and man-machine interfaces

Panel E: AI in banking, finance and accounting

Panel F: AI in policy analysis.

The following list describes only a few possible uses, some of which are further analyzed by dedicated papers in this volume:

- Multiple criteria budget analysis
- KBS to configure an econometric model prior to estimation
- Diagnostics of econometric models
- KBS to evaluate alternative forecasts wrt qualitative selection criteria or policy goals
- Integration of scenarios with econometric models; judgmental forecasts combined with model-based forecasts
- Processing commercial loan applications
- Options and currency trading
- Providing commercial customer advice, e.g. lease vs purchase of capital goods
- Analysis of investment partofolios, e.g. advice on accounting for yield, risk, liquidity and security; screening for securities, options, etc...
- Consumer banking, e.g. advice on retirement savings, credit lines, etc...
- Terminal based services: resolution of accounts, enhanced brokerage services, instant loan, cash-management
- Insurance analysis, e.g. designing and selecting an insurance program
- Screens for insurance claims: social security, casualty coverage, etc...
- Intelligent word processors, with knowledge based retrieval and filing functions
- Selection of new products and services
- Manufacturing planning and scheduling
- Project planning and scheduling
- Security or document access screens
- Strategy analysis in international politics and business
- Policy analysis: crisis warning
- Knowledge based filing of past cases and judgments in law.

4. CONCLUSION

There is still a long way to go, though, as the human resources, as well as software tools needed are not yet fully available.

Most importantly, there is not yet a basis for comparison with more traditional notions. This is why future research and implementations will be real challenges.

ACKNOWLEDGEMENTS

INTERNATIONAL PROGRAM COMMITTEE FOR THE WORKSHOP AND REVIEWERS

L.F. PAU (CH), Chairman
S. AIDA (J)
J.P. ANTUN (Mexico)
J. CLIFFORD (USA)
E.J. DAVISON (CDN) (IFAC-Theory)
J. Mc DERMOTT (USA)
P. DEVIJVER (B) (IAPR)
H. DONALDSON (UK)
G. FEICHTINGER (Austria)
T. HERBORD NIELSEN (DK)
H.J. LUEHTI (CH) (IFORS)
O. MORAVCIK (CS)
K. MORIK (FRG)
J. MYLOPOULOS (Canada)
B. NEUMANN (FRG)
T. NISHIDA (J)
H.E. POPLE (USA)
A.H.G. RINNOOY KAN (NL) (MPS)
W. SCHAUFELBERGER (CH) (IFAC-SECOM)
H.J. SCHNEIDER (FRG)
L. STEELS (B) (ECCAI)
P.A. TINSLEY (USA)
T.L. WILLIAMS (USA)
A.B. WHINSTON (USA)

WORKSHOP SPONSORS

ORGANIZER

Swiss Association of Automatic Control (SGA/ASSPA)

SPONSORS

* International Federation of Automatic Control (IFAC) (sponsor)
  - Economic and Management Systems Committee (main sponsor)
  - Theory Committee
  - Social Effects Committee
  - Systems Committee
* International Federation of Operations Research Societies (IFORS) (co-sponsor)
* International Federation of Information Processing (IFIP) (co-sponsor)

WITH THE PARTICIPATION OF:

* ECCAI: European Coordinating Committee for Artificial Intelligence
* Association for Computer Machinery
* IEEE Computer Society (IEEE-CS)
* Institute of Electrical and Electronics Engineers (IEEE Region 8)
* International Association for Pattern Recognition (IAPR)
* Mathematical Programming Society (MPS)
* Battelle Memorial Institute (BMI)

AND THE SUPPORT OF

Union Bank of Switzerland

CONTENTS

Artificial Intelligence in Economics and Management
L.F. Pau (Editor)

ARTIFICIAL INTELLIGENCE IN ECONOMICS--EXPERT SYSTEMS MODELLING OF MICROECONOMIC SYSTEMS

Elizabeth Hoffman
Purdue University

James R. Marsden
University of Arizona and
University of Kentucky

V. S. Jacob
Purdue University

Andrew Whinston
Purdue University

Expert systems provide a means to overcome the limitations of pure mathematical modelling of microeconomic systems. In addition, they can serve as data generators in analyses aimed at determining the impact of institutional changes or bidder strategy modifications. The present paper outlines these uses of expert systems, emphasizing the ability of expert systems to incorporate critical behavioral information and relationships.

I. INTRODUCTION

In attempts to avoid the limitations and problems inherent in naturally occurring data, economists have used detailed mathematical models or "process models" as data-generating tools (see Griffin [1972, 1974], Marsden, Pingry, and Whinston [1974a,b]). Data generation using process models involves repeated solution of economic optimization problems over varying parameters. The constraints for these optimization problems consist of mathematical representations of the relevant physical processes. Despite the advantages over naturally occurring data pointed out by the cited authors, there remains the serious limitation on the process model approach associated with the problem of adequately modelling complex human behavior within such a rigid mathematical framework.

Our purpose in the present paper is to suggest that the expert system framework can be used to generalize the process model approach resulting in a rule-based representation of microeconomic systems. As their name implies, expert systems have generally been constructed as a means for determining expert level solutions, usually to problems involving diagnosis, design, planning, or interpretation. Here, we suggest a different use for expert systems, highlighting their usefulness in modelling economic systems and as a data generating technique. With successful modelling, such generated data can provide an intriguing new means for testing economic theories and for studying the impact of proposed policy changes.

We focus on two major issues: 1) defining a rule-based representation scheme for process models, and 2) using such a representation for modelling and analyzing microeconomic systems. Because of required brevity, a third key issue, verification, is left for another time. Section II outlines the structure of process models and expert systems and presents our view of the expert system as a generalization of process models. Section III provides a characterization of a microeconomic system (following Smith [1982]) and our analysis of the appropriateness of modelling certain such systems as expert systems. Section IV contains auction market examples of the procedure we posit. This is followed by our summary and conclusions including suggested uses for our approach and brief comments on some ongoing work in model verification and application.

II. PROCESS MODELS, EXPERT SYSTEMS, AND THE LINKING FRAMEWORK

a. Process Models

Initially used by engineers to represent the physical process of production, process models have been adopted by economists to study economic issues in production. From early linear programming representations to more general mathematical programming representations, the process model approach has been focused on deriving useful implications from the rigor and accurate structure of the detailed mathematical model (see Chenery [1949], Tsao and Day [1971], and Bever, Marsden, Salas-Fumas, and Whinston [1982a,b]). But it is this very aspect of past process modelling that leads to the discomforting disadvantage that processes which cannot be mathematically represented cannot be modelled. This problem has major impact whenever one is attempting to model decision processes involving important behavioral aspects.

There is a second problem which arises with the traditional mathematical modelling representation scheme of process models. The solutions which generate the data are obtained using single valued criteria or objective functions. This conflicts with the multiple goals typical in behavioral decision problems.

b. Expert Systems

Expert systems have the common property with process models that they require detailed knowledge about the problem domain before they can be constructed. But in the expert system framework, one is not confined to a strictly mathematical representation for modelling the system under consideration. This aspect of expert systems has been exploited in numerous applications in the medical area, resulting in such systems as MYCIN (see Shortliffe [1976]), PUFF (see Aikens et al. [1984]), and others. The continued use and success of these systems illustrates the capability of expert systems to handle problems which are not mathematical by nature, a capability largely derived from the expert system's use of symbol manipulation for problem solving.

The power and versatility of the expert system stems from the separation of its three components: 1) knowledge about the problem domain, 2) information about the current problem or 'task specific' knowledge, and 3) the control strategy which manipulates the knowledge sets. This separation of the three components required for a computer-based solution enables solution of diverse problems within a given problem area and facilitates the extensive analyses of individual problems. The breadth of possibilities depends, of course, upon the comprehensiveness of the knowledge base, the collection of facts, and the heuristics, which represent the decision processes typically used by experts to solve problems. Though the domain knowledge can be represented in several ways (see Barr and Feigenbaum [1981]), we focus here on rule-based systems because of their convenience for describing economic systems. Rule-based expert systems evolved from a general class of computational models known as production models (see Newell and Simon [1972]). Following computation in the production system framework, rule-based expert system computation involves a process of applying transformation rules in a sequence determined by the task specific input data. Our concern here is the form of representation and its advantages for our analysis. For details on production systems and their use in artificial intelligence, see Newell and Simon [1972], Waterman and Hayes Roth [1978], and Davis and King [1976].

The rules in a rule-based system have the form:

IF [condition] THEN [action].

In general, the condition part of a rule can by any pattern that can be matched against a stated current database containing facts or assertions concerning the problem being solved. Once a match is made, the action part of the rule can by executed, possibly resulting in the addition of new facts to the database or in modifications of facts previously in the database. This matching process is conducted by the rule interpreter, with rule execution taking place in a recognize-act cycle (see Duda et al. [1979]). The rule interpreter checks the condition part of the rules, looking for one that matches the current database. When a match is found, the action that is associated with the rule is executed. In a large system, often more than one rule could 'fire' any recognize-act cycle. Since the system is required to choose one rule, an additional phase called the conflict resolution phase is incorporated, forming a generalized recognize-act cycle (or recognize-conflict resolution-act (RCRA) cycle). The strategy used by the rule interpreter to perform this RCRA cycle is called the control strategy, with the three most common forms being data driven (DD), goal driven (GD), and mixed (M) strategies. A DD control strategy executes rules only when their conditions match the information in the current database. In systems using this type of strategy, one usually begins by entering information about the current problem as facts in the database. If these facts match the condition part of a rule, the rule is applied. If no match is found, however, the system is typically set to ask the user for more information. If more than one rule is applicable, then the system uses a conflict resolution strategy. Barr et al. [1981] provide a list of commonly used conflict resolution strategies while McDermott [1980] illustrates use of such a strategy in the RI system.

In contrast to the data driven strategy, the GD strategy is structured to only consider rules that are applicable to a particular goal. Achieving a goal implies showing that the fact statements or conditions required for the goal to be achieved are indeed true. This implies that initially all rules whose actions achieve the goal are 'gathered together'. One rule is then chosen by utilizing a conflict-resolution strategy and its conditions are examined to see if the rule is applicable. If there is no information in the database about the conditions, the determination of its truth becomes a new subgoal. The process progresses in this manner until the original goal is established to be true or false. An example of a system using this strategy is MYCIN (see Shortliffe [1976]).

A mixed strategy attempts to combine the DD and GD strategies to eliminate some of the disadvantages of using each singly. For example, a DD strategy's firing of one rule after another based on the match achieved could well be viewed by the user as aimless wandering about the system. The GD strategy, on the other hand, is slower and does not allow the user to steer it by volunteering relevant information about the problem. The mixed strategy alternates between the two, using information volunteered by the user to determine a goal and then querying the user for additional information while working on the problem (see, for example, the variant used in PROSPECTOR (Duda et al. [1979]).

We have focused on rule-based systems for two reasons. 1) The rules are modular: they do not call each other directly. This allows the addition or deletion of rules without an impact on other rules, a capability of considerable importance in modelling economic systems since data on such systems are constantly changing as government regulations and the general environment change. 2) The representation scheme seems to be a natural way to integrate mathematical and nonmathematical modelling involving important institutional rules.

c. Expert Systems as Generalized Process Models

There is a common thread that ties process models and the rule-based production system framework within which we viewed expert systems--that is the structure of the transformation rules that link the initial state (inputs) to the goal state (outputs). In process models, the transformation links are provided in purely mathematical forms. As such, they are but a subset of rule-based expert systems, which can accommodate pure mathematical rules as well as more general pattern description based rules of action. The generalization of the process model production transformation to incorporate behavioral modelling sets expert systems apart from pure mathematical process models as means of modelling systems with key behavioral aspects. As noted in our introduction, previous authors have detailed the usefulness of process models as a data-generating technique. The more general expert system representation provides us with this data generating ability in an even wider area of application. In the next section we focus on the use of expert systems to model and generate data for one particular area, microeconomic systems.

III. MODELLING MICROECONOMIC SYSTEMS USING AN EXPERT SYSTEM FRAMEWORK

Smith [1982] provides a general characterization of microeconomic systems (S) utilizing two major components, an environment (e), and an institution (I), or S = (e,I). In what follows we outline Smith's representation, highlighting the key fact that the system is represented in a rule-based framework and thus directly amenable to our intended expert system representation.

Smith defined the microeconomic environment by: $e = (e^1,e^2,\ldots,e^n)$ where e^i represents the characteristics of each agent i. The ith agent is characterized by the vector: $e = (u^i,T^i,w^i)$, where u^i is the agent's utility function, T^i is the technology or knowledge endowment, and w^i is the commodity endowment. Each is defined on the k dimensional commodity space R^k. The environment therefore specifies the set of initial characteristics.

The institution (I) specifies the rules of private property under which agents may communicate and exchange or transform commodities for modifying initial endowments in accordance with private tastes and knowledge. The microeconomic institution is defined by the collection of individual property right characteristics, where $I = (I^1,I^2,\ldots,I^n)$. Each agent's property rights are defined by:

$$I^i = (M^i,h^i(m),c^i(m),g^i(t_0,t,T))$$

where M^i is the set of messages sent by i, $h^i(m)$ is the allocation rule which states the final commodity allocation to i as a function of the messages m sent by all agents, where $m = (m^1,m^2,\ldots,m^n)$ and $m^i \varepsilon M^i$. $h^i(m) \varepsilon H = (h^1(m),h^2(m),\ldots h^n(m))$ is the set of allocation rules. $C^i(m)$ is the rule which states the payment to be made by agent i as a function of the messages sent by all agents. $c^i(m) \varepsilon C = (c^1(m),c^2(m),\ldots,c^n(m))$ is the set of cost imputation rules. $g^i(t^0,t,T) \varepsilon G = (g^1(t^0,t,T),\ldots g^n(t^0,t,T))$ is the set of adjustment process rules. These rules consist of a starting rule specifying the initial conditions, transition rules governing the sequencing and exchange of messages, and a stopping rule.

Given the above characterization of a microeconomic environment, the outcome behavior of agent i in a static description of the economy e is defined by a function $B^i(e^i/I)$ which yields the allocation determining message m^i sent by agent i with characteristics e^i, given the property rights of all agents defined by I.

In a dynamic description of the economy, agent i's response behavior can be defined by $m^i(t) = F^i(m(t-1), e^i,I)$, which gives message response m^i at point t to earlier messages m(t-1) by all agents. This response behavior could follow an optimal decision rule or a rule of thumb.

This rule-based form of Smith's characterization of microeconomic systems provides us with the direct link to pursue our earlier suggestion of representing such systems as expert systems.

IV. MODELLING MICROECONOMIC SYSTEMS--EXAMPLES OF EXPERT SYSTEM REPRESENTATION

Before presenting our examples, we briefly consider the analogous nature of an expert system diagnostic problem to the problem of determining outcome behavior in a microeconomic system.

A typical diagnostic problem involves determining a diagnosis given certain observed symptoms, the diagnosis being based on knowledge about diseases and their effects. In other words, the diagnosis is based on the rules which govern normal bodily functions and rules about diseases and their effects. This can then be represented as D(SY/K), i.e., the diagnosis based on the symptoms (SY) given the knowledge required for diagnosis (K).

In a microeconomic system, the problem one is faced with is similar in that the object of interest is the outcome behavior, which is based on environmental features, given the institutional rules under which the individual functions, i.e., $B^i(e^i/I)$. This implies that the knowledge base would need to have the set of rules which characterize the institution, i.e., the allocation rules, cost computation rules, and process adjustment rules. In addition to this, the knowledge base should have details about the choices which are possible under various environmental conditions. The knowledge base could also contain information about such aspects of behavior as minimizing cost or maximizing utility and the process for computing each.

The above suggests that a microeconomic system can be modelled within an expert system framework. To illustrate the feasibility of doing so, we consider two examples of microeconomic systems--a first price sealed bid auction and an English auction model--and outline a rule-based framework for modelling each.

The modelling problem is really a two stage problem. Stage one involves modelling the auction process, while stage two involves modelling the decision process for bid determination, given the auction process. The integration of the two stages would lead to an expert system which can be used either as a data generation tool or as an actual decision aid.

An auction consists primarily of a set of individuals bidding on an object that has been put up for sale by an auctioneer. The manner in which bidding takes place determines whether the auction is static (one bid per bidder) or dynamic (bid revision permitted, revisions based upon current updated information). We begin with an example of a static process followed by one involving bidding dynamics.

a. First Price, Sealed Bid Auction (FPSB)

The FPSB auction process involves all bidders submitting their bids. The item bid upon is awarded to the highest bidder who pays the amount bid while the other bidders pay nothing. Assuming, for simplicity, one seller and two bidders, the initial state can be described as follows:

a) seller has an object called 'A';
b) bidder 1's endowment is V_1; he values the object at V_1* and bids V_1';
c) bidder 2's endowment is V_2; he values the object at V_2* and bids V_2';

The final state can be described as follows:

a) the highest bidder receives A, and his endowment is reduced from V_i to V_i-V_i';

b) the loser retains his initial endowment of V_i;
c) the seller gets V_i'.

Two rules model the above process:

RULE 1: IF [there is an object to be auctioned] AND [bid V_i' is greater than bid V_j'] THEN [award object to bidder i].
RULE 2: IF [i is awarded the object] AND [i's endowment is V_i] THEN [i's endowment becomes V_i-V_i'].

Thus, given the initial state, application of RULE 1 followed by RULE 2 moves us from the initial state to the goal state. Modelling the decision process, that is determining what bid should be made for an object, is a more complicated procedure requiring expert knowledge. This topic is considered in brevity later in the paper and it is the focus of ongoing research. (Interested readers are encouraged to write for further information.)

b. The English Auction

Since the FPSB auction model is a static model, modelling it is far simpler than modelling continuous auction systems where an agent may alter his bid in response to other bids or to the failure of a bid to be accepted. Modelling such systems requires transition rules in addition to the usual cost and allocation rules. We illustrate such modelling using a simple English auction format.

The English auction proceeds as follows:

i) the bidding process begins with a call for an opening bid;
ii) an accepted and announced bid remains standing until it is displaced by a new higher bid;
iii) the process stops when no new overbid can be elicited from the agents and the object is awarded to the agent who bid last at the last bid price.

Again, for simplicity, let us consider a single seller, two bidders, and one object to be auctioned off. The initial state can be characterized as follows:

a) seller has object 'A';
b) seller calls for opening bid;
c) agent 1 has endowment V_1;
d) agent 2 has endowment V_2;
e) standing bid = 0.

Since this is a dynamic model, as agents change bids in response to the environment, there can be several intermediate stages before a goal state is reached. A typical intermediate state could be summarized as follows:

a) call for new bid that must exceed standing bid;
b) agent 1 has endowment V_1;
c) agent 2 has endowment V_2;
d) standing bid = X_i, where i corresponds to agent i.

The goal state can be characterized as:

a) standing bid = X_i;
b) no response to call for new bid;
c) i awarded object at price = X_i;
d) i's endowment reduced from V_i to V_i-X_i;
e) loser (agent j) retains endowment.

The following rules could be used to model the auction process just described:

RULE 1: IF [object is to be auctioned] THEN [call for bid].
RULE 2: IF [standing bid is X_i] AND [new bid is X_j] AND [$X_j > X_i$] THEN [standing bid is X_j] AND [call for new bid].
RULE 3: IF [standing bid is X_i] AND [call for new bid unanswered] THEN [award object to agent i].
RULE 4: IF [object is awarded to agent i] THEN [i's endowment reduced from V_i to V_i-X_i].

The bidding process using these rules can be summaried in the following manner. Initially the global database contains information about the object being auctioned and the endowments of the two agents. RULE 1 is now activated and the database is updated to depict the call. If a bid is tendered, then RULE 2 is fired and the current database would depict one of the intermediate states. RULE 2 models the transition between the intermediate states. RULE 3 models the transition from an intermediate state to the goal state. RULE 4 completes the transition by computing the changes in the endowments.

In modelling the above auction process, we assumed that the bids were external and that the rules depicted the state change once the bids were known. Modelling the generation of bids, i.e., modelling the decision processes which generates the bids, is a more complex procedure. We briefly outline the issues for the English auction model, sacrificing details and completeness for brevity.

Typically, a bid would be announced based on the information the decision maker has about the current state, namely, the resources available to him, the current standing bid, and the value to him of the object being auctioned. Additional rules would be required to handle the cases where different information is available prior to the bidding, e.g., information regarding competitor's resources or valuations. A simple bid generating rule would be:

BID RULE: IF [standing bid is X_i] AND [resources $V_i > X_i$] AND [value of object to i is $V_i^* > X_i$] THEN [bid V_i' with $V_i' < V_i^* < V_i$].

Integrating rules from the auction process and decision processes together in one knowledge base would give rise to a process model form of expert system that could be used to generate data for any variety of specified initial conditions. In the next brief section we consider some of the general issues in the actual decision making (bid-determination) process.

c. The Decision Process

Einhorn and Hogarth [1981] view the human decision process as consisting of four interacting subprocesses--information acquisition, evaluation, action, and feedback/learning. Current expert systems are capable of performing the first three components in reasonable ways. However, the learning capabilities of current systems are at best superficial compared to that of the humans they are intended to model. In the context of our auction systems, we will here view the final stage of the process as purely a feedback process in which the acceptance or rejection of a bid is made known to the bidder. The learning/feedback state is considered as a post-final state phenomenon since typically the decision maker has little, if any, control once an action has been taken.

Consider modelling the decision process for an organization bidding for a specific object, say, an offshore oil lease on a specified plot. The initial phase includes:

1) INFORMATION ACQUISITION
   i) details about the auction process, the institutional rules;
   ii) details about the object being bid upon--key individual characteristics;
   iii) likely or expected returns from obtaining the object;
   iv) details of the financial status of the organization itself;
   v) details about competitors.

2) INFORMATION EVALUATION
   The primary information in the knowledge base focuses on strategies to determine bids based on information acquired in step (1) above. Pertinent knowledge here would include information about where certain strategies are applicable--about the links between the information obtained in (1) and associated optimal strategies.

The key feature of an expert system is that in determining the bid, one is not bound solely to optimal strategies for bid determination. Consider, for example, where our sample organization refuses to bid on projects within a certain state no matter how attractive the project is or how reasonable the optimal bid is. In the rule-based expert system, addition of a simple rule (e.g., IF [project is in OHIO] THEN [do not bid]) takes account of this or any myriad of other similar nonmathematical, but important situations.

Once the evaluation stage determines the desired bid, two task stages remain:

ACTION: Submission of bid and determination of the auctioneer response.

FEEDBACK: In a static process, the feedback information on whether a bid is accepted has value only for updating the information set, e.g., the organization's financial status. In a dynamic system, however, the feedback information is potentially useful for evaluating the next step--determining whether to submit a new bid or to stop bidding.

In the offshore oil lease setting, we might use two expert systems in tandem. The first would analyze the data on the site specific information while the second would take information fed from the first expert system and combine it with additional information to determine the optimal bid.

V. THE EXPERT SYSTEM AS A DATA GENERATION TOOL

Once in place, an expert system model can be used as a data-generating technique for economic policy analysis. For example, with the institution fixed, we can study variations in the generation of optimal bids as we vary the characteristics of the individual or organization determining the bids. Such an approach contrasts with that often used in experimental economics in which the behavior of experimental subjects is assumed representative of behavior in nature. Our approach is to model a microeconomic system as an expert system and use it to generate outcomes assuming a variety of behaviors of decision makers.

This approach allows us to simulate a range of possible behaviors for comparison with naturally occurring data. It also allows us to test the sensitivity of the expert system's recommendations to changes in the presumed behavior of decision makers.

VI. CONCLUSION

We conclude by pointing out that two important ingredients are missing from our presentation--a consideration of the verification of a given expert system representation and a detailed numerical example. The former is the topic of a current companion paper. The latter is the focus of our current efforts involving offshore oil leasing in the U.S. outer continental shelf. The offshore oil leasing area particularly attracted our attention since we have been able to obtain detailed micro data on all lease sales (and all resulting drilling, production, and revenue) since the inception of the program.

We model microeconomic systems so that we can use such models to develop information for formulating and/or analyzing economic policy. Expert systems are particularly well suited for such modelling and can provide us with the means to incorporate critical behavioral information which has, by necessity, been excluded from strictly mathematical model representations.

REFERENCES

1. Aikins, Janice S., Kunz, J. C., Shortliffe, E. H., and Fallat, R. J. (1984), "PUFF: An Expert System for Interpretation of Pulmonary Function Data," in Readings in Medical Artificial Intelligence, W. J. Clancey and E. H. Shortliffe (eds.), Addison-Wesley, Reading, Mass., 444-462.
2. Barr, Aaron and Feigenbaum, E. A. (eds.) (1981), The Handbook of Artificial Intelligence, William Kaufmann, Los Altos, Cal., Vol. I, 141-222.
3. Bever, R. C., Marsden, J. R., Salas-Fumas, V., and Whinston, A. B. (1982a), "Verifying the Usefulness of Process Models Applied to Forecasting," Electric Power Research Institute, Final Project Report EA-2441, Palo Alto, Cal.
4. ____________ (1982b), "Aggregate Summary Functions: Heterogeneity and the Use of Random Coefficient Models," Advances in Applied Microeconomics, Vol. II, 38-60.
5. Chenery, H. B. (1949), "Engineering Production Functions," Quarterly Journal of Economics, Vol. 63, pp. 407-431.
6. Davis, R. and King, J. (1976), "An Overview of Production Systems," in Machine Intelligence, 8, E. W. Elcock and D. Michie (eds.), Wiley, New York, 300-332.
7. Duda, R., Gaschnig, J. and Hart, P. (1979), "Model Design in the Prospector Consultant System for Mineral Exploration," in Expert Systems in the Micro-Electronic Age, Donald Michie (ed.), Edinburgh Univ. Press, Edinburgh.
8. Einhorn, Hillel J., and Hogarth, Robi M. (1981), "Behavioral Decision Theory: Processes of Judgement and Choice," Ann. Rev. Psychology, 32, 53-88.
9. Griffin, James M. (1972), "The Process Analysis Alternative to Statistical Cost Functions," American Economic Review, 62, 46-56.
10. ____________ (1977), "Long-Run Production Modelling with Pseudo-Data: Electric Power Generation," Bell Journal of Economics, 8 (1), 112-127.
11. Marsden, J. R., Pingry, D. E., and Whinston, A. B. (1974a) "Engineering Foundations of the Production Function," Journal of Economic Theory, 9, 124-140.
12. ____________ (1974b), "The Process Analysis Alternative to Statistical Cost Functions: Comment," American Economic Review, 64, 773-776.
13. McDermott, J. (1980), "R1: An Expert System in the Computer Systems Domain," Proc. First Annual Nat'l Conf. on Artificial Intelligence, Stanford Univ., Palo Alto, Cal., pp. 269-271.
14. Newell, A., and Simon, H. A. (1972), Human Problem Solving, Prentice Hall, New York.
15. Shortliffe, E. H. (1976), Computer Based Medical Consultations: MYCIN, North Holland, New York.
16. Smith, Vernon L. (1982), "Microeconomic Systems as an Experimental Science," American Economic Review, 72, 923-955.
17. Tsao, C. S., and Day, R. H. (1971), "A Process Analysis Model of the U.S. Steel Industry," Management Science, 17 (10), B588-B608.
18. Waterman, D. A., and Hayes, Roth F. (eds.) (1978), Pattern Directed Inference Systems, Academic Press, New York.

Artificial Intelligence in Economics and Management
I.F. Pau (Editor)

A THEORETICAL BASIS FOR EXPERT SYSTEMS

H. Keith Hall, James C. Moore and Andrew B. Whinston

Krannert Graduate School of Management
Purdue University
West Lafayette, Indiana 47907
U.S.A.

In recent years, a great deal of research has been devoted to the expert system approach to computer-based problem solving.[1] Since there are so many different facets to the problem of developing expert systems (including the language for representing expert knowledge, the ability to provide users with an explanation system, the system's acquisition of expert knowledge, etc.) it is perhaps not too surprising that the decision-theoretic basis for expert system models, has received relatively little attention. In this paper we take a step toward remedying this deficiency by extending the framework of classical decision theory to provide a theoretical basis for an "ideal" expert system. In view of the fact that there may be many difficulties associated with finding an optimal solution ("ideal expert system") in applications, we also consider the development of a "satisficing" solution which we believe has many advantages over traditional production-rule based approaches to expert systems.

1. INTRODUCTION

Decision theory has typically characterized "best" decisions based upon the underlying assumption of a rational, utility maximizing decision-maker. He is seen to make inferences about an uncertain domain after obtaining information about critical parameters that affect the consequences of his decision. Inferences are based upon a set of beliefs about the likelihood of the environment, as embodied in a subjective probability distribution. The acquisition of infomation may be any activity such as experiments, tests, questions, etc., as long as it generally reduces uncertainty by altering these beliefs. If this framework is extended to incorporate the sequential gathering of (costly) infomation from different sources prior to making a final decision, then such a process may involve the formulation of an a priori strategy for collecting information and making a decision, as is necessary in an expert system. The formulation of what decision theory would describe as an optimal strategy in such a model would therefore correspond to the construction of an "ideal" expert system that computes only "best" solutions. In the next section we construct such a model; an extension of that presented in Marschak and Radner (1972). We have omitted all of the proofs in what follows, but they may be found in Moore, Hall, and Whinston (1985).

2. AN "IDEAL" EXPERT SYSTEM

We suppose that a state of the environment can be specified by the values of ℓ unobservable parameters, $\theta = (\theta_1,\ldots,\theta_\ell)$, and m observable parameters, $z = (z_1,\ldots,z_m)$. Thus the state space is given by

$$X = Z_1 \times \cdots \times Z_m \times \Theta_1 \times \cdots \times \Theta_\ell \equiv Z \times \Theta,$$

where we suppose each Θ_i and each Z_j is a finite set.[2] For example, in the case of medical diagnosis, the value of θ_i might correspond to the presence ($\theta_i = 1$) or absence ($\theta_1 = 0$) of the ith disease, while the values of the z_j's would represent symptoms and personal characteristics of a patient.

We suppose that there is a finite set, $D = \{d_1,\ldots,d_p\}$, of final decisions available to the decision-maker;[3] who receives a gross payoff $\omega(\theta,d)$, where $\omega: \Theta \times D \to \mathbf{R}$. Thus the gross payoff is a function of the unobservable parameters, $\theta = (\theta_1,\ldots,\theta_\ell)$, and the final decision taken, while (as will be specified in more detail shortly) obtainable information is directly pertinent only to Z. Information on Z can, however, be used to make inferences about Θ on the basis of a known probability density function, $\phi: Z \times \Theta \to [0,1]$, which defines a probability measure by

$$\pi(Y) = \sum_{(z,\theta)\in Y} \phi(z,\theta) \quad \text{for } Y \subseteq Z \times \Theta.$$

Let $A = \{0,1,\ldots,n\}$ be the set of initial actions (or experiments) available to the decision maker where $a = 0$ represents no information collection. Associated with each $a \in A$ is a finite set of information signals, Y_a, which we can write as:

$$Y_a = \{1,2,\ldots,n(a)\};$$

and a single-valued function mapping Z onto $Y_a, \eta_a: Z \to Y_a$.[4] We then define for $a = 0,1,\ldots,n$ and $y = 1,2,\ldots,n(a)$

$$M_{ay} = \{z \in Z | \eta_a(z) = y\} = \eta_a^{-1}(y)$$

and $M_a = \{M_{a1},\ldots,M_{an(a)}\}$ for $a = 0,1,\ldots,n$.[5] We shall call any non-empty partition of a subset of Z, $B \subseteq Z$, an <u>information structure on B</u>.

<u>Definition 1</u>. Let $B \subseteq Z$ be non-empty, and let $a \in A$. We define the information structure <u>induced</u> on $\overline{B}$ by a, $\iota(B,a)$, as:

$$\iota(B,a) = \{B\cap M_{a1}, B\cap M_{a2},\ldots,B\cap M_{an(a)}\}\setminus\{\emptyset\}.$$

<u>Definition 2</u>. Let $B \subseteq Z$ be non-empty, let $\mathcal{B} = \{B_1,\ldots,B_k\}$ be an information structure on B, and let $\alpha: \mathcal{B} \to A$ (we shall refer to such a function as an <u>action function on $\mathcal{B}$</u>). The <u>refinement</u> of $\mathcal{B}$ by α, $R(\mathcal{B},\alpha)$, is defined by:

$$R(\mathcal{B},\alpha) = \bigcup_{j=1}^{k} \iota[B_j,\alpha(B_j)].$$

<u>Definition 3</u>. Let $B \subseteq Z$ be non-empty, and let $\mathcal{B}_1$ and $\mathcal{B}_2$ be information structures on B. We shall say that $\mathcal{B}_1$ is as fine as $\mathcal{B}_2$ (or that $\mathcal{B}_1$ is a refinement of $\mathcal{B}_2$), and write $\mathcal{B}_1 \geq \mathcal{B}_2$, iff:

$$(\forall\, B' \in \mathcal{B}_1)(\exists\, B'' \in \mathcal{B}_2): B' \subseteq B''.$$

<u>Remark</u>. If B is non-empty subset of Z, $\mathcal{B}$ is an information structure on B, and α is an action function on $\mathcal{B}$, then $R(\mathcal{B},\alpha)$ is an information structure on B and a refinement of $\mathcal{B}$.

<u>Assumption</u>: The decision maker can take up to r information-gathering actions, where $1 \leq r \leq n$. Since we include the null information action in A (and its associated cost will be assumed to be zero), we can, without loss of generality, assume that the decision maker takes exactly r information-gathering actions.

<u>Definition 4</u>. A <u>feasible strategy</u>, σ, is a sequence of r + 1 pairs:

$$\sigma = \langle(\mathcal{B}_1,\alpha_1),(\mathcal{B}_2,\alpha_2),\ldots,(\mathcal{B}_r,\alpha_r),(\mathcal{B}_{r+1},\delta)\rangle$$

satisfying:

1. $\mathcal{B}_1 = \{Z\}$

2. a. $\alpha_t: \mathcal{B}_t \to A$ for $t = 1,2,\ldots,r$.

   b. $\mathcal{B}_{t+1} = R(\mathcal{B}_t,\alpha_t)$ for $t = 1,\ldots,r$.

3. $\delta: \mathcal{B}_{r+1} \to D$.

We shall denote the set of all feasible strategies for a particular decision problem $\mathcal{D}$ by "$\Sigma(\mathcal{D})$."[6]

A sequence of action functions can be seen to create, a priori, a sequence of partitions on Z, each a refinement of the previous partition in the sequence. The element of a given partition in the sequence in which the "true" state of the environment falls will determine the exact sequence of signals that the decision maker will receive from the sequence of action functions generating the partition. If a sequence of action functions, its associated sequence of partitions, and a final decision function defined on the last partition in the sequence are chosen a priori, then a feasible strategy is formed. The decision maker in effect generates the information structure from which he will make his final decision.

Example Let $Z = \{(z_1,z_2) \in \mathbf{R}^2 | 0 \le z \le 2 \text{ for } i = 1,2\}$,[7] $A = \{0,1,2,3\}$, and $\mathcal{M}_a = \{M_{a1},M_{a2}\}$ for $a = 1,2,3$, where

$$M_{11} = \{z \in Z | 0 \le z_1 \le 1\} \quad M_{12} = \{z \in Z | 1 < z_1 \le 2\}$$

$$M_{21} = \{z \in Z | 0 \le z_2 < 1\} \quad M_{22} = \{z \in Z | 1 < z_2 \le 2\}$$

$$M_{31} = \{z \in Z | z_2 - z_1 \ge 0\} \quad M_{32} = \{z \in Z | z_2 - z_1 < 0\}.$$

Let $r = 2$ and consider the feasible information-gathering strategies α and α^* where

$$\mathcal{B}_1 = \mathcal{B}_1^* = \{Z\},\ \alpha_1(Z) = \alpha_1^*(Z) = 1,$$

$$\mathcal{B}_2 = \mathcal{B}_2^* = \{M_{11},M_{12}\},$$

$$\alpha_2(M_{11}) = 2, \alpha_2(M_{12}) = 3,$$

$$\alpha_2^*(M_{11}) = 3, \alpha_2^*(M_{12}) = 2.$$

In decision-tree format, these two strategies can be represented as

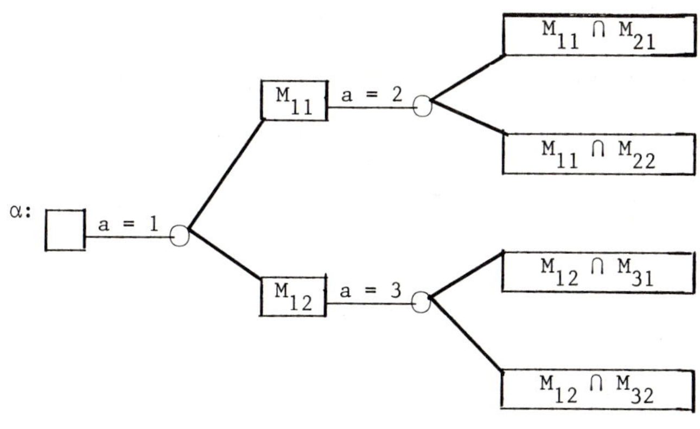

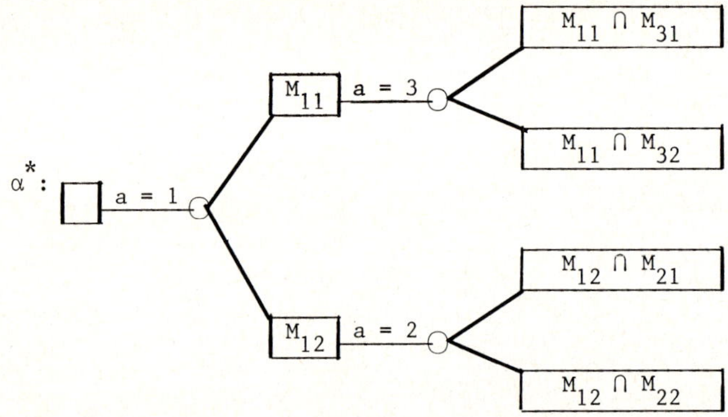

Thus the final information structures yielded by the two strategies are

$$\mathcal{B}_3 = \{M_{11}\cap M_{21}, M_{11}\cap M_{22}, M_{12}\cap M_{31}, M_{12}\cap M_{32}\},$$

and

$$\mathcal{B}_3^* = \{M_{11}\cap M_{31}, M_{11}\cap M_{32}, M_{12}\cap M_{21}, M_{12}\cap M_{22}\};$$

which the reader will note are quite different, despite the fact that the two strategies make use of the same set of initial actions.

□

Definition 5. Let $\sigma = \langle(\mathcal{B}_1,\alpha_1),\ldots,(\mathcal{B}_r,\alpha_r),(\mathcal{B}_{r+1},\delta)\rangle$ be a feasible strategy and $q \in \{2,\ldots,r+1\}$. For each $B \in \mathcal{B}_q$, we define $a^q(B)$ as the sequence (of length q-1) of actions taken by the strategy σ along the path that yields B. Thus: $a^q(B) = \langle a(1,B),\ldots,a(q-1,B)\rangle$, where "a(t,B)" denotes the action taken at step $t (t = 1,\ldots,q-1)$ along the path that yields B.

Assumption. We suppose that, with each $a \in A$ is associated a nonnegative cost, c(a), and that c(0) = 0.

In a given realization of our decision problem, the application of a feasible strategy, $\sigma = \langle(\mathcal{B}_1,\alpha_1),\ldots,(\mathcal{B}_r,\alpha_r),(\mathcal{B}_{r+1},\delta)\rangle$ will result in the determination that $\hat{z}$, the true state, is an element of some $B \in \mathcal{B}_{r+1}$. The cost of determining that $\hat{z} \in B$ will be the sum of the costs of actions taken along the path yielding B:

$$C(B) = \sum_{t=1}^{r} c[a(t,B)]. \tag{1}$$

Consequently the expected informational cost of strategy σ is given by:

$$\Gamma(\sigma) = \sum_{B\in\mathcal{B}_{r+1}} \pi(B)c(B). \tag{2}$$

Given a feasible stragety, $\sigma = (\alpha,\mathcal{B},\delta)$, we denote the expected gross payoff for σ by "$\Omega(\sigma)$," that is

$$\Omega(\sigma) = \sum_{B\in\mathcal{B}} \sum_{z\in B} \sum_{\theta\in\Theta} \phi(z,\theta)\omega[\theta,\delta(B)]. \tag{3}$$

We can now more formally state the goal of our decision problem, as follows.

Objective: Choose $\sigma^* = (\alpha^*,\mathcal{B}^*_{r+1},\delta^*)\in\Sigma(\mathcal{D})$ such that for all $\sigma = \langle\alpha,\mathcal{B},\delta\rangle \in\Sigma(\mathcal{D})$, we have:

$$\Omega(\sigma^*) - \Gamma(\sigma^*) \geq \Omega(\sigma) - \Gamma(\sigma). \tag{*}$$

Definition 6. If $B \subseteq Z$ is non-empty, we define the potential gross payoff associated with B, $\nu(B)$, and the conditionally optimal decision set for B, $D^*(B)$,

$$\nu(B) = \underset{d \in D}{\text{Max}} \sum_{z \in B} \sum_{\theta \in \Theta} \phi(z,\theta|B)\omega(\theta,d)$$

$$D^*(B) = \{d \in D | \sum_{z \in B} \sum_{\theta \in \Theta} \phi(z,\theta|B)\omega(\theta,d) = \nu(B)\}.$$

The following is then easily proved.

Proposition 1. If $\sigma = <(\mathcal{B}_1,\alpha_1),\ldots,(\mathcal{B}_r,\alpha_r),(\mathcal{B}_{r+1},\delta)> \in \Sigma(\mathcal{D})$ is optimal for $\mathcal{D}$, then for each $B \in \mathcal{B}_{r+1}$ we have $\delta(B) \in D^*(B)$. Furthermore, $\Omega(\sigma) = \sum_{B \in \mathcal{B}_{r+1}} \pi(B)\nu(B)$.

Definition 7. We define the finest information structure obtainable from A, $\mathcal{B}^A$, by:

$$\mathcal{B}^A = \{\bigcap_{a=1}^{n} M_{a\ell}, \bigcap_{a=1}^{n-1} M_{a\ell} \cap M_{n2}, \ldots, \bigcap_{a=1}^{n-1} M_{a\ell} \cap M_{n,n(a)}, \bigcap_{a=1}^{n-2} M_{a\ell} \cap M_{n-1,2} \cap M_{n\ell}, \ldots, \bigcap_{a=1}^{n} M_{an(a)}\} \setminus \{\emptyset\}.$$

We shall say that a strategy $\sigma = <(\mathcal{B}_1,\alpha_1),\ldots,(\mathcal{B}_r,\alpha_r),(\mathcal{B}_{r+1},\delta)>$ yields $\mathcal{B}^A$ if $\mathcal{B}_{r+1} = \mathcal{B}^A$.

Lemma 1. If $\sigma = <(\mathcal{B}_1,\alpha_1),\ldots,(\mathcal{B}_r,\alpha_r),(\mathcal{B}_{r+1},\delta)>$ is feasible, then $\mathcal{B}^A \geq \mathcal{B}_{r+1}$.

Because of Lemma 1 the following is essentially a special case of the theorem on p. 54 of Marschak and Radner (1972).

Proposition 2. Suppose $\hat{\sigma} = <(\hat{\mathcal{B}}_1,\hat{\alpha}_1),\ldots,(\hat{\mathcal{B}}_r,\hat{\alpha}_r),(\hat{\mathcal{B}}_{r+1},\hat{\delta})>$ is such that $\hat{\mathcal{B}}_{r+1} = \mathcal{B}^A$ $\hat{\delta} \in D^*(\hat{\mathcal{B}}_{r+1})$. Then for any $\sigma = (\mathcal{B}_1,\alpha_1),\ldots,(\mathcal{B}_r,\alpha_r),(\mathcal{B}_{r+1},\delta)> \in \Sigma(\mathcal{D})$, we have

$$\Omega(\sigma) \leq \Omega(\hat{\sigma}) = \sum_{D \subset \mathcal{B}_{r+1}} \pi(B)\nu(B).$$

While, by Proposition 2, a strategy of the form $\hat{\sigma}$ maximizes the gross payoff, it may not maximize the net payoff as in our objective equation (*) above. That is, the expected cost of such a strategy may be sufficiently higher than some alternative feasible strategy, σ^*, as to more than offset the (possibly) higher expected gross payoff from $\hat{\sigma}$. Also, since our decision problem is constrained to to have $r \leq n$ information actions, there may be no feasible strategies which result in the finest information structure given A. Nonetheless, Proposition 2 will be used in Section 3 to develop a class of "satisficing strategies" which approximate an optimal solution.

3. APPLICATION TO EXPERT SYSTEMS

There are three types of expert knowledge that must be acquired to implement our ideal expert system. First is the knowledge of the problem domain that is necessary to identify a set of critical parameters, identify a set of possible decisions (problem solutions), and calculate the a priori likelihoods of each of the various states of the environment. Second is the knowledge of the information-acquisition abilities of the system or system user which, combined with knowledge of the domain, is necessary to identify the set of information-gathering actions and measurable parameters, and to calculate the conditional probabilities of the measurable parameters (z), given the state of the environment (θ). And lastly, knowledge of the desirability of the outcomes (and therefore the correctness) of the possible final decisions is needed to specify a payoff function to guide the decision process.

The ease with which the environmental parameters may be identified will vary with different problem domains. Generally, however, one would expect that expert knowledge that may easily be represented in production rules form will also have a fairly developed set of critical parameters already identified by expert sources. Knowledge of the system or system user's abilities to collect information on the decision problem under study, together with knowledge of the domain, allows the identification of the set of available information-gathering actions (A) and the set of observable parameters ($Z = Z_1 \times \ldots \times Z_m$). In most applications a practical method of constructing the density function, ϕ, would be to construct the marginal density function, $f(\theta)$, develop the conditional probability function, $g(z|\theta)$, and then obtain the joint density function, ϕ, by calculating

$$\phi(\theta,z) = g(z|\theta)f(\theta) \quad \text{for } (\theta,z) \in \Theta \times Z.$$

Generally we would expect that information on both the marginal density function, $f(\theta)$, and the conditional density function, $g(z|\theta)$, would be available in published sources; however, in applications both functions would need to be checked in consultation with an expert.

The last type of knowledge needed to implement our model as an expert system is knowledge of the desirability of the outcomes of the different decisions. Although the identification of the set of critical and measurable environmental parameters, set of possible decisions, and set of informational actions already involves some of this knowledge,[8] we require a much more precise measure of the desirability of the outcomes to estimate a payoff function. The importance of using knowledge of desirability of the possible outcomes of the decision to guide the solution process comes from the recognition that collecting information is costly and this must be weighed against its potential benefits (in possibly making a better decision).[9] However, this may be the most difficult knowledge to acquire, in the detail necessary to fully specify our model. For this reason, we close this section by discussing a class of strategies which do not require the specification of a payoff function, yet still produce good solutions.

To obtain our satisficing strategy, we first (as discussed above), obtain a specification of the states of both the unobservable and the observable environment, Θ and Z; the probability density function, ϕ; the set of possible final decisions, D; the set of information-gathering actions, A; and the partition of Z and cost associated with action a, M_a and $c(a)$, respectively. Next, using the partitions of Z, M_a, for all $a \in A$, the finest information structure obtainable from A, $\mathcal{B}^A$, must be calculated.[10] We then elicit from an expert source the best decisions, $d \in D$ for each element of $\mathcal{B}^A$; thus obtaining a decision strategy $(\mathcal{B}^A,\delta^*)$, where $\delta^*: \mathcal{B}^A \to D$. If this choice of decision is assumed to be guided by maximizing the expected value of an underlying gross payoff function, then we have obtained an element of the conditional optimal decision set for each $B \in \mathcal{B}^A$. That is, $\delta^*(B) \in D^*(B)$ for all $B \in \mathcal{B}^A$.

Third, those elements of $\mathcal{B}^A$ with the same best decision, $\delta^*(B)$, may be grouped together to create the coarsest partition of Z possible that may result in the same expected gross payoff as $\mathcal{B}^A$. Formally, this partition, $\mathcal{B}^D$, is defined by

$$\mathcal{B}^D = \{B_d | d \in D^*\}.$$

where $B_d = \delta^{-1}(d) = \bigcup_{B \in B(d)} B$ and $B(d) = \{B \in \mathcal{B}^A | \delta(B) = d\}$. Since a new decision function on $\mathcal{B}^D$ may be defined such that

$$\delta^D(B) = \delta^*(\bar{B})$$

where $\bar{B} \in \mathcal{B}^A$, $B \in \mathcal{B}^D$, and $\bar{B} \subset B$; by Proposition 2 above, any feasible strategy that yields B^D (i.e., $R(B_r,\alpha_r) \geq \bar{\mathcal{B}}^D$) maximizes the expected gross payoff.

Lastly, we need to find those strategies, if any, that yield $\mathcal{B}^D$. Letting $\Sigma^D \subseteq \Sigma(\mathcal{D})$ denote this set of strategies, we then find that strategy, σ^D, such that

$$(\forall\ \sigma \in \Sigma^D): \Gamma(\sigma) \equiv \sum_{B \in \mathcal{B}_{r+1}} \pi(B)C(B) \geq \sum_{B \in \mathcal{B}^D_{r+1}} \pi(B)C(B) \equiv \Gamma(\sigma^D).$$

Since r may be less than n, Σ^D may be empty. If this is the case the following may be done.

First, follow the above steps for r = n and find some $\sigma^+ = <(\mathcal{B}_1^+,\alpha_1^+),\ldots,(\mathcal{B}_n^+,\alpha_n^+),(\mathcal{B}_{n+1}^+,\delta^+)>$ such that[11]

$$(\forall\ \sigma \in \Sigma^{D+}): \Gamma(\sigma) \geq \Gamma(\sigma^*).$$

At the rth step of this strategy, for each $B \in \mathcal{B}_{r+1}^+$ one of the following two things are true. a) $B \subseteq B_d$ for some $d \in D^*$. Since we may define $\delta^{++}(B) = d$, no further information is required for this subset of Z. b) There exists no $d \in D^*$ for which $B \subseteq B_d$. Here we must consult again with our expert source to find out whether, having arrived at B, it would be feasible to conduct further information-gathering activities; or whether a final decision should be made at that point, and if so, which one.

Proceeding in this way, we will obtain a new (generally truncated) strategy

$$\sigma^{++} = <(\mathcal{B}_1^{++},\alpha_1^{++}),(\mathcal{B}_{r^{++}}^{++},\alpha_{r^{++}}^{++}),(\mathcal{B}_{r^{++}+1}^{++},\delta^{++})>$$

which will satisfy: $r \leq r^{++} \leq n, \mathcal{B}_{r+1}^{++} = \mathcal{B}_{r+1}^{+}$, and $\mathcal{B}_t^{++} = \mathcal{B}_t^{+}$, and $\alpha_t^{++} = \alpha_t^{+}$ for $t = 1,2,\ldots,r$. The strategy σ^{++} will be "good" in the sense that (a) it is consistent with the expert's preferences (judgments) and (b) it should come close to the goal of maximizing expected gross payoff (in terms of the expert's implicit gross payoff function) at minimum expected cost.

Footnotes

[1]See, for example, Davis, Buchanan, and Shortliffe (1977), Davis, et al. (1981), McDermott and Steel (1981), and Holsapple, Shen, and Whinston (1982), respectively. Also, see Bonczek, Holsapple, and Whinston (1981) for an exploration of management applications of expert systems.

[2]We do not exclude the possibility that we may have $\Theta_i = Z_j$ for some i and j.

[3]In our medical example, the elements of D would correspond to possible treatments.

[4]Thus information is noiseless with respect to Z; that is, for each $z \in Z$ there is a single signal receivable from z if experiment a is performed.

[5]For $a = 0, n(0) = 1$, and $M_0 = \{M_{01}\}$, where $M_{01} = Z$. Note that an information action will generally not be noiseless with respect to θ and that a set of signals, Y_a is related to θ by a conditional probability density function $h_a : Y_a \times \theta \to [0,1]$ where

$$h_a(y|\theta) = \sum_{z \in M_{ay}} \phi(z,\theta) \quad \text{for } \theta \in \Theta, \text{ and } y \in Y_a.$$

[6]We shall often find it convenient to regard a feasible strategy, $\sigma = <(B_1,\alpha_1),\ldots,(B_r,\alpha_r),(B_{r+1},\delta)>$ as being composed of two parts:

i. the <u>information-gathering strategy</u>: $\alpha = <(B_1,\alpha_1),\ldots,(B_r,\alpha_r)>$,

ii. the <u>decision strategy</u>, (B_{r+1},δ).

[7]Strictly speaking, of couse, this example is not legitimate, since Z is not finite. It is, however, very convenient.

[8]The importance of identifying these environmental parameters lies in their effect on the outcome of the decision and in their effect on the desirability of the outcome. Therefore, if expert sources have already identified the parameters, then they will have done so with the set of possible decisions, the potential outcomes of the decisions, and the desirability of these outcomes at least implicitly in mind.

[9]When a human expert goes through the process of collecting information he/she implicitly makes judgments about the desirability of the possible outcomes. These judgments weigh the likelihood of the existence of particular states of the environment by their potential effect on the goodness of the decision.

[10]Note that by Definition 7 this may be achieved by calculating the final information structure of any non-sequential strategy using all $a \in A$.

[11]Note that this strategy always exists since a simple non-sequential strategy involving all $a \in A$ will generate strategy in Σ^{D+}.

References

Bonczek, R. H., C. W. Holsapple and A. B. Whinston (1981). Foundations of Decision Support Systems, Academic Press, 1981.

Buchanan, B. G. and R. O. Duda (1982). "Principles of Rule-Based Expert Systems," to appear in Advances in Computers, (M. Yovits, ed.), Vol. 22, August 1985.

Davis, R., B. G. Buchanan, and E. H. Shortliffe (1977). "Production Rules as a Representation of a Knowledge-Based Consultant Program," Artificial Intelligence, 8, 15-45.

Davis, R. and J. J. King (1984). "The Origin of Rule-Based Systems in AI," in Rule-Based Expert Systems, (G. B. Buchanan and E. H. Shortliffe, eds.), Addison-Wesley.

Davis, R. et al., (1981). "The Dipmeter Advisor: Interpretation of Geological Signals," Proc. Seventh Int'l. Joint Conf. Artificial Intelligence, August.

DeGroot, H. M. (1970). Optimal Statistical Decisions, McGraw-Hill, Inc.

Gordon, J. and E. H. Shortliffe (1984). "The Dempster-Shafer Theory of Evidence," Chapter 13 in Rule-Based Expert Systems, (B. B. Buchanan and E. H. Shortliffe, eds.), pp. 272-292.

Holsapple, C. W., S. Shen and A. B. Whinston (1982). "A Consulting System for Data Base Design," International Journal Information Systems, Vol. 7, no. 3 March, 281-296.

Ishizuka, M., K. S. Fu, and J. T. P. Yao (1982). "Inference Procedures Under Uncertainty for the Problem-Reduction Method," Information Sciences, 28, 179-206.

Marschak, J. and R. Radner (1972). Economic Theory of Teams, Yale University Press.

McDermott, J. and B. Steele (1981). "Extending a Knowledge-Based System to Deal with Ad Hoc Constraints," Proc. Seventh Int'l. Joint Conf. Artificial Intelligence, 824-828.

Moore, J. C., H. K. Hall, and A. B. Whinston (1985). "Theoretical Foundations of Expert Systems."

Nau, D. S. (1983). "Expert Computer Systems," IEEE, February, 63-85.

Shortliffe, E. H. and B. G. Buchanan (1975). "A Model of Inexact Reasoning in Medicine," Mathematical Biosciences, 23, 351-379.

Shortliffe, E. H., R. Davis, S. G. Axline, B. G. Buchanan, C. C. Green and S. N. Cohen (1975). "Computer-Based Consultations in Clinical Therapeutics: Explanation and Rule Acquisition Capabilities of the MYCIN System," Computers and Biomedical Research, 8, 303-320.

Suwa, M., A. C. Scott, and E. H. Shortliffe (1984). "Completeness and Consistency in a Rule-Based System," Chapter 8 in Rule-Based Expert Systems, (B. B. Buchanan and E. H. Shortliffe eds.), pp. 159-170.

Artificial Intelligence in Economics and Management
L.F. Pau (Editor)

OVERVIEW OF ROME: A REASON-ORIENTED MODELING ENVIRONMENT

Donald W. Kosy and Ben P. Wise

The Robotics Institute
Carnegie-Mellon University
Pittsburgh, Pennsylvania 15213

The ROME system is an experimental decision support system generator that incorporates facilities originally developed for "expert" artificial intelligence systems. Like other DSS generators, it provides a set of tools for building, running, and documenting mathematical models of business activities. Beyond that, however, the system includes explicit differentiation between hard facts and softer information such as assumptions and expectations, a set of procedures for evaluating and explaining results, and a natural language user interface. In this paper, we discuss the representation of knowledge in ROME and show how it is used to answer questions, explain trends, detect anomalous values, and assess the credibility of model assumptions.

1. INTRODUCTION

In recent years, it has become very much easier to build computerized planning models for use in business decision making. Systems embodying such models have come to be called "decision support systems" (DSSs) and by using a decision support system generator [10], one can construct models in a few hours or days that would have taken weeks or months otherwise. At the same time, artificial intelligence (AI) techniques have emerged from the laboratory which have proven to be quite effective in solving certain classes of real-world problems. It has therefore been suggested [5,9,11] that there may be considerable value in combining these technologies to yield more powerful DSSs than are currently available.

The ROME system is an experimental DSS generator which has been built to investigate the application of AI techniques to quantitative business analysis. Its name is an acronym which is meant to characterize the approach we have taken. As a "modeling environment", ROME is like other DSS generators in that it provides a set of tools for building, running, and documenting mathematical models of business activities. A hierarchically structured database is part of that environment and an English-like command interface is used to access both the tools and the data. More importantly, however, ROME is "reason-oriented" in that it includes explicit differentiation between hard facts and softer information, such as assumptions and expectations, and procedures for evaluating and explaining the results it produces. A major goal of our research to date has been to realize a system that can explain why a result should be believed or give reasons why it should be challenged.

2. BACKGROUND: THE PLAN REVIEW PROBLEM

Our interest in evaluation and explanation was originally motivated by a study [7] of long range resource planning at a large US computer firm, which we will call EESCO. A *resource plan* is essentially a quantitative projection of the amounts of resources that will be needed to produce the volume of goods a firm expects to sell in future years. The major resources in EESCO's plan, for example, were labor, factory floor space, raw material, facilities, capital equipment, and expense funds. Projections of resource needs are used by a firm to allocate resources currently held and to make decisions on acquiring new ones.

Creating resource projections involves a combination of calculation and judgment that can be represented in a quantitative planning model with judgmental parameter values. Although it may be large, this model is simply a set quantitative relationships among variables, expressed by formulas and conditional statements, together with a set of input data. The formulas encode such things as accounting relationships between price and cost, aggregation of resource subtotals into totals, and the relative amounts of each type of resource required to produce a unit of product. The data include product parameters, manufacturing process parameters, and forecasts of resource price levels. Judgment is involved in the forecasts and in characterizing the resource demands of new products and processes.

Since there are many ways to design a manufacturing process for a given product, planners will normally choose a design that is responsive to various *goals* the firm has set for itself. EESCO's goals, for example, included increases in productivity, improved customer service, and maintenance of a stable workforce in spite of substantial changes in product types and volumes. These goals affect the specification of planned processes and these specifications, in turn, are reflected in the planning model parameters.

As in many large firms, the overall planning task at EESCO was decomposed into a hierarchy of subtasks corresponding to the different levels of the organizational hierarchy. As projections at lower levels were generated, they were reviewed and then consolidated into projections for the parent level. If approved at the parent level, these projections were frozen into final plans to be submitted to the next level up. For example, if several products were manufactured in the same plant, a plan for each product would be developed, reviewed at the product level, consolidated into a plant plan, reviewed at that level, and then, if approved, submitted for consolidation at division level.

At all levels, the resource plans themselves were displayed as arrays of numbers where the columns specified planning periods (e.g. years) and the rows showed the projections for each type of resource for each period. The labor section of a hypothetical plan for one of EESCO's plants is shown below.

Marysville	FY82	FY83	FY84	FY85	FY86	FY87
dl	95	127	85	38	46	54
il	68	87	69	49	51	51
year end people	163	214	154	87	97	106
ave people		189	184	121	92	102

Figure 1: Part of a Resource Plan for EESCO's Marysville Plant

The review steps in the planning process turned out to be very important to its success. Reviews were performed by planning managers who were ultimately held accountable for the plans they submitted to the next level up. They recognized that a plan is only as good as the assumptions it is based on and so one purpose of their review was to identify and assess those assumptions. In particular, reviewers wanted to make sure that assumptions used at lower levels matched their own assumptions about how the firm operated so that there would be no inconsistencies in combining lower level results into an aggregate. If an inconsistency was detected, an explanation would be sought from the lower level planner.

They also recognized that for a plan to be acceptable at the next higher level, it must be responsive to organizational goals. At EESCO, goals for one level did not necessarily have to be met by all lower levels. However, it was important that they be met by the combination of lower level values in the aggregate. Hence, a second purpose of the review was to evaluate aggregate results against goals and, if there were a mismatch, to negotiate revisions in lower level plans that would eliminate it.

While there are a number of DSS generators that could have been used to build and run the planning models at EESCO, and one, in fact, was being used, none of them provides much help for the review process. In particular, none distinguishes assumed relationships from necessary ones, none can really explain the results produced, and none has any facilities for evaluating results against established goals or norms. The ROME project was initiated to investigate what might be done to fill this gap.

3. THE ROME SYSTEM

The approach we have taken in ROME is to provide a modeling system in which results can be evaluated and explained by comparative analysis. More specifically, results can be evaluated by comparing them to expectations, and results can be explained by comparing derivations of differences. These operations are facilitated by a database structure that allows inheritance of symbolic information and a user interface that allows natural expression of expectations and questions.

As shown in the figure below, the system itself consists of four major components: a database, an interface module called ROMULUS, an explanation component called ERGO, and an evaluation component called REMUS.

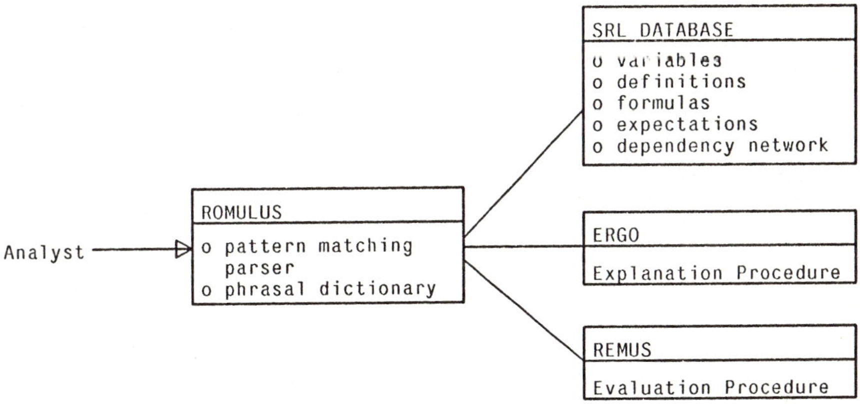

Figure 2: ROME Components

In the following sections, we describe each of these components in turn.

4. THE DATABASE

The database contains all the non-procedural knowledge ROME uses and is organized around the set of variables comprising a planning model. The variables are arranged in a hierarchical network and are represented in the database by records called *schemata* using the frame-style language SRL [14]. This hierarchy represents a categorization of variables into classes, subclasses and instances according to their level of specificity. The figure below shows part of the tree of variables for the resource plan shown in Figure 1.

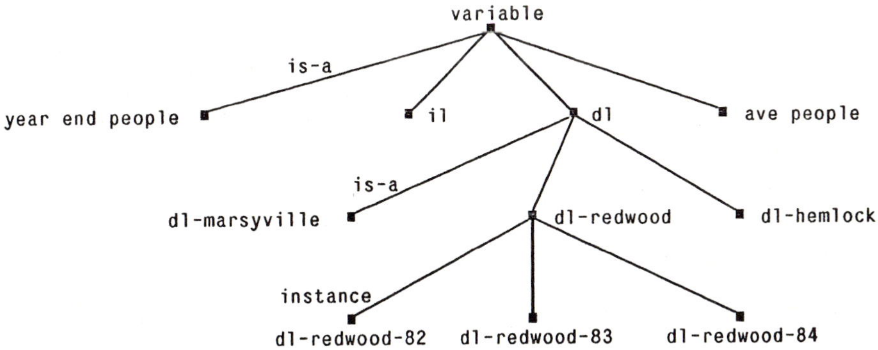

Figure 3: Part of a Tree of Variables

At the top are the different types of variables. At the next level, a variable is differentiated into subclasses according to the real-world entity it relates to, such as a particular product, plant, company, or whatever. We call such entities *anchors*. At the bottom level, each instance of a variable is associated with an evaluation context, such as a time period. The bottom level is thus equivalent to a set of two dimensional arrays where each element is indexed by anchor and context.

Unlike an array, however, the *is-a* and *instance* links in the tree are used to propagate information from higher to lower levels by "inheritance". In SRL, information about a schema is represented by storing symbolic values in *slots* attached to the schema. Information is said to be inherited when a slot in a one schema is automatically filled with a value taken from another schema where the schemata are related by a chain of *is-a* and *instance* links. Thus, in ROME, if information about a variable is stored at the class level, such as a formula for computing its value, all subclasses and instances of that variable will inherit this same formula. Furthermore, there is no restriction on making one class of variable a subclass of another class so that information about the latter may be inherited by the former. For instance, IL and DL might be made subclasses of the class "labor" and would then inherit information from this more abstract level.

Properties of variables may be linked into the tree at any level, and lower level properties normally supersede higher level ones. For instance, a DL formula for product 2 will be the same for every period unless it is overridden by a different formula at the instance level. However, the inheritance procedure may also be directed to augment lower level properties with properties from higher levels. This kind of inheritance is used for expectations and goals.

The content of the database represents the knowledge ROME has about variables, values, formulas, and the real-world activities they describe. Properties of variables include their definition (verbal or arithmetic), their numerical values in different contexts, the source of those values (input or formula), and whether the variable is taken to be endogenous or exogeneous to the system being modeled. Input variables may be further described as "controllable" if the decision-maker using the model can change (or negotiate a change in) its value in the real world.

Values have a modality property which indicates whether they are empirical facts, estimates based on other variables, or simply assumptions. Likewise, formulas are categorized as being either definitions, estimation equations, or assumptions. Definitions are exact equalities, e.g. "sales = volume * selling price". Estimation equations, on the other hand, are not exact and are used to characterize a process without actually simulating or defining it. Estimates of endogenous variables can be viewed as approximations of their values while estimates of exongenous variables can be viewed as predictions. Examples of estimation formulas include regression equations, trend extrapolation, use of growth-rate factors, etc. All other formulas that are not definitions or estimations are considered to be assumptions.

Knowledge about what a variable describes can be represented in the database in two ways. First, actual values the variable has had in the past can be stored as facts. Second, expected or desired values can be specified by expressions that denote norms or goals, respectively. A *norm* in ROME is a relationship among variables that "should" hold true under "normal" circumstances according to experts in the domain of the model. A *goal* is a statement of an organizational objective or policy that can be expressed in terms of model variables. Norms and goals are used by REMUS to evaluate model results and, as part of that process, may be used to infer formulas for variables that are needed for the evaluation but are not explicitly present in the model.

To keep track of derived information, a dependency network [2] is used to link properties to their sources. A dependency is a record that contains the justification for a slot's value in terms of the action that produced the value plus the inputs to that action. Examples of actions that set values are communication with the user, execution of a formula, and inheritance from a higher level. Inputs corresponding to these actions are the content of user input, values of variables contained in a formula, and the is-a/instance chain that allowed inheritance, respectively. Using these dependencies, the system can tell, for example, what variables affect what other variables and this, in turn, provides the information ERGO needs to analyze and explain model results.

5. ROMULUS

ROMULUS stands for Reason-Oriented Modeling Using a Language Understanding System and this component acts as the intermediary between the user and the other components. Its responsibilities include initial processing of user inputs, maintenance of the database, and control of the output display. As a "service module" for the rest of the system, our main goal for ROMULUS has been that it be unobtrusive: It should be fast, flexible, forgiving, informative, and easy to learn without training.

Like other natural language interfaces [6,12], ROMULUS is designed to simulate understanding in a limited domain by recognizing all likely forms of expression for a limited number of ideas. This recognition is performed at the sentence level by a pattern-matching parser [1] in conjunction with a large number of grammar rules. Every grammar rule is a triple consisting of a lefthand side, a righthand side, and an arrow between them. A pattern to be matched is expressed by a sequence of expressions comprising terminal symbols, non-terminal symbols and operator expressions. Some sample grammar rules (for a "why" question) are shown below:

```
(why <aux> <focus-item> <change> (!setting := ?<adjunct>) ?%qmark)
=>
(why-change !tense !focus !change !setting)

        <aux> -> ((!tense := (&i present (do | does | is | are))) |
                  (!tense := (&i past (did | was | were))))
        <focus-item> -> (!focus := (&u <change>))
        <change> -> ((!change := change) | go (!change := (up | down)) |
                     (!change := (&i up (increase | rise)))|
                     (!change := (&i down (decrease | fall))))
        <adjunct> -> ((in | for | at) (+ ~%qmark))
```

Non-terminal symbols are marked by angle brackets, operator expressions by parentheses, and terminals are left unadorned. Variables to be bound to constituent strings when a pattern is matched are indicated by an exclamation mark.

Rather than continuing with a formal description, it is easier to see how a rule works by tracing through its application. For example, if the first word in an input sentence is *why*, the parser will try to apply the first rule above (and all other rules whose first pattern element can match the terminal symbol *why*). If the next word matches the pattern specified by <aux> (for auxiliary verb), the variable **!tense** will be set. A word will match <aux> if it is one of the terminals *do*, *does*, *is*, or *are*, in which case **!tense** is bound to *present*, or if it is one of *did*, *was*, or *were*, in which case **!tense** is bound to *past*. Next, the non-terminal <focus-item> can be matched by any string of words that is followed by a string that matches <change>. If this process can be continued until all of the input is matched, the righthand side of the top level rule will be executed using the variable bindings made during the match. For instance, if the input is *Why did Marysville year end people go up in 83*, the routine "why-change" will be called with bindings **!tense** = *(present)*, **!focus-item** = *(Marysville year end people)*, **!change** = *(up)*, and **!setting** = *(in 83)*.

The next task is to find referents for the phrases that have been extracted from the input. A referent is a schema in the database such as a variable, anchor, or context, and the association is made by a phrase interpreter using a phrasal dictionary. Unlike a typical natural language system, wherein the vocabulary is fixed, the ROMULUS interpreter must be able to deal with whatever terminology the user happens to employ. Hence, it does not attempt to determine what a phrase means, but only what it refers to. Interpretation proceeds by (1) segmenting a phrase into parts using syntactic cues, (2) determining the referent of each part, and (3) assembling a retrieval request for the whole phrase based on the semantic type of each referent in it. This procedure is flexible enough to recognize that

Marysville year end people in FY83
year end people at Marysville in 83
yep(mr) in 83
year end people(83,mr)

all refer to the same variable, if the dictionary contains appropriate entries.

The dictionary entries for words and phrases are simply pointers to whatever schemas they refer to. This makes it easy to represent synonyms, abbreviations, and acronyms as just other names for the same schema. Moreover, since dictionary entries can be phrases, the interpreter can almost always guess the appropriate correction for a misspelled word in a phrase by examining the other words around it and finding the phrase that matches most closely. The algorithm used for spelling correction is taken from [4].

In general, the interface to a modeling system must accept three sorts of inputs: questions, commands, and declarations. The current ROMULUS grammar includes interrogative forms for asking questions about variables, getting advice on functions the system can perform, and asking why results came out the way they did. It includes imperative forms for controlling the display and requesting evaluations. The remaining forms specify the syntax of declaratives which are used to define variables, express formulas, establish goals and norms, assign values to input variables, and declare all other properties of variables. Examples of declarations related to the variables in Figure 1 are shown in Figure 4, where hemlock and redwood are the names of two products manufactured at Marysville:

```
Define dl to be the number of in-house direct labor EESCO employees at year end
Define il to be the number of in-house indirect labor EESCO employees at year end
Define year end people to be dl + il
Define ave people to be the average number of plant employees during a year
Estimate ave people(y) to be (year end people(y) + year end people(y-1))/2
Estimate dl to be roundup(dl-hrs * 1000 / hrs/shift/yr)
Declare marysville, redwood, and hemlock to be anchors
Use mr to refer to marysville
Use rw to refer to redwood
Use hm to refer to hemlock
Define dl(mr) to be dl(rw) + dl(hm)
Define il to be plant mgmt + product il
Define dl-hrs to be std hrs + n-std hrs
Declare fy82 values to be factual
Let std hrs(rw) = 0 44.40 73.60 50.79 62.68 77.21
Let std hrs(hm) = 85.12 91.13 22.56 0 0 0
```

Figure 4: Definitions and Declarations

System output is displayed on a split screen. The top portion shows a spreadsheet display of model results very much like that shown in Figure 1. Each column is headed by the name of the evaluation context (fiscal years in Figure 1) and the name of the anchor for the values being displayed is shown at the upper left. Such displays are produced by a *show* command and any calculations are performed when they are needed to show the results. The bottom portion is used to display user inputs, answers to questions, explanations, and the results of REMUS's evaluations. Thus, the top portion is a report of results and the bottom portion shows the dialogue that has occurred so far.

The overall effect is to give the user the impression that he is conversing with an analyst about the results shown in the report. After the declarations shown above have been processed, the conversation below exemplifies the kinds of questions ROMULUS can answer.

```
> What does "dl" mean?
It stands for direct labor.

> How is direct labor defined?
That represents the number of in-house direct labor EESCO employees at year end.

> How is it calculated?
In general, the formula is:
        dl = roundup(dl-hrs * 1000 / hrs/shift/yr)        [estimate]
```

Note that pronouns, such as the word *it*, are allowed to refer back to previously mentioned items. Determining the referent of a pronoun is easy in this environment because interrogative and imperative forms in English clearly establish a focus of interest. Output generation is also easy because everything the system can say can be cast in the form of output templates to be instantiated as needed. Although all the techniques ROMULUS uses are simple, combining them with a large number of patterns (grammatical, phrasal, etc.) allows the interface to be much more flexible and forgiving than in other modeling systems.

6. ERGO

ERGO stands for Explaining Results Generated by Others and its function is to answer "why" questions about numbers. In asking a "why" question, a person is expressing a desire to have something clarified that he doesn't understand. In the case of numbers, what needs to be clarified is how the numbers were derived and why the derivation produces the results observed.

We can divide results to be explained into two categories. The first category comprises *explicit results*, which are those that appear explicitly in the output of a model and are produced directly by formulas. ERGO takes a very simple and direct approach to explaining explicit results: it simply displays the formula and the values of subordinate variables. For example, ERGO's answer to the question *Why does dl(mr) equal 128 in 83?* in our example model would be that *dl(rw) = 56 and dl(hm) = 72 and dl(mr) = dl(rw) + dl(hm)*. Thus, a "why" question about a variable's values is treated as a "how" question about its derivation, and the answer is simply the derivation itself. This approach is very similar to that taken by MYCIN [3], which explains its conclusions by exhibiting the rules used and the certainty factors of subordinate clauses. There are a number of similarities between the formulas in a model and the rules in an expert system, and so the explanations can be similar as well. Although simple, this technique is important because it saves the user from having to search the model himself to find out where a result came from.

The second, more interesting, category comprises *implicit results*, which are those that come from comparisons the user makes between values. Implicit results are referenced in questions like *why does dl(mr) go up in 83?* and *why is there a dip in year end people in 85?*. Answering such questions involves explaining differences. For example, the difference to be explained for a direction question such as *Why does dl(mr) go up in 83?* is the difference between the value of the variable in the given context, 83, and its value in the previous context, 82. We call the first value the *focus value* and the second the *referent value*.

The procedure ERGO uses to explain differences is based on comparing derivations. To be comparable, the derivations must involve the same formula, say g, so that the difference, Δy, comes from evaluating g in the focus context vs the referent context:

$$\Delta y = g(a_f, b_f, c_f, \ldots) - g(a_r, b_r, c_r \ldots)$$

The subscripts on the arguments denote the two different contexts. We will let S denote the set of variables referenced in g: $S = \{a, b, c, \ldots\}$. Since all ROME variables are two dimensional, one can easily specify comparisons across columns, across anchors, or across both, by asking questions that specify the appropriate indices. For instance, to ask why DL for the redwood product is greater than DL for hemlock, the question form would be: *Why is dl(rw) greater than dl(hm) in 83?*. The comparison in this case would be between variables subscripted (rw,83) and variables subscripted (hm,83) in the formula that computes the value of DL. The formulas for the different instances of DL would be the same because they both would be inherited from the general formula for DL.

The first step in the explanation procedure is to find a set of variables X, where $X \subseteq S$, which is sufficient to account for Δy. To do that, we define a measure of significance, $\varepsilon(X,y)$, which measures the *effect* of variables in X on y in the focus context relative to the referent context. The definition is:

$$\varepsilon(X,y) \triangleq y_f - g(Z)$$

where the vector Z contains values of variables in X evaluated in the referent context and values for all other variables in S evaluated in the focus context. By successively choosing values of X to be first individual variables in S, then pairs, then triples, and so on, the derivation of the value of $\varepsilon(X,y)$ is made closer and closer to the derivation of Δy. When the derivations are close enough that the value of $\varepsilon(X,y)$ is a substantial fraction (80%) of the total difference Δy, we conclude that the effect of the variables in X is large enough to explain the difference. Variables in S but not in X are taken to be insignificant with respect to this difference.

Given the set of explanatory variables X, the second step is to express the explanation in words. In general, the answer will include (1) the differences that account for Δy, (2) the formula g, (3) identification of the primary explanatory variable(s) and (4) a qualification, which may express counteracting, reinforcing, or insignificant effects. Like the responses ROMULUS produces, ERGO's answers are generated from templates that are just sufficient to express in English the information that must be conveyed. To illustrate, if the input question is *Why did dl(mr) go up in 83?*, the answer would be:

> *Dl(mr) goes up in 83 because dl(rw) goes up and dl(mr) = dl(rw) + dl(hm). Although dl(hm) also changes, its effect was insignificant. Would you like me to continue?*

The explanation can be continued all the way down to the lowest level of the model, i.e., its exogenous variables. A more complete description and justification of both steps of this procedure is given in [8].

7. REMUS

The purpose of REMUS is to Review and Evaluate a Model's Underlying Structure. Of all ROME components, the design of this one has been most strongly influenced by the resource plan review problem at EESCO. First, it uses an encoding of evaluation criteria that is independent of the model itself. The reason for this is simply that such criteria depend much more on the aims of the reviewer than on the model he is reviewing. In ROME, evaluation criteria are expressed by statements of goals and norms. Second, it was the case at EESCO that some important criteria involved variables that were not explicitly shown on the resource plan. However, their values could be inferred from variables that were shown plus the reviewer's knowledge of the domain of the model. For this reason, ROME allows criteria to be phrased in terms of "generic variables", if desired, which a reviewer may link to variables in a specific model. Finally, it was also the case for some important variables that reviewers had no criteria. When this situation arose, reviewers would first search for related variables they could evaluate, perform the evaluation, and then assess the impact of their evaluation on the original variable. To capture this aspect of plan review, the REMUS review procedure capitalizes on the hierarchical structure of resource plans to search for evaluable variables at lower levels in the derivation tree if needed.

The main steps in this procedure are shown below. To evaluate a variable *v*:

1. If there are criteria for the values of *v*, apply them and state conclusions. Check equalities before inequalities.
2. Find variables that explain the trend using ERGO and the formula for *v*. If there is no formula but there is an equality norm, use that. Call this set of variables S.
3. If there are variables in the formula which have criteria but are not in S, add them to S.
4. Recursively evaluate the variables in S.

The main conclusions that may be drawn are as follows:

1. If criteria are met, REMUS says so.
2. If a goal is not met, REMUS calls it "problematic".
3. If there is a moderate difference (< 30%) between a value and a norm, it is "OK".
4. If there is a large (> 30%) difference between a value and a goal, it is "extraordinary". If there is a large deviation from a norm, it is "odd".
5. If the effect on *v* of a large deviation in a lower level variable can be determined, REMUS suggests that *v* may be "too high" or "too low".

This procedure can be continued until it reaches exogenous variables. If the initial variable *v* is at the subclass level, then each instance in the context sequence is evaluated in turn. A fuller discussion may be found in [13].

To use this procedure, one must declare the evaluation criteria in the form of goals and norms. For example, one goal at EESCO was that new products should be manufactured more efficiently than old products, or at least no less efficiently. This goal may be expressed to ROME as:

```
Declare comparable product to be an anchor variable
Declare current year to be a context variable
We want Resource Used/Unit to be no more than Resource Used/Unit(comparable
        product,current year)
```

One such resource, for example, might be the amount of labor used per unit of output. In accounting, labor usage is measured in hours required, given some manufacturing process and a "standard" volume of output:

```
Define Standard Hours/Unit to be Total Standard Hours / Q-produced
Declare Standard Hours/Unit to be a measure of Resource Used/Unit
Expect Total Standard Hours to equal Standard Hours/Unit * Q-produced
Declare Standard Hours/Unit to be exogenous
```

Of course there may be many such criteria, but one will suffice for illustration.

Notice that the variables just mentioned are not specific to the model defined in Figure 4. Rather, they represent quantities that are more or less universal in manufacturing operations and the relationships between them are essentially generic. As a textual convention, we have distinguished these generic variables by capitalizing their names. Relationships among them are expressed by declaring expected equalities. If variables in a specific model are made instances of generic ones, the corresponding relationships will be inherited. This may be done as follows:

```
Declare std hrs to be a measure of Total Standard Hours
Declare build schedule to be a measure of Q-produced
Let comparable product(rw) = hemlock
Define current year to be 82
```

If a generic variable is not linked to any specific one it will be instantiated directly for any relevant anchors and contexts. This will be the case here for Standard Hours/Unit.

To show how this all works, we close with a sample evaluation:

```
> Evaluate dl(mr)
There are no evaluation criteria for dl(mr).  However, dl(mr) goes up in 83 because
dl(rw) goes up and dl(mr) = dl(rw) + dl(hm).  Although dl(hm) also changed, its effect
was insignificant.  Would you like me to continue? Y

Dl(rw) goes up in 83 solely because dl-hrs(rw) goes up and dl = roundup(dl-hrs * 1000 /
hrs/shift/yr).  Would you like me to continue? Y

Dl-hrs(rw) goes up in 83 because std hrs(rw) and n-std hrs(rw) both go up and dl-hrs =
std hrs + n-std hrs.  The increase in dl-hrs was due primarily to the increase in std
hrs. Would you like me to continue? Y

By norm 1, we expect std hrs to equal Standard Hours/Unit * build schedule.
This appears to be so for rw in 83.  Would you like me to continue? Y

By goal 1, we want Standard Hours/Unit to be no more than Standard Hours/Unit(hm,82).
This appears to be so for rw in 83.  But we also find Standard Hours/Unit(rw) to be much
less than Standard Hours/Unit(hm,82) in 83.  This seems extraordinary.  So dl(mr) may
be too low.  Would you like me to continue?
```

If the user answers *yes* at this point, evaluation will continue with the next column. It might have continued with an explanation of the increase in n-std hrs(rw), but this is an input variable with no known equality relationships and so there was no way to continue from there.

8. CONCLUSIONS

It can be argued that current DSSs support decisions in three ways. First, they automate some of the clerical component of an analyst's activities thereby enabling him to explore a broader range of options than would otherwise be possible. Second, they provide structural frameworks for some types of decisions in the form of computational models. Third, within the context of a model, they provide a free-flowing interaction with the system thereby introducing the possibility of helping the analyst arrive at a better understanding of the problem.

The support they provide is limited, however. For one thing, their clerical function does not extend much beyond calculating and formatting. Not much attention is paid to input validation, assumption checking, or keeping track of intermediate results. Nor is there much in the way of mechanisms by which results could be explained or justified to users who were not familiar with what a particular model does. If a user is skeptical of the results he gets, it is up to him to search for reasons to believe or challenge them.

In ROME, we have attempted to go beyond these limits by adding several AI-inspired capabilities to a traditional DSS base. Using ROMULUS, for example, an analyst can ask questions about properties of variables other than their values, which would not be possible with a strictly numerical system. Using ERGO, he can get explanations of results. Using REMUS, he can review the results in light of assumptions and check them against evaluation criteria.

These capabilities have been implemented using two basic AI techniques: search and hierarchical knowledge representation. The comparative analysis that ERGO performs, for example, requires searching through combinations of variables to find a set that accounts for a difference. The evaluations made by REMUS require a search for variables that are related to the variable being evaluated. Hierarchical representation has been important in linking individual variables to more abstract or generic classes whose properties should be inherited by the individuals.

Given the framework we have set up in ROME, there seem to be many opportunities for further research. For one, both explanations and evaluations are currently limited to one context at a time, e.g. one column. But, given a set of explanations or evaluations, it might be possible for the system to produce summary statements from them, or generalizations, that would identify what was significant about a whole series of values. Second, the technique of comparative analysis might be extended to explaining the results of what-if scenarios, or to finding the causes of differences between the actual performance of a firm and what was planned or budgeted. Thus, it may be possible to provide much better support for budget-variance analysis, for instance, than is currently available. Finally, we are very interested in whether the techniques implemented in ROME are robust enough for practical use. While we have tested the system on a few small models, it remains to be seen whether the concepts and procedures will scale up to larger, more complex models where explanation and evaluation should be especially valuable. These are among the issues we are currently exploring.

REFERENCES

[1] Boggs, W.M, Carbonell, J.G., and Monarch, I., "The Dypar-I Tutorial and Reference Manual," Computer Science Department, Carnegie-Mellon University, 1984.

[2] Charniak, E., Riesbeck, C.K., and McDermott, D.V., "Data Dependencies," in *Artificial Intelligence Programming*, Hillsdale, N.J.: Lawrence Erlbaum Associates, 1980.

[3] Davis, R., *Applications of Meta Level Knowledge to the Construction, Maintenance and Use of Large Knowledge Bases*, PhD Thesis, Computer Science Department, Stanford University, July 1976.

[4] Durham, I., Lamb, D.A., Saxe, J.B., "Spelling Correction in User Interfaces," *CACM*, V. 26, No. 10, pp. 764-773, October 1982.

[5] Gorry, G. and Krumland, R., "Artificial Intelligence Research and Decision Support Systems," in *Building Decisions Support Systems*, J. Bennet (ed.), Addison-Wesley, 1982.

[6] Hendrix, G.G., Sacerdoti, E.D., Sagalowicz, D., and Slocum, J., "Developing A Natural Language Interface to Complex Data," *ACM Transactions on Database Systems*, V. 3, No. 2, pp. 105-147, June 1978.

[7] Kosy, D.W., and Dahr, V., "Knowledge-Based Support Systems for Long Range Planning," The Robotics Institute, Carnegie-Mellon University, 1983.

[8] Kosy, D.W., and Wise, B.P., "Self-Explanatory Financial Planning Models," *Proceedings of AAAI-84*, pp. 176-181, August 1984.

[9] Scott Morton, M.S., "Expert Support Systems -- The Next Generation of Decisions Support," *National Conference on Decision Support and Expert Systems*, George Washington University School of Government and Business Administration, Washington, D.C., April 1985.

[10] Sprague, R.H., Jr., "A Framework for the Development of Decision Support Systems," *MIS Quarterly* **4**, December 1980, pp 1-26.

[11] Sprague, R.H., Jr., "Knowledge Based DSS: A Research Progress Report," *Transactions Second International Conference on Decision Support Systems*, G. Dickinson (ed.), June 1982.

[12] Waltz, D.L., "An English Language Question Answering System for a Large Relational Database," *CACM*, V. 21, No. 7, pp. 526-539, July 1978.

[13] Wise, B.P., and Kosy, D.W., "Model-Based Evaluation of Long-Range Resource Allocation Plans," *This volume.*

[14] Wright, M., and Fox, M.S., "SRL/1.5 User Manual," The Robotics Institute, Carnegie-Mellon University, 1982.

Artificial Intelligence in Economics and Management
L.F. Pau (Editor)

DECISION SIMULATION (DSIM) - ONE OUTCOME OF COMBINING EXPERT SYSTEMS AND DECISION SUPPORT SYSTEMS

Kenneth J. Fordyce
Gerald A. Sullivan

International Business Machines Corp.
Poughkeepsie, NY 12602, U.S.A.

This paper outlines one role for expert systems (ES) in decision support systems (DSS). This combination results in a hybrid system called Decision Support / Decision Simulation (DSIM). Examples are presented.

INTRODUCTION

In the past year reporting in the popular press has improved the general availability of facts about artificial intelligence (AI). The image being generated portrays AI as a powerful new tool. Like other tools, AI allows a human to easily control and direct power sources in accomplishment of a task by providing cognitive amplification or augmentation.

Research in AI generally falls into one of two major categories: (1) making machines more useful to humans, and (2) understanding intelligence. Since we are practitioners with interest and experience in implementations of AI which function as tools in support of the decision maker, the focus of this paper is 'increased usefulness'. Specifically, the implications that expert systems (ES) subarea of AI has in the arena of decision support systems (DSS).

The paper will proceed as follows: A review of computer based decision support tools. A working definition of ES. A description of the role of ES in DSS and and a definition of Decision Support / Decision Simulation (DSIM). Some examples of expert systems being developed by us. Finally, an estimation of what can be accomplished in the future. Our work is done in APL (Sullivan and Fordyce 1985).

COMPUTER-BASED DECISION SUPPORT TOOLS OR AIDS

One primary use of computers is to support decision making at all levels of an organization. Over the past 30 years a number of distinct "software technologies" have developed to provide decision support tools or aids by "harnessing" the computer. Builders of application systems to provide decision support integrate specific tools from each of the technologies to meet the needs of the group of decision makers they are servicing. Expert or knowledge based systems can be viewed as one of the newest decision support software technology. These technologies are:

1. Data Base Query
   Tools in this group enable the user to easily and flexibility retrieve factual information. The information may be historical, real-time, or future projections. Facts are divided into two components: a class and a specific instance. For example, price would be class of facts (the variable name), and $8.50 would be a specific instance (the value of the variable for a certain situation). The facts are organized into data bases. The relationships among the facts is used to structure the data base.

2. Normative Models
   Tools in this group provide the user a recommended action or generate new knowledge. The facts are organized into a set of algebraic or differential equations. Many of these tools come from operations research, statistics, and engineering. For example, statistical techniques might provide a confidence interval or a regression model from a set of facts, linear programming might tell the user how to distribute his product among four warehouses, and an engineering model might tell the user at what temperature to operate his kiln or what size furnace to install.

3. Simulation
   Tools in this group enable the user to project the outcome of specific set of actions. This is called "what if" analysis. The facts are organized into a network which represents the actual flow of events. Flowcharts are most often used to initially represent the flow. The simulation is made operational when the flow is encoded into computer code. Simulation can be split into three groups: engineering, management science and financial planning.

4. Visual Aids
   Tools in this group help the user understand the information by providing a variety of graphical or pictorial (icons) representations of the information.

5. Networks
   Tools in this group help the user obtain information from another computer system or send information to another information system.

6. Expert or Knowledge-Based Systems
   Tools in this group provide the user a recommended action or generate new knowledge. This is the same function as normative models, but the methods used are much different, and the problems addressed are usually

those for which modeling is inappropriate. The facts are usually organized into rules, frames, and/or networks. The logical relationships among the facts as understood by a human expert(s) is used to build these structures. This collection of information is called a knowledge base. Some type of "reasoning mechanism" is used to extract the appropriate facts from the knowledge base to satisfy a request. This reasoning mechanism usually has the ability to explain why it recommended a certain action.

REVIEW OF EXPERT SYSTEMS

There are a number of sub-specialities within the AI field. They include: vision, Robotics, speech recognition, human problem solving, natural language interfaces, and knowledge-based expert systems. The last two have the most immediate potential impact on decision support systems.

The goal of the artificial intelligence (AI) field is to develop computational approaches to intelligent behavior (Gevarter 1983). Some of the earliest work done in the AI field got computers to play games like chess and checkers. Of particular importance is getting machines to solve problems or carry out tasks by enabling them to purposefully manipulate symbols, recognize and appropriately respond to patterns, and/or learn or adapt in a manner similar to human beings. Additionally, AI includes the productive merging of symbol manipulation and pattern recognition by the computer, with the computers ability to carry out extensive computational algorithms quickly and accurately.

Knowledge-based expert systems (ES) is defined (Rauch 1984) to be a class of computer programs intended to serve as consultants for decision making. These programs use a collection of facts, rules of thumb, and other knowledge about a limited field to help make inferences in the field. They differ substantially from conventional computer programs in that their goals may have no algorithmic solution, and they must make inferences based on incomplete or uncertain information. They are called expert systems because they address problems normally thought to require human specialists for solution, and knowledge-based because researchers have found that amassing a large amount of knowledge, rather than sophisticated reason techniques, is responsible for the success of the approach. A predecessor of knowledge-based expert systems is decision tables (Decision Tables 1978). The process of building an expert system is called knowledge engineering. Knowledge engineering is a subarea of problem situation analysis (Sullivan and Fordyce 1983). The following drawing depicts the general makeup of a rule-based expert system.

```
                                      ------------------
                                      | KNOWLEDGE BASE  |     ----------
                                      | rules for the   |<--| EXPERT |
                                      | problem domain  |     ----------
                                      ------------------
                                            |   |
--------      ---------------         ------------------
|       |<--| answers        |<---  |  INFERENCE       |
| USER  |   | and            |--->  |  MECHANISM       |
|       |-->| explanation    |      ------------------
--------      ---------------               |   |
                                      ------------------
                                      | DATA BASE        |     --------------
                                      | specific facts   |<--| data         |
                                      | or observations  |   | collection   |
                                      ------------------       --------------
```

Knowledge-based expert systems and techniques enable information system builders to move problem domain knowledge information from the human to the computer. Benefits can accrue to an organization in four ways (Rychener 1985):

1. Provide expertise when human expertise is not available
2. Provide expertise more uniformly, and sometimes faster
3. Assist experts in making decisions in complex situations
4. Characterize the problem domain

The expert systems of the 1980's now function productively in such diverse areas as medical diagnosis, mineral & oil exploration, tactical targeting, equipment fault locating, computer operation and configuration, and management of manufacturing operations. Sullivan and Fordyce (1984) has a more detailed description of expert systems.

ES AND DSS

To understand how the ES and DSS combination can help the decision maker, we have to characterize the role. Typically, the decision maker is faced with the need to select from a stream of alternatives by some deadline, those actions which maximize the chance of success and minimize the chance of failure.

Success can be something as mundane as increasing corporate market share, or as humane as saving a patient's life. In both cases there are alternative ways to attack the problem. Usually there is a mass of data available. The decision window may be such that:
the time needed to reduce the data to information relevant to the decision, exceeds the time for which the opportunity to act exists.

Present decision support techniques can help assemble the data into information, if the decision maker speaks its language. Then the information can be used by the decision maker to generate a series of alternatives available. Last, the decision maker can use a simulation language to project the outcome of each decision. In many cases the patient has probably died, or didn't need treatment to survive in the first place.

In situations where the decision window is too small to thoroughly analyze a problem with today's support technology, the decision maker relies on his experience with similar situations in the past. This experience base allows the decision maker to rapidly sort relevant input from non-relevant, to rapidly arrive at a choice, and take action on that basis. The experience base is difficult and costly to build. It is not easily transferable from one mind to another. Thus experts tend to be in short supply.

For a computer to fully augment the decision maker's expertise two conditions are necessary:

1. The computer must be made to understand the data and problem well enough to reduce the flow to a structured series of the available alternatives with an explanation of their consequence
2. The language barrier must be eliminated

The first condition is something ES can help with. Natural language interfaces (NLI) can help with the second.

Until recently, system applications which aimed at helping the decision maker have been bound to traditional computational methods. The actions taken by the computer being limited to only those which the systems analysts and programmers anticipated might be necessary.

Current techniques provide for gathering the expertise of successful decision makers and characteristics of the environment, and then making it available in an untiring, constantly available, and adaptable (non-procedural) form called the expert system. The domain knowledge provided by expert systems will add structure to the data. Such systems can assist in finding the appropriate computational algorithm or data set, a solution for problems where the computational algorithm alone is not sufficient and explain its reasoning.

Additionally, current work in natural language interfaces and nested windows significantly ease communication between humans and machines.

Expert systems are one of the key tools in moving DSS into the next step in the evolution from passive data storage to highly active systems that participate in the decision making process. Figure 1 contains the hierarchy. This last step is called Decision Support / Decision Simulation (DSIM). In DSIM data is increasingly extended into more compact and useful information. DSIM combines traditional DSS, quantitative analysis, graphics and simulation, data base management and query, and expert systems. It integrates all six decision support technologies to provide the decision maker a more powerful decision aid.

INFORMATION ACTIVE

DSIM - DECISION SUPPORT / SIMULATION

DSS - DECISION SUPPORT SYSTEMS

MIS - MANAGEMENT INFORMATION SYSTEMS

DB - DATA BASES

DATA PASSIVE

Figure 1
Management System Hierarchy

DSIM is not limited to answering the questions:
What is the present status of some activity, or
what if I change the value assigned to a variable in a model?
DSIM is able to formulate alternatives, predict logical outcomes, and answer the question why.

Many of the new support systems are moving in the DSIM direction. For example Kosy (1984), Fox (1984), Brown (1985), Bard (1985), Wiig (1985), Hagaman (1985), and Duchessi (1985). This direction is also reflected in some the latest expert system shells, languages, and consulting businesses. Examples are Inference Corporation's ART (1984), Intellicorp's KEE (1984), IBM's APL2, many of the recent enhancements made to LISP and PROLOG.

LOGISTICS MANAGEMENT SYSTEMS

The manufacturing environment is one of constant flux. Rarely do short-term operational assumptions hold true long enough to be implemented completely. Recovery and redirection are more the rule than the exception. A system for logistics management is a closely coupled clustering of decision support systems (including expert system components) to aid the decision maker in coping with this environment. As is the case with decision support systems in general, this class of system assists the decision maker by providing structure to the rather unstructured problems facing him in managing a large scale logistics network like the ones found in major manufacturing operations.

Logistics is controlling the manner in which the manufacturing process unfolds. The floor manager must get the right parts to the right place on the right tool at the right time. There are wide variety of unique final assemblies. Some achieve their uniqueness from the processes used to construct them, others by the components from which they are assembled. Each follows a unique path through the process flow. Current hi-tech manufacturers are dealing with processes whose control tolerances are expressed in microns and nanoseconds. Required processes and tooling are often so technologically advanced as to be on the very edge of possibility. These factors combine to form the antithesis of the predictable operating environment. Thus, although the problems encountered by the decision maker are composed of a set of basic parts, their variety is limitless.

Expert systems have the ability to approach the problem by machine application of codified knowledge obtained from experts in floor control and management. This rules base is coupled with data reflecting the current state of the line. The actual state is compared to the planned, or desired state. If a variance exists between the two, the system uses the rules to develop a response to the situation. A logistics management systems would, include the following components:

- Status repeater and alert mechanism.
  A cluster of rules determine when a particular happening on the line should have attention directed towards it. It also determines when attention to the problem should be escalated. This information is made available to the decision maker through animated graphics and windows.
- Log Analysis
  After evaluating the the log maintained by roving inspect, this component makes recommendations about altering the inspection strategy.
- Recovery Generator
  This component will recommend actions to decision makers when a variance from plan has occurred. For example, if a process fails, a machine goes down, or the queue builds up past acceptable limits.
- Review of past and present states of line activity.
  Using graphical information representation (animated modeling), portrays various levels of activity in the line.
- Future projection of the line.
  A manager can input a recovery plan he devised in response to a current problem and then run the projection to see the probable outcome of his proposed reaction to the problem. In developing the projection, the system will simulate the activity of the entire system to portray interactions of scheduling, WIP, internode impacts, goals met, and goals missed.

The first purpose of a logistics management system is to enable various levels of management to view the manufacturing floor in real time without having to physically visit it. The second is to help cope with the complexity and size of the operation being managed. Such a system would be a hybrid of a number of expert subsystems and several traditionally procedural modules running under a software bus architecture.

Survey of the literature has established that there is a need for more support in logistics management than currently exists. It is not a matter of gaining expertise. The needed expertise exists today. The problem is growing more unmanageable because the increase in need for this expertise is coupled with competitive pressure to cut cost by reducing the number of people on hand to apply it. Expert systems evidence great potential to handle this situation. Integration of traditional manufacturing control systems with adaptive systems capable of functioning at an expert floor manager level is the premise on which logistic management systems are predicated.

AUTOMATED LEDGER BOOK (ALB)

ALB is a worksheet model generator with an equation solving / analyzing expert system component. The analyst models the problem using algebraic notation to describe the relationships that exist between the variables involved. These relationships, or rules, make up the flow of the analysis. The system then employs an algebra inference engine coupled with the rules of algebra to understand the structure of the analysis. Depending on the data involved, ALB will develop an execution strategy for resolving the relationships. The order will be dependent on the data and structure, but independent of any procedural implications. The problem is always resolved in the minimum number of cycles. A full explanation is always available.

Let's look at an example. A farm manager wants to calculate profit and cost ratio for his apple crop. The equations in his model are:

EQ 1: REVEN = SOLD x PRICE
EQ 2: VCOST = SEED + FERT + LABOR
EQ 3: FCOST = MACHD + TAX
EQ 4: EXPEN = VCOST + FCOST
EQ 5: PROFT = REVEN - EXPEN
EQ 6: RATIO = EXPEN / SOLD

Initially the user wants the output variables calculated, but then he may want to specify an output variable, and have an input variable calculated. For example, the farm manager may wish to calculate PROFT, SOLD, PRICE, MACHD, and FCOST based on REVEN, EXPEN, RATIO, SEED, FERT, LABOR, VCOST, and TAX.

ALB will determine the following sequence of calculations will find PROFT, SOLD, PRICE, MACHD, and FCOST without any new instructions from the user.

- solve equation 2 for VCOST
- solve equation 4 for FCOST
- solve equation 3 for MACHD
- solve equation 5 for PROFT
- solve equation 6 for SOLD
- solve equation 1 for PRICE

Another question the farm crop manager might have is: "What the input variables effecting profit"

ALB would provide the following answer:

```
PROFT =  REVEN   -   EXPEN
     REVEN =  SOLD x PRICE
     EXPEN = VCOST + FCOST
          VCOST = SEED + FERT + LABOR
          FCOST = MACHD + TAX

- PROFIT IS A FUNCTION OF
  SOLD  PRICE  SEED  FERT  LABOR  MACHD  TAX
```

CONCLUSIONS

Today's technology can and does measurably support the decision maker. Exploitation of AI in DSS/DSIM is largely a matter of implementation. It is academia's role to produce people capable of understanding, building and using what technology provides. It is industry's role to develop and use the tools responsibly.

REFERENCES

Bard, Y., "APLPIE - An APL Programmed Inference Engine," IBM Cambridge Scientific Center, Cambridge, MA 02142, 1985.

Brown, J., Cook, J., Groner, L., and Eusebi, E., "Logic Programming in APL2," IBM Santa Teresa Lab, San Jose, Calif. 95150, 1985.

Decision Tables: A Systems Analysis and Documentation Technique (2nd ed.), IBM, White Plains, NY., 1978.

Duchessi, P., "The Conceptual Design of a Knowledge-Based System for Aggregate Planning," School of Business, Suny at Albany, Albany NY 12222, 1985.

Fox, M. and Smith, S., "ISIS - a Knowledge Based System for Factory Scheduling," Expert Systems. vol. 1, no. 1, pp. 25-50, July 1984.

Gevarter, W., "Expert Systems: Limited But Powerful," IEE Spectrum, pp. 39-45, August 1983.

Hagaman, W. et al., "MEDCAT: An APL Program for Medical Diagnosis, Consultation, and Teaching," Proceedings of the 1985 Conference.

Kosy, D. and Wise, B. "Self-Explanatory Financial Planning Models," Proceedings of the 1984 National Conference on Artificial Intelligence.

Rauch, H. "Probability Concepts for an Expert System Used for Data Fusion." AI Magazine. vol. 5, no. 3, pp. 55-60, Fall 1984.

Rychener, M., "Expert Systems for Engineering Design," Expert Systems. pp. 30-44, vol. 2, no. 1, January 1985.

Sullivan, G. and Fordyce, K., "A Decision Support System Paradigm." IBM, H20/906, Poughkeepsie, NY 12602, 1983.

Sullivan, G. and Fordyce, K., "A Review of Expert Systems," IBM, H20/906, Poughkeepsie, NY 12602, 1984.

Sullivan, G. and Fordyce, K., "AIDA: Artificial Development Aids for APL," Proceedings of the 1985 APL Conference.

Wiig, K., "The Arthur D. Little Artificial Intelligence Applications Center," Cambridge, MA 02140, 1985.

Artificial Intelligence in Economics and Management
L.F. Pau (Editor)

DECISION SUPPORT SYSTEM USING FUZZY REASONING AND EVALUATION

Nakaji HONDA*, Futoshi SUGIMOTO**, Masatomo TANAKA* and Shuhei AIDA*

* Department of Communication Systems
University of Electro-Communication
Chofu-shi, Tokyo 182, JAPAN

** Department of Information and Computer Sciences
Toyo University
Kawagoe-shi, Saitama 350, JAPAN

This paper proposes a decision support system which realize a reasonable decision making in complex systems management. The proposed system consists of two portions; data processing and data base. The data processing portion involving both reasoning and evaluation procedures is formulated by fuzzy methods, and can deal with linguistic data which is essential in the complex systems. The efficiency of the system is verified in the application to a job finding problem.

INTRODUCTION

Recently, reasonable decision making has become more and more important problem for the management of complex systems, e.g., industrial systems, social systems, environmental systems, etc.. Some studies on human decision process have been undertaken to model it and analyse mathematically(Fishburn (1979), Raiffa (1968)). However, the models obtained by these studies might not always be applied in practical decision making because it includes various ambiguous factors, i.e., short information, vague conditions, ill-defined structure, etc., especially in the case of complex systems management. It is much efficient to use a man-machine interactive system, namely, decision support system (DSS) which attains a decision making through iterative interaction of decision maker (DM) with computer.

In this paper, a decision support system is proposed to realize a reasonable decision making, where the DM is supported to understand the decision making process by the interaction with computer, and a final decision is then made by the DM. Here, computer presents various information which is required for the decision making to the DM. The system mainly consists of two portions; data processing and data base. In the system, linguistic approach based on fuzzy set theory is applied in both reasoning and evaluation procedures of the data processing portion. Fuzzy reasoning has two separate approaches; one is Zadeh's approach(Zadeh (1975)) which is termed as fuzzy direct reasoning (FDR) in this paper, and the other Tsukamoto's one(Tsukamoto (1979)) termed as fuzzy indirect reasoning (FIR). The system can use the two approaches according to the characteristics of decision making. A linguistic approach is suitable for the evaluation of alternatives because it facilitates the understanding of the DM, and is adopted in the evaluation procedure of the system(Kickert (1978)). The data base of the system contains the data required for decision making and some fuzzy reasoning rules. The system is applicable in the decision problems which include ill-defined factors and also when need some subjective judgements of the DM, e.g. job finding problem investigated in this paper, election problem, investment problem, etc.. This is because the system can appropriately introduce a partial judgement of the DM into decision making process.

The second section of this paper describes the structure of the proposed decision support system along with both reasoning and evaluation procedures. The third section deals with an application of the system to job finding problem.

CONSTRUCTION OF DECISION SUPPORT SYSTEM USING FUZZY METHODS

Fundamental Structure of the Decision Support System

The decision support system (DSS) proposed in this paper mainly consists of two portions; data base and data processing, and fundamental structure of the system is shown in Fig. 1. The data base portion of the system is to store some data sets required for decision making, and several fuzzy reasoning rules in the form of "if - -, then - -.". The rules contain the values of several membership functions which are used for the processing in fuzzy reasoning. Data base plays an important role in the decision making process, and it largely effects the system performance. In the system, a relational data base for personal computer is used, and it supplies the data not only for the data processing portion but also directly for DM. Therefore, the DM can also use only the data base portion.

The data processing portion has the reasoning and evaluation procedures formulated by fuzzy methods. The formulations are effective to deal with linguistic data such as "very good", "more or less bad", and so on, as the fuzzy methods are considered to be suitable for the linguistic data processing. It is also because the linguistic data with ambiguity would be essential rather than numerical and definite one in the decision making of complex systems.

In the procedures of the system, first, DM has to choose some alter-

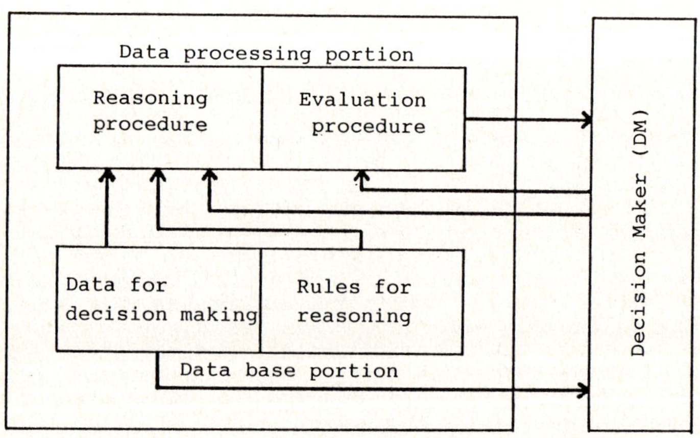

Fig. 1 Fundamental structure of the Decision Support System (DSS)

natives which come from the decision making problem, refering to information offered by the data base, and to determine attributes or aspects of the alternatives. Next, the performance of each aspect is derived in the form of rating from various environmental data about the problem by using suitable fuzzy reasoning rules. Finally, the evaluation of the respective alternatives is performed by fuzzy operation, which multiplies the obtained ratings by weights of the aspect. Here, the weight means the degree of importance with respect to each aspect, and is given by the DM.

The DM makes a final decision by investigating the evaluation results of each alternative. If the DM would not be satisfied with the result, he can iteratively revise some input data, e.g., weight, rules, etc., through the interaction, and can attain to a more satisfactory result.

Fuzzy Reasoning

Fuzzy reasoning based on fuzzy set theory has been studied as a quantitative model of representing human reasoning and thinking processes, and is applicable in the decision making process for deriving useful information from various environmental data. Fuzzy reasoning shows that when an implication R = "If x is A, then y is B" and a premise P = "x is A'" are given, conclusion Q = "y is B'" is deduced, where A, A', B and B' are fuzzy subsets and are characterized by respective membership functions $\mu_A(x)$, $\mu_{A'}(x)$, $\mu_B(y)$ and $\mu_{B'}(y)$. A need not necessarily be identical with A' and same in B with B'. Two separate approaches, i.e., FDR and FIR mentioned in the previous section exist in the fuzzy reasoning, and are compared to derive their characteristics below.

In FDR, implication is defined using fuzzy relation R with membership function $\mu_R(x,y)$ by the following equation

$$B = A \circ R \qquad (1)$$

where $\circ$ denotes composition of fuzzy relation. The operation of their membership function is as follows,

$$\mu_B(y) = \bigvee_{x \in X} (\mu_A(x) \wedge \mu_R(x,y)) \qquad (2)$$

where $\vee$ and $\wedge$ are maximum and minimum operations, respectively. The reasoning by Eq.(1) is called compositional rule of inference. Conclusion Q' = "y is B'" is derived from premise P' = "x is A'" by using Eq.(1). Various definitions of fuzzy relation R are proposed, for example, Mamdani's definition(Mandani (1974)) is as follows,

$$R = A \times B, \qquad (3)$$

where Eq.(3) means the following operation of membership functions,

$$\mu_R(x,y) = \mu_A(x) \wedge \mu_B(y). \qquad (4)$$

A diagram of FIR is shown in Fig. 2. Let propositions P and Q, and implication R be as follows:

P = "u_1 is small",
Q = "u_2 is large",
R = "P $\longrightarrow$ Q",

where R is assumed to be very true, and "small" and "large" are definded as fuzzy subsets S^* and L^* respectively. When a premise P' = "u_1 is very small" is given, where "very small" is defined as fuzzy subset S, it is investigated below how conclusion Q' = "u_2 is L" is

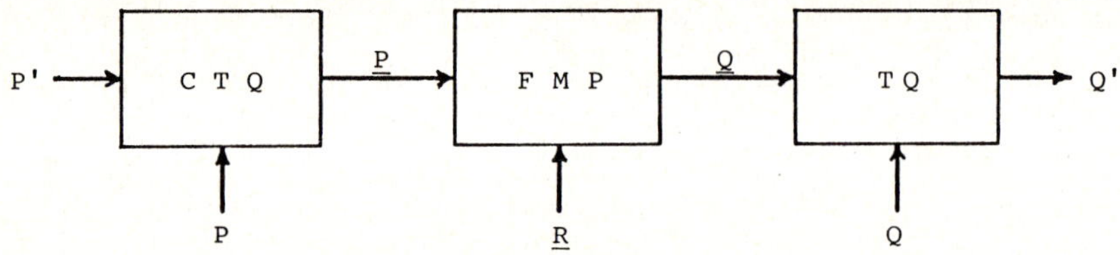

CTQ : Converse Truth Qualification

FMP : Implication (Fuzzy Modus Ponens)

TQ : Truth Qualification

P,Q : Fuzzy Propositions

P' : Primise

Q' : Conclusion

$\underline{R}$: Linguistic Truth Value of Implication

$\underline{P}$,$\underline{Q}$: Linguistic Truth Values of P and Q

Fig. 2 Diagram showing FIR process

deduced. First, using the Converse Truth Qualification (CTQ), Linguistic Truth Value (LTV) $\underline{P}$ of the premise P' is determined, and then by substituting to LTV $\underline{R}$ of implication R and LTV $\underline{P}$ into the following logic equation:

$$\underline{R} = (1 - \underline{P} + \underline{Q}) \wedge 1,$$

LTV $\underline{Q}$ of conclusion Q can be obtained. Finally, a fuzzy set L is determined from the obtained LTV $\underline{Q}$ by using Truth Qualification (TQ). Thus "u_2 is large" can be obtained if fuzzy subset is "large".

Two fuzzy reasoning approaches mentioned above have their respective characteristics. In FDR, the reasoning process is formulated in a simple form as shown in Eq.(1), and the reasoning function is represented to aggregate it into fuzzy relation R and compositional rule. FDR is, therefore, comparatively easy to identify the membership function $\mu_R(x,y)$ of R and is possible to be utilized as an effective tool. The treatments in advance is required for identifying a lot of compositional rules of FDR. On the other hand, in FIR, its reasoning process is logically clear as shown in Fig. 2, and it is comparatively easy to handle the reasoning process. It is consequently useful to investigate the human reasoning mechanism in decision making process. On the contrary, FIR's operation is more difficult than FDR's one.

In the system proposed in this paper, the fuzzy reasonings are applied to derive the rating of aspect from various conditions. The reasoning process is formed by two types of model as shown in Fig. 3. In the reasoning section of the figure, a set of compositional rules and a part of membership functions required are previously prepared in the data base. The other part of membership functions are created through the iterative interaction of the DM with the system.

Multi-stage reasoning is applied in such a case where the several conditions requrired for the reasoning have different priority to each other, and reasoning are sequentially performed according to the

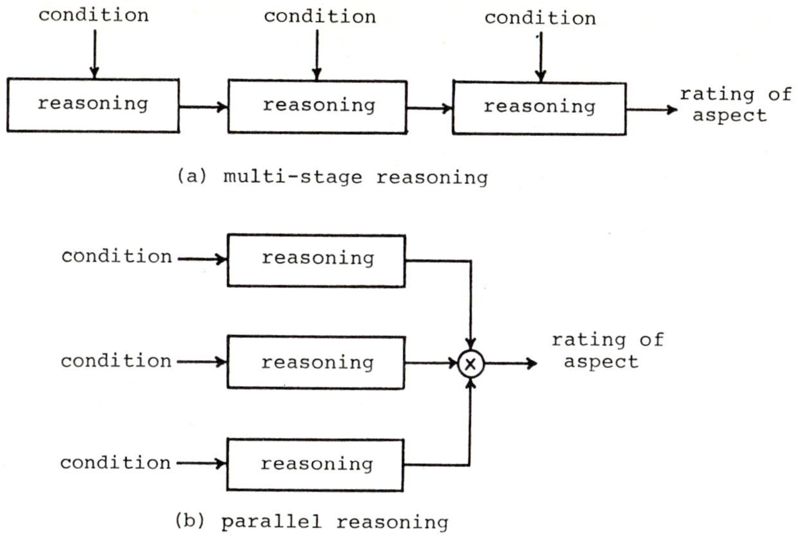

Fig. 3 Two types of reasoning procedures used in the DSS

order of its priority. The rating of current stage is deduced from the rule defined as follows:

> If pre-rating is A and if current conditions is B, then current rating is R.

In parallel reasoning, ratings are derived with each condition which has the same priority, and a final rating is obtained by using AND operation for them.

Evaluation of Alternatives

It is a very difficult problem to choose one among the alternatives with multi-aspects which have not equal importance to each other. In this problem, a simple and well-known approach is to obtain the weighted average rating for each alternative by the following equation:

$$\bar{r}_i = \frac{\sum_{j=1}^{n} w_j \cdot r_{ij}}{\sum_{j=1}^{n} w_j}$$

and to compare the obtained ratings over the alternatives and choose the most suitable one. Here, r_{ij} denotes the rating of aspect C_j, and w_j its weight. In this approach, it is assumed that the rating and weight of the above equation are available for numerical data. However, in practical decision making of complex systems, the rating and weight can be very ofen obtained only as linguistic form, i.e., some words, such as "very high", "moderately important", and so on. Fuzzy method is applicable in such linguistic processing for evaluation of the alternatives. The evaluation using fuzzy method(Baas

(1977), Tong (1980)) is briefly described below.

Let $A_1, A_2, ---, A_m$ denote alternatives and $C_1, C_2, ---, C_n$ the different aspects of the alternatives. It is assumed that the fuzzy rating of aspect C_j of alternative A_i is represented by a membership function $\mu_{Rij}(r_{ij})$, where r_{ij} takes its values on the real domain **R**. Similarly, the relative importance of aspect w_j is a fuzzy variable as well, represented by the membership function $\mu_{Wj}(w_j)$, where w_j also takes its values on **R**. In order to determine the fuzzy evaluation of alternative A_i based on the fuzzy ratings and weights, we consider a function g for mapping $\mathbf{R}^2$ into **R**. The function g is defined by

$$g(z) = \frac{\sum_{j=1}^{n} w_j \cdot r_{ij}}{\sum_{j=1}^{n} w_j}$$

where $z = (w_1, w_2, ---, w_n, r_1, r_2, ---, r_n)$. On the product space $\mathbf{R}^2$, a membership function μ_{Zi} is defined as follows:

$$\mu_{Zi}(z) = [\bigwedge_{j=1}^{n} \mu_{Wj}(w_j)] \wedge [\bigwedge_{j=1}^{n} \mu_{Rik}(r_k)]$$

where $\wedge$ is minimum operation. Through the mapping $g{:}\mathbf{R}^2 \longrightarrow \mathbf{R}$, the fuzzy set $Z=(\mathbf{R}^2, \mu_{Zi})$ induces a fuzzy set $R=(\mathbf{R}, \mu_{Ri})$, with membership function

$$\mu_{Ri}(\bar{r}) = \sup_{z:g(z)=\bar{r}} \mu_{Zi}(z), \quad \bar{r} \in R.$$

Fuzzy set characterized by this membership function is the weighted average rating of alternative A_i, and is called suitability set. Therefore, evaluation of the alternatives is performed by comparing the obtained suitability sets to each other.

In the proposed system, the membership functions which characterize the ratings of the aspects are obtained by using fuzzy reasoning

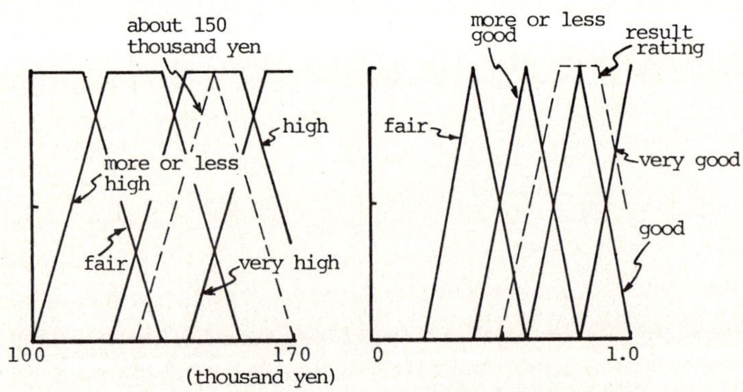

(a) membership functions of initial salary

(b) membership functions of linguistic ratings

Fig. 4 Examples of linguistic ratings derived from FDR

explained in previous section. On the other hand, the weights for the aspects are selected in the form of linguistic expressions which are presented to the DM by the system. The membership functions corresponding to the linguistic expressions are prepared in the data base of the system.

APPLICATION OF DECISION SUPPORT SYSTEM

In this section, the decision support system described in the previous section is applied to a job finding problem for university students. The system is to supply information required for the job finding to the students and to support their decision making of finding the most satisfactory job.

Here, four kinds of job related to electronics engineering were selected as alternatives, and are as follows:

A_1 : manufacturing company employee,
A_2 : operator of telecommunications,
A_3 : government employee,
A_4 : system engineer.

The aspects used for the evaluation of the alternatives are as follows:

C_1 : economic conditions,
C_2 : stability,
C_3 : status,
C_4 : working conditions.

The ratings of the above aspects were derived from conditions corresponding to the aspect using the specified reasoning rules. The conditions in the respective aspects are initial salary for C_1, the authorized capital for C_2, and the number of paid holidays for C_4. However, the rating of C_3 was directly obtained from the data collected through some questionaires supplied to the students. In the reasoning rules of C_2, since the government office has no capital, a extra rule, "if alternative is A_3, then rating of C_2 is very good" was added. The reasoning rules and the data collected through the questionaires had been stored in the data base.

The reasoning process to derive the rating of C_1 is described below. First, the membership functions corresponding to the linguistic evaluation of the initial salary, i.e., "very high", "high", "more or less high" and "fair" were obtained from the student who was finding a job through the iterative inquiries about his sense of value to money. An example of membership functions for the evaluation of the initial salary is shown in Fig. 4(a). Next, the rating of C_1 was derived from the reasoning rules as follows:

If x is very high, then r is very good,
If x is high, then r is good,
If x is more or less high, then r is more or less good,
If x is fair, then r is fair,

where x is the initial salary and r is the rating of C_1. Four ranks of rating, e.g., "very good", "fair", etc., were also defined by fuzzy sets, and were characterized by membership functions as shown in Fig. 4(b). When the initial salary is "about 150 thousand yen", the rating of C_1 was obtained as a fuzzy set illustrated in Fig. 4. Then the economic conditions may be said to be "good".

The ratings of other aspects C_2 and C_4 could be obtained by the same procedure mentioned above. At the same time, the weights of the

Table 1 Examples of linguistic ratings

	C_1	C_2	C_3	C_4
A_1	fair	more or less good	good	fair
A_2	very good	more or less good	good	fair
A_3	more or less good	very good	very good	good
A_4	very good	fair	good	more or less good

Table 2 Examples of linguistic weights

C_1	C_2	C_3	C_4
fair	important	very important	more or less important

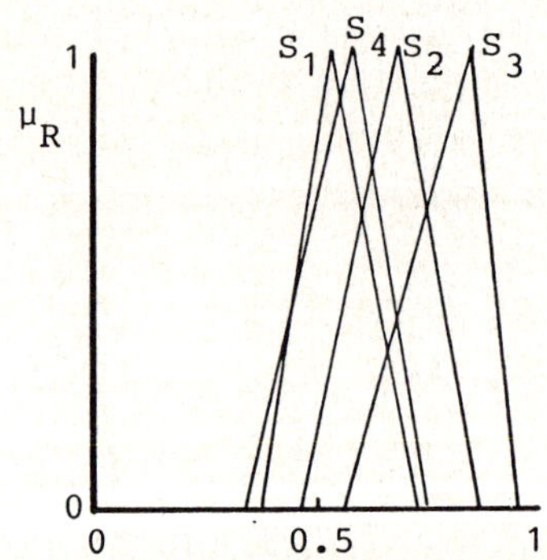

Fig. 5 Examples of suitability sets of alternatives

aspects might be obtained through the iterative interaction. Examples of the ratings and the weights of a certain student are shown in Table 1 and Table 2, respectively. The suitability sets which showed the student's satisfaction for jobs were obtained by the fuzzy operation described in previous section. The obtained suitability sets of the student are shown in Fig. 5. From the figure, it can be infered that the government employee is recommendable to this student as the most suitable job. If the result differs from what the student feels, he can try again and again the job finding after reforming the membership functions, the reasoning rules, the weights of the aspects and so on. Throughout these iterative interaction of the student with the system, he may attain to a satisfactory job.

CONCLUSION

In this paper, a decision support system using fuzzy reasonings and evaluation was proposed to solve various decision making problems with multi-aspect in complex systems. The proposed system was applied to a job finding problem and its efficiency was tested. In the system, it is possible to deal with linguistic data which is essential in the decision making of complex system, by using the fuzzy methods. Decision maker can attempt to change some parameter and input data of the system for obtaining a satisfactory result through iterative interaction with computer.

The problem of how data base and man-machine interface are made is very important to construct decision support system. For this, we are studying on application of effective visual data representations and linguistic approaches in the system.

REFERENCE

[1] P. C. Fishburn: Utility Theory for Decision Making (Roberte Krieger, New York, 1979).
[2] H. Raiffa: Decision Analysis (Addison-Wesley, Mass., 1968).
[3] L. A. Zadeh, Fuzzy Logics and Approximate Reasoning, Synthese, 30 (1975) 407-428.
[4] Y. Tsukamoto: An Approach to Fuzzy Reasoning Method, in Advances in Fuzzy Set Theory and Applications (North-Holland, Amsterdam, 1979).
[5] W. J. M. Kickert, Social Sciences Division: Fuzzy Theories on Decision-Making (Martinus Niihoff, Boston, 1978).
[6] E. H. Mamdani, Application of Fuzzy Algorithms for Control of a Simple Dynamic Plant, Proc. IEE 121-12 (1974) 1585-1588.
[7] S. J. Baas and H. Kwakernaak, Rating and Ranking of Multiple-Aspect Alternative Using Fuzzy Sets, Automatica, vol.13 (1977) 47-58.
[8] R. M. Tong and P. P. Bonissone, A Linguistic Approach to Decision making with Fuzzy Sets, Trans. Systems, Man and Cybernetics, vol.SMC-10, No.11 (1980) 716-723.

Artificial Intelligence in Economics and Management
L.F. Pau (Editor)

OPTIMAL FUZZY HIERARCHICAL DECISIONS

Bart Kosko

VERAC, Incorporated

9605 Scranton Road

San Diego, California 92121

U. S. A.

A general multiobjective decision algorithm is developed for evaluating objects in a criteria hierarchy given fuzzy decision input. The AI techniques used are knowledge representation theory (fuzzy sets, logic, and reasoning) and expert systems theory (forward chaining inference). A formal hierarchy theory is developed. Fuzzy theory is reviewed. The fuzzy hierarchical decision (FHD) algorithm is developed from the fuzzy decision work of Bellman, Zadeh, Yager, and Kosko, and stated in full generality. Candidate applications for the FHD algorithm include the salary review problem in a corporate hierarchy of vice-presidents, managers, supervisors, and technical staff. Other managerial and finance applications--as well as cognitive processing hierarchy applications--are under development at VERAC.

I. INTRODUCTION

How can a decision be reached when different knowledge sources state their different opinions in uncertain terms? This is the problem of fuzzy multiobjective decision making with multiple decision makers. In general the objectives are ordered or hierarchical, the data is non-numeric, and a "best" or optimal decision is sought.

A common but vexing example is the selection of a new product design. Hundreds of managers, analysts, and cost estimators contribute their knowledge in the form of directives, requirements, studies, and critiques. Design criteria are myriad and hierarchical, ranging from "Maximize profit!" on down to establishing which design uses fewest ball bearings. Moreover, the knowledge sources have varying levels of expertise in different evaluation subdomains.

In this and all hierarchical multiobjective decision problems a key relationship holds among the decision criteria. For any level in the hierarchy except the highest, <u>the criteria in a given level are evaluated with respect to the criteria in the next highest level</u>. The highest level in the hierarchy always has one criterion in it (such as "Maximize profit," "Win the war," "Propagate genes") and is assumed to have maximum value. The decision objects in the lowest level are viewed as degenerate criteria.

Below a formalism is developed to represent these hierarchical relationships. Fuzzy theory is used for generality, since it subsumes as a special case criteria evaluations given in ordinal values. A between-level linear ranking scheme is used for maximal evaluation speed. Optimal fuzzy decisions are defined in terms of fuzzy sets and combined with a general knowledge combination scheme for aggregating disparate knowledge responses with varying degrees of credibility. The FHD (Fuzzy Hierarchical Decision) algorithm is then explicitly stated.

II. HIERARCHY THEORY

Hierarchies are naturally occurring efficient structures. Miller's empirical law of cognitive psychology that the human mind can simultaneously consider at most 7 ± 2 objects underlies the need for hierarchical formalisms in cognitive models and AI systems. This is especially true for multiperson management decision models. Any management decision model that requires a manager to concurrently process an arbitrary number of decision objects will quickly pass into infeasability as the 7 ± 2 bound on decision objects is exceeded.

Hierarchical prioritization models are rare. Saaty (1977) has developed an elegant hierarchical critera evaluation theory based on the Perron-Frobenius eigenvector theorem (which guarantees the existence of a unique positive eigenvalue with maximum modulus and corresponding all-positive eigenvector) for positive matrices. Saaty exploits the theorem to retrieve the vector (eigenvector) of underlying values given relative numeric rankings of decision objects. But the conditions needed to satisfy the theorem--pairwise rank comparisons of decision objects elicited as ratios of positive numbers--severely limit the theory's generality and hence applicability. Moreover, for n decision objects, Saaty's pairwise procedure is nonlinear in ranking time--it increases no slower than n^2 increases.

The present theory requires only a general hierarchical structure and partially ordered ranks. Indeed the ranks can be fuzzily partially ordered (wherein reflexivity sort of holds, transitivity often holds, anti-symmetry usually holds, etc.). In particular the ranks can be ordinal values like <u>more</u> or <u>less</u>. The hierarchical structure is defined as follows.

A <u>hierarchy</u> H is a collection of $n + 1$ <u>levels</u> $L_0, L_1, \ldots, L_n$. Each level L_i consists of m_{L_i}-many abstract objects $O^1_{L_i}, \ldots, O^{m_{L_i}}_{L_i}$. Level L_{i+1} is higher (on some meta-level precedence ordering) than level L_i. The highest level L_n contains exactly one object, $O^1_{L_n}$. A <u>rank set</u> R is a finite (or, more generally, bounded) partially ordered set $\{r_0 \precsim r_1 \precsim \cdots \precsim r_k\}$. Let $w\colon H \to R$ be an arbitrary <u>weight function</u> defined on the H-levels; i.e., $w\colon L_i \to R$ for all i. Let $w_{O^p_{L_i}}(O^q_{L_{i-1}})$ denote the weight of the qth (criterion) object, $O^q_{L_{i-1}}$, in level L_{i-1} with respect to the pth (criterion) object, $O^p_{L_i}$, in level L_i, where subscripts obey $1 \le i \le n$, $1 \le p \le m_{L_i}$, $1 \le q \le m_{L_{i-1}}$. Enumerating this weight function fills n-many <u>object evaluation matrices</u> $C_1, \ldots, C_n$, where matrix C_i has dimension $m_{L_{i-1}} \times m_{L_i}$.

III. FUZZY THEORY REVIEW

The grounding intuition of fuzzy theory is that <u>all things admit of degrees</u>. This can be applied to set theory by permitting degrees of set membership. In particular, the zero-one valued indicator function I_A of set A (which equals 1 if element x is in A, 0 if not) can be generalized to, say, a unit-interval-valued membership function $m_A\colon A \quad 0, 1$. Fuzzy set operations are then defined in terms of fuzzy set membership functions (as in fact they have always been so defined but simply with unobtrusive two-valued nonfuzzy set membership functions). In particular, fuzzy set intersection, union, and complementation are respectively defined in terms of minimum (or, more generally, t-norm or triangular norm), maximum (t-conorm), and order-reversing operators. Analogous to fuzzy set theory there is a (multi-valued) fuzzy logic with analogously defined operations of fuzzy conjunction, disjunction, negation, and implication. In fuzzy theory as in abstract integration theory (Lebesgue integration, say), emphasis is put on the range not the domain of defining functions.

Fuzzy decision theory stems from the path-breaking work of Bellman and Zadeh (1970). Their key insight is that a decision is a confluence of goals and constraints. They interpret the goals and constraints as subsets of some space of decision alternatives. This leads to the formal model:

$$\begin{aligned} \text{DECISION} &= \text{Confluence(GOALS, CONSTRAINTS)} \\ &= \text{Conjunction(GOALS, CONSTRAINTS)} \\ &= \text{Intersection(GOALS, CONSTRAINTS)} \\ &= G_1 \cap \ldots \cap G_n \cap C_1 \cap \ldots \cap C_m . \end{aligned}$$

Hence the membership function m_D of the decision set D is given by

$$m_D = \min_{i,j} (m_{G_i}, m_{C_j})$$

for $i = 1, \ldots, n$; $j = 1, \ldots, m$. The decision is fuzzy if any of the goal or constraint subsets is fuzzy.

IV. FUZZY HIERARCHICAL DECISION ALGORITHM

The Bellman-Zadeh fuzzy decision theory doesn't allow the goals and constraints--the criteria--to have different importance weights in the rank set R. (The default assumption is that they all have maximal weight r_k.) Let criterion C have weight w(C). If w(O) is the weight of an object evaluated with respect to criterion C, then how can w(O) be conditioned on w(C)? More precisely, we seek some conditioning function z such that z(w(C), w(O)) gives the weight of object O when evaluated with respect to criterion C which is itself weighted or perturbed by w(C). Of course we require $z(r_k, w(O)) = w(O)$.

Yager (1981) proposes the function $z(w(C), w(O)) = \max(-w(C), w(O))$, where the order-reversing negation operator is defined on R by $-r = r_{k-i}$. Yager's argument for this choice of z is simple but sound. He interprets the conditioning of w(O) on w(C) literally as the conditional $w(C) \Longrightarrow w(O)$. A classical material-implication interpretation then leads to -w(C) OR w(O), which in turn leads to the fuzzy set interpretation max(-w(C), w(O)). Then applying the Bellman-Zadeh decision theory leads to the decision function

$$m_D = \min_i \max(-w(C_i), w(O)) ,$$

where the minimum is taken over the i criteria (all the objects in level L_i). For m objects, the optimal decision is simply the highest-valued conditional decision,

$$D^* = \max_j \min_i \max(-w(C_i), w(O_j)) .$$

In Kosko (1985), a knowledge combination function ϕ is constructed that turns out to generalize the Bellman-Zadeh decision theory in the sense that ϕ is a general confluence operator that decreases to the intersection operator as uncertainty increases. Such a ϕ is given by

$$\phi(l, m) = \min(m , 1 - m + l) ,$$

where l and m are the respective minimum and maximum over the decision or criteria objects. An immediate property is that $\phi \geq l$. A provable property is that ϕ decreases to l as the uncertainty increases (in the random sampling case, as the number of samples increases). A step back shows that, when restricted to goal and constraint subsets of some space of alternatives, $l = m_D$, the Bellman-Zadeh decision operator. More generally, given a weight vector $w = (w_1, \dots, w_n)$ for the random variables (knowledge responses, criteria weights, etc.) $^1X_1, \dots, {}^nX_n$, the weighted ϕ, ϕ^w, is determined as follows:

$$\phi^w(l, m) = \phi(l^w, m^w)$$

$$= \min(m^w , 1 - m^w + l^w) ,$$

where
$$l^w = \min_i z_i^l(w_i, X_i) = \min_i \max(-w_i , X_i) ,$$

$$m^w = \max_i z_i^m(w_i, X_i) = \max_i \min(w_i, X_i) .$$

For large sample sizes (several criteria objects), it is still the case that $\phi^w \geq l^w$ and that ϕ^w decreases to l^w with probability one. Another step back reveals that l^w is equivalent to the Yager conditional decision function m_D derived above. Hence in some sense the Yager decision function represents a worst-case assumption about the environmental uncertainty. ($m_D = m^w$ represents a best-case assumption.) In what follows we will use the Yager decision function (see Yager (1981) for a detailed analysis of its properties), remembering that for full generality a more general conditional confluence operator such as ϕ^w should be used.

The FHD (Fuzzy Hierarchical Decision) algorithm is produced by combining the fuzzy decision theory we have developed with hierarchical formalism developed above. The intuition behind the FHD algorithm is that value is propagated down a hierarchy. Criteria at the second highest level are ranked with respect to the criterion at the highest level. These weighted criteria are then used to rank the criteria at the third highest level, and so on down to the lowest-level criteria, the decision objects. In this manner, the FHD algorithm is the control structure of an expert-system inference engine, where decision output is propagated by forward chaining (descending hierarchy levels). Arbitrary knowledge bases can be connected to this hierarchical inference engine, and we assume for simplicity that sufficient evaluation knowledge is available. (The knowledge-combination scheme developed in Kosko (1985) is a general method for obtaining such decision information when the knowledge sources differ in their credibilities in different knowledge domains. Any knowledge combination scheme, such as the Dempster-Shafer scheme, can be used.)

Let $C_1, C_2, \dots, C_n$ be the object evaluation matrices, where matrix C_i can be denoted component-wise as $(c^i_{pq})^{1 \leq p \leq m_{L_{i-1}}}_{1 \leq q \leq m_{L_i}}$. Let the m_{L_0}-by-1 vector D_0 denote the sought-after vector of hierarchically weighted decision objects. Then the FHD algorithm can be stated as follows.

A. INPUT: $C_1, \dots, C_n$.

B. OUTPUT: D_o .

C. THROUGHPUT:

C.1. Form the $m_{L_{n-1}}$-by-1 vector D_{n-1} by putting $D_{n-1} = C_n$.

C.2. Set $j = n - 1$.

REPEAT UNTIL $j = 0$:

Form the $m_{L_{i-1}}$-by-1 vector D_{i-1} from A_{i-1} and D_i by taking row minima of the matrix

$$\begin{array}{c} \\ O^1_{L_{i-1}} \\ \vdots \\ O^{m_{L_{i-1}}}_{L_{i-1}} \end{array} \begin{array}{c} \begin{array}{ccc} O^1_{L_i} & \cdots & O^{m_{L_i}}_{L_i} \end{array} \\ \left(\begin{array}{ccc} \max(-d^i_1, c^{i-1}_{11}) & \cdots & \max(-d^i_{m_{L_i}}, c^{i-1}_{1m_{L_i}}) \\ \vdots & & \vdots \\ \max(-d^i_1, c^{i-1}_{m_{L_{i-1}}1}) & \cdots & \max(-d^i_{m_{L_i}}, c^{i-1}_{m_{L_{i-1}},m_{L_i}}) \end{array} \right) \end{array}$$

I.e., put

$$D_{i-1} = \begin{pmatrix} \min\limits_{1 \le q \le m_{L_i}} \max(-d^i_q, c^{i\ 1}_{1q}) \\ \vdots \\ \min\limits_{1 \le q \le m_{L_i}} \max(-d^i_q, c^{i-1}_{m_{L_{i-1}}q}) \end{pmatrix}.$$

Then set $i = i - 1$.

C.3. Exhibit D_0.

C.4. End.

The FHD algorithm can be applied to any level in the hierarchy H. The advantages of the FHD algorithm are that, because of its underlying fuzzy and hierarchical generality, can be applied to numerous complex disions problems, it programs easily, it involves no statistical aggregation and hence data washout is avoided, it requires only fuzzy ordinal decision input not necessarily numbers, and it requires only linear list rankings.

V. APPLICATIONS TO MANAGEMENT AND FINANCE

The FHD algorithm can be applied to innumerable multiobjective multiperson fuzzy decision problems. Space does not permit a detailed numeric example. A heuristic sketch can be given of a promising set of applications: the delicate multiobjective decision problem of determining salary reviews in large corporations. Here the organizational hierarchy typically consists of a vice-president, managers, supervisors, and technical staff. The decision-criteria hierarchy consists of three levels:

corporate objectives, managerial performance criteria, and technical performance criteria. These levels can themselves be further decomposed into other levels. The FHD can also (and has been) fruitfully applied to new-concept design selection, where there is a hierarchy of corporate objectives and production constraints, and to individual and group (e.g., mutual fund) portfolio selection, where there is a hierarchy of wealth and risk preferences and budget constraints. A related military application is to tactical target prioritization. Targets are evaluated ("prioritized") with respect to strike objectives (defense suppresion, offensive counter air, interdiciton, etc.), strike objectives are evaluated with respect to mision phases (early and late, say), and mission phases are evaluated with respect to the overall mission ("Achieve ..."). At VERAC, the FHD algorithm is being applied to hierarchical cognitive processing and artificial neural systems. Here resonant causal or neural activation in one network (generalized hierarchy level) propagates activation and inhibition down to other networks. The empirical and theoretical consequences of such hierarchical networks are under investigation.

REFERENCES

(1) Bellman, R. E., and Zadeh, L. A. "Decision Making in a Fuzzy Environment." Management Science, 1970, 17, pp. 141 - 164.

(2) Kosko, B. "Fuzzy Knowledge Combination." Presented to the 1st Congress of the IFSA (International Fuzzy Systems Association) in Mallorca, Spain, July, 1985.

(3) Saaty, T. L. "A Scaling Method for Priorities in Hierarchical Structures." Journal of Mathematical Psychology, 1977, 15, pp. 234 - 281.

(4) Yager, R. R. "A New Methodology for Ordinal Multiobjective Decisions Based on Fuzzy Sets." Decision Sciences, October 1981, Vol. 12, No. 4, pp. 589 - 600.

Artificial Intelligence in Economics and Management
L.F. Pau (Editor)

A "DOWN - TO - EARTH" MANAGERIAL DECISION MAKING VIA A FUZZY-LOGIC-BASED REPRESENTATION OF COMMONSENSE KNOWLEDGE

Janusz Kacprzyk

Systems Research Institute
Polish Academy of Sciences
ul. Newelska 6
01-447 Warsaw, Poland

A further "softening" of some multicriteria decision making models is discussed. The use of Zadeh's fuzzy logic based representation of commonsense knowledge in terms of dispositions, i.e. propositions with implicit fuzzy linguistic quantifiers, is advocated. Basically, the derived models seek an optimal solution best satisfying, e.g., most of the important objectives. The "softening" makes the models closer to a practical human perception of their purpose which should facilitate implementations.

1. INTRODUCTION

Importance of decision making, which is certainly the most crucial element in any managerial activity, has implied many attempts of its formal, mathematical treatment. The developed decision making models have reached some maturity by, e.g., efficiently reflecting uncertainties of stochastic, fuzzy, etc. types, or multiple aspects as, e.g., the existence of multiple objectives, decision stages and decisionmakers.

While applying those models serious difficulties may often occur which are usually attributed to an inherent discrepancy between "soft" reality and "hard" conventional mathematical tools. A "softening" of the models have been strongly advocated (e.g., Checkland, 1972; Rapoport, 1970). Fuzzy sets may play here some role (Kacprzyk, 1983b) as a tool to formalize imprecision.

In the paper we further "soften" some fuzzy multicriteria decision making models. We use some elements of natural languages which are the only fully natural human communication means. In particular, we use some elements of a simple and elegant fuzzy-logic-based representation of commonsense knowledge due to Zadeh (1983b). Its main element is a disposition, i.e. proposition with an implicit fuzzy linguistic quantifier. For instance, a disposition "winter days are cold" should be read, e.g., "most winter days are cold". Its manipulation is then through some fuzzy-logic-based calculi.

The use of the above mentioned commonsense knowledge has proven to be fruitful in various decision making models: multicriteria (Yager, 1983a; Kacprzyk and Yager, 1984a, 1984b), multistage (Kacprzyk, 1983a, 1984c), group and consensus formation (Kacprzyk, 1985a, 1985b), etc. In this paper we discuss its use in multicriteria decision making models. Basically, we derive models which determine an optimal solution (option) best satisfying, say, most of the important objectives (criteria). This seems to make the models more human-consistent, hence "down-to-earth", which should in turn facilitate their use in decision support systems, and help in their implementations.

Our notation is standard. $A \subsetneq X$ is a fuzzy set in X characterized by its membership function $\mu_A(x)$. If $X = \{x_1,\ldots,x_n\}$, then A is written $A = \mu_A(x_1)/x_1 + \ldots + \mu_A(x_n)/x_n$. Moreover, $a \wedge v = \min(a,b)$, $\bigwedge_{i=1}^{n} a_i = a_1 \wedge \ldots \wedge a_n$, $a \vee b = \max(a,b)$, and $a^* = \arg\max_{a \in A} f(a)$ means to find a^* which maximizes $f(a)$ with respect to $a \in A$.

2. ZADEH'S REPRESENTATION OF COMMONSENSE KNOWLEDGE

In Zadeh's (1983b) approach commonsense knowledge is equated with a collection of dispositions, i.e. propositions with implicit linguistic quantifiers. For instance, a disposition "winter days are cold" really means, e.g., "most winter days are cold" where "most" is a linguistic quantifier. Representation and manipulation of commonsense knowledge boils down to the restoration ("identification") of the quantifiers and processing of the dispositions. The traditional logical systems cannot be used for that due to the existence of linguistic quantifiers, hence Zadeh (1983a, 1983b) - assuming that the linguistic quantifiers are represented by fuzzy sets, which will also be assumed throughout the paper - has developed a fuzzy-logic-based calculus of linguistically quantified propositions. An alternate calculus is due to Yager (1983a). A similar approach appeared also in Lesmo, Saitta and Torasso (1984).

The point of departure is a linguistically quantified proposition, exemplified by "most experts are convinced", and generally written as

$$QY\text{'s are } F \tag{1}$$

where Q is a linguistic quantifier (e.g., most), Y is a set of objects (e.g., experts) and F is a property (e.g., convinced).

Importance B can also be introduced yielding

$$QBY\text{'s are } F \tag{2}$$

e.g., "most of the important experts are conviced".

Basically, the problem is to find truth(QY's are F) knowing each truth(y_i is F), $y_i \in Y$, or in case of (2) - to find truth(QBY's are F). Fuzzy logic can be used for that purpose, and two calculi will be presented below.

2.1. The algebraic (consensory) method

This classical method is due to Zadeh (1983a, 1983b). The linguistic quantifier is here assumed to be a fuzzy set in $[0,1], \subsetneq [0,1]$. For instance, Q = "most" can be given as

$$\mu_{\text{"most"}}\, x = \begin{cases} 1 & \text{for } x \geqslant 0.8 \\ 2x - 0.6 & \text{for } 0.3 < x < 0.8 \\ 0 & \text{for } x \leqslant 0.3 \end{cases} \tag{3}$$

In the paper we will use only the proportional fuzzy quantifiers, e.g., "most", "almost all", etc. For the absolute quantifiers, e.g., "about 5","much more than 10", etc. the reasoning is similar.

Property F is defined as a fuzzy set in Y, $F \subsetneq Y$. If $Y = \{y_1, \ldots, y_p\}$, then truth(y_i is F) = $\mu_F(y_i)$, i=1,...,p.

The calculation of truth(QY's are F) is based on the nonfuzzy cardinalities, ΣCounts, of the respective fuzzy sets and proceeds in two steps:

$$r = \Sigma\text{Count}(F)/\Sigma\text{Count}(Y) = \frac{1}{p} \sum_{i=1}^{p} \mu_F(y_i) \tag{4}$$

$$\text{truth}(QY\text{'s are } F) = \mu_Q(r) \tag{5}$$

To introduce importance, B = "important" is defined as a fuzzy set in Y, B Y, such that $\mu_B(y_i) \in [0,1]$ is a degree of importance of y_i: the higher its value the more important y_i. We rewrite "QBY's are F" as "Q(B and F) Y's are B" which leads to the following counterparts of (4) and (5):

$$r' = \sum_{i=1}^{p} (\mu_B(y_i) \wedge \mu_F(y_i)) / \sum_{i=1}^{p} \mu_B(y_i) \tag{6}$$

$$\text{truth}(QBY\text{'s are } F) = \mu_Q(r') \tag{7}$$

"∧" may be replaced, e.g., by any t-norm (Kacprzyk and Yager, 1984b).

Example 1. Let Y = "experts" = {X,V,Z}, F = "convinced" = 0.1/X+ +0.6/V+0.8/Z, Q = "most" be given by (3), B = "important" = 0.2/X+ +0.5/V+0.6/Z. Then, r=0.5, r'=0.9, and truth("most experts are convinced") = 0.4, truth("most of the important experts are convinced") = 1.

Instead of the nonfuzzy cardinalities, the fuzzy cardinalities, may also be used (Zadeh, 1983a).

Finally, let us introduce the concept of a nondecreasing quantifier defined as

$$r_1 > r_2 \Rightarrow \mu_Q(r_1) > \mu_Q(r_2) \quad \text{for each} \quad r_1, r_2 \in [0,1] \tag{8}$$

which is important in our context. "Most" (3) is evidently nondecreasing. The method may be viewed to yield a consensory like aggregation of the pieces of evidence "y_i is F".

2.2. The substitution (competitive) method

This alternative method is proposed by Yager (1983a). (Lesmo, Saitta and Torasso (1984) is also close in spirit.) As previously, $Y = \{y_1, \ldots, y_p\}$ and $F \subsetneq Y$. We denote P_i: "y_i is F", i=1,...,p, and

$$\text{truth } P_i = \text{truth } (y_i \text{ is } F) = \mu_F(y_i) \tag{9}$$

We introduce the set

$$V = \{v\} = 2^{\{P_1, \ldots, P_p\}} \tag{10}$$

where {v} is $\{P_{k1}, \ldots, P_{km}\}$ written as $\{P_{k1}$ and ... and $P_{km}\}$; v and

$\{P_{k1}$ and ... and $P_{km}\}$ will be used interchangeably. We assume $Q \subseteq V$. Each v is seen to have the truth

$$\mu_T(v) = \text{truth}\ (P_{k1}\ \text{and...and}\ P_{km}) = \text{truth}\ P_{k1} \wedge \ldots \wedge \text{truth}\ P_{km} = \bigwedge_{i=1}^{m} \text{truth}\ P_{ki} = \mu_F(y_{k1}) \wedge \ldots \wedge \mu_F(y_{km}) = \bigwedge_{i=1}^{m} \mu_F(y_{ki}) \quad (11)$$

Now

$$\text{truth}(QY\text{'s are F}) = \max_{v \in V}(\mu_Q(v) \wedge \mu_T(v)) \quad (12)$$

If $B \subseteq Y$ is importance, then

$$\text{truth}\ (QBY\text{'s are F}) = \max_{v \in V}(\mu_Q(v) \wedge \bigwedge_{i=1}^{m} (\mu_B(y_{ki}) \rightarrow \mu_F(y_{ki}))) \quad (13)$$

where "$\rightarrow$" is an implication operator (Yager, 1983b). If, e.g., $a \rightarrow b = (1-a) \vee b$, then

$$\text{truth}\ (QBY\text{'s are F}) = \max_{v \in V}(\mu_Q(v) \wedge \bigwedge_{i=1}^{m} (1-\mu_B(y_{ki})) \vee \mu_F(y_{ki}))) \quad (14)$$

Example 2. If we take the same data as in Example 1, and Q="most" is given as

$$\mu_{\text{"most"}}(v) = \begin{cases} 1 & \text{for} \quad v \in \{P_1 \text{ and } P_2 \text{ and } P_3\} \\ 0.7 & \text{for} \quad v \in \{P_1 \text{ and } P_2,\ P_1 \text{ and } P_3,\ P_2 \text{ and } P_3\} \\ 0.3 & \text{for} \quad v \in \{P_1,\ P_2,\ P_3\} \end{cases} \quad (15)$$

then

truth ("most experts are convinced") = 0.6
truth ("most of the important experts are convinced") = 0.8

Notice that the substitution method may yield different results than the algebraic.

Particularly important is the monotonic quantifier defined as

$$v_1 = v_2 \text{ and } v_3 \Rightarrow \mu_Q(v_1) > \mu_Q(v_2) \vee \mu_Q(v_3) \quad (16)$$

for each $v_1, v_2, v_3 \in V$. "Most" given by (15) is evidently monotonic. The monotonic quantifiers are close in spirit to the nondecreasing ones.

The substitution method may be viewed to provide a competitive like aggregation of the pieces of evidence "y_i is F".

The two above calculi will be applied for "softening" some fuzzy multicriteria decision making models.

Among other approaches to the representation and manipulation of commonsense knowledge, those default-reasoning (logic) - related seem to be promising due to their intuitive appeal and constructiveness. For some details, see, e.g., Reiter (1980), Reiter and Criscuolo (1981, 1983) or Ferreny and Prade (1985); let us notice that the last is explicitly based on possibility theory. Finally, let us notice that issues discussed here, i.e. those involving commonsense knowledge, are related to imprecise, uncertain (in a non-probabilistic sense), vague, etc. reasoning which is of utmost importance in artificial intelligence and related fields. For a survey, see, e.g., Prade (1983); an interesting approach is that used in MYCIN (Shortliffe and Buchanan, 1975).

3. INTRODUCTION OF COMMONSENSE KNOWLEDGE INTO MULTICRITERIA DECISION MAKING UNDER FUZZINESS

Multicriteria decision making under fuzziness may be meant as follows. $A = \{a\} = \{a_1,\dots,a_q\}$ is a set of possible alternative decisions (options) and $0 = \{0_1,\dots,0_p\}$ is a set of fuzzy objectives (fuzzy constraints and/or fuzzy goals). The degree to which $a \in A$ satisisfies $0_i \in 0$ is given by truth (0_i is satisfied (by a)) $= \mu_{0_i}(a)$.

Traditionally, it is postulated (e.g., Bellman and Zadeh, 1970) that $a \in A$ satisfy "0_1 and ... and 0_p", i.e. <u>all</u> the fuzzy objectives; the degree of that satisfaction is given by the fuzzy decision

$$\mu_D(a|\text{"all"}) = \text{truth } (0_1 \text{ and... and } 0_p \text{ are satisfied}) =$$

$$= \text{truth } (\text{"all" } 0\text{'s are satisfied}) = \text{truth } (0_1 \text{ is satisfied}) \wedge \dots$$

$$\dots \wedge \text{truth } (0_p \text{ is satisfied}) = \mu_{0_1}(a) \wedge \dots \wedge \mu_{0_p}(a) \tag{17}$$

The problem is to find an optimal decision $a^* \in A$, such that

$$a^* = \arg\max_{a \in A} \mu_D(a|\text{"all"}) \tag{18}$$

The requirement to satisfy "all" the fuzzy objectives may be viewed too rigid and restrictive for practical purposes. An idea to replace "all" by some milder requirement specified by a linguistic quantifier Q, say "most", appeared in Yager (1983a) and Kacprzyk and Yager (1983a, 1983b). Basically, it consists of seeking an optimal decision that best satisfies Q (e.g., "most") fuzzy objectives.

We introduce first the fuzzy sets: S = "satisfied" $\subseteq 0$, such that $\mu_S(0_i)$ = truth (0_i is satisfied (by a)) $= \mu_{0_i}(a)$, $i=1,\dots,p$, and B = "important" $\subseteq 0$, such that $\mu_B(0_i) \in [0,1]$ is the degree of importance of objective 0_i: from 0 denoting "unimportant at all" to 1 denoting "definitely important", through all intermediate values. Q is a fuzzy linguistic quantifier.

The fuzzy decision is now written as

$$\mu_D(a|Q) = \text{truth } (Q0_i\text{'s are satisfied (by a)}) \tag{19}$$

in case of not accounting for importance, and

$$\mu_D(a|Q,B) = \mu_D(a|Q, \text{"important"}) = \text{truth}(QB\ 0_i\text{'s are satisfied (by a)}) = \text{truth } (Q\text{"important" } 0_i\text{'s are satisfied}) \tag{20}$$

in case of accounting for importance.

The corresponding problems are to find $a^* \in A$, such that, respectively:

$$a^* = \arg\max_{a \in A} \mu_D(a|Q) \tag{21}$$

$$a^* = \arg\max_{a \in A} \mu_D(a|Q,B) \tag{22}$$

For the solution of these problems we will use the two calculi given in Section 2.

3.1. Solution by the algebraic method

Let us solve the more general problem (22), i.e. find $a^* \in A$, such that

$$a^* = \arg\max_{a \in A} \mu_D(a \; Q,B)$$

Due to (6) and (7), we obtain

$$r(a) = \sum_{i=1}^{p} (\mu_B(O_i) \wedge \mu_{O_i}(a)) / \sum_{i=1}^{p} {}_B(O_i) \tag{23}$$

$$\mu_D(a|QB) = \mu_Q(r(a)) \tag{24}$$

and

$$a^* = \arg\max_{a \in A} \mu_Q(r(a)) \tag{25}$$

Notice that if we do not wish to account for importance, we set $\mu_B(O_i) = i$ for each $O_i \in O$, and (23) becomes

$$r(a) = \frac{1}{p} \sum_{i=1}^{p} \mu_{O_i}(a) \tag{26}$$

while (24) and (25) remain the same.

It is easy to see that it is difficult to say something about the solution of (25) for a general Q.

However, for a nondecreasing Q we obtain a solution by solving (Yager, 1983a; Kacprzyk and Yager, 1984a, 1984b)

$$a^* = \arg\max_{a \in A} \mu_D(a|QB) = \arg\max_{a \in A} \sum_{i=1}^{p} (\mu_B(O_i) \wedge \mu_{O_i}(a)) / \sum_{i=1}^{p} \mu_B(O_i) \tag{27}$$

Example 3. Let: $A = \{a_1, a_2, a_3\}$, $O_1 = 1/a_1 + 0.7/a_2 + 0.1/a_3$, $O_2 = 0.2/a_1 + 1/a_2 + 0.5/a_3$, $O_3 = 0.2/a_1 + 0.3/a_2 + 1/a_3$, Q="most" be given by (3), and B="important"$=0.3/O_1 + 0.8/O_2 + 1/O_3$. Then, due to (23): $\mu_D(a_1|.,.)=0$, $\mu_D(a_2|,,.)=1$, and $\mu_D(a_3|.,.)=0.9$, i.e. $a^* = a_2$.

3.2. Solution by the substitution method

Let us solve the more general problem (22), i.e. find

$$a^* = \arg\max_{a \in A} \mu_D(a|Q,B)$$

If we denote P_t: "O_t is satisfied (by a)", $V=\{v\}=\{P_{k1}$ and ...

and $P_{km}\} = 2^{\{P_1,\ldots,P_p\}}$, and $a \to b = (1-a) \vee b$, then by following (9) - (14), we obtain

$$a^* = \arg\max_{a \in A} \max_{v(a) \in V} (\mu_Q(v(a)) \wedge \bigwedge_{i=k1}^{km} ((1-\mu_B(0_i) \vee \mu_{0_i}(a))) \quad (28)$$

Its solution is difficult (Yager, 1983a) but for the case without importance, i.e. $\mu_B(0_i)=1$, for all $0_i \in 0$, we have a nice property (Yager, 1983a; Kacprzyk and Yager, 1984a, 1984b): if (1) Q is monotonic, (2) $\mu_Q(v) \in \{b_1,b_2,\ldots,b_s\}$ and $b_1<b_2<\ldots<b_s$, and (3) d_i is the i-th largest element of $\{\mu_{0_i}(a),\ldots, \mu_{0_p}(a)\}$, then

$$a^* = \arg\max_{a \in A} \max_{i=1,\ldots,s} (d_i \wedge b_i) \quad (29)$$

Example 4. For the same data as in Example 3, we obtain: $\mu_D(a_1|.)= =0.3$, $\mu_D(a_2|.)=0.7$, and $\mu_D(a_3|.)=0.5$, hence $a^*=a_2$.

4. CONCLUDING REMARKS

In the paper we presented an idea of introducing some elements of Zadeh's representation of commonsense knowledge into a conceptual model of multicriteria decision making under fuzziness. We obtain a "softer" formulation of the models which seems to better reflect a practical human perception of the essence of the modeled situation and of the very meaning of a solution.

A promising application of the models can be an extension of Kacprzyk and Straszak's (1984) fuzzy multistage decision making (control) model for the determination of regional development policies. The model considers regional development in terms of a multi-indicator life quality index evolving over a planning horizon. Due to an inherent "softness" of the life quality index and the very nature of economic planning, the introduction of some linguistic quantifiers into "cost/benefit"assessment schemes of the model as, e.g.,"... for most of the life quality indicators..." or "... for almost all the control stages..." seems quite natural. The problem will be considered in a separate work.

The models proposed should help attain a better synergy between the human decision maker and decision support system employing them. This should greatly help in implementations.

We feel that the discussed approach to make decision making models more human - consistent is a promising direction of great practical importance and should be further pursued.

LITERATURE

Bellman R.E. and L.A. Zadeh (1970) Decision-making in a fuzzy environment, Manag. Sci. 17, 151-169.
Checkland P.B, (1972) Towards a system-based methodology of real world problem solving J. Syst. Eng. 3.
Ferreny H. and H. Prade (1985) A possibility-theory-based approach to default and inexact reasoning. Comp. and Art. Intelligence 4, 125-136.
Kacprzyk J. (1983a) A generalization of fuzzy multistage decision-

-making and control via linguistic quantifiers. Int. J. Control, 38, 1249-1270.

Kacprzyk J. (1983b) Multistage Decision-Making under Fuzziness: Theory and Applications, Verlag TÜV Rheinland, Cologne.

Kacprzyk J. (1984a) Collective decision making with a fuzzy majority. Proc. 5th WOGSC Congress. Paris.

Kacprzyk J. (Guest Ed.) (1984b) Special Issue on Fuzzy Sets and Possibility Theory in Optimization Models, Control and Cybern. 13, 4.

Kacprzyk J. (1984c) A generalized formulation of fuzzy multistage decision making and control under fuzziness. In Sanchez E. and M.M. Gupta (Eds.), Proc. IFAC Symp. on Fuzzy Inf., Knowledge Representation and Dec. Anal., Marseille, Pergamon, Oxford.

Kacprzyk J. (1985a) Some "commonsense" solution concepts in group decision making using fuzzy linguistic quantifiers. In Kacprzyk and Yager (1985).

Kacprzyk J. (1985b) On some fuzzy cores and "soft" consensus measures in group decision making. In Bezdek J. (Ed.) The Analysis of Fuzzy Information. CRC Press (forthcoming).

Kacprzyk J. and A. Straszak (1984) Determination of "stable" trajectories of integrated regional development using fuzzy decision models. IEEE Trans. on Syst., Man and Cybern. SMC-14, 310-313.

Kacprzyk J. and R.R. Yager (1984a) "Softer" optimization and control models via fuzzy linguistic quantifiers, Inf. Sci. 34, 157-178.

Kacprzyk J. and R.R. Yager (1984b) Linguistic quantifiers and belief qualification in fuzzy multicriteria and multistage decision making, In Kacprzyk (1984b), 155-174.

Kacprzyk J. and R.R. Yager (1985) Management Decision Support Using Fuzzy Sets and Possibility Theory. Verlag TÜV Rheinland, Cologne.

Lesmo L., L. Saitta and P. Torasso (1984) Evaluation of quantified expressions in expert systems. Proc. 5th WOGSC Congress, Paris.

Prade H. (1983) A synthetic view of approximate reasoming techniques. Proc. 8th Int. Joint Conf. on AI, Karlsruhe; 272-279.

Rapoport A. (1970) Modern systems theory - an outlook for coping with change. In General Systems Yearbook, Soc. for Gen. Syst. XV.

Reiter R. (1980) A logic for default reasoning. Art. Intelligence 13, 81-132.

Reiter R. and G. Criscuolo(1981) On interacting defaults Proc. 7th Int. Joint Conf. on Art. Intelligence, Vancouver, 270-276.

Reiter R. and Criscuolo G. (1983) Some representational issues in default reasoning. Comp. and Maths. with Appls. 9, 15-27.

Shortliffe E.H. and B.G. Buchanan (1975) A model of inexact reasoning in medicine. Math. Biosci. 23, 351-379.

Yager R.R. (1983a) Quantifiers in the formulation of multiple objective decision functions. Inf. Sci. 31, 107-139.

Yager R.R. (1983b) On the implication operator in fuzzy logic, Inf. Sci. 31, 141-164.

Zadeh L.A. (1983a) A computational approach to fuzzy quantifiers in natural languages, Comp. and Maths. with Appls. 9, 149-184.

Artificial Intelligence in Economics and Management
L.F. Pau (Editor)

A USER-FRIENDLY PROPOSITIONAL FORMALISM FOR A MANAGERIAL DSS-GENERATOR

R. Maes
J.E.M. van Dijk

Universiteit van Amsterdam
Vakgroep Bedrijfsinformatica & Accountancy
Jodenbreestraat 23
1011 NH Amsterdam
The Netherlands

Abstract
The starting-point of this paper is that the transparency of a large number of managerial decisions is highly obscured by their logical complexity. The logical component of a managerial DSS-generator is outlined. Its main features are a human-oriented propositional formalism and a powerful yet simple intermediate representation scheme. It is indicated how this scheme can be used to introduce pattern recognition techniques.

1. Introduction

In the past, many attempts have been made to introduce formal techniques into managerial decision making. A major disadvantage of these contributions is their inability to cope with the very decision making process itself. Instead, they constrain themselves to delivering data and/or standard models, the results of which are still to be integrated by the manager in his own mental model of the decision situation.

Practical experiences reveal that problems with the analysis and the formal description of at least a part of the managerial decisions are due to the logical complexity of the decision process, i.e. to the inextricable intertwinement of the individual decision rules linking observations and outcomes.
Typical examples include decisions made according to prescriptions laid down in laws, regulations, judgements (e.g. in the case of the approval of credits) and others. A common characteristic of these decisions is that they are all based on the evaluation of a large number of influencing factors. It has been noted elsewhere (see, e.g., [5]) that the reduction of the concepts, relationships and rules involved in this evaluation process to a formally tractable system, and the subsequent (semi-)automatic deduction of new relationships and/or rules is a major task of every research effort aiming at the elucidation and the support of managerial thinking.

Our claim is that the development and the use of managerial decision support systems can be enhanced by the availability of a DSS-generator that assists in revealing the implicit decision rules and in extending the explicit ones. In this way, the decision process is basically split up in:

(1) Building a DSS, the rules of which can be either entered by the manager himself (the decision modeler) or can be prompted by the DSS-generator and subsequently be approved by the manager.
(2) Using the DSS. The task of any particular decision maker in this phase is to fill in the 'holes' explicitly left open by the DSS.

As a matter of course, the managers involved in (1) - the decision modeler - and in (2) - the decision maker(s) - need not to be the same. This means, among others, that the DSS can be used as an adaptable tool for communicating directives throughout the organization.

Now, what demands can be made upon this DSS-generator? Its foremost function is to be of use in structuring and formalizing managers' 'soft knowledge'. This means that:

(a) The DSS-generator should have a user-friendly interface ('a language') for the (semi)-formal description of managerial knowledge by the decision modeler. The importance of a user-friendly interface is also stressed by Michalski : "In concept acquisition, the main interest is in derivation of symbolic descriptions that are human-oriented, i.e. that are easy to understand and easy to use for creating mental models of the information they convey."([13])

(b) The DSS-generator should be able to extend the cognitive capabilities of the decision modeler by analyzing the intermediate representation of the latter's decision processes. Possible directions of assistance include checking the internal consistency of the decision specification and signalizing likely decision rules not yet 'discovered' by the modeler.

In figure 1.1, the outline of a DSS-generator that fully meets both requirements is given. The decision modeler is assumed to translate (part of) his informal mental model into a (semi)-formal equivalent. The latter model in its turn is translated into an intermediate model (the so called Decision Grid Chart model), that can be both optimized and analyzed. The result of the analyzing process consists of suggestions for extending, refining and/or correcting the intermediate model. The end result of this interactive process is translated into the final model, viz. the DSS to be consulted by the decision makers.

In the remaining paragraphs, the logical part of this DSS-generator is dealt with. It is a further elaboration of the ideas as they were developed in [7] and laid down in the PRODEMO system ([9]). It should be noted that the term 'procedural', that was freely used in [9], is a rather misleading denotation of the rule-selecting mechanism that is activated in managerial decision making processes.

The following aspects are discussed:

1. In the second paragraph, a human-oriented propositional formalism is proposed. This formalism is aimed at bridging the gap between 'natural' logic, as it is encountered in everyday decision making processes, organizational prescriptions and others on the one side and its final DSS-encoding, viz. in the form of production rules, on the other side. It is our belief that the simple logical AND/OR- operators of production systems languages, (that were also used in the PRODEMO system, see [9]), are not well suited for coping with the cognitive and psychological problems encountered in decision analysis and decision modeling.
   In a further stage, this propositional formalism can be included in a much more general, user-friendly language for the representation of managerial knowledge. The importance of this work to be done was also stressed by Lee : "The real work (...) would be to develop a predicate calculus specialized to the problems of administration." ([5]).

2. In paragraph 3, a powerful yet simple intermediate representation formalism, the extended decision grid chart, is presented. Existing algorithms, taken from the research on decision tables, can be used to optimize the intermediate model according to different criteria. Readers who are unfamiliar with decision tables, are referred to [11].

3. The suitability of the decision grid chart for supporting the interactive decision analysis is investigated in paragraph 4. It is indicated how generalization and specialization rules, as they are used in concept acquisition and pattern recognition, apply. In paragraph 5, some further perspectives and conclusions are given.

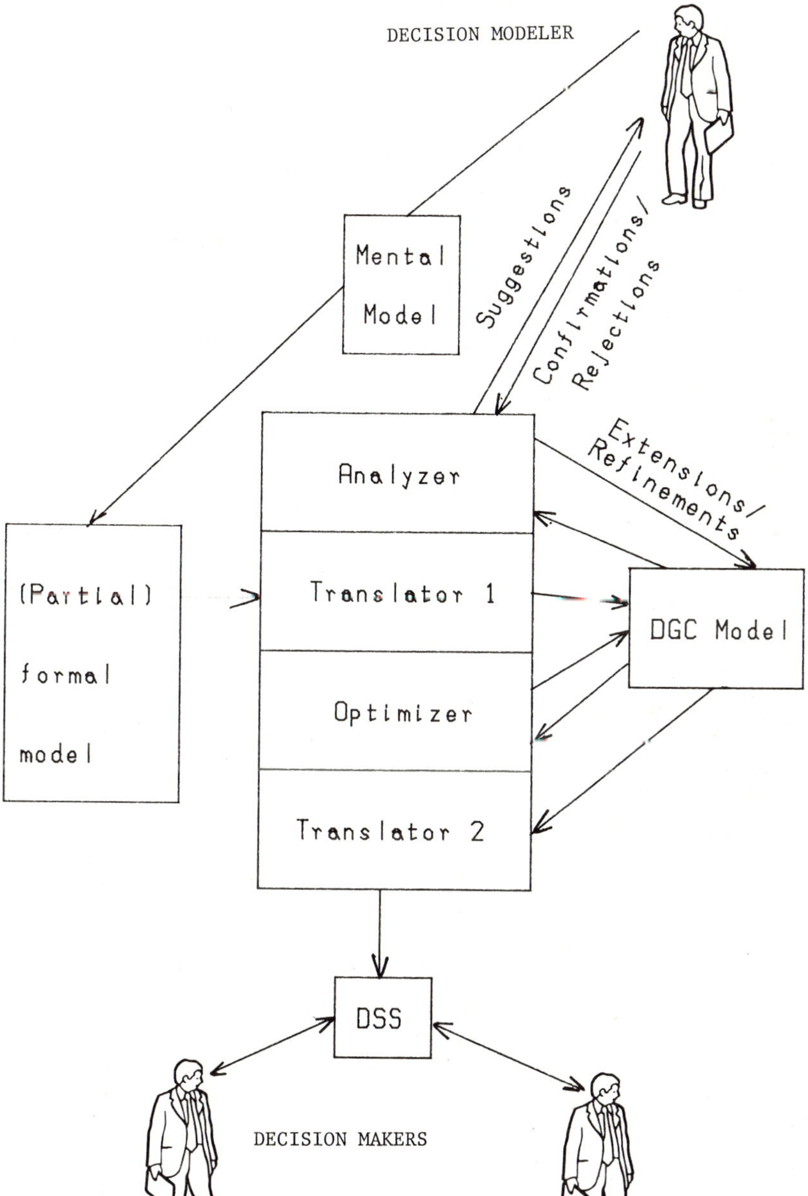
DECISION MODELER
Mental Model
Suggestions
Confirmations/ Rejections
Analyzer
Extensions/ Refinements
(Partial) formal model
Translator 1
DGC Model
Optimizer
Translator 2
DSS
DECISION MAKERS

Fig. 1.1

2. The propositional formalism

2.1 Presuppositions

The formalism we are proposing, is aimed at describing the relationships between the properties of the relevant environmental conditions and the outcome of the decision(s). Further, it should be possible to describe interrelations between these conditions as well as between the possible outcomes of the decisions (the 'actions'). In the rest of the paragraph, we assume that the following conventions hold true:

1. The decision modeler has previously specified at least a part of the relevant conditions and their states. Practical experiences with the PRODEMO system (see [9]) reveal that an interactive decision analysis, where the decision modeler is systematically focused on the individual combinations of condition states, contributes to the completeness (in terms of conditions and their states) of the resulting model. In this paragraph, environmental conditions are referred to by a positive integer. Their actual state is specified by the use of a letter; for sake of reference, the alphabetical order is assumed.

   Ex.: 1b refers to the second ('b') state (value) of the first ('1') condition.

   Remark further that the different states of a condition are supposed to be mutually exclusive.

2. It is assumed that every action (outcome of the decision) takes on one of the following three truth-values:

   - execute
   - don't execute
   - undefined

   The third value refers to our instantaneous (i.e. at the moment of the description) inability to describe the actual outcome of that part of the decision process (= that combination of condition states). It is similar to the truth-value 'undefined' as proposed by Colmerauer and Pique ([3]); it is further comparable to the classical law of the excluded middle ('the principium tertii exclusi') as it was introduced by Brouwer ([2]) and discussed by Wittgenstein ([17], pp 266-281). As a matter of fact, one of the purposes (if not the main purpose) of the modeling process is to eliminate these instances of indefiniteness. Instances still left open at the end of the modeling process, are passed on as 'open holes' to the decision makers.

   Remark further that, generally spoken, an action can have more than two (execute/don't execute) 'normal' values or states.

   Ex. : Give a discount of x %, where x equals 2,5 or 10.

   We assume, for sake of simplicity, that every multi-valued action has been transformed previously into an equivalent set of two-valued actions. We refer to actions by means of positive integers.

3. A regular propositional statement consists of a condition part and an action part. The following sequence is used in the next (sub)paragraphs:

   <action part> <propositional operator> <condition part>

2.2. Logical and propositional operators

The logical and propositional operators allow (1) to group simple operands into more complex conglomerates and (2) to relate conditions and actions. We discern four types of operators:

1. The logical NOT-, AND-, OR- and XOR-operators.

   The AND-operator can be used in the condition part as well as in the action part.

   Ex. : 1a AND 3c

   By the fact that we assume that the states of a single condition are mutually exclusive, one can easily ascertain that the following composed conditional operand is idle :

   1a AND 1b

   The OR-operator only has sense in the condition part. The following convention relieves the notational scheme :

   1abc ≡ 1a OR 1b OR 1c

   The exclusive OR can always be replaced by a combination of OR-, AND- and NOT-operators.

   Ex. : 1a XOR 3c ≡ (1a OR 3c) AND NOT (1a AND 3c)

2. The causal operators

   These operators separate the action part from the condition part. We discern the following operators :

   - '<-'-operator (logical consequence)

   Ex. : 1 <- 2a AND 3b

   Meaning: action 1 has to be executed if the conditional expression following the '<-'-operator holds true. However, other causal statements may still set bounds to this statement.

   - '<- <-'-operator (imperative consequence)

   Ex. : 1<- <-2b

   Meaning: action 1 has to be executed if condition 2 takes its second value. Every other causal statement limiting this statement reveals a contradiction.

   - '(<-)'-operator (potential consequence)

   Ex. : 1 (<-) 2c AND (3a OR 4ab)

   Meaning: action 1 <u>can</u> be executed under the specified conditions. As such, this indicative statement has no sense : it doesn't give any definite answer whether action 1 should be executed or not. This operator has to be amplified by the use of the intensive consequence/ cause-operator to be discussed hereafter.

- '[ ]'-operator (intensive consequence or cause)
As opposed to the foregoing operators, this complementary operator can occur both in the action part and in the condition part.

Ex. 1 : 1 (<-) [2c]	Meaning: <u>only if</u> the second condition takes its third value, then action 1 can be executed (i.e., the execution is impossible in all other cases).
Ex. 2 : [1] <- 2c	Meaning: if the second condition takes its third value, then action 1 <u>and no other action</u> should be executed.

2.3. The limitators

These supplementary operators allow to interrelate the individual logical statements.

Ex. :
(1) 3 <- lab
(2) 1 : NOT 3 <- 2a
(3) 2 <-3a : 1

Meaning:
- The statement following the 'ref :'-limitator, as in statement (2), only holds for the conditional state defined by the conditional part of the statement referred to by 'ref'. Consequently, statement (2) has to be interpreted as:

NOT 3 <- 2a AND lab

- The ':ref'-limitator (as in statement(3)) indicates that the statement preceding the ':'-symbol holds true as far as the statement referred to by 'ref' doesn't hold. Consequently, statement(3) has to be interpreted as:

2 <- 3a AND NOT lab

Remark that both operators limit the applicability of the statement in which they appear. The 'ref:'-operator, however, at the same time limits the statement referred to by 'ref', whereas the ':ref'-operator can be considered as rendering a completion of the statement referred to by 'ref'. Both limitators are very handy for representing generale rule/exception-situations.

2.4. Operators for describing interdependencies

The following operators are sufficient to represent in a handy way any logical interdependency of conditions as well as of actions:

- '->'-operator (implication)

Ex. 1 : la AND 2a -> 3a	Meaning : if the first combination of condition states holds true, then condition 3 must take its first state.
Ex. 2 : 1 -> 2 XOR 3	Meaning : if action 1 is executed, then either action 2 or action 3 (but not both) has to be executed.

- 'IMPOS'-operator

Ex. : la AND 2a -> IMPOS	Meaning: the combination of condition states preceding the ->-operator is impossible.

- 'EXCL'-operator

Ex. : 1 AND 6 AND 7 -> EXCL — Meaning : actions 1, 6 and 7 are mutually exclusive, i.e. only one of these actions can be executed for a combination of condition states.

- 'IEXCL'-operator

Ex. : 1 AND 6 AND 7 -> IEXCL — Meaning : one and only one (imperative exclusiveness) of the actions has to be executed for every combination of condition states.

Remark that the following identity holds :

(1 AND 4 ->IEXCL) ≡ ((1 AND 4 ->EXCL) AND (NOT 1 AND NOT 4 ->IMPOS))

2.5. A remark

The formal operators that were presented in the preceding subparagraphs all have a precise meaning; as such, they differ to a great extent from the natural linguistic usage as found in the specification of decision situations. As a consequence, the translation of natural language sentences into formal conditional statements might be a precarious yet clarifying experience.

As far as the decision logic is concerned, one might replace the formal operators by the following expressions in natural language:

<-<-	ALWAYS IF
<-	IF
(<-) [ ]	ONLY POSSIBLE IF
<- [ ]	ONLY IF
<-<- [ ]	IF AND ONLY IF

3 The extended decision grid chart

The decision grid chart (DGC) or decision matrix was proposed by Strunz ([15]) as a handy tool for representing the relations between the conditions and the outcomes of the decision process (called the 'actions'). In [8], its basic format was extended and a powerful algorithm for minimizing the number of rules of a DGC was developed. A simple example of an extended DGC is given in figure 3.1.

	1	2	3	4	5	6	7	8	9	10	
											Rule number
C1	1	1	2	2	3	3	-	3	-	-	
C2	Y	-	Y	N	-	-	-	Y	-	Y	
C3	N	-	-	Y	-	Y	-	-	Y	-	
C4	-	Y	-	-	N	-	N	-	N	N	
C5	N	-	Y	-	-	-	-	-	N	-	
	A1	A2		A3	A4		A5	Impossible			Action

Fig. 3.1

It can be seen that the DGC is merely a special form of a multiple hit decision table, i.e. a decision table with mutually nonexclusive rules. Rule no. 2 of the DGC of figure 3.1, e.g., means that action A2 should be executed every time condition C1 takes its first value and condition C4 holds true (Y-entry). A

don't care-entry ('-') means that the condition is irrelevant for the given decision rule. Rule no. 3, on the other hand, stipulates yet another situation (combination of condition states) where the same action should be applied. Remark that two or more DGC rules, even when dealing with the same action, may be overlapping (as is the case in rules 5 and 6).
The last three rules of the DGC of figure 3.1, marked by the 'Impossible'-action, in fact represent the interdependencies of the conditions. In natural logic, these interdependencies can be either impossibilities or implications.

The extended DGC has proven, e.g. in the PRODEMO system, to be a powerful mechanism for the intermediate representation of decision logic.

In particular:

1. The extended DGC is able to represent any relations between conditions and actions and any logical interdependencies of conditions, provided we introduce the notion of a negation of an action in the DGC. This means that every rule of a DGC can be governed by an action (as in figure 3.1) or by the negation (don't execute') of an action. The latter convention means a further extension of the DGC-concept. The interdependencies of actions, in their turn, can be dealt with by the use of a simple separate action matrix, similar to the 'Impossible'-part of the extended DGC.
2. There exist efficient algorithms for the manipulation of DGCs. In [8], e.g., a powerful algorithm for the contraction of DGCs was presented. This and similar algorithms enable to reduce the description of the decision process to its most efficient form. What is more important is that the DGC allows for the decision modeler to guarantee the syntactic completeness and consistency of the description under development. A very common practice to validate completeness and consistency is to transform the DGC into the equivalent decision table; algorithms performing this transformation were presented in [6].
3. The procedural execution of the decision process is postponed till the moment of the actual decision making. Numerous algorithms exist for the optimization of this execution according to several criteria such as the (weighted) number of conditions to be tested or the number of decision rules to be traversed (see, e.g., [10] and [14]).
4. The DGC is very well suited for the application of generalization and specialization rules as they are applied in pattern recognition and knowledge acquisition. We refer to the next paragraph for an elaboration of this topic.

4. The application of A.I.-techniques

A very straightforward procedure for the specification of decisions can be derived from figure 1.1: the decision modeler transforms his/her mental model into a set of formal statements; these statements in their turn, are transformed into a set of equivalent DGC-rules. It was indicated in the forgoing paragraph that this internal representation scheme allows to optimize the intermediate and/or final DGC.

As long as the set of decision rules brought into the DGC is incomplete and/or syntactically inconsistent we can further use techniques taken from A.I. to refine the DGC model in a semi-automatic way. Basically there are two types of errors that may occur during the modeling of the decision process:

- type 1: not to execute an action that should be executed and
- type 2: to execute an action that should not be executed.

To prevent type 1 errors, new decision rules must be generated. In the sequel, we suppose that, due to the inherent complexity of the decision situation, the modeler is unable to specify the complete decision by himself. If supplementary rules are generated by the DSS-generator, type 2 errors might be introduced; in that case, the generalization was inappropriate and one can take one of the following way outs:

- either, one can consider the generalization as a mere suggestion; if an inconsistency is detected (either by the DSS-generator itself or by the decision modeler), then the suggestion is dropped;
- or one can set limits to the applicability of the generated rule (and hence remove the inconsistency) by a further specialization of this rule.

An extreme example of specialization is the case where no generalization is possible at all, i.e. where all new combinations of condition values for a particular decision rule have to be fully specified.

Michalski has outlined a number of generalization rules in [12] and [13]. In what follows, we describe the generalization rules that are most suitable to be applied in a DGC:

1 - 'dropping condition' rule

Ex.: 1 <- 1a and 2c can be generalized into: 1 <- 1a

```
c1  a          c1   a
c2  c          c2   -
-----          ------
Ax  1          Ax   1
```

This rule can very easily be applied in DGCs. However, if the value set of condition 2 has x elements, then (x-1) possible errors of type 2 (executing action 1 while it should not be executed) might be introduced. Notice further that if the original DGC-rule is derived from a single logical expression (as is the case in the example given above), then it is rather unlikely that the 'dropping condition' generalization rule is the appropriate rule to be selected (provided we assume a 'conservative' decision modeler, i.e. a modeler who only enters rules he can be sure of).

2 - 'adding alternative' rule

Ex.: 1 <- 1b, generalization: 1<- 1b or 2a

```
c1  b        c1  b  -
c2  -        c2  -  a
-----        --------
Ax  1        Ax  1  1
```

In this case, we have to add a decision rule to the DGC. As a matter of fact, the generated rule is not disjunct from the existing rule (both rules contain the situation 1b <u>and</u> 2a). The 'adding alternative' rule can be applied in many circumstances; it is self-evident that in case the 'if and only if'-construction is used (e.g. 1 <- <- [1b]), this type of generalization is inappropriate.

3 - 'extending reference' rule

Ex.: 1 <- 1c, generalization: 1 <- 1bc

```
c1   c           c1  b   c
c2   -           c2  -   -
--------         ---------
Ax   1           Ax  1   1
```

If b and c are the only values in the domain of condition 1, then the entry of condition 1 becomes a don't-care value ('dropping condition' rule).

4 - 'turning conjunction into disjunction' rule
Ex.: 4 <- 1a and 2a, generalization: 4 <- 1a or 2a

```
c1  a        c1 a  -
c2  a        c2 -  a
-----        -------
Ax  4        Ax 4  4
```

One decision rule is split in two not disjunct rules.

5 - 'inductive resolution' rule

```
Ex.: 1 <- 1b and 2c  }
                     }        generalization: 1 <- 2c or 3a
     1 <- 1a and 3a  }
```

```
c1   b  a        c1   - -
c2   c  -        c2   c -
c3   -  a        c3   - a
---------        --------
Ax   1  1        Ax   1 1
```

6 - 'extension against' rule

```
Ex.: 2 <- 1c and 2a          }
                             }    generalization: 2 <- not 2b
     (not 2) <- 3a and 2b    }
```

```
c1  c   -             c1  -
c2  a   b             c2  (not b)
c3  -   a             c3  -
------------          --------
Ax  2  (not 2)        Ax  2
```

Remark that if a and b are the only values in the domain of condition 2, we get one decision rule after the generalization; otherwise we get more rules.

Extensions of the value set of a condition can not be proposed by the system; if extentions are necessary, they have to be given by the decision modeler.

Developing a generalized strategy of generalization, that is a good strategy for all kinds of decision problems is a cumbersome task that needs further research. In fact we have to make four selections:

- Which decision rule will be modified?
- Which component/condition in that rule will be modified?
- Do we have to generalize <u>or</u> to specialize?
- Which generalization or specialization rule must be applied?

Some simple heuristics that might apply are:
- If a rule is entered as: (for example) 3 <- 1a <u>and</u> 2c
  then do not apply the 'dropping condition' rule to this decision rule.
- If a rule contains the operator: "if and only if"
  then no generalization rule is applicable.
- If we want to minimize the number of rules
  then apply either the 'dropping condition' rule, the 'inductive resolution' rule or the 'extension against' rule first.
- If we want to minimize the number of condition tests
  then do not apply the 'adding alternative' rule.

- If a condition has a small value set
  then modify this component before modifying conditions with large(r) value sets.
- Change one condition value at a time.

See [1], [4] and [16] for more heuristics.

5. Perspectives and conclusions

Using the components of the DSS-generator, as described above, the decision modeler can formalize the logical part of his decision process without assistance of knowledge engineers. The generator is capable to support the DSS during its entire life cycle. If changes occur, the new situation is simply reanalyzed and optimized by the generator. Algorithms, as they are known from the research on decision tables can be applied.

Two of the biggest problems in knowledge acquisition are completeness and interpretation. As far as these problems are due to the logical part of the decision process they are avoided by applying the generator, because the DSS-generator guarantees both syntactical completeness and internal consistency.

The strong point of our proposal are:

- A very simple formalism, consisting of two types of operators, enabling to express logical expressions in a consistent and unambigious way.
- Using the decision grid chart we can introduce generalization rules taken from the research on pattern recognition problems.
- The DGC allows to use existing algorithms for simplifying the description of the decision process.

References

1. Bell, D.A., Decision Trees, Tables and Lattices, Pattern Recognition (ed. Batchelor), Plenum Press, New York & London, 1978, pp. 119-141.

2. Brouwer, L.E.J., De Onbetrouwbaarheid der Logische Principes, Tijdschrift voor Wijsbegeerte, No. 2, 1908, pp. 152-158.

3. Colmerauer, A. & J.F. Pique, About Natural Logic, Advances in Database Theory, Vol. 1 (ed. H. Gallaire, J. Minker & J.M. Nicolas), Plenum Press, New York, 1981, pp. 343-365.

4. Davis, R. & D.B. Lenat, Knowledge-Based Systems in Artificial Intelligence, McGraw-Hill, New York, 1982, 490 pp.

5. Lee, R.M., Application Software and Organizational Change: Issues in the Representation of Knowledge, Information Systems, Vol. 8, No. 3, 1983, pp. 187-194.

6. Maes, R., An Algorithmic Approach to the Conversion of Decision Grid Charts into Compressed Decision Tables, Communications of the ACM, Vol.23, No. 5, May 1980, pp. 286-293.

7. Maes, R., Bijdrage tot een Kritische Herwaardering van de Beslissingstabellentechniek, Doctoral Thesis, Catholic University of Leuven, 1981, 397 pp.

8. Maes, R., On Minimizing Decision Grid Charts, Angewandte Informatik, Vol. 24, No. 9, 1982, pp. 451-456.

9. Maes, R., J. Vanthienen & M. Verhelst, Practical Experiences with the Procedural Decision Modeling System, Processes and Tools for Decision Support (ed. H.G. Sol), North Holland, 1983, pp. 139-154.

10. Maes, R. & J.E.M. van Dijk, Criteria and New Algorithms for Contracting Decision Tables, forthcoming.

11. Metzner, J.R. & B.H. Barnes, Decision Table Languages and Systems, Academic Press, New York, 1977, 172 pp.

12. Michalski, R.S., Pattern Recognition as Rule-guided Inductive Inference, IEEE Transactions on Pattern Analysis and Machine Intelligence, Vol. PAMI-2, No. 4, July 1980, pp. 349-361.

13. Michalski, R.S., J.G. Carbonell & T.M. Mitchell (eds.), Machine Learning, Tioga Publ. Co., Palo Alto, 1983.

14. Moret, B.M.E., M.G. Thomason & R.C. Gonzalez, Optimization Criteria for Decision Trees, University of New Mexico, Albuquerque, Technical Report CS81-6, 1981, 14 pp.

15. Strunz, H., The Development of Decision Tables via Parsing of Complex Decision Situations, Communications of the ACM, Vol. 16, No. 6, June 1973, pp. 366-369.

16. Waterman, D.A., Generalization Learning Techniques for Automating the Learning of Heuristics, Artificial Intelligence, Vol. 1, No. 1, 1970, pp. 121-170.

17. Wittgenstein, L., Remarks on the Foundations of Mathematics, 3rd revised ed., Basil Blackwell, Oxford, 1978, 444 pp.

Artificial Intelligence in Economics and Management
L.F. Pau (Editor)

A SYSTEM FOR NATURAL LANGUAGE COMMUNICATION BETWEEN A DECISION MODEL AND ITS USERS

Robert W. Blanning

Owen Graduate School of Management
Vanderbilt University
Nashville, Tennessee 37203
USA

There are two principal applications of artificial intelligence to management: the development of natural language query processors for decision models and the construction of expert systems for management. In this paper we address the first of these topics and examine its relationship to the second. In addition, we introduce MERLIN, a natural language query processor for a simple decision model, and we describe briefly the design strategies used in the development of MERLIN.

INTRODUCTION

The growing number of applications of artificial intelligence (AI) methodology to non-management domains--such as the development of expert systems for medical diagnosis and of natural language query processors for database management systems--has led to suggestions that AI technology may be of direct assistance to managers who must make decisions and implement them (Bonczek, Holsapple, and Whinston (1981), Fox (1983), Gorry and Krumland (1983), Reitman (1982)). There appear to be two principal applications of AI to management. The first is the development of natural language query processors for decision models--such as financial models, marketing models, production scheduling models, etc. (Blanning (1984d)). These systems, which are still undergoing development, would allow a user to access a decision model in a natural language (such as English), rather than in a well-structured query language. The second is the development of expert systems for management (ESMs) that would capture the expert knowledge of experienced managers and apply it to specific decision tasks (Blanning (1984e)). Several ESMs have been developed at universities and industrial research laboratories, and many ESMs may achieve commercial implementation during the next decade (Blanning (1985, 1984a, 1984c)).

The purpose of this paper is to examine the first of these two topics and discuss its relevance to the second. In doing so we introduce MERLIN, a natural language query processor for a simple decision model (Blanning (1984b)). In Section II we outline the features of an ideal natural language model query processor. MERLIN possesses some, but not all, of these features. In Section III we describe MERLIN, explain the design strategies used in its construction, and present an example of its use. In Section IV we examine the state of the art in ESM development and examine its relationship to natural language model query processing.

NATURAL LANGUAGE MODEL QUERY PROCESSING

During the past two decades substantial research has been done on natural language processing and its application to database query processing (Tennant (1981), Waltz (1982), Rich (1984)). The input to a natural language database query processor is a query, stated in a natural language, whose answer requires the accessing or processing (e.g., summarizing) of information contained in a database. The output is the same query stated in a structured query language that is then processed by a file processing or database management system. The query processor parses the query and attempts to resolve ambiguities. The ambiguities may include misspellings, lexical (or word sense) ambiguities, and ambiguities resulting from anaphora--that is, reference within a query to information contained in an earlier part of the same query or in previous queries. Examples of anaphora are pronoun reference, paraphrase (i.e. the use of different phrases to refer to the same entity or action), and ellipsis (the omission of words whose meaning is understood by the user and therefore, must be inferred by the system). In some cases the ambiguities are resolved directly by the system, and in other cases the system queries the user to resolve them. Many such query processors have been constructed for research purposes, at some of which are now commercially available (Harris (1984)).

The issues in the design of natural language model query processors are similar, although the variety of functions to be performed by decision models are more complex than those to be performed by database management systems. One simplifying factor is that it is possible to take a relational view of models, similar to the established relational view of data (Blanning (1983)). That is, a model is viewed as a virtual relation with input and output attributes, just as a file is viewed in relational database theory as a stored relation with key and content attributes. Thus, the target language of a natural language model query processor can be based on a relational view of models with appropriate requirements for relational completeness.

The requirements for relational completeness are examined in detail in (Blanning (1984d, 1984e)) and are summarized here. There are three requirements for relational completeness of model query languages. The first is execution: one or more input or output attributes of the model are identified and values are assigned. The operation of execution results in values for the remaining attributes that satisfy the relationships in the model. This corresponds to selection and projection in relational database theory. The second operation is optimization: one or more input attributes (the decision variables), a single output attribute (the objective function), and a maximum or minimum designator are identified, and the remaining input attributes are assigned values. The operation determines the optimal values of the decision variables and the resulting outputs. The third operation is sensitivity analysis, which determines the rate of change of one attribute (usually an output attribute) with respect to another attribute (usually an input attribute). MERLIN performs only the first of these operations, and further work will be needed to incorporate the other two. However, it contains extensive procedures for the resolution of ambiguities, as is demonstrated below.

MERLIN: A NATURAL LANGUAGE MODEL QUERY PROCESSOR

MERLIN is a natural language model query processor for a simple decision model. Written in UCI LISP, it runs on a DEC System 10 at Vanderbilt University under the TOPS-10 operating system. The model has two inputs, a sale price (PRICE) and a unit cost of production and distribution (COST); an intermediate variable, the resulting sales volume (VOL); and two outputs, total expense (EXPENSE) and revenue net of expenses (PROFIT). The relationships in the model are as follows: (1) VOL = 1000 - 50 x (MIN (20, PRICE)), (2) EXPENSE = COST x VOL, and (3) PROFIT = (PRICE - COST) x VOL. The input attributes (PRICE and COST) in these equations must be nonnegative. Thus, EXPENSE will always be nonnegative, although PROFIT need not be. If a negative number appears in the query, MERLIN sets it to its absolute value and tells the user that it has done so.

The user of MERLIN specifies the input attributes and requests the values of the output attributes, and MERLIN responds. The user may misspell words in the query, paraphrase the words with synonyms (e.g., INCOME for PROFIT), and make anaphoric reference. For example, if the user enters "CHANGE IT TO 7," then MERLIN will identify the input attribute to be changed (which is the last input attribute previously mentioned) and take the appropriate action. MERLIN contains rules for the resolution of more complex ambiguities, some of which are illustrated below.

MERLIN is based on three design strategies. The first is semantic filtering. MERLIN looks only for certain key words (interrogative words, input attribute names, output attribute names, and numbers) and their permitted misspellings and synonyms, and it ignores all other words. This strategy has an obvious advantage: MERLIN need not have an enormous vocabulary and need not ask users to define words it does not understand. But it also has a disadvantage: in some cases MERLIN may incorrectly interpret a query. For example, if the user were to enter "THE PRICE WILL CHANGE AT 5 PM," then MERLIN, having no concept of time, would assume that the user is trying to set PRICE to 5.

The second strategy is rule-based inference. The inference mechanism attempts to infer the user's intent from the filtered query. It is designed to minimize the likelihood that a well intentioned user familiar with MERLIN's problem domain would ask a question to which MERLIN would respond inappropriately. The rules are described below.

The third strategy is partial understanding with feedback. Like many of the natural language query processors that have been developed for database systems, MERLIN determines when any ambiguities are apparently unresolvable by analysis of the query as stated and interrogates the user in an attempt to disambiguate the query. In order to facilitate its interrogation, MERLIN assigns to each user query one of four levels of confusion, as follows:

LEVEL I: all ambiguities are resolved to the satisfaction of MERLIN.

LEVEL II: there is a single ambiguity that can be resolved if the user will answer a simple question (e.g., "PLEASE TELL ME THE PRICE").

LEVEL III: MERLIN understands a part of the query but cannot communicate its lack of understanding with a simple question (e.g., "I ASSUME THAT THE COST IS 6 BUT PLEASE REPHRASE THE REST OF YOUR QUESTION").

LEVEL IV: MERLIN is completely confused and asks that the entire query be rephrased.

The situation-action rules applied to the filtered query determine the proper level of confusion and thus, the most appropriate system response. MERLIN makes use of five sets of rules. If none of the rules obtain, then MERLIN identifies a LEVEL IV ambiguity and asks the user to rephrase the query. The five types of rules are:

TYPE A RULES: The first set of rules examines the query in order to determine whether any output attribute values should be printed, and if so, which of them should be printed. There are three components of the Type A rules. The first component states that if any output attribute names are mentioned in the query, then the corresponding attribute values are printed as a part of the system response. The second component states that if no attribute names (input or output) appear in the query but an interrogative word (WHAT or HOW) appears, then all output attribute values are printed. Third, if no output attribute names appear but at least one input attribute name and value appear and the query contains an interrogative word, then all output attribute values are printed.

TYPE B RULES: These rules attempt to match input attribute names with their corresponding values in the query. They are invoked only if the number of input attribute names and the number of numerical values in the query are equal, and the vector of numerical values is assigned to the vector of named attributes in the order in which they appear in the query.

TYPE C RULES: These are invoked when the query contains one or more input names without any numerical values. It is assumed that the user is asking for the values of the mentioned attributes, which are then printed. In both the Type B and Type C rules, if an input attribute name is repeated (i.e., appears more than once in a single query), then MERLIN interrogates the user to resolve the ambiguity.

TYPE D RULES: These are the opposite of the Type C rules--they are invoked when at least one numerical value but no input attribute names are found in the query. This is assumed to be an anaphoric reference to input attribute names that have appeared in previous queries, and the anaphora is resolved. If more numbers appear in the query than there are input attributes in the model (in this case 2), then MERLIN conducts a dialogue with the user in an attempt to resolve the ambiguity.

TYPE E RULES: These are a combination of Type D and Type B rules. They are invoked when anaphoric reference to an input attribute name and an assignment of a value to a name both occur in a single query. However, if an attempted anaphora occurs after an assignment, MERLIN interrogates the user about it.

A sample MERLIN session appears in Figure 1. The user logs in, runs the LISP interpreter, loads the file containing MERLIN, and executes a driver function. MERLIN welcomes the user and displays a prompt (*). The first question illustrates the semantic filtering of misspellings and paraphrase (e.g., MONY is a misspelling of MONEY, which is a synonym of PROFIT). The remainder of the conversation illustrates MERLIN's ability to resolve ambiguities, and the final question ("WHAT IS THE PRICE OF PROGRESS") illustrates the ability of an ignorant or malicious user to cause MERLIN to respond inappropriately.

EXPERT SYSTEMS FOR MANAGEMENT

The successful construction of expert systems in such non-management domains as medical diagnosis and geological prospecting (Hayes-Roth, Waterman, and Lenat (1983), Weiss and Kulikowski (1984)) has led to the development of a variety of ESMs, which may be grouped into four categories. To date, most ESM development has taken place at universities and industrial research laboratories, and none of the systems described below is commercially available. The four categories of ESMs are (1) resource allocation (e.g., portfolio management and capital budgeting), (2) problem diagnosis (e.g., auditing and financial statement analysis), (3) scheduling (e.g., of meetings) and assignment (e.g., of personnel to job slots), and (4) information management (Blanning (1985, 1984a, 1984c)). The latter refers to the use of inferential (i.e., theorem proving) and other techniques to determine whether and how available files and programs can be combined to respond to a user query.

```
AUGUST 15  1984

WELCOME - I AM MERLIN
PLEASE ASK ME A QUESTION
TO CONTINUE A LINE END IT WITH A BLANK SPACE
PLEASE DO NOT USE ANY PUNCTUATION MARKS
TO RETURN TO MONITOR TYPE GOODBYE OR BYE

*DEER MARLON IF MY PRIEC IS FIVE AND 4 IS MY COS
*HOW MUDH MONY WOLD I MAK

THE PROFIT IS 750

*WHAT PRICE ARE YOU ASSUMING

THE PRICE IS 5

*CHANGE IT TO 8

I UNDERSTAND

*NOW WHAT HAPPENS

THE EXPENSE IS 2400
THE PROFIT IS 2400

*WHAT IF THE COST IS 5 AND 7

I DO NOT UNDERSTAND WHAT THE COST IS TO BE
PLEASE TELL ME

*6
```

FIGURE 1: A MERLIN Conversation

```
I UNDERSTAND
I ASSUME THAT THE PRICE IS STILL 8
IS THAT CORRECT ?

*PERHAPS

PLEASE TELL ME THE PRICE

*HORSEFEATHERS

I DO NOT UNDERSTAND
I ASSUME THAT THE COST IS 6
BUT PLEASE REPHRASE THE REST OF YOUR QUESTION

*TO HIM WHO IN THE LOVE OF NATURE HOLDS COMMUNION WITH
*HER VISIBLE FORMS SHE SPEAKS A VARIOUS LANGUAGE

I DO NOT UNDERSTAND YOUR QUESTION
PLEASE REPHRASE IT

*WHAT IS THE PRICE OF PROGRESS

THE PRICE IS 8

*GOODBYE MERLIN

GOODBYE
```

FIGURE 1: A MERLIN Conversation (continued)

The literature on ESMs suggests two possible enhancements to MERLIN or a MERLIN-like system (other than the obvious one of incorporating optimization and sensitivity analysis features). The first is the incorporation of information about the decision processes of the managers who will use it. For example, if MERLIN were to be used for resource allocation, the input sentences might differ from those that would be inputted if the system were to be used for problem diagnosis. With this additional information MERLIN might be able to answer queries that would arise naturally in a problem context rather than those that require the user to know the input and output attributes of the model--for example, "WHAT PRICE SHOULD I CHARGE?" or "IS A COST OF 10 ACCEPTABLE?"

A second enhancement is suggested by the literature on information management. MERLIN is based on a single model. However, most organizations maintain a large number of files and models. Futhermore, there may be more than one information source of a given type (e.g., several files containing redundant or contradictory data or several potentially useful data analysis procedures or decision models) that could be used to prepare a response. An enhanced MERLIN might detect this, inform the user that there are several possible ways to respond to the query, and elicit further information that would be helpful in selecting an appropriate strategy.

CONCLUSION

We have presented the design of a natural language query processor for a simple decision model. The most striking feature of this processor is the large amount of semantic filtering done before the inferential mechanism is invoked. The syntactic structure of the query is almost completely obliterated, and the inferential mechanism is permitted to access only a few key words. The advantages and disadvantages of this approach were discussed in Section III. Whether this approach will be effective for models with larger numbers of input and output attributes or for systems that perform optimization or sensitivity analysis is not clear. However, there is a reason for believing that this approach may be useful in more general areas of model management.

In relational data management each tuple in a relation corresponds to a single entity in the real world, and the functional dependency between key and content attributes represents a relationship between the indentifier assigned to each entity and the value of the attributes of that entity. In model management there is a single entity in the real world corresponding to each relation, and the functional dependency between input and output represents a causal relationship between certain attributes of the entity (Blanning (1983)). It is possible that the causal, as opposed to the assigned, nature of the functional dependencies in model management imposes a structure on the queries presented to a model query processor that permits substantial semantic filtering. This is the premise on which MERLIN is based. Additional research is needed to determine whether this approach will be effective in more complex cases.

Another area in which research might be done is menu-based natural language query processing. In this case a user would be shown a sequence of sets of words and would form a query by selecting one word from each set in the sequence. The sets might consist of interrogative words, the names of input and output attributes, and the names of operations to be performed. In addition, the user would be allowed to enter numbers representing attribute values. This approach has been implemented for database systems (Tennant (1984)), and it offers several advantages. For example, spelling errors are eliminated, as are ambiguities, and the user cannot present a query that is outside of the processor's problem domain. This more structured approach may also be useful in natural language model query processing.

ACKNOWLEDGEMENT

This work was supported by the Dean's Fund for Faculty Research of the Owen Graduate School of Management of Vanderbilt University.

REFERENCES

[1] Blanning, R. W., Expert systems for management: research and applications, Journal of Information Science 9 (1985) 153-162.

[2] Blanning, R. W., Management applications of expert systems, Information & Management 7 (1984) 311-316 (a).

[3] Blanning, R. W., MERLIN: System and User Manual, Working Paper 84-132, Owen Graduate School of Management, Vanderbilt University (1984) (B).

[4] Blanning, R. W., Issues in the design of expert systems for management, Proceedings of the National Computer Conference (AFIPS Press, Reston, 1984) (c).

[5] Blanning, R. W., Conversing with management information systems in natural language, Communications of the ACM 27 (1984) 201-207 (d).

[6] Blanning, R. W., Language design for relational model management, in: Chang, S-K. (ed.), Management and Office Information Systems (Plenum, New York, 1984) (e).

[7] Blanning, R. W., Issues in the design of relational model management systems, Proceedings of the National Computer Conference (AFIPS Press, Reston, 1983).

[8] Bonczek, R. H., Holsapple, C. W., and Whinston, A. B., Foundations of Decision Support Systems (Academic Press, New York, 1981).

[9] Fox, M. S., The intelligent management system: an overview, in: Sol, H. G. (ed.), Processes and Tools for Decision Support (North-Holland, Amsterdam, 1983).

[10] Gorry, G. A. and Krumland, R. B., Artificial intelligence research and decision support systems, in: Bennett, J. L. (ed.), Building Decision Support Systems (Addison-Wesley, Reading, 1983).

[11] Harris, L. R., Experience with INTELLECT: artificial intelligence technology transfer, The AI Magazine 5 (1984) 43-50.

[12] Hayes-Roth, F., Waterman, D. A., and Lenat, D. B. (eds.), Building Expert Systems (Addison-Wesley, Reading, 1983).

[13] Reitman, W., Applying artificial intelligence to decision support: where do good alternatives come from? in: Ginzberg, M. J., Reitman, W. and Stohr, E. A. (eds.), Decision Support Systems (North-Holland, Amsterdam, 1982).

[14] Rich, E., Natural language interfaces, Computer 17 (1984) 39-47.

[15] Tennant, H., Menu-based natural language understanding, Proceedings of the National Computer Conference (AFIPS Press, Reston, 1984).

[16] Tennant, H., Natural Language Processing (Petrocelli, New York, 1981).

[17] Waltz, D. B., The state of the art in natural language processing, in: Lenhert, W. J. and Ringle, M. H. (eds.), Strategies for Natural Language Processing (Lawrence Erlbaum, Hillsdale, 1982).

[18] Weiss, S. M. and Kulikowski, C. A., A Practical Guide to Designing Expert Systems (Rowman and Allenheld, Totowa, 1984).

Artificial Intelligence in Economics and Management
L.F. Pau (Editor)

INTELLIGENT CONTROL and INTELLIGENT MANAGEMENT for LARGE SCALE SYSTEMS

Tu Xu-Yen

Chinese Association of Artificial Intelligence

Due to the complexity of large scale system, there are many problems to be solved. However it is very difficult and expensive those problems only by traditional methodology of system theory. This paper try to find a new way to solve the above problems through the combination of artificial intelligence, large scale system theory and microcomputer technique. Three schemes are given: Multilevel Self-Optimalizing Control (msoc), Multilevel Fuzzy Control (MFC) and Multilevel Expert System (MES).

INTRODUCTION

Now, the "Artificial Intelligence" (AI) and the "large scale system theory" both are very active fields, but they are developing seperately.

Due to the complexity of large scale systems, there are many problems to be solved.

However, it is very difficult and expensive to solve those problems only by the traditional methodology of the System Theory.

So that, the Subject Matter of this paper is to explore the "New Way" ---

The Combination of the "Large Scale System Theory", "Artificial Intelligence" and "Microcomputer Technique"

Namely :

The Intelligent Control, Intelligent Management and Intelligent Decision -Making for Large Scale Systems.

(1) The Problems on Large Scale Systems

There are many problems on large scale system theory and its application to be solved. For example:

1) Contradiction between Model and Method

The lack of appropriate mathematical model of the object is the troublesome but usual obstruction in system theory and its applications. The accuracy and reliability of model are contradictory to the effectiveness and practical computability of the method.

2) Non-classical Information Pattern

Due to the decentralization of subsystem the non-classical information pattern is present, i.e. information decentralization and control decentralization. But the traditional methodology of system theory is based on the classical information pattern, i.e. information centralization and control centralization.

3) Uncertainty

The uncertainty of large scale systems may be formed by the fuzziness, randomness, uncertainly-know and drift.

4) Activity

Many large scale systems are active systems, in which, the active element is the human element, such as the human operator, manager... etc. The passive element is computer, machine... etc.

How to promote the advantages: Creatability, Flexibility, ..., and to overcome the shortage: Weariness, Forgetfulness, Sentimentality,... of the active elements are the interesting open problems on control, management and decision-making of large scale systems.

(2) Possibility of New Way

The new way, to solve the problem of large scale systems, can be explored from the combination of Artificial Intelligence, Large scale system theory and Microcomputer Techniques.

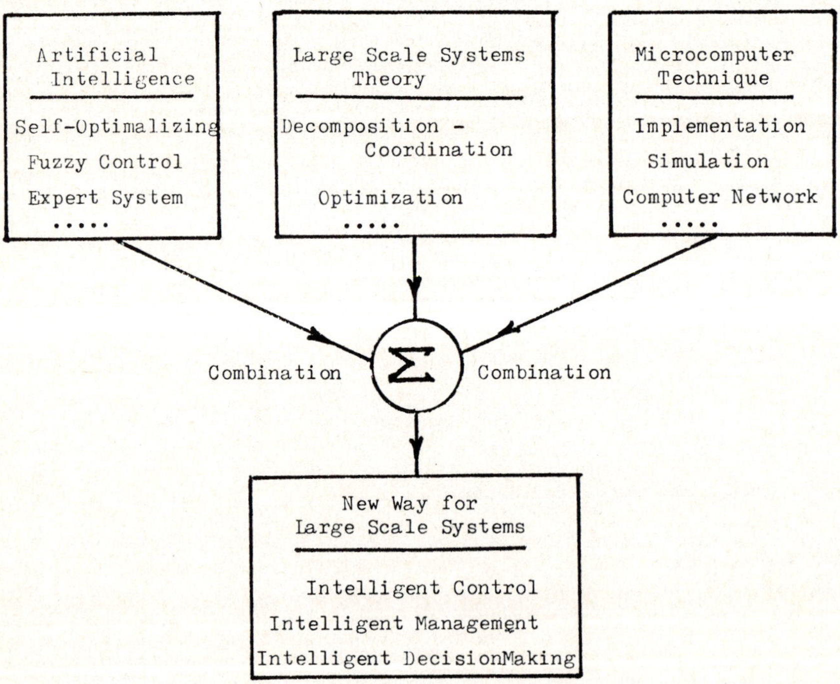

(3) Multilevel Self-optimalizing Control

See reference (18)

(4) Multilevel Fuzzy Control

See reference (19)

(5) Multilevel Expert System (MES)

As the scheme of the intelligence decision-making for the large scale system, we suggest the multilevel expert system:

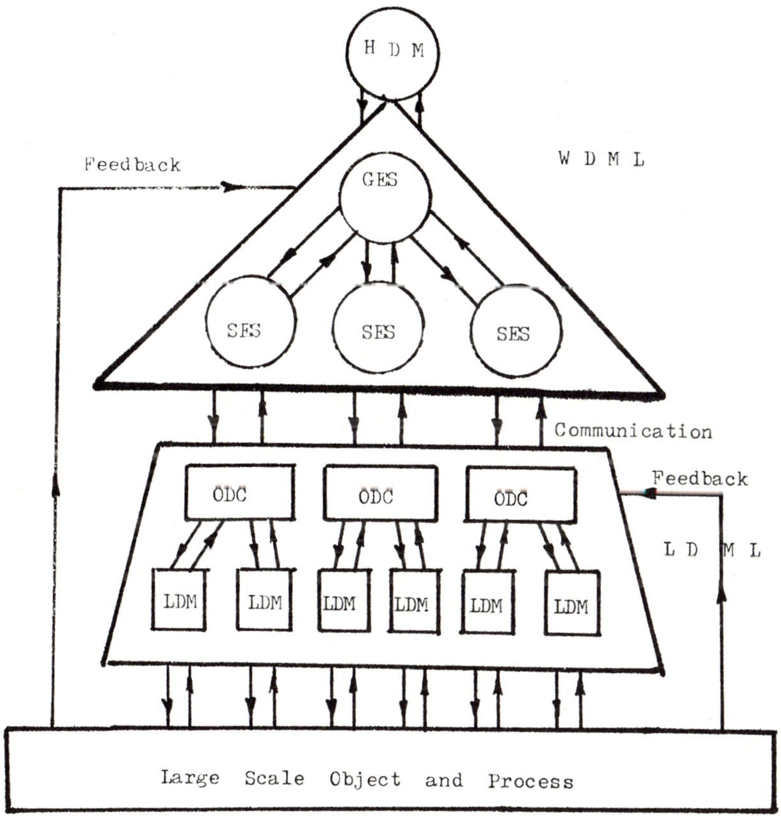

** Design of the MES Scheme

The MES scheme is obtained from the combination of the "Decomposition-Coordination" method and the "expert system" in artificial intelligence.

It can be used for the decision-making of the special large scale system such as a city, a province or a nation ... etc.

The MES scheme is designed with the multilevel hierarchical structure. Its macro-structure has two levels:

1) Whole Decision-Making Level (WDML)
2) Local Decision-Making Level (LDML)

Between the WDML and LDML the reliable communication is necessary in order to exchange the information about the commands from WDML and the reaction of LDML.

The direct feedbacks from the controlled object to WDML and LDML are useful for the effective decision making in time.

The MES can be implemented by the computer center and the microcomputer network.

**Whole Decision Making Level (WDML)

The WDML is a "man-machine" system.

It is also with the multilevel hierarchical structure and consists of the human decision makers (HDM) such as the leader, president ... etc, and the group of artificial intelligence expert system, i.e. the general expert system (GES) and some special expert system (SES), such as the systems engineering expert system and the industrial, agricultural ... expert system.

The principal function of the WDML is to solve the whole, long term and strategical problems, usually, it is related with the heuristic, uncertain and large scale decision making.

** Local Decision Making Level (LDML)

The LDML is designed also with the multilevel hierarchical structure.

It consists of :

LDM--Local Decision Makers
ODC--Optimal Decision Makers (Coordinators)

The principal function of the LDML is to solve the local, short term and tratical problems, usually, it is related with the formulary, certain and small scale decision making.

CONCLUSION

In this paper, the intelligent control, intelligent management and the intelligent decision making for the large scale system are discussed.

Three schemes for the intelligent control,management and decision making of large scale system have been proposed:

1) Multilevel self-optimalizing control (MSOC)
2) Multilevel Fuzzy Control (MFC)
3) Multilevel Expert System (MES)

It may be seen that the new way to solve the problem of large scale systems can be obtained from the combination of artificial intelligence, large scale system theory and microcomputer techniques.

REFERENCES:

(1) Athans,M., Advances and Open Problems on the Control of Large Scale Systems. Proc. 7th IFAC World Congress, 1978.
(2) Vamos,T., Automatic Control and Artificial Intelligence. Proc. 7th IFAC world Congress, 1978.
(3) Fu,K.S., Learning Control Systems and Intelligence Control Systems: An Intersection of Artificial Intelligence and Automatic Control. IEEE Trans. AC-16, No.1, 1971
(4) Mendel,J.M. and Zapalac,J.J., The Application of Technique of Artificial Intelligence to Control System Design. Advances in Control Systems, Leondes,C. T., (eds), 1968
(5) Zadeh,L.A., Fuzzy Set. Inform. & Control, 8,1965
(6) Nilsson,N.J., Principles of Artificial Intelligence, 1980
(7) Ho,Y.C., Decision, Control and Games, 1979
(8) Simon,H.A., The New Science of Management Decision, 1977
(9) Rosenbrock,H.H., Seeking an appropriate Technology, IFAC--Symposium on Systems Approach to Appropriate Technology Transfer, 1983
(10) Mamdani,E.H., Application of Fuzzy Algorithms for Control of Simple Dynamic Plant, Proc. IEE, Vol.121, 1974
(11) Procyk,T.J. & Mamdani,E.H., A Lingustic Self-Organizing Process Controller, Automatica, 15, pp15-30, 1979
(12) Tsien,H.S. & Song,J., Engineering Cybernetics, 1980
(13) Dai,X.Y., Self-optimalizing Control and its Application, Metallurgic Automation No.2, 1980
(14) Li,B.S. & Liu,Z.J., The Application of Fuzzy Set Theory to the Design of a Class of Controllers, Acta Automation Sinica, No.1, 1980
(15) Tu,X.Y., Theory of an Harmonically Acting Control System with a Large Number of Controlled Variables, Proc. 1st IFAC World Congress, 1960
(16) Tu,X.Y. & Guo,R.J., Intelligence Control and its Applications, Automation,1977
(17) Tu,X.Y., Some Problems of Large Scale System Theory, Acta Automation Sinica, No.1, 1977
(18) Tu,X.Y., An New Approach to Flexible Automation of Large Scale Systems, IFAC--Symposium on Systems Approach to Appropriate Technology Transfer, 1983
(19) Tu,X.Y. & Hu,X.M., The Fuzzy Control for Large Scale Systems, Institute of Automation, Acadmia Sinica, 1982
(20) Tu,X.Y. The Intelligent Control for Large Scale Systems, Institute of Automation, Hebei Academy of Sciences, 1984

Artificial Intelligence in Economics and Management
L.F. Pau (Editor)

MODEL-BASED EVALUATION OF LONG-RANGE RESOURCE ALLOCATION PLANS

Ben P. Wise and Donald W. Kosy

The Robotics Institute
Carnegie-Mellon University
Pittsburgh, Pennsylvania 15213

When corporate planning is decentralized, the plans produced by each sub-organization must be reviewed and evaluated to make sure they are reasonable and acceptable to the organization as a whole. This paper considers three ways of automating the evaluation task, two based on rules combined with qualitative arithmetic, and one based on a microeconomic model combined with quantitative reasoning and a search procedure. We found that the knowledge encoded in the rules could be derived from the model and its application could be controlled by the procedure. Moreover, quantitative reasoning can deal with reinforcing and counteracting effects, which qualitative arithmetic cannot. This approach has been used as the basis for the REMUS module in the ROME system.

1. INTRODUCTION

In many large firms, the task of estimating future resource needs is decomposed into a hierarchy of subtasks corresponding to the different levels of the organizational hierarchy. As estimates at lower levels are generated, they are reviewed and then consolidated into estimates for the parent level. If approved at the parent level, these estimates become plans which guide future resource allocation decisions.

While considerable attention has been given to methods for generating resource plans (e.g. mathematical programming), not much has been given to methods for reviewing or approving them. Traditionally, these activities have been performed by planning managers who are held accountable for the consistency, completeness, and overall acceptability of plans made for their organizational units. We were asked to develop a knowledge-based system to assist in the plan review activity; this paper describes what we learned from that project and what resulted from it. The most interesting result was that it was possible to recast the knowledge initially expressed to us in a large number of if-then rules into a general procedure plus a declarative model based on economic production functions. Using this knowledge in conjunction with a fairly general evaluation strategy was sufficient to reproduce most of the expert behavior we observed.

2. EVALUATING RESOURCE PLANS

To develop an appropriate algorithm and knowledge representation, we began with verbal protocols elicited from a manufacturing plant planning manager as he reviewed several resource plans. The plans were displayed as spreadsheets of numbers where the columns specified planning periods (fiscal years) and the rows showed the projections for each type of resource for each period. There were also rows containing projections of output levels, inventory levels, breakdowns of shipments by type of customer, etc. (see [5] for details). During the course of the reviews, the manager described what features of the plans caught his eye, which seemed odd, what he had expected to find, how he explained away some oddities, and so forth.

His overall goal in this activity was to evaluate a plan against three basic criteria. The first was <u>credibility</u>: projected requirements should be consistent with known relationships and limits. E.g., an increase in output with no corresponding increase in raw material purchase implies something strange is going on. The second was <u>responsiveness</u>: projected performance measures should meet goals. E.g., a shortfall in desired productivity level means that either the goal is unattainable or someone did not pay enough attention to it. The third was completeness: all resource needs should be properly included in the plan. For example, an increase in projected productivity without some projected expenditure on process improvement almost certainly implies somebody forgot to include it in the plan. In short, every effect should have a cause, the effects should be those desired, and all effects of a particular cause should be accounted for[1].

For each item in the plan, the manager's evaluation proceeded as follows. First, if there were any corporate goals for the item, he would check the values shown against them, since these were the easiest criteria to apply. If a goal was not met, he would note it and continue. Often, however, there would be no specific goal for an item. He would then check whether the values seemed "reasonable" relative to his expectations about what the values ought to be. To do that, he would first characterize the values by various features, such as whether they struck him as high or low, or whether the trend was increasing or decreasing. He would then hypothesize features in other items that these initial ones would lead him to expect, and check for the presence of these other features.

If all expected features checked out, then the manager would conclude that the original item was probably all right and move on. If one were absent, however, he would then begin checking the assumptions implicit in his initial hypothesis. These assumptions typically involved items not shown in the plan, such as proportionality coefficients and minor terms in an aggregate sum. The usual assumption was that these had remained constant. For example, if *Output* rose, then he would expect the number of *production-employees* to also rise, assuming that the two would maintain a constant ratio. If that expectation failed, he would then check the assumption by looking for an expenditure on process improvement, which would account for how the output per person ratio could have increased. If, in turn, that failed, the original item was taken to be problematic and was placed on a list of concerns to be taken up with the planner responsible.

The links between features were originally classified as two separate rules of the form *if X, then Z* and *if X and not-Z, then Y*. In practice, *X*, *Y*, and *Z* were conjunctions, as in the rule *if production-employees rose and output rose, then expect material-spending up and inventory up*. (He expected inventory to rise because of a policy that inventory was to be held at approximately one fifth of output.) Noting this pattern of pairs of rules, we were led to adopt Doyle's formalism of *if X, unless Y, then Z* rules, rather than the usual *if X, then Z* rules [4]. Sixty-three such rules were found, enough to reproduce the observed behavior. Doyle's formalism differs from *if (X and not-Y), then Z* in that the latter must explicitly, and perhaps slowly, verify that Y is false. The former checks only whether Y has already been proven false. Only if Z turns out to be false will a thorough check of Y's truth or falsity be undertaken. If Y is chosen carefully, this not only allows non-monotonic reasoning, as Doyle explains, but can also be faster.

This rule-set had three severe -- and related -- problems:

- it was far too small;
- the knowledge expressed did not seem to be the "basic" knowledge involved;
- its reliance on qualitative, rather than quantitative, description rendered it quite weak.

First, in a rule like *if X, unless Y, then Z*, each variable in *X*, *Y*, and *Z* could be either positive, zero, or negative (+,0,-), and either rising, constant, or falling (r,c,f). Clearly, the number of possible combinations of signs and slopes, each with its own rule, climbs exponentially. Although our set of sixty-three was enough to reproduce observed behavior, it was only a tiny fraction of those needed to produce all the slight variations on that behavior.

Second, the rules did not seem to represent empirical correlations, as in a system like MYCIN [3], or situation-action pairs, as in R1 [8]. Rather, every rule seemed to have a "deeper" justification in terms of

[1] In addition, if the basic criteria were met, the manager was also interested in what the projections implied about resource acquisition or disposal. We will not be concerned here with this aspect of the review.

known relationships among manufacturing resource variables. For instance, the justification for the rule *if Output rose, expect production-employees up* would be that the quantity of factor-inputs to a production process should be roughly proportional to the quantity of output produced. So, if output is projected to rise, projections of labor should rise also. Thus the rules as stated do not stand on their own as fundamental facts.

Finally, the rules could not properly handle many situations which a human reviewer could handle easily. For example, if three items in a plan were related by $A = B + C$, it is clear that if both B and C rise, then A will also rise. In this case, qualitative arithmetic (to be abbreviated henceforth as QA) is unambiguous: (r) + (r) = (r). But if B rises and C falls, then A could do anything: (r) + (f) = (?), where (?) means 'unknown'. Thus, any extended chain of reasoning with QA may rapidly be dominated by (?)'s. However, our planning manager could easily see that if B rose by 20, and C fell by 1, then A should rise, and he would rely on this inference subsequently. Hence, we began working directly with numbers and quantitative equations.

The use of equations solves the three problems just mentioned. First, since the relationships are fully spelled out, almost all the permutations of the qualitative rules can be automatically subsumed by ordinary arithmetic. Second, since equations are essentially statements of facts about the activities represented by the variables in them, they constitute the "deeper" knowledge that motivated the original rules. Third, the effects of differences in magnitudes can readily be propagated along a chain of equations, again, by arithmetic. However, using equations introduces three new problems related to knowledge acquisition: (1) what functional forms do these equations have? (2) what are their parameter values? and (3) aren't equations too precise to reproduce the kind of reasoning people use? Our solutions to these problems are presented in the next two sections.

3. A MANUFACTURING RESOURCE UTILIZATION MODEL

Our first step was to divide the activities in a manufacturing plant into three generic subactivities: manufacture of commodities, acquisition of new capital, and technical improvements to existing capital, as in the figure below. These subactivities were each represented as linear relations between quantities of inputs and of output, i.e. as Leontieff production functions. While fairly simple, these Leontieff functions were sufficient to reproduce our planning manager's reasoning.

The most important process is the manufacture of final product. The elements of the input vector, I_Q, are machine hours, floor space-hours, materials-spending and man-hours; they are linearly related to output, Q, subject to capacity constraint, C, by the relations of equation 1, where α is the vector of resource-per-unit requirements.

$$I_Q = \alpha * Q, \; Q < C \tag{1}$$

Growth and technical change are represented as two separate processes, outside the one for production, for two reasons. First, they are not necessary for output; a factory can produce products without process improvements, but not without raw materials. Second, they produce not material outputs but changes in the parameters of the production process. Technical change alters the α-vector; growth alters the capacity constraint.

The equation for technical change is equation 2. It is linear in the percent improvement, and in the amount of equipment improved:

$$I_\alpha = \beta * (C * \Delta\alpha_i / \alpha_i) \tag{2}$$

The equation for capital growth is equation 3, where ΔC is the change in capacity, and I_C is a vector with elements of indirect labor for design and installation, and direct capital costs.

$$I_C = \gamma * (\Delta C) \tag{3}$$

Equations were also added for cost-accounting, measuring performance, and miscellaneous relations like volume discounting of purchases, increased pay for overtime, the learning-curve effects on productivity, and so on. In effect, these were a financial scaffolding built on top of a three-part physical model.

The above three equations bring up a difficult, fundamental question: since the parameter values did not explicitly appear in the plans, how could we get numerical values for the parameter vectors α, β, γ? Our

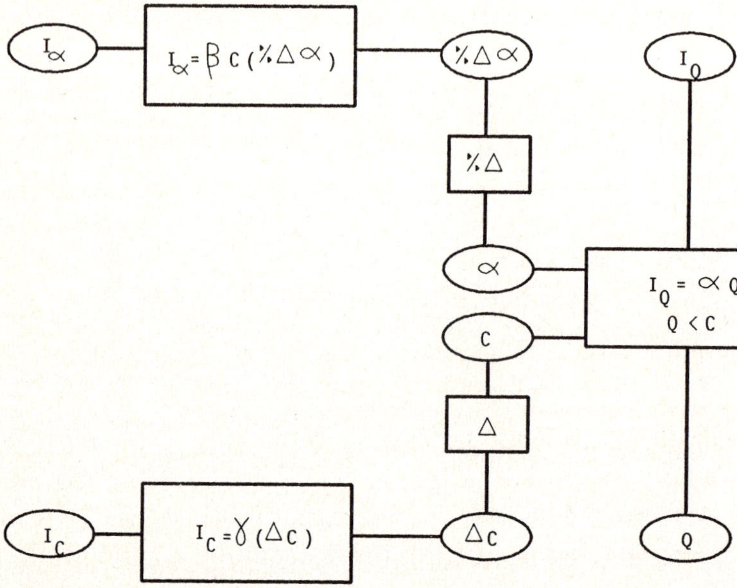

The manufacturing, growth, and change models

answer comes from the observation that these values embody expertise in much the same sense that rule-strengths embody expertise in rule-based expert systems. This analogy suggests that they might be elicited directly. Or, they might be estimated statistically from data, such as past history or the current plan. Estimation from historical data might reveal, for example, that the current plan assumes unusual productivity over its entire span. Estimation from the current plan might reveal outliers.

In our case, however, the estimation process was trivial. Taking a cue from our human reviewer, we simply used values of parameters taken from current plant operations, which were readily available. Of course these would be quite unsuitable if we tried to use them to generate resource projections, since they would not take into account the characteristics of the products and manufacturing process being projected. However, for purposes of comparison, they provided the kinds of ballpark estimates that human reviewers used.

4. QUANTITATIVE REASONING

Given the set of equations and parameter values just described, the linkage between features initially represented by rules could now be made by arithmetic operations on variables. In particular, it was now possible to determine the influence of variables on each other by tracing through the graph of relationships induced by the equations. However, since the human reviewer was only concerned with the most significant influences, it was important to be able to disregard "insignificant" effects during the reasoning process. To do that, we developed a numeric influence measure which is fully described in [6]. We called the measure ε, and it measures how much a set of variables effects a single variable, in the change between two contexts. If $A = F(B,C)$, and the two contexts are 1 and 2, with $A_1 = F(B_1,C_1)$ and $A_2 = F(B_2,C_2)$, then B's influence on A is defined by equation 4.

$$\varepsilon(A,\{B\}) = F(B_2,C_2) - F(B_1,C_2) \qquad (4)$$

Likewise, the effect of both variables, {B C}, is measured by 5:

$$\varepsilon(A,\{B\ C\}) = F(B_2,C_2) - F(B_1,C_1) \qquad (5)$$

The two contexts could be two different years of a plan, or actual versus goal, or any other pair of contexts for which the variables were all related by the same F. To drop insignificant effects, and also allow for competing effects, we did not require a perfect match between ε and the the change in A, ΔA. Rather, we said that a set X accounted for ΔA if inequality 6 held, where τ was empirically set at 0.8.

$$1/\tau > \varepsilon(A,X)/\Delta A > \tau \qquad (6)$$

This measure is not limited to linear or even monotonic influences, unlike correlation, and it does not assume a single unique influence, unlike partial derivatives. The slack in 6 also allows minor estimation inaccuracies to pass unnoticed.

A procedure for using this measure that matches the planning manager's review strategy can be stated as follows. Given a feature for one variable, start tracing back, breadth first, via all equations involving that variable, collecting the influences that account for the feature, until an "adequate cause" is found. If the tracing requires checking a variable whose value is not shown on the plan, find a suitable surrogate, and check it, where a surrogate is a variable whose value is shown that is functionally related to the missing variable. If a cause is found, but the relevant variable is not shown on the plan, check to make sure that its other expected effects, beside the initial feature, are present.

One additional kind of knowledge must be included in a model in order to use this procedure to find an "adequate cause" of observed features. A list of equations is not inherently directional, but causality is. Hence it is necessary to provide an ordering on the variables that indicates their precedence. This precedence was implemented by labeling equations as "aggregation", "definition", "policy", or "physical constraint". An example aggregation would be the relation between total productivity and the various factor productivities, or between total labor and each sub-type of labor. An example definition would be that total productivity is the amount of output over the total value of all inputs. An example policy would be that inventory should be 20% of the yearly output, or that productivity should improve according to a learning curve with a pre-planned rate of improvement. Each of the three basic manufacturing plant processes are "physical constraints". The "aggregation" and "definition" labels serve as flags to make sure that the superordinate variable is explained in terms of the subordinate variables, not vice versa. If a variable is connected to a "policy" equation, there is no need to go beyond, because one or another of the variables in such an equation must be controllable (in order that the policy be implementable), and hence can be stopped at. Finally, to identify the end of a causal chain, certain variables were labeled as exogenous. No attempt is made to find causes for features of these since they are taken to be outside the system being modeled.

As a very simple illustration of how this procedure reproduces the planning manager's reasoning, consider the rule *if employee-hours up, then expect material-spending up and output up*. Once "employee-hours up" has been noticed, that is traced to the exogenous variable, Q. However, no variable in the plan shows the value of Q in terms of volume of output produced. Rather, what is shown is the dollar volume of output, which is related to Q by price. Hence, the procedure checks the dollar output variable and, as a double-check, the other inputs (e.g. material-spending) required to produce plant output are also checked.

As a more complex example, *if total-space up, employee-hours constant, and distribution-space constant, then expect production-space up, output up, and capital-for-operations-improvement positive*. First, since total-space is defined as the sum of production-space and distribution-space, then the total rising with distribution-space constant requires production-space to rise. Second, while one input factor (space) rose, others (employee-hours) have stayed constant, hence the α-vector must have changed, and so the trace would proceed to examine inputs to the technical change process. In the original rule-set, the presence or absence of countering effects had been reflected by using multiple rules, one for each combination of missing and countering effects. These were later incorporated into the "unless.." clauses. For example, if *output* rose, increases in each input were expected. If output rose and an input did not rise, then a change in the α-vector was sought, because that is the only remaining term in $\alpha_i{*}Q = I_i$. Because α's were not listed in the plan, expenditure for capital improvements was checked, because that was a reliable surrogate, and hence a good check for whether the expected countering effect was actually present. Thus, the elicited rule actually embodies two distinct analyses, which the above procedure reproduces in sequence.

Clearly the graph-searching strategy can trace whatever combinations are present, without needing a special rule for each one. However, one should note that this procedure is not exactly the same thing as what the manager described. That is, when asked how he reviewed resource plans, he gave many specific rules. Our general procedure traces influences, and mentions in sequence those variables that appear on the plan as it encounters them in the equational model. These turn out to be the same variables that the planning manager mentions in his rules.

Our quantitative approach to explaining numerical results contrasts strongly, and instructively, with that of Bouwman [1,2]. Bouwman's domain was also quantitative data about a manufacturing concern, but the reasoning was performed entirely in QA. His system basically scans the data, and, for each equation in the model, forms an expectation about the term it defines. For example, if $A = B + C$, B rose, and C rose, then A is expected to rise also. These expectations were then fitted together into chains, and those confirmed by the data were cited as explanations, discarding those contradicted by the data or simply not addressed by it. Our approach differs in that it begins at a variable and works out from there, rather than doing a complete scan before putting the pieces together. More importantly, Bouwman did not include cases where QA gives ambiguous results. While this strategy does prevent domination by (?)'s, it also rules out more accurate analyses when the numbers are available. For example, if A depends mainly on B and C, but only slightly on D, then our significance test will detect that and not follow D. QA would consider D to be just as important as B and C, unless D were omitted from the equation entirely. But then, it would be misled in those cases where D actually was important. Thus, Bouwman's approach is more dependent on a powerful and parsimonious model of a firm than is ours. It relies on the significant factors to have already been picked out when the model was specified, as it has no means of picking them out on a case-by-case basis. In the resource plans we examined, however, the relative magnitudes of the variables were crucial in deciding which lower level variables to explore next.

In summary, we discovered that the original sixty-odd highly specific rules could be generated by general knowledge about arithmetic applied over and over, in different ways, to a more or less generic model of how resource variables are related in a manufacturing plant, as expressed by simple equations. This is in marked contrast to a system like MYCIN, where rules express empirical correlation but are not linked to a model. The use of arithmetic contrasts with a system like Bouwman's, which reasons purely qualitatively, not quantitatively.

5. THE REMUS EVALUATION PROCEDURE

A version of the model and reasoning procedure just described has been adapted for use in the REMUS module of the ROME system[7]. ROME is an experimental decision support system generator that allows specification of planning models in terms of variables and algebraic formulas. Models may be executed and the results displayed in spreadsheet form. The purpose of REMUS is to Review and Evaluate a Model's Underlying Structure by comparing results to evaluation criteria. Generic models -- such as the one for manufacturing resource utilization -- and quantitative reasoning are used to support the evaluation process.

Two sorts of evaluation criteria may be declared: norms and goals. A *norm* is a relationship among variables that "should" hold true under "normal" circumstances according to experts in the domain of the model. A *goal* is a statment of an organizational objective or policy that is likewise expressible in terms of model variables. Norms and goals are declared in ROME by *expect* and *want* statements, respectively.

To illustrate, the three production functions in the manufacturing model are relationships that should hold true in a manufacturing plant. Expanding out the vectors in equation 1, and using somewhat more mnemonic variable names, yields the following set of norms:

```
Expect Direct Labor Hours to equal Labor Hours/Unit * Q-produced
Expect Total Materials Cost to equal Material $/Unit * Q-produced
Expect Total Floorspace Hours to equal Floorspace Hours/Unit * Q-produced
Expect Total Machine Hours to equal Machine Hours/Unit * Q-produced
Expect Q-produced to be no more than Plant Capacity
```

Equation 2 has two components which may be expressed as follows:

```
Expect abs(%change(Labor Hours/Unit(y))) to equal Project Hours(y-1) /
```

```
          Plant Capacity(y) * Labor Hours per Unit Productivity Change(y-1)
  Expect %change(Labor Hours/Unit(y)) to equal Addon Capital Expense (y-1)/
          Plant Capacity(y) * Capital Cost per Unit Productivity Change(y-1)
```

Equation 3 may be expressed similarly.

Regarding goals, there may of course be many for a particular plant at a particular time. However, there are two that tend to apply generically to manufacturing resource plans. The first is that new products should be manufactured more efficiently than comparable current products, or at least no less efficiently. This goal, applied to labor efficiency, may be expressed to ROME as:

```
Declare comparable product to be an anchor variable
Declare current year to be a column variable
We want Labor Hours/Unit to be no more than Labor Hours/Unit for a
        comparable product in the current year
```

The second goal is that productivity should improve at a desired rate as a function of the amount of production experience that has accumulated for a given product. This relationship is known as a "learning curve", and one way to state the goal is:

```
Define Cumulated-Q(y) to be Cumulated-Q(y-1) + Q-produced(y)
Define Cumulated Direct Labor Hours(y) to be Cumulated Direct Labor Hours(y-1)
        + Direct Labor Hours(y)
Declare y1 to be a column variable
Define y1 to be the first year of production of the product
Let Cumulated-Q(y1-1) = 0
Let Cumulated Direct Labor Hours(y1-1) = 0
Define %Additional-Q(y) to be Cumulated-Q(y) / Q-produced(y1)
Define LCRF to be the desired learning curve cost reduction factor
Define Alpha to be log2(LCRF)
We want Direct Labor Hours(y) to be no more than
        Cumulated-Q(y) * %Additional-Q(y) ↑ Alpha * Labor Hours/Unit(y1)
        - Cumulated Direct Labor Hours(y-1)
```

To actually check these goals, their parameter values (e.g. comparable product, current year, LCRF) must be set. We will do this in a moment.

The main steps in the REMUS evaluation procedure that applies the above criteria are shown below. To evaluate a variable *v*:

1. If there are criteria for the values of *v*, apply them and state conclusions. Check equalities before inequalities.
2. Find variables that explain the trend in *v* using the formula for *v* given in the planning model. If there is no formula but there is an equality norm in the generic model, use that. Call this set of variables S.
3. If there are other variables in the formula which have evaluation criteria but are not in S, add them to S.
4. Recursively evaluate the variables in S.
5. If there is no formula for *v* (S is empty), go on the the next variable to be evaluated.

This procedure may be continued until it reaches exogenous variables. The main conclusions that may be drawn are as follows:

1. If criteria are met, say so.
2. If a goal is not met, conclude that *v* is "problematic".
3. If there is a moderate difference (< 30%) between a value and a norm, conclude that *v* is "OK" with respect to that norm.
4. If there is a large (> 30%) difference between a value and a goal, it is "extraordinary". If there is a large deviation from a norm, it is "odd".
5. If the effect on *v* of a large deviation in a lower level variable can be determined, suggest that *v* may be "too high" or "too low".

The boundary between moderate and large differences is taken from Bouwman [1].

This procedure differs from the one described in the previous section in several respects. First, criteria are applied whenever possible. This tends to focus attention on every issue that may affect the top level variable being evaluated. Second, all explanatory variables are found at once, using the ε measure and test 6. This contrasts with the hypothesize / check assumptions / find countering factor strategy. Moreover, explanation paths are pursued depth first, rather than breadth first. Both of these make it easier to express each step of the evaluation in words. Finally, REMUS makes no default assumptions about the values of variables not shown on a plan. Rather, these assumptions must be stated explicitly, if needed. The reason for this is to make sure the user knows what assumptions are being used, and to sidestep the problem of choosing good surrogate variables.

One thing remains to be done before we can use this procedure to evaluate a specific resource plan and that is to link the criteria to the particular variables in that plan. Consider the portion of a resource plan shown below:

==========redwood==========	1985	1986	1987	1988	1989	1990
production spending	1.40	4.87	4.79	3.45	4.73	5.85
mfg dl $	0.0	2.49	4.08	2.86	3.90	4.94
other dl $	1.37	2.38	.71	.58	.82	.92
mfg employee-hours	0.0	44.40	73.60	50.79	62.68	77.21
other employee-hours	31.40	42.50	12.80	10.30	13.20	14.40
labor rate	44.47	56.00	55.44	56.38	62.27	64.02
process improvement hrs	0.0	0.0	0.0	0.0	0.0	0.0
capital for improvement	0.0	0.0	0.0	0.0	0.0	0.0
output $M	0.0	36.75	62.16	52.06	65.36	81.13
avg price		.25	.21	.19	.19	.19

"Redwood" is the name of a new product that is to be introduced in 1986. The relationships in the planning model that generated these results are as follows:

```
Define production spending to be mfg dl $ + other dl $
Estimate mfg dl $ to be mfg employee-hours * labor rate / 1000
Estimate other dl $ to be other employee-hours * labor rate / 1000
```

All the other values are input. Dollar values are expressed in millions except for labor rate, and labor hours are expressed in thousands.

The variables in this plan may be linked to variables in the generic model given above by declaring them to be "kinds" or "measures" of the corresponding generic variables. The norms and goals from the generic model will then become norms and goals for the planning variables by a process of "inheritance" described in [7]. The ROME statements expressing these correspondences are:

```
Declare mfg employee-hours to be a kind of Direct Labor Hours
Declare capital for improvement to be a kind of Addon Capital Expense
Declare process improvement hrs to be a kind of Project Hours
Assume Q-produced to equal output $M / avg price
Declare labor rate, Labor Hours/Unit and Q-produced to be exogenous
Define Labor Hours/Unit to be Direct Labor Hours / Q-produced
```

Several other facts that bear on the evaluation are also known. The current product being produced in 1985 is called "Hemlock" and the labor needed to manufacture it is 640 hours/unit. For the new product, Redwood, being introduced in 1986, it is desired that productivity improve by 10% for each doubling in cumulative output. The production process for Redwood will be similar to that for Hemlock. This information can be stated as follows:

```
Define current year to be 1985
Let Labor Hours/Unit(hemlock,1985) = .64
Let comparable product(redwood) = hemlock
Define y1(redwood) to be 1986
We want LCRF(redwood) to be .9
Let Labor Hours per Unit Productivity Change(redwood) =
        Labor Hours per Unit Productivity Change(hemlock)
Let Capital Cost per Unit Productivity Change(redwood) =
        Capital Cost per Unit Productivity Change(hemlock)
Let Plant Capacity(redwood) = Plant Capacity(hemlock)
```

We are now in a position to evaluate several variables in the plan. However, we will only show the evaluation for one -- production spending -- since the others will be evaluated along the way:

```
> Evaluate production spending(redwood) for 1989
There are no evaluation criteria for production spending(redwood) in 1989.  However,
redwood production spending goes up in 1989 because mfg dl $ and other dl $ both go
up and production spending = mfg dl $ + other dl $.  The increase in production
spending was due primarily to the increase in mfg dl $. Would you like me to
continue?  Y

Redwood mfg dl $ goes up in 1989 because mfg employee-hours and labor rate both go up
and mfg dl $ = mfg employee-hours * labor rate / 1000.  The increase in mfg dl $ was
due primarily to the increase in mfg employee-hours.  Would you like me to continue? Y

By norm 1, we expect redwood mfg employee-hours to equal Labor Hours/Unit * Q-produced.
Assuming Q-produced = output $M / avg price, this appears to be so in 1989.

By goal 2, we want redwood mfg employee-hours to be no more than Cumulated-Q(y) *
%Additional-Q(y) ↑ Alpha * Labor Hours/Unit(y1) - Cumulated Direct Labor Hours(y-1).
This appears to be so in 1989.  But we also find redwood mfg employee-hours to be
much less than that value in that year.  This seems extraordinary.  So redwood
mfg employee-hours may be too low in 1989, which means mfg dl $ may be too low, which
means production spending may be too low.  Would you like me to continue? Y

By norm 6, we expect abs(%change(redwood Labor Hours/Unit(y))) to equal process
improvement hrs(y-1) / Plant Capacity(y) * Labor Hours per Unit Productivity
Change(y-1).  This seems to be OK in 1989.

By norm 7, we expect %change(redwood Labor Hours/Unit(y)) to equal capital for
improvement(y-1) / Plant Capacity(y) * Capital Cost per Unit Productivity Change(y-1).
This seems to be OK in 1989.

By goal 1, we want redwood Labor Hours/Unit to be no more than Labor Hours/Unit
(hemlock,1985).  This appears to be so in 1989.  But we also find redwood Labor
Hours/Unit to be much less than that value in that year.  This seems extraordinary.
So, again, mfg employee-hours may be too low in 1989, which means mfg dl $ may be too
low, which means production spending may be too low.  Would you like me to continue?
```

The procedure would now go on to evaluate Q-produced, labor rate, and other dl $. It can be seen from the above, however, that the 1989 projection for mfg employee-hours is quite optimistic. This, in turn, diminishes the credibility of the mfg dl $ and production spending values that depend on it.

6. CONCLUSIONS

Evaluating a resource plan may be viewed as a process by which a reviewer compares what he knows or believes to what he is told by the numbers in a plan. For a computer program to perform such comparisons, it must use some representation of a reviewer's knowledge and beliefs. While our initial representation of this knowledge was in terms of if-then rules, we discovered that relatively simple linear-equation models could be used to encode the same information at a more fundamental, structural level. We also developed an algorithm for exploring equational models, and the influence measure necessary to make quantitative, but still approximate, inferences from them.

Although, in this paper, we have confined our attention to evaluating resource plans, the issues involved are very much related to the general problem of model validation. Hence, it may not be surprising that parts of the evaluation strategy we induced from a human reviewer's protocols are similar to more formal model validation techniques. For example, in hypothesizing variables that should change when a change is observed in a given variable, a human reviewer is performing a kind of sensitivity test. In comparing the value of a variable against what that value would be for current plant operations, he is essentially trying to verify that the planning model would produce correct results for a known test case. Finally, the entire strategy rests on the principle that values can best be judged by comparing them to other values that have independent justification.

The chief strength of the REMUS procedure is that it allows evaluation of a result even if there are no criteria directly applicable to it. By descending to subordinate variables that affect a given variable, this procedure conducts a search for criteria that may be relevant based on functional relationships. Moreover, because the variables in a given planning model can be linked to expected relationships, a given set of criteria can be transferred to other models in the same domain. Together, these mechanisms provide a means of using relatively general, structural models to make judgments about specific cases.

REFERENCES

[1] Bouwman, M.J., *Financial Diagnosis: A Cognitive Model of the Processes Involved*, PhD Thesis, Graduate School of Industrial Administration, Carnegie-Mellon University, 1978.

[2] Bouwman, M.J., "Human Diagnostic Reasoning by Computer: An Illustration from Financial Analysis," *Management Science*, V. 29, No. 6, pp. 653-672, June 1983.

[3] Davis, R., *Applications of Meta Level Knowledge to the Construction, Maintenance and Use of Large Knowledge Bases*, PhD Thesis, Computer Science Department, Stanford University, July 1976.

[4] Doyle, J., "Methodological Simplicity in Expert System Construction: Judgments and Reasoned Assumptions," *The AI Magazine*, V. 4, No. 2, pp. 39-43, Summer 1983.

[5] Kosy, D.W., and Dahr, V., "Knowledge-Based Support Systems for Long Range Planning," The Robotics Institute, Carnegie-Mellon University, 1983.

[6] Kosy, D.W., and Wise, B.P., "Self-Explanatory Financial Planning Models," *Proceedings of AAAI-84*, pp. 176-181, August 1984.

[7] Kosy, D.W., and Wise, B.P., "Overview of ROME: A Reason-Oriented Modeling Environment," *This volume.*

[8] McDermott, J., "R1: A Rule-Based Configurer of Computer Systems," *Artifial Intelligence*, V. 19, No. 1, pp. 39-88, September 1982.

Artificial Intelligence in Economics and Management
L.F. Pau (Editor)

DECISION SUPPORT SYSTEM FOR MANAGEMENT OF OIL PIPELINE

Chen Zhao-ying

Institute of Automation, Academia Sinica
Beijing, P.R.China

This paper summarizes the main portion of a research program concerned with Decision Support System for Management of Oil Pipeline (DSS-MOP). Research in the program has focused on the new methodology for the development of DSS, called Heuristic Optimization Technique. This methodology combines artificial intelligence with optimization technology to carry out the required decision making function, promising the transport of oil in great quantities at reasonable costs.

INTRODUCTION

In 1982, the research project "Optimization of Crude Oil Pipeline Operation" was organized in order to expand and modernize facilities for tranaporting the crude from field to port. The author has been involved in the research project from the beginnig. Before then, researches for optimization of oil pipeline operation seemed to focus attention on building mathematical model and generating optimal solution for given problems where the objectives, data and constraints can be prespecified. The author decided not to follow this way.

As we went on with our research, we recognized that the optimization problem of oil pipeline is complex and ill-structured to decision makers. We have developed the Decision Support System for Management of Oil Pipeline (DSS-MOP), which is a supportive tool for managers under their own control. DSS-MOP is designed with emphasis on extending the range and capability of manager's decision making instead of on generating optimal solutions for given types of problems.

Besides the usual problems in DSS design, DSS-MOP poses the following questions:
1. How can the DSS-MOP be used by no-professional people ?
2. How can we develop the useful optimization methodology to aid managers to generate the satisfying and effective solutions in a changing environment.
3. How to design the manager-acceptable software packages with retaining a versatility often found only in pipeline systems under manual operation ?
4. How to implement the full DSS-MOP in a microcomputer ?

These questions imply specific requirements in design methodology,in the DSS-MOP functions and in the DSS-MOP structure.

HEURISTIC OPTIMIZATION TECHNIQUE (HOT)

Optimization plays a large role in today's pipeline system by allowing the transport of oil in great quantities at reasonable costs. The subject of optimization for management of pipeline is an area of practical interest in which little has been done and reported. This is primarily due to the following difficulties:

1. Changing environment. For example, heat loss and soil conditions vary from

summer to winter, and operating modes are sufficiently flexible to allow selecting one of fifteen modes.

2. Changing requirements of managers. Different manager will have different requirements. Some may make decision with emphasis on minimizing operating cost; others on reliability and stability of operating process (e.g., the ability to resume operation after shutdown);still others on flexibility to changing environment.

3. Ill-structured problem. Optimization for pipeline operation is a good example of ill-structured problem. This problem consists of three subproblems(P_1 -P_3) and four goals (G_1-G_4), which intersect and interact in various ways.

P_1 — The problem to develop long term management plan of transport oil.
P_2 — The problem to develop short term operating plan of oil pipeline.
P_3 — The problem to develop coordinative decision for top level managers to evaluate the plans of P and P .
P_1 and P_2 cannot be solved simultaneously; P_1 and P_3, P_2 and P_3 support each other.

G_1 — To guarantee to fulfil the task of transporting oil.
G_2 — To minimize the cost of heating.
G_3 — To minimize the cost of pumping.
G_4 — To minimize the probability of operating accidents.

Any goal is involved in several subproblems, and a lot of alternatives are produced in solving any subproblems. But, it is not clear which alternatives will attain any given goal, then we have an ill-structured problem (cf. Figure 1).

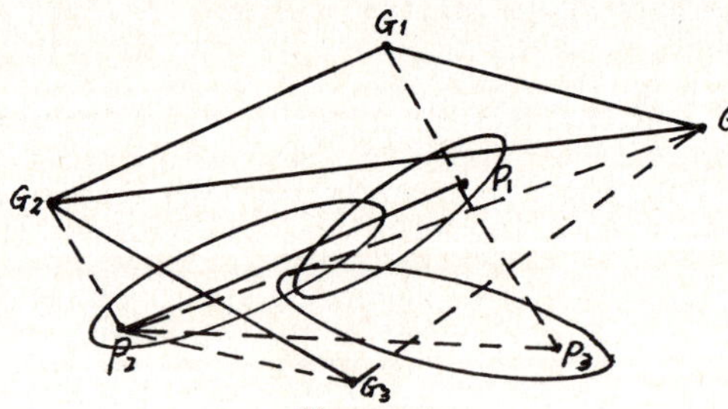

Figure 1
An Ill-Structured Problem

The point is that we have great difficulty in developing a perfect mathematical model for this ill-structured problem with a changing environment and requirements of managers. Although the improvement in technology of model building may offer some new means to approach more complex problems, it often accompanied by increased complexity and instability of the systems to be studied, and this limits the effectiveness of problem solving through models.

This difficulty is solved by developing Heuristic Optimization Technique (HOT), replacing traditional optimization methods. HOT differs from most of traditional optimization methods in many ways. To illustrate HOT, this section summarizes its typical characteristics:

1. To make no difference between objectives and constraints in model building. Since pipeline designers generally know reasonable upper and lower bounds on key parameters, the ranges of controllable and uncontrollable variables can be specified as the constraints in model building.

2. User satisfaction. User satisfaction is separate from optimization. HOT provides final results based on decision maker's preferences instead of predefine

objectives. From a theoretical point we cannot generally prove optimization of solutions; for practical application, HOT is relatively fast and simple method that yields acceptable answers within a reasonable computer time.

3. Heuristic graph-search method. Since the range of variable can be specified, the solution can be represented by graph-search procedures. For many task it is possible to use task-dependant information to help reduce search. So heuristic graph-search method of artificial intelligence is an extremely valuable tool for determining user-satisfying solutions.

In order to apply heuristic informations to order the alternative solutions, we use the evaluation function for computing the "promise" of an alternative. The evaluation function is based on manager's experience, in sight of the physical problem, decision maker's preferences and some other important aspects. Suppose we denote the evaluation function by symbol f, then f(n) gives the value of the function at alternative n. The selection of heuristic function is crucial in determining the heuristic power of HOT (cf.[2]).

An evaluation function which is given by HOT for management decision of oil pipeline is

$$f(n)=h(n)+w\ g(G_1,G_2,G_3,G_4)$$

where h(n) is an estimate of difference between alternative n and optimal solution, which has been suggested based on the manager's experience and engineering knowledge of oil pipeline, $g(G_1,G_2,G_3,G_4)$ represents the decision maker's preferences. The weight of g and h in evaluation function can be controlled by a positive number w.

So that selection of a suitable heuristic function permit one to balance production, costs, risks, benefits and values in decision making.

To summarize, though many questions relating to HOT are still left open, it is believed that this method can broaden our capability to make decision with incomplete knowledge.

DESIGN OF DSS-MOP (cf.[4])

1. Structure of DSS-MOP

DSS-MOP is two-level hierarchical in structure (cf. [1]). The first level (lower-level) is specific software for programed decision, which provides DSS-MOP with capabilities to carry out highly specialized tasks and to help managers become more rational in their recurrent decision-making. In our research, recurrent decision-making means the optimal allocation of pressure in oil pipeline, which is a multi-stage decision so that Dynamic Programming is an appropriate method for use. The kernel of this specific software consists of following parts:

(a) Packages for building dynamic programming. The key of building the model is to apply heuristic graph-search method of Artificial Intelligence.
(b) Packages of dynamic programming algorithm.

The second level (top level) is the software for non-programed decision, the aim of which is to provide DSS-MOP with capabilities to resolve complex and unexpected problems and thus to aid managers when they make decision about unforeseen and ill-structured problems. This software is also effective for multiple criteria decision making. To achieve this aim the software of top-level consists of the following parts:

(a) Packages for interaction between managers and computer. It permits managers to introduce their own experiences and requirements into decision process.

(b) Packages for HOT, which permits managers to evaluate alternative decisions and compare them.

(c) Packages for modification of dynamic programming model. It permits managers to modify some parameters in dynamic programming model to adapt to changing requirements of mangers and changing environment.

2. Function of DSS-MOP

The function of DSS-MOP can be represented in terms of three time horizons: short term function, mediate term function and long term function.

Short term function implies to provide effective direct assistance to managers to search for answers of optimal allocation of pressure on the spot.

Mediate term function implies adaption to individual differences and environmental conditions. In the broad sense, the DSS-MOP is an adaptive system.

Long term function focuses on the future. For long range, the most valuable information which DSS-MOP can provide is the extrapolation or projection of data, so as to encourage the users to explore new problems.

The software system of DSS-MOP which was programmed in FORTRAN language is currently running on a IBMPC-XT computer at the Institute.

CONCLUTION

Decision Support System is still at an initial stage of development, specially for China, where exists few of DSS, and no decision support laboratory. The major problem faced by DSS designers in China is that of manager's understanding and accepting.

REFERENCES

[1] Simon, H.A., The New Science of Management Decision (Prentice-Hall, New Jersey, 1977).

[2] Nilsson, N.J., Principles of Artificial Intelligence (Tioga Publishing Company, Palo Alto, 1980)

[3] Pohl, I., Practical and theoretical consideration in heuristic search algorithms, Machine Intelligence 8 (1977) 55-72

[4] Chen Zhao-Ying, DSS for Management of oil pipeline from Tieling to Dalian, Research Report, Institute of Automation, Academia Sinica (1984)

Artificial Intelligence in Economics and Management
L.F. Pau (Editor)

AN EXPERT SYSTEM KERNEL FOR THE ANALYSIS OF STRATEGIES OVER TIME

L.F. PAU

Battelle Institute
7, rte de Drize
CH-1227 Carouge
Switzerland

An expert system Kernel in Prolog has been developed aiming at the analysis of time dependent strategies, as encountered in economic/business planning, policy analysis, etc... The inference engine of this Kernel is based on the notion of transactions among asset types, with different settlement terms and constraints. General asset types accounted for include: physical, monetary, policy and information assets. The user only adds his domain dependent assets, transaction classes and constraints.
The Kernel implementation allows for the interaction with external data bases, tables and econometric/ simulation models. The examples to be introduced cover: planning an information campaign, currency rate adjustements.

<u>Notation</u>

AI	:	artificial intelligence
KBS	:	knowledge based system
OR	:	operations research

1. INTRODUCTION

In many knowledge based planning problems, it is both essential and difficult to represent time dependency. (1,3):

Typical difficulties of traditional, as well as first generation KBS approximating the former, are the following:

i decoupling quantitative forecasting models (typically for monetary and physical assets only) from qualitative scenarios (typically about policies); the first-mentioned forecasting models can be either graphical charting, econometric, or O.R. models.

ii incompleteness of "fundamental analysis" in terms of not balancing off the possible causality relations (e.g. in financial analysis, policy analysis, information flow analysis).

iii no systematic hypothesis generation in scenario analysis, or delphi models.

iv predominant description of time-dependency only through the time-dependency of monetary, physical, or policy aggregates; (e.g: macroeconomic aggregates, accounting aggregates).

v these aggregates are often selected as to characterize market equilibria, disregarding the market tâtonnement or disequilibrium processes.

vi general semantic nets are hard to design for time dependent processes.

This research was motivated by the need to find an internal structure, and inference mechanism, for time-dependent events, which would:

- first, achieve a better unification between specialized processes (qualitative and quantitative resp.)

- next, allow for writing a KBS kernel, largely domain independent, to allow for powerful implementations in a diversity of cases having common time-dependency properties.

The generic applications are to be found in economic planning, business planning, policy planning problems having in common a mixture of time-dependent qualitative and quantitative goals or constraints.

2. INTERNAL STRUCTURE OF THE INFERENCE ENGINE

2.1. Methodology

The time dependent evolution of many organizations (company, public body, nation) involve jointly the following:

Asset types

	1.	Monetary assets
	2.	Physical assets
(i, j)	3.	Policy assets
	4.	Service and information/intelligence assets

Actions and events are reflected at any time by transactions between asset types. Regardless of the nature of the specific assets which are considered, but which fall into one of the previous four classes, transactions between pairs of them, can in a broad sense be categorized as follows:

Transactions between assets

(at corresponding prices or utilities)

(i,j) Asset types	1	2	3	4
1	Financial			
2	Investment	Barter		
3	Aid	Legal Control	Negociation	
4	Access	Insurance	Assistance	Intellectual

2.2 Attributes of a transaction

Besides the asset types involved (i, j), a transaction is characterized by the following attributes:

i settlement terms: immediate, fixed horizon, futures, hedges, options, initiated

ii logical constraints on transaction sequences (represented through scripts)

iii valued constraints on transaction duration

iv transaction costs expressed as a vector with 4 components for each of the 4 asset types by which the costs are payable, as well as transaction cost settlement terms (immediate, fixed horizon).

2.3 Inference procedures

The strength of the proposed internal structure of the inferences relying on transactions between different asset types, is that it does allow for the joint implementation in the kernel of several different reasoning procedures:

1. backward chaining: it allows e.g. for transactions to be settled now in view of future goals

2. forward chaining: it allows e.g. for transaction costs and choices to be settled after the transaction decision

3. successive refinement of hypotheses: it allows for constraints on transaction assumptions, sequences, durations and existence, to be logically chained together

4. hypothetico-deductive and hierarchies of object classes: it allows e.g. to have time-dependent hierarchies for the same transaction: immediate, futures, hedges, options, initiate

5. process model for attribute values: it incorporates e.g. externally implemented (e.g. COBOL, FORTRAN) accounting calculations, econometric estimation, risk evaluation, clustering (2).

2.4 Knowledge representation

The object types with frame representations considered are:

1. asset types (i, j)
2. transactions betweeen assets (at corresponding prices or utilities)
3. settlement terms for the transactions, and transaction costs
4. goals expressed as target values for selected assets (at intermediate, final or undetermined dates).

2.5 Domain data

The user of the kernel will in each instance specify explicitely application dependent object frames and the corresponding attribute values, through a menu driven interface module.

3. KERNEL IMPLEMENTATION

The kernel development has been carried out in PROLOG on VAX/VMS 780. The interface module 2.5 is not completed.

PROLOG was selected because PROLOG's backtracking is very close to many policy making needs through exhaustive search on logical outcomes.

This kernel development has essentially consisted in:

* writing a set of general PROLOG predicates, with attribute fields and evaluation functions, to describe all transaction combinations and attribute forms of Section 2.2.

* studying the logical coherence of such sets of predicates, establishing basically that no such coherence can be achieved (in terms of depth-first backtracking) without incorporating explicitely the asset types i, j: 3,4 (political, information), regardless of the problem dependent knowledge.

The strength in this approach resides in:

- the above mentioned coherence over all transaction/action classes and settlement terms,
- the ease whereby the user can, in each instance, specify his own asset types (problem dependent), and the attribute values, by adding the corresponding predicates into the proper domain
- the exhaustivity of all causality effects intrinsic to the handling of general transaction types by the kernel.

4. TWO EXAMPLES

Two examples are treated, namely:

4.1 an information campaign in international politics

4.2 currency rate adjustments.

4.1 Information campaign: examples of rules

The specific case was a political campaign aiming at promoting one viewpoint in the public.

* The goals to be attained consist in reducing the set of logical bindings between policy assets in a predefined way (e.g. enforce a decision favorable on one issue). This transcribes into an attribute logical filter applied to alternative information propagation channels.
* If the logical filter predicate is to hold true, the required information and service assets (4) must be in place before.
* For the information and service assets to operate properly, physical assets (2) must be used to create bindings on possible policy assets negating the attribute logical filter.
* For (2) to operate, monetary assets must be diverted to controlling all types of transactions on service and information assets, without appearing as touching at political assets.

4.2 Currency rate adjustments: examples of rules

* If the markets for (1) assets are perfect, the real prices (after inflation), reflected by the transactions, must be equal regardless of the country, e.g. a price difference can be due to an inflation rate difference (difference in i. for assets (1)).
* The nominal interest rate for a currency (rate i. for assets (1) in a given country), is equal to the sum of a real interest rate and of an anticipated inflation rate for that country (related to i. for assets (3))

* Currency rate differences between instantaneous rates and futures must be equal to the differences between real interest rates.

* The political premium in terms of interest rate on political assets (3) is equal but opposite to the real interest rate difference for assets (1), between the same pair of countries.

* The interest rate for assets (4) is the behavioural interest rate, sum of those on assets (1) and (3).

5. CONCLUSIONS

Whereas classical approaches have experienced difficulties (see Section 1), this KBS kernel eliminates some of them by stressing a common internal structure and the logical coherence between transaction predicates among different asset types.

Especially, the application examples have shown that the logic predicate coherence can only achieved by including explicitely political (3) and information (4) assets. This demonstrates the global approach to be relevant to such strategy problems.

Specific implementations will continue to strenthen the kernel robustness. These include cases in:

- commodity pricing by producers and suppliers
- threat analysis (security policy).

References

1. R. Wilensky, Planning and understanding, Addison Wesley, Reading, MA, 1983.

2. L.F. Pau, P. Valstorp, Feature extraction in the time-domain: application to the analysis of financial strategies over time, in: K.S.Fu, A. Whinston (Ed), "Pattern recognition thoery and applications", Noordhoff, Leyden, 1977, 75-90.

3. L.F. Pau (Editor), Artificial intelligence in economics and management, North Holland, Amsterdam, 1985.

Artificial Intelligence in Economics and Management
L.F. Pau (Editor)

EXPERT SYSTEM IN FINANCIAL ANALYSIS

B.Iwasieczko, J.Korczak, M.Kwiecień, J.Muszyńska

Academy of Economics
Wrocław, Poland

The current methods of analysis of financial situation of a company applying for credit have often been criticized. The main problem of crediting is the use of the appropriate methods of analysis and in order to decide as to who should receive credit, taking into consideration finance policy, economy, solvency, risk, etc. The present paper proposes an expert system which supports a bank-officer in credit-worthiness analysis of a company which would like to get credit. This system is currently in progress.

INTRODUCTION

Complexity and economic importance of the financial analysis as well as its useability are the main reasons of taking up the studies on expert system. We assume that our system will act as an expert when allowing a credit by the bank. In central-planned system of economy, a bank is only an institution which can allow a credit to companies. Financial and credit policy of the state as well as a credit plan are set by the Parlament /Seym/. The assumptions of financial and credit policy formulate the state financial policy which the banks are obliged to follow in relation to the borrowers. A given company can get a credit only from this branch bank in which it has its basic bank account.

The procedure of entering into a credit contract assumes conducting negotiations. Within their scope, the borrower should prove the fact of possessing the credit-worthiness by means of data showing the state and workable prospects of conducting activities in such time, for which the credit is to be granted.

Bank reserve is limited. Only the companies which have credit-worthiness can get the credit. According to legal and financial rules, the borrowing power can be understood as the current and anticipated effectiveness of managing and financial position which ensures solvency and repayment. The analysis of credit-worthiness is complex. It should be estimated not only for a day on which the credit is granted but also for the whole period of credit repayment. The idea of credit-worthiness involves the ascertainment as well as the prognosis of financial situation of the borrower. The preparation of expertise is a difficult task for a bank-officer. He must define the problem properly, choose adequate data and methods of analysis, make a diagnosis and then explain his opinion. That means that a bank-officer should explain to the borrower what reasons and results make the basis of the diagnosis. This procedure requires from the bank-officer the knowledge of an expert. In fact it is not so, as the realities of economic practice show.

The research on expert system in crediting is in progress now in Academy of Economics, Wrocław. The problem has been defined (a credit-worthiness analysis), the definition of economic knowledge scope and specification of algorithms of financial analysis have been formulated. At present we are in the course of experiments on bringing into operation the system in the scope of balance-sheet analysis.

IDENTIFICATION OF BALANCE DATA

The company that endeavours to obtain a credit is obliged to deliver to a bank: a credit application and its motivation, the account of the possessions (balance-sheet) together with account of the effectiveness of its work (account of losses and profits), and economic plan (Korczak and Kwiecień (1985)).

The credit has an acknowledged character, therefore the bank grants it on the results of the investigation of the borrower's property. As concerns the sum of the credit the bank evaluates the reliability concluded by the company on the basis of information comprised in the balance sheet, of the estimation of economy effectiveness (losses and profits) and of economic plan.

The economic purport of balance sheet and its structure are the basic sources of information for evaluation of property and financial situation of the company and of effectiveness of its activities. The balance sheet is a general financial statement of real state of all assets (i.e. of the means which the company has at its disposal) as well as current liabilities, long-term liabilities, fixed capital (i.e. the source of assets) for a given day.

The relations between the groups of assets and liabilities can be investigated in horizontal and vertical scheme. Reading (analysing) the balance sheet vertically and horizontally, bank-officer looks for an answer to the following question the borrower has: are there real prospect for retaining credit-worthiness over whole period until the date of return payment of all the credits taken up in the bank. The analysis of the balance sheet enables the evaluation of the changes taking place, of financing the property of the company in relation to the fixed standards of estimation of deviations and irregularities in order to make a diagnosis. Figure 1 depicts simplified structure of balance sheet specifying the items which are indispensable in the latter part of this paper. The detailed bålance discription is contained in Bednarski (1979), Fedak and Skrzywan (1984), Waśniewski (1983).

Assets	Liabilities
1. Property, plant and equipment 2. Stores and receivables 2.1. Raw materials 2.2. Goods 2.3. Finished goods 2.4. Cash 2.5. Current receivables	1. Fixed capital 2. Floating credit for financing the needs connected with running of business 3. Current liabilities 4. Profit

Figure 1
Balance sheet

From the view-point of expert system, the balance is one of important moduls of economic knowledge, defining the financial situation of the company in terms of granting credits. Taking into account complexity of economic knowledge as well as the procedures of analysis, we shall confine our considerations to some essential problems. Now we shall write down the balance structure (Figure 1) in GVL notation Dietterich and Michalski (1983), Nilsson (1980) and then in MuLISP language together with chosen functions of expert system.

The contents of the balance sheet in GVL notation is as follows:

balance sheet (company) = {[statement-unit], [statistics-number], [period], [date-of-issue], [assets], [liabilities], [account-of-economy-effectiveness], [complementary-data]} (1)

DOM (statement-unit) = {text} (2)

DOM (statistics-number) = {number} (3)

DOM (period) = {quarter, half-year, year} (4)

DOM (day) = {1,2,...,31} (5)

DOM (month) = {1,2,...,12} (6)

DOM (year) = {85,86,...} (7)

date-of-issue (balance sheet) = {[year], [month], [day]} (8)

[[month (date-of-issue (balance sheet)) = 3] √ [month date-of-issue (balance sheet)) = 9]] =>[period (balance sheet) = quarter] (9)

[month (date-of-issue (balance sheet)) = 6] =>[period (balance sheet) = half-year] (10)

[month (date-of-issue (balance sheet)) = 6] =>[period (balance sheet) = year] (11)

assets (balance sheet) = {[group-A], [group-B], [group-C], [group-D], [group-E], [group-F], [initial-state], [final-state], [position]} (12)

liabilities (balance sheet) = as above (13)

account of economy effectiveness (balance sheet) = as above (14)

complementary data (balance sheet) = as above (15)

Each term occourring in assets definition (see description 16) has been defined in GVL notation, for example:

group-C (assets) = {[name], [initial-state], [final-state], [stores], [materials], [goods], [finished-goods-and-products-work-in], [supplies-for-example-purchase-cost], [notes-payable], [assets-diminshing-fixed-capital-in-work]} (16)

name (group-C (assets)) = [stores and notes payable] (17)

DOM (name) = {text} (18)

DOM (position) = {001,002,...,176} (19)

position (group-C (assets)) = 015 (20)

The generalized definition of the balance sheet in GVL notation allows to make easily the implementation of the system within other programming languages as PASCAL, PROLOG or generators of expert systems. The definition of the balance sheet in MuLISP language can be presented as follows:

```
(DEFUN BALANCE-SHEET (LAMBDA (B SU SN SP DI ASS LIA AEE CD)
(PRINT STATEMENT UNIT) (SETQ SU (READ))
(PRINT STATISTICS NUMBER) (SETQ SN (READ))
(PRINT STATEMENT PERIOD) (SETQ SP (READ))
(PRINT DATE OF ISSUE) (SETQ DI (READ))
(SETQ ASS (ASSETS)) (SETQ LIA (LIABILITIES))
(SETQ AEE (ACCOUNT-OF-ECONOMY-EFFECTIVENESS))
(SETQ CD (COMPLEMANTARY-DATA))
(SETQ B (LIST  SU SN SP DI ASS LIA AEE CD)) ))                    (21)

(DEFUN ASSETS (LAMBDA (ASS IS FS)
(PRINT ASSETS) (A-GR-A) (A-GR-B) (A-GR-C) (A-GR-D) (A-GR-E) (A-GR-F)
(FIS) (SETQ IS (READ)) (FFS) (SETQ FS (READ))
(SETQ ASS (LIST IS FS AGA AGB AGC AGD AGE AGF))                   (22)

(DEFUN A-GR-C (LAMBDA (AGC NAME IS FS)
(PRINT ASSETS GROUP C) (SETQ NAME STORES AND NOTES PAYABLE)
(PRINT NAME) (STORES) (NOTES-PAYABLE) (ASSETS-DIMINISHING-FIXED-CAPITAL-
-IN-WORK) (FIS) (SETQ IS (READ)) (FFS) (SETQ FS (READ))
(SETQ AGC (LIST NAME IS FS L16 L40 L46)) ))                       (23)
```

ANALYSIS OF BALANCE DATA

The general schema of the system actions in the field of financial analysis is presented in Figure 2.

Let us return to a balance analysis. Its results provide answers to many questions (Korczak and Kwiecień (1985)), for example:
1. what is the general financial situation of the company?,
2. what is its payment situation?,
3. has the capitals been property engaged in financing the property elements?

The idea is to start from the goal state and apply those investigations that can contribute to the goals. As soon as a function's preconditions are true, it is applied and new state is generated. A new subgoal is added to the list of goals to be achieved (Michaelsen, Michie and Boulanger (1985)).

The first step in any consultation is to choose a goal for the investigation. In this paper we will present the first phase of the analysis of balance data (II level in Figure 2) called INV-OF-GE-FIN-SIT investigation of general financial situation. This phase has 7 conceptually distinc interrelated modules. The relations between modules depend on the outputs (diagnosis) from each investigation.

The system is goal-directed. This means that the system creates explicit hierarchy of goals during execution and colects diagnosis related to each goal. The system objective is to find a way of achieving the current goal and to elaborate diagnosis resulting from analysis and explanations.

In the MuLISP program the fragment of balance data analysis (Figure 2) is defined in the following way:

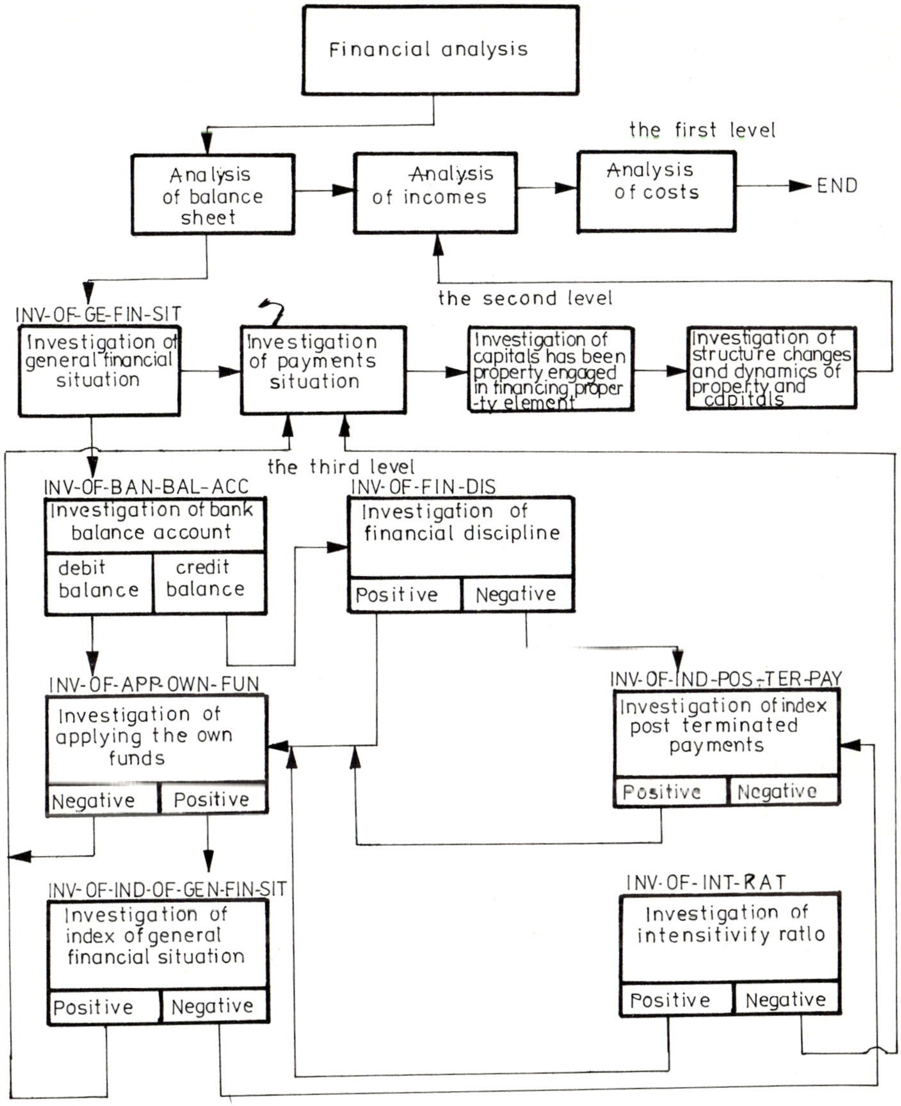

Figure 2
Schema of financial analysis

Legend: Over the symbols of the third level of analysis are the names of the functions which are the same as in MuLISP program.

```
(DEFUN INV-OF-GE-FIN-SIT (LAMBDA NIL (SAVE-GOAL NAME RULES)
(INV-OF-BAN-BAL-ACC) (COND ((EQ BANK-BALANCE-ACCOUNT DEBIT)
(INV-OF-APP-OWN-FUN) (INV-OF-IND-OF-GEN-FIN-SIT))
((INV-OF-FIN-DIS)) ) (SAVE-DIAGNOSIS GOAL) ))                    (24)

(DEFUN INV-OF-BAN-BAL-ACC (LAMBDA (BANK-BALANCE-ACCOUNT)
(SAVE-GOAL NAME RULES) (COND ((ZEROP (CADDR LP55))
(SETQ BANK-BALANCE-ACCOUNT CREDIT))
((SETQ BANK-BALANCE-ACCOUNT DEBIT)) ) (SAVE-DIAGNOSIS GOAL) ))   (25)

(DEFUN INV-OF-APP-OWN-FUN (LAMBDA (C D) (SAVE-GOALS NAME RULES)
(SETQ C (TIMES (QUOTIENT (MIDDLE OWN-FUN) (MIDDLE FIXED-ASSETS)) 100))
(SETQ D (TIMES (QUORIENT (MIDDLE LIA) (MIDDLE WORKING-ASSETS)) 100))
(SAVE-DIAGNOSIS GOAL) ))                                         (26)

(DEFUN INV-OF-IND-OF-GEN-FIN-SIT (LAMBDA (IOGFS)
(SAVE-GOAL NAME RULES) (SETQ IOGFS (QUOTIENT C D))
(SAVE-DIAGNOSIS GOAL) ))                                         (27)
```

The advantages of that approach are: easier construction hierarchy of analysis in the structure of program, and efficiency of control strategy procedures.

Knowledge base of this expert system can be thought of as a collection of sets containing: production rules, goal hierarchy, hipotheses and dictionary. Production rules relate both to knowledge about financial analysis and to principles and modes of crediting as well. Production rules are organized hierarchically according to the goal structure (Thompson and Thompson (1985)). The results of investigations that were carried out (Figure 2) is a set of diagnosis describing general financial situation of company. The set of diagnosis is created by the interpreter of production rules that additionally on the basis of data chooses a way of reasoning, controles a sequence of actions, and explains mechanism of balance data analysis to a bank-officer.

Let us consider in order to illustrate the inference mechanism the following example. Suppose that the system realizes the function [24]: INV-OF-GEN-FIN-SIT and after ending the function [25]: INV-OF-BAN-BAL-ACC has returned information that the saldo of bank account is debit. According to the definition this part of function [24], after the condition has been satisfied the first function to be carried out is the function [26]: INV-OF-APP-OWN-FUN. Makro SAVE-GOAL writes in the hierarchy of goals the current goal: "investigation of using funds" and pointers to relevant production rules: R20, R21. After the calculation of index of own funds application

$$C = \frac{\text{own funds}}{\text{fixed assets + investment fund}} \cdot 100 \qquad (28)$$

the following production rules will be executed:
Rule 20

IF $C \geq 100$ THEN correct structure of assets, or (29)

Rule 21

IF $C < 100$ THEN incorrect structure of assets. (30)

Macro SAVE-DIAGNOSIS of the function [26] writes in the stack a diagnosis depending on condition part of rules.

The second function called by the definition [24] is INF-OF-GEN-FIN-SIT [27]. Calculated in this function index of general financial situation explains the finance source of assets and their structure. As it did before, macro SAVE-GOAL writes the current goal in hierarchy of goals and pointers to production rules. After the calculation of index the following rule will be executed:
Rule 24

IF IOGFS ≥ 100 THEN correct financing of assets, or (31)

Rule 25

IF IOGFS ≤ 100 THEN incorrect financing of assets. (32)

Macro SAVE-DIAGNOSIS saves relevant diagnosis resulting from the employed rules.

Finally, the system has completed all subgoals of the function [24] with the set of diagnoses concluded from the functions [25], [26], [27]. The last task to be performed is macro SAVE-DIAGNOSIS, which generalizes the diagnoses obtained from the lower level using production rules related to goal of the function [24]. A good example is the following production rule:
Rule 11

IF (free financial means on bank account) and

(correct financing of assets) and

(correct structure of assets)

THEN good financial situation (33)

The same reasoning process can be carried out when saldo of bank account is credit (function 25). In that case financial discipline should be investigated.

CONCLUSION

In the present paper we have outlined some of the issues involved in achieving better computer-supported balance data investigation. This is only a part of the expert system in financial analysis implemented in MuLISP version under CP/M 2.2. and preliminarily tested on APPLE II (Webster (1985)). In order to realise the whole system several problems should be resolved, e.g. knowledge aquisition and learning strategy should be improved, and economic explanation should be developed. These are the issues to be approached at the next step of our study.

References:

[1] Bednarski, L., Analiza ekonomiczna (Państwowe Wydawnictwo Ekonomiczne, Warszawa, 1979).

[2] Dietterich, T.G. and Michalski, R.S., A Comparative review of selected methods for learning from examples, in: Machine learning (Tioga Publishing Company, Palo Alto, 1983).

[3] Fedak, Z. and Skrzywan, S., Rachunkowość przedsiębiorstwa przemysłowego (Państwowe Wydawnictwo Ekonomiczne, Warszawa, 1984).

[4] Korczak, J. and Kwiecień, M., System Ekspert w kredytowaniu przedsiębiorstw w: materiałach konferencyjnych Komputerowe wspomaganie decyzji gospodarczych (Polska Akademia Nauk, Katowice, 1985).

[5] Michaelsen, R.H., Michie, D. and Bonlanger, A., The technology of expert systems, Byte. 4 (1985) 303-312.

[6] Nilsson, N.J., Principles of artificial intelligence (Tioga Publishing Company, Palo Alto, 1980).

[7] Thompson, B.A. and Thompson, W.A., Inside an expert system, Byte. 4 (1985) 315-330.

[8] Waśniewski, T., Analiza finansowa w przedsiębiorstwie przemysłowym (Państwowe Wydawnictwo Ekonomiczne, Warszawa, 1983).

[9] Webster, R., Experts systems an microcomputers, Computers and Enics. 3 (1985) 69-73.

Artificial Intelligence in Economics and Management
L.F. Pau (Editor)

A Prototype Expert System for Credit Evaluation

Arie Ben-David[1]
Manager, O.&M. Department,
Barclays Discount Bank, Ltd.
Tel-Aviv, 61012, Israel

Leon Sterling[1]
Department of Applied Mathematics
The Weizmann Institute of Science
Rehovot, 76100, Israel

The world of banking and finance is an untapped market for expert systems technology. To demonstrate the applicability of the technology in this domain we developed a prototype expert system for Credit Evaluation. This paper describes a simplified version of the prototype which accurately reflects the program structure, but with sensitive bank information removed. The program uses ordinal scales to represent the qualitative reasoning of bank experts. The prototype has been tested so far on the data of a dozen real world clients. According to our experts, it gave reasonable results, which encourage further investments in the prototype in order to make it (actually, a version of it) a working system.

1. Introduction

There is an abundance of literature about Expert Systems [4],[5],[6],[15],[19]. The written material reflects the confusion about the cost effective use of this Artificial Intelligence (AI) technology. There is little dispute that some systems (although very few and created at high cost) do operate at a highly talented expert level [3],[9]. Severe critics doubt however that the technology will find widespread use.

There are currently very few working Financial Expert Systems of which we are aware, most of them are experimental [1],[11],[16]. We decided to check the applicability of research in expert systems to the financial field by building a prototype system ourselves. From reading the literature it is almost impossible to distinguish facts from beliefs.

The potential benefits of a financial expert system include the following:

- When linked to existing databases, the rules can be applied to identify potential threats among present debitor customers.
- A combination of human experts with a good Expert System can lead to a better decision making process.
- A good system can help in the reduction of bureaucratic processes within the bank, and to increase the control of management over the organization.
- The use of both rules of thumb and 'conventional' bad debt analysis can achieve better results than one kind alone.
- The time spent by experts on trivial and straightforward cases can be lessened. Good experts are rare.
- The service to the customers can be improved by shortening the request/reply cycle, by defining the authorities according to the risk and not only according to the sums.

Even the most severe critics admit that the financial community is one of the most promising commercial application areas for Expert Systems. Because of the huge amounts of money involved in the financial community business environment, even a modest improvement in the decision process can have a considerable positive yield over these very expensive systems [3],[9].

The following sections describe the prototype, outlining some of its major components and the programming environment. Our descriptions are in terms of actual Prolog code to emphasize the close relation between the representation of knowledge in the program and

---

1: Authors' current address: Department of Computer Engineering and Science, and Center for Automation and Intelligent Systems Research, Case Western Reserve University, Cleveland, Ohio 44106 USA

the banking concepts themselves. The reader unfamiliar with Prolog is referred to [2] for details of the language. However the features of the program can be understood independent of the programming language.

The system is written in C-Prolog, and runs at 1000 LIPS under Unix on a Vax 750. It currently contains more than 350 rules. The response time to a request to evaluate a client is on the order of a few seconds (in a multiuser environment).

2. An Overview of the System

The actual system is constructed of seven modules, each dealing with a different aspect of the client's profile. The modules deal for example with financial stability, collateral offered by the client, his reputation (from his banker's point of view), his ability to cover regular payments, the profitability to the bank while dealing with him, the profitability to the bank from a special deal, and the resources available to the bank.

In addition to these modules the system contains a database of rules for evaluating the results of the modules, an interpreter for the rules which gives the final recommendations, a consistency checker for the incremental addition of evaluation rules by the expert, an interactive explanation facility which gives the user an easy way to follow the reasoning used by the program to form its conclusions, a bank database with details about available funds and resources, marginal yields, risk policy, and the like, and a client's database with details about each client.

The top level control structure of the system has the form given in Figure 2.1. The basic relation is **credit(Client,Answer,RuleNumber)** where **Answer** is the reply given to the request by **Client** for credit. **RuleNumber** is the number of the principal rule used during the final evaluation phase, computed by the relation **evaluate.** The code given has three modules, **collateral, financial_rating** and **bank_yield.** There is a preliminary check that no essential data is missing (in this case the system prompts the user how to enter the data from the terminal) and that the client is worth considering in the first place. This is determined by the predicate **ok_profile(Client).**

```
credit(Client,Answer,RuleNumber):-
   ok_profile(Client),
   collateral(Client,CRating),
   financial_rating(Client,FRating),
   bank_yield(Client,Yield),
   evaluate(profile(CRating,FRating,Yield),Answer,Rulenumber).
```

Figure 2.1: The top-level control structure

Within each module the standard backward reasoning of Prolog is used. There were two main reasons to accept this simple depth first search strategy in all the modules. Firstly, our domain experts were unable to express any directed search policy. An important principle in building the system was to conform to the experts' way of reasoning as they expressed it, and not to enforce any artificial behaviour upon the system. Secondly, this control suffices! The nature of the rules which were expressed by the experts, enabled us to cover a large problem space with relatively few rules, so this naive (but natural according to our experts) search strategy led to a reasonable response time. These important features will be discussed more deeply in section 5.

Some of the modules in the prototype are more advanced than others. This is for two reasons. Firstly there are natural differences existing among the various subsystems, which affect the complexity of the area. Secondly we concentrated upon the harder financial areas consisting of relatively large amounts of knowledge. Thus, for example, the collateral module is well developed (although still not complete), while the profitability module is primitive.

In the following two sections we look more closely at the collateral evaluation module and the financial stability module.

3. Collateral Evaluation

The purpose of this important module is to estimate what will be left for the bank should the client be unable (or unwilling) to pay his debt. The relative importance of this module will depend on the particular banking organization. In general, the less a bank relies upon collateral, the more carefully it must analyse other client factors such as financial stability, reputation from the bank's point of view, and estimation about the industry.

The module reflects a particular expert's point of view rather than any universal truth. Within the bank there is no consensus about this subject. Some people tend to be conservative and some are prepared to take considered risks. An Expert System can thus reflect the management's policy towards collateral (as well as towards other issues), and to improve the auditing tasks. Furthermore, there are many kinds of banking organizations, each with its specific client population, and its unique attitude towards collateral.

The style of the collateral evaluation is reflected in the program in Figure 3.1. Let us look at its essential features. The relation **collateral** determines a rating for a particular client. The first step is to determine a profile for the client. This is done with the predicate **collateral_profile** which classifies the client's collateral as first class, second class or unliquid, and gives the percentage which each cover of the amount of credit the client requested. The relation uses facts in the both the bank and client databases. Sample facts shown in Figure 3.1 indicate, for example, that local currency deposits are a first class collateral.

The profile is evaluated to give a rating by **collateral_evaluation.** It uses 'rules of thumb' exemplified in Figure 3.1 to give a qualitative rating of the collateral: as excellent, good, etc. The first collateral_evaluation rule, for example, reads that the rating is excellent if the coverage of the requested credit amount by first class collateral is greater than or equal to 100 per cent.

```
collateral(Client,Rating) :-
  collateral_profile(Client,FirstClass,SecondClass,Unliquid),
  collateral_evaluation(FirstClass,SecondClass,Unliquid,Rating).

collateral_evaluation(FirstClass,SecondClass,Unliquid,excellent) :-
  FirstClass >= 100.
collateral_evaluation(FirstClass,SecondClass,Unliquid,excellent) :-
  FirstClass > 70, FirstClass+SecondClass >= 100.
collateral_evaluation(FirstClass,SecondClass,Unliquid,good) :-
  FirstClass+SecondClass > 60,
  FirstClass+SecondClass < 70,
  FirstClass+SecondClass+Unliquid >= 100.

collateral(local_currency_deposits,first_class).
collateral(foreign_currency_deposits,first_class).
collateral(negotiate_instruments,second_class).
collateral(mortgage,unliquid).
```

Figure 3.1: Sample code in the collateral evaluation module

Several features of the code in Figure 3.1 bear further discussion and emphasis. Firstly, there can be many profiles which give a specific rating such as excellent. Secondly, the terminology used in the program is the terminology of the experts. This makes the program (almost) self-documenting to the experts, and means they can modify it with little help from the knowledge engineer. Allowing people to think in domain concepts also greatly facilitates debugging efforts.

Finally, the apparent naivete of the evaluation rules is deceptive. There is a lot of knowledge and experience hidden behind these simple numbers. Choosing poor values for these numbers may mean suffering severe losses.

4. Financial Evaluation

The financial evaluation module evaluates the financial stability of the client. It uses items taken mainly from the balance and profit/loss sheets. A simplified version of the module is given as a program segment in Figure 4.1. The financial rating is also qualitative. A weighted sum of financial factors is calculated by **score** and used by **calibrate** to determine the qualitative class.

```
financial_rating(Client,Rating) :-
  financial_factors(Factors), score(Factors,Client,0,Score), calibrate(Score,Rating).

score([(Factor,Weight)|Fs],Client,Acc,Score) :-
  value(Factor,Client,Value), Acc1 is Acc+Weight*Value, score(Fs,Client,Acc1,Score).
score([],Client,Score,Score).

financial_factors([(net_worth_per_assets,5),(last_year_sales_growth,1),
     (gross_profits_on_sales,5), (short_term_debt_per_annual_sales,2)]).

calibrate(Score,bad):-Score =< -500.
calibrate(Score,medium):- -500 < Score, Score < 150.
calibrate(Score,good):- 150 =< Score, Score < 1000.
calibrate(Score,excellent):- Score >= 1000.
```

Figure 4.1: An example of the top level financial evaluation

The financial evaluation does not assume a fixed weight for each factor. For example, if the short term debt per annual sales reaches a certain value, the experts think it is important enough to modify both the score and weight either higher or lower. In some cases severe enough findings will lead to a negative answer, irrespective of the remaining features of the client.

The overall modularity of the program makes it easy to replace these financial calculations. Incorporating statistical techniques for estimating bad debts, for example, could be easily done.

5. Ordinal Scales for Qualitative Reasoning

The rules naturally supplied by our experts all made a qualitative judgement with respect to an implicit ordinal scale. For example, the financial stability of a client was described as ‘sound’, ‘very weak’, and so on. Concepts that could be determined quantitatively were then mapped to qualitative terms by the experts.

This is a general phenomenon in all the modules we have dealt with. The financial world is too complicated to be expressed only with the numbers and ratios constantly being calculated. In order to make judgements, experts in the financial domain tend to think in qualitative terms with which they are more comfortable.

The outcome is also one of several possibilities on some ordinal scale. The final phase of the credit evaluation determines which outcome on the scale is appropriate given the client's profile. This section discusses the necessary machinery for doing this.

There is a latent problem with using ordinal scales. Building a client profile using ordinal scales leads to a large number of individual cases potentially having to be specified. If each of N modules have M possible outcomes, there are N^M possibilities to be specified.

In a real world application the number of possible profiles of a client is very high. For example, in our prototype there are on the order of 10000 possibilities. It is reasonable to anticipate that this number will increase by one or two orders of magnitude in a real system.

It is infeasible to have a separate rule for each possibility. Not only is the knowledge acquisition the major problem for so many rules, but the search involved in finding the correct rule may be prohibitive.

In our prototype, rules are defined in such a way as to cover many cases at once. For the system a small number, approximately 25, suffices to cover all the test cases. We believe that in general, since human experts are able to make judgements, a tractable number of rules can be found.

Let us consider the rules in some detail. Figure 5.1 gives three sample rules. Rules have the form **rule(Conditions,Conclusion,N)** where **N** is the number of the rule, **Conclusion** is its conclusion, and **Conditions** is a list of conditions that describe the cases the particular rule covers. This list is made up of terms of the form **cond(Factor,Relation,Rating)**, insisting that the rating from the factor named by **Factor** bears the relation named by **Relation** to the rating given by **Rating.** Rule 1 in Figure 5.1 reads that if the collateral rating is excellent (**be** stands for better than or equals), the financial rating is good or better, and the yield is better or equal than reasonable, then the credit officer should approve the credit request. **We** stands for worse than or equal and **eq** means equal.

```
rule([cond(collateral,be,excellent),cond(finances,be,good),cond(yield,be,reasonable)],
        give_credit,1).
rule([cond(collateral,eq,good),cond(finances,eq,good),cond(yield,be,reasonable)],
        consult_your_superior,2).
rule([[cond(collateral,we,moderate),cond(finances,we,bad)],refuse_credit,3).
```

Figure 5.1: Recommendation rules

There are currently approximately 25 evaluation rules of this type. In a complete system there should be more, but we have decided to accumulate them slowly. It is not a simple task, even for an excellent expert, to express many sensible and consistent rules even over a long period of time.

Rules can be added, deleted and modified independently of each other. Furthermore they are totally independent from the rules interpreter. Let us see how this interpreter operates. Our rules interpreter gives the best conservative answer it can.

The rules interpreter is recursively instantiated by the appropriate result of each module and compared against the rules. It must determine whether a rule implicitly applies to a profile which is not explicitly written because of the reasons given above.

The predicate **evaluate(Profile,Answer,Rulenumber)** determines the final answer **Answer** that will be given according to the client's profile **Profile** determined in the previous modules. For this toy example, the profile is represented as a structure **profile(Collateral,Finance,Yield)** where **Collateral**, **Finance** and **Yield** are the ratings determined by the respective modules. **Rulenumber** is the number of the rule used to decide the answer. The predicate **verify(Conditions,Profile)** checks the relation between the corresponding symbols in the rule and the ones that are associated with the **Profile** of the client as specified by Conditions. **scale** returns the relevant scale symbols, while **select** returns the appropriate symbol of the factor under the ordinality test which is performed by **compare.**

The **evaluate** predicate compares every symbol occurring in a rule with each corresponding symbol of the client profile. If and only if all the client's factors symbols are better than or equal to the corresponding factors symbols in the rule, **Answer** will be instantiated and the search will stop. This strategy supplies reasonable answers only when there are a sufficient number of rules and provided the search is in descending order of answer symbol values (in other words, the rules with the higher answer symbols must be evaluated first): ordering of the rules is important. Otherwise you will get funny answers since any good customer factors symbols are better than those of the corresponding symbols in a rule which refer to your worst client and naturally gives a "do not dare to bother me again with a client like this" answer. A slower (but a cleaner) alternative solution is to add a meta-interpreter to control the search, as described in [20].

There are advantages to inferences such as these, since the more rules present, the more delicate can the differentiation be between the clients. Nonetheless the system can begin to produce reasonable answers in an early stage of the project, so you can keep the experts alert and interested in the project relatively quickly.

```
evaluate(Profile,Answer,RuleNumber) :-
  rule(Conditions,Answer,RuleNumber), verify(Conditions,Profile).

verify([cond(Type,Comp,Rating)|Conds],Profile) :-
  scale(Type,Scale), select(Type,Profile,Fact), compare(Scale,Comp,Fact,Rating),
                                   verify(Conds,Profile).
verify([],Profile).

scale(collateral,[excellent,good,moderate]).
scale(finances,[excellent,good,medium,bad]).
scale(yield,[excellent,reasonable,poor]).

select(collateral,profile(C,F,Y),C).        select(finances,profile(C,F,Y),F).
select(yield,profile(C,F,Y),Y).

compare(Scale,eq,Rating,Rating).
compare(Scale,be,Rating1,Rating2) :- precedes(Scale,Rating1,Rating2).
compare(Scale,we,Rating1,Rating2) :- precedes(Scale,Rating2,Rating1).

precedes([R1|Rs],R1,R2).
precedes([R|Rs],R1,R2) :- R = R2, precedes(Rs,R1,R2).
```

Figure 5.2: An example of the rules interpreter

In order to help the experts to define a consistent set of rules we considered this ordinal model in a broader context. A rule is interpreted as a boundary condition and has to be consistent with its predecessors. The following two meta-rules were used for consistency, and each rule must satisfy them both.

Consistency Rule 1: If all of client A's factors are better than or equal to client B's, then the outcome of client A must be better than or equal to that of client B.

Consistency Rule 2: If all of client A's factors are equal to or between the corresponding factors of clients B and C then the outcome of A must be equal to or between those of B and C.

To estimate whether the outcome space could be covered by a reasonable number of rules, a simulation program was written in Algol and run on a Burroughs 7800. Each of the possible values for a given scale were assigned equal probability. (In practice this is unlikely to be the case.) Rules were generated at random, and added to the current rule set if they were consistent with it. Results indicated that an order of magnitude of one hundred rules covered most of the possibilities for this problem.

6. The Explanation Facility

It is crucial to give the user a convenient and a friendly way to follow the reasoning process [4],[5]. We wrote a domain independent explanation facility using a meta-interpreter, as described by Sterling [20].

The explanation facility enables the user to traverse any branch of the proof tree he wishes. Sometimes the user may wish to know why a certain answer was given by the system, and he can choose among the predicates in a prompt. There can be as many prompts as one wishes, each group can belong to a totally different Expert System. The user can choose any head of a clause which interests him, then the meta-interpreter looks for the body, proves it, and explains all the arguments of the body. In addition it notifies the user whether an argument is itself a head of a lower level branch (in this case the user can enter a number which appears near the instantiated head to get an explanation for a lower level subtree) or a fact. System predicates or uninteresting goals can be omitted from the displayed explanation simply by defining them as unprintable.

7. Prolog as a Development Language for Expert Systems

At the beginning of the project we looked for an appropriate programming environment to write the prototype. The alternatives included Lisp, Prolog, any of the available 'off-the-shelf' Expert Systems Shells or a 'conventional' programming language such as Algol, Pascal or C. Prolog provided the fastest and the cheapest way to write the prototype.

The choice was very fortunate. Prolog is a very powerful tool for symbolic computation and can deal with the necessary arithmetic. It is relatively easy, even for a new user of Prolog, to formulate the rules in a natural way and he does not have to deal with many syntax problems. Complex rules can easily be expressed in the language. The naive but computer-aware user can quickly use Prolog to write an interesting toy expert system without any prior or special training.

Using Prolog, the user is free to concentrate on issues of knowledge representation and acquisition rather than search strategies. This allows rapid feedback to be presented to the experts, maintaining their interest and commitment.

Another reason for rapid feedback is the natural program development style of the language. One can naturally develop a top down program. This feature is very important while writing Expert Systems for the reason that Expert Systems cannot be defined in advance. Typically the expert does not know a priori how he thinks, and the system inevitably develops somewhat by trial and error.

Another important feature of Prolog is the easy ability of meta-programming. It can be used to define any search strategy the user wishes and to write explanation facilities. This flexibility comes at a price. Meta-interpreters slow down the computation speed.

Prolog still lacks today the rich programming environment of the Lisp machines, but if you intend to write an expert system, we highly recommend you should seriously examine Prolog among other alternatives. You may conclude, in many circumstances, that its exceptional power in building Expert Systems will compensate for its shortcomings.

8. Conclusions and Future Directions

A major aim of building the prototype was to give a good, direct estimation about the usefulness of Expert Systems to problem solving in the financial domain.

One should treat such Expert Systems in finance as a very sophisticated Decision Support System. While the "conventional" DSS offer a convenient way to represent data, Expert Systems also allow the user to interpret simultaneously different kinds of data within the database with an appropriate explanation regarding how a conclusion has been made.

Our program does this interpretation quite successfully, and as was mentioned above, the system responded well to a dozen real world cases, as well as to many hypothetical cases. It should not, however, be regarded as a fully automatic system for evaluating credit requests.

Of course, one should not expect Expert Systems to replace the best credit officers or actuaries. Their main use is to assist the management to identify risks among clients - most of the details about them are probably in some kind of database.

Our experts believe that although the prototype is far from perfect, it is more sophisticated now than any 'conventional' DSS they know. They wish to develop the prototype further into a working system to be used in the bank's credit department. They believe that a special type of an Expert System will be cost effective even to a small bank. The general idea is that such a system will assist identifying risks among the borrowers.

In general, we believe developing Expert Systems to be a costly project, due mainly to the difficulty of knowledge acquisition, and knowledge maintenance. However the larger the financial organization is, the more it can invest in development. Expert Systems can assist organizations to reduce their costs by their ability to rapidly reason about large quantities of data, to enforce regulations and policies, and to reduce the number of mid-management staff. The specific considerations vary with each organization and environment.

Constructing the prototype was a valuable experiment. The resultant system can serve as a tool for testing ideas about credit evaluation, and to help build further expert systems in the financial domain in other subjects and organizations. It consists of all the necessary elements for a larger system, and we suggest its development is a good example of expert system construction.

Finally, we summarize our main conclusions.

1. Expert knowledge about giving credit can be embedded in computers. To do properly, it is a costly project to develop and maintain. Nonetheless implementations can be cost effective in many circumstances.

2. The qualitative nature of the expert's reasoning can be captured with rules based on ordinal scales. Such rules ease the search process, and make knowledge acquisition easier.

3. Prolog has proved to be an excellent tool for developing the prototype.

4. Excellent domain experts are the major key to a successful system.

5. A well constructed prototype is a useful testbed for many ideas. For example, a direction of future research is to provide this system with learning capabilities. Every reasonable conclusion given can become a new rule, which will be taken into account by subsequent analysis.

Bibliography

[1] AI is Here, Businessweek, July 9th (1984).

[2] Clocksin & Mellish, Programming in Prolog, (Springer-Verlag, 1981).

[3] Alexander, T., Why Computers Can't Outthink the Experts, Fortune, August 20 (1984).

[4] Feigenbaum, E.A., McCorduck, P., The Fifth Generation, (Addison Wesley, 1983).

[5] Hayes-Roth, F., Waterman, D.A., Lenat, D.B., Building Expert Systems, (Addison Wesley, 1983).

[6] Hayes-Roth, F., Knowledge-based Expert Systems, A Tutorial. Computer, September (1984).

[7] Hartley, R.T., Krib: Computer Fault Finding Through Knowledge Engineering, Computer, March (1984).

[8] Littleford, A., A MYCIN-like Expert System in Prolog, in Proceedings of the 2nd Intnl. Logic Programming Conference, Uppsala, Sweden (1984)

[9] Martins, G.R., The Overselling of Expert Systems, Datamation, November (1984).

[10] McDermott, J., Bachant, J., R1 Revisited, Four Years in the Trenches, AI Magazine, Fall (1984).

[11] Michaelson, R., Michie, D., Expert Systems in Business, Datamation, November (1983).

[12] Niwa, K., Sasaki, K., Ihara, H., An Experimental Comparison of Knowledge Representation Schemes, The AI magazine, Summer (1984).

[13] Pecora, V.J. Jr., EXPRS, A Prototype Expert System Using Prolog for Data Fusion, The AI Magazine, Summer (1984).

[14] Rauch, H.E., Probability Concepts For an Expert System Used for Data Fusion, The AI Magazine, Fall (1984).

[15] Rich, E., The Gradual Expansion of AI, Computer, May (1984).

[16] Roos, J.L., AI and Macro Economy an Application, in Proceedings IJCAI-8, Karlsruhe, Germany, (William-Kaufmann, 1983).

[17] Sauers, R., Walsh, R., On The Requirements of Future Expert Systems, in Proceedings IJCAI-8, Karlsruhe, Germany, (William-Kaufmann, 1983).

[18] Sergot, M., Prospects for Representing the Law as Logic Programs, A.P.I.C. Studies in D.P. No. 16. (1982).

[19] Smith, R.G., On the Development of Commercial Expert Systems, The AI Magazine, Fall (1984).

[20] Sterling, L., Expert Systems = Knowledge + Meta-Interpreter, Technical Report CS84-17, Weizmann Institute of Science, Rehovot, Israel,(1984).

[21] Stolfo, S.J. et al., ACE: an Expert System for Telephone Cable Maintenance, in Proceedings IJCAI-8, Karlsruhe, Germany, (William Kaufmann 1983).

[22] Tate, P., The Blossoming of European AI, Datamation, November (1984).

Artificial Intelligence in Economics and Management
L.F. Pau (Editor)

MARKETS AS LOGIC PROGRAMS

Ross M. Miller

Boston University
School of Management
704 Commonwealth Avenue
Boston, Massachusetts 02215
U.S.A.

This paper examines how the market mechanism may be represented as a logic program. In this representation markets are viewed as systems that follow rules (in the form of Horn clauses) in pursuit of a specific goal. The logic program representation of a market mechanism carries with it the potential to build directly into the mechanism the satisfaction of constraints and optimality conditions. In addition, it provides a very compact and flexible way to program computerized markets as demonstrated by a Prolog example of New York Stock Exchange trading rules.

I. INTRODUCTION

Some recent advances in the field of Artificial Intelligence were aided by the ease with which certain kinds of knowledge, such as that required for an expert system, are readily represented by the constructs of formal logic. Not only can knowledge be represented with formal logic, but computational processes can be "programmed in logic." This paper demonstrates how economic mechanisms, particularly markets, can be represented as logic programs, and thereby exploit the ability of logic both to represent knowledge and to describe computational processes.

This paper starts with a brief introduction to logic programming as implemented by the Prolog language. (The Edinburgh version of Prolog is used in this paper. All programs included in this paper were developed and tested using C-Prolog 1.5 on a Digital Equipment Corporation VAX 11/780.) Those familiar with logic programming can skip that section. The next section gives a general description of how to represent economic mechanisms with logic programs, followed by a logic program for a double auction. Finally, the potential for building optimality into the logic program and some concluding remarks are presented.

II. LOGIC PROGRAMMING

Logic programming embodies the notion that it is possible to perform computations from a description in logic of the values one wishes to compute. For example, in first-order logic the Fibonacci numbers can be represented by following formulas which serve to define the function Fib:

(2.1a) $n=0 \implies Fib(n) = 1$

(2.1b) $n=1 \implies Fib(n) = 1$

(2.1c) $n>1 \implies Fib(n) = Fib(n-1) + Fib(n-2)$

Logic programming languages, such as Prolog (Clocksin and Mellish [3]), make explicit the procedural interpretation of formulas by essentially requiring that all formulas take the form of Horn clauses--a restriction that does not reduce the expressiveness of first-order logic and facilitates the proof of assertions by resolution (see Kowalski [4] and Lloyd [6] for the necessary formalizations). A Horn clause is any formula of the form

$$A_1 \text{ and } A_2 \text{ and } \ldots A_N \implies B,$$

where $A_1, \ldots A_N$ and B are atomic formulas. Prolog syntax emphasizes the procedural interpretation of the Horn clauses by expressing them as:

$$B :- A_1, A_2, \ldots A_N.$$

The validity of the formula B (the head of the Horn clause) is determined by invoking A_1 through A_N (the tail) in order. The formula B is then true if each formula in the tail is shown to be true.

In Prolog, the definition of Fibonacci numbers becomes:

(2.2a)
```
fib(0,1).
```

(2.2b)
```
fib(1,1).
```

(2.2c)
```
fib(M,N) :- M>1,
            M1 is M-1, M2 is M-2,
            fib(M1,N1), fib(M2,N2),
            N is N1+N2.
```

where fib is a predicate that takes two arguments such that fib(M,N) is true only if N=Fib(M). The first two formulas, (2.2a) and (2.2b), are tailless Horn clauses, known as facts, that state that the first two Fibonacci numbers are equal to 1. These formulas correspond to (2.1a) and (2.1b), respectively. The third formula, (2.2c), gives a rule that lists conditions that other Fibonacci numbers must meet.

A Prolog database is a collection of facts and rules. The database may be "queried" by presenting it with a goal. The goal

(2.3)
```
?- fib(2,X).
```

is satisfied when the variable X is instantiated to the value of Fib(2), the Fibonacci function defined above. (Note that Prolog variables start with upper-case letters.) Prolog attempts to satisfy the goal by finding an instantiation of variables in the head of some clause that matches the goal. The only formula that can match goal (2.3) is the rule (2.2c) with M instantiated to 2. Rule (2.2c) is satisfied by instantiating M1 to 1, M2 to 2, N1 to 1, N2 to 1, and N to 2. Hence, goal (2.3) is satisfied with X instantiated to 2.

III. REPRESENTING ECONOMIC MECHANISMS WITH LOGIC

The purpose of this section is to demonstrate that general economic mechanisms can be represented by logic programs. An example of such a representation is given in the next section.

An economic system consists of a collection of agents (consumers, firms, etc.) and a mechanism that determines the allocation of goods among agents. Agents are capable of taking actions. Actions may be thought of as messages that are sent to the mechanism. The range of messages is limited to those expressible in the language available to each agent. An action may be represented by the predicate action as follows:

action(Agent,Type,Conditions),

where Agent is the name of the agent, Type is the type of action, and Conditions is an object that specifies parameters relevant to the particular action. Hence, the actions of agents can be represented as facts. "Nature" may also be considered as an agent whose actions indicate the time or other possible states of nature.

An economic mechanism consists of goals and rules. The mechanism works by trying to achieve its goals by deriving inferences from its rules and from the facts generated by the actions of agents. When the mechanism achieves a goal, this "result" is added to the database as another fact or rule. Results can specify the set of agents who are permitted to read them. Included in the results is the outcome of the mechanism, i.e., the allocation of goods to agents. Results also indicate the current state of the mechanism.

This approach to representing economic mechanisms is similar to Vernon Smith's (1982) formulation of a microeconomic system as a basis for a theory of experimental economics. The types of rules that Smith incorporates into his mechanism--allocation rules, imputation rules, and adjustment process rules--are expressible in the above framework. While there are several technical differences that come up in comparing these approaches, (e.g., the restriction of logic programs to deal with objects that have finite representations and the possibility of non-determinism in logic programs), the spirit of these approaches is similar.

IV. A LOGIC PROGRAM FOR THE DOUBLE AUCTION

One of the simplest economic (market) mechanisms is the double auction. Smith (1982) describes the double auction as follows:

> After the market opens an auction for a unit begins with the announcement of a price bid by any buyer or a price offer by any seller. Any subsequent bid (offer) must be at a higher (lower) price to be admissible. Once a bid (offer) has been made public, that is, is "standing", it cannot be withdrawn. A binding contract occurs when any buyer (seller) accepts the offer (bid) of any seller (buyer). The auction ends with a contract. If the standing bid (offer) was not part of the contract (for example, if a buyer other than the one with the standing bid accepted the standing offer), the maker of that bid (offer) is no longer bound to it unless the bid (offer) is now re-entered. Following a contract a new auction begins when a new price bid (offer) is announced. . . . This process continues until the market "day" comes to an end.

The double auction captures the essential procedures of many centralized securities and commodities markets. (Smith's description is paraphrased from Leffler and Farwell's classic book on the stock market [5]).

A logic program based on the above description of the double auction is given in Table I. The first predicate that is defined, **go,** contains the goals that drive the market. Starting Prolog off with the goal

?- go.

will cause it to read the next action from an agent, using the built-in predicate **read,** and add that action to the (end of the) database, using the built-in predicate **assertz.** The mechanism then attempts one of the following: to make a trade, to post a bid, or to post an offer. (Semicolons in the tail of a clause

TABLE I

LOGIC PROGRAM FOR STOCK EXCHANGE DOUBLE AUCTION

```
go:-read(X),assertz(X),
    (dotrade(Buyer,Seller);placebid(Buyer);placeoff(Seller);true),
    (retract(X);nl),
    go.

dotrade(Buyer,Seller):-takebid(Seller,Price),openbid(Buyer,Price),
                       retract(openbid(Buyer,Price)),
                       retract(takebid(Seller,Price)),
                       (openoff(Seller,Anyprice);
                           retract(openoff(Anyseller,Anyprice));true),
                       assertz(trade(Buyer,Seller,Price)),
                       write(trade(Buyer,Seller,Price)).

dotrade(Buyer,Seller):-takeoff(Buyer,Price),openoff(Seller,Price),
                       retract(openoff(Seller,Price)),
                       retract(takeoff(Buyer,Price)),
                       (openbid(Buyer,Anyprice);
                           retract(openbid(Anybuyer,Anyprice));true),
                       assertz(trade(Buyer,Seller,Price)),
                       write(trade(Buyer,Seller,Price)).

placebid(Buyer):-bid(Buyer,Price),
                 not(openbid(Oldbuyer,Oldprice)),
                 assertz(openbid(Buyer,Price)),
                 write(openbid(Buyer,Price)),
                 retract(bid(Buyer,Price)).

placebid(Buyer):-bid(Buyer,Price),
                 openbid(Oldbuyer,Oldprice),
                 Price>Oldprice,
                 assertz(openbid(Buyer,Price)),
                 write(openbid(Buyer,Price)),
                 retract(openbid(Oldbuyer,Oldprice)),
                 retract(bid(Buyer,Price)).

placeoff(Seller):-offer(Seller,Price),
                  not(openoff(Oldseller,Oldprice)),
                  assertz(openoff(Seller,Price)),
                  write(openoff(Seller,Price)),
                  retract(offer(Seller,Price)).

placeoff(Seller):-offer(Seller,Price),
                  openoff(Oldseller,Oldprice),
                  Price<Oldprice,
                  assertz(openoff(Seller,Price)),
                  write(openoff(Seller,Price)),
                  retract(openoff(Oldseller,Oldprice)),
                  retract(offer(Seller,Price)).
```

function as a "logical or" with predicates evaluated from left to right until one succeeds.) If the trade or posting has not already retracted the agent's action, the third line of **go** makes sure that it is retracted. The built-in predicate **true** in the second line of the definition of **go,** as well as the **nl** (newline) in the third line, always succeeds, so that the goal **go** always succeeds. Finally, the goal invokes itself to repeat the cycle.

The **read** predicate can be replaced with a predicate that parses natural language input and/or receives input from a number of different sources. (The Prolog predicate **read** is limited to reading Prolog clauses.) Some unspecified external system must handle the task of sequencing the actions that are read into the database.

The state of the market prior to any action is described by the standing bid and offer. The predicate **openbid** represents the standing bid. The fact

```
openbid(Buyer,Price).
```

means that the buyer represented by the variable Buyer has a bid open at the price represented by the variable Price. The Price variable may be a list of attributes in instances where there is more than one type of good. Implicitly, trade occurs in a single unit at a time. If **openbid** is not in the database, then there is no standing bid. Similarly,

```
openoff(Seller,Price).
```

gives the current standing offer.

During the processing of an action, the state of the market also consists of the current bids and offers that are either made or being taken. The placing of a bid and the making of an offer are represented, respectively, as

```
bid(Buyer,Price).
```

and

```
offer(Seller,Price).
```

The acceptance of a bid or offer are represented, respectively, as

```
takebid(Seller,Price).
```

and

```
takeoff(Buyer,Price).
```

The Price variable in takebid and takeoff is redundant when a homogeneous object is for sale; however, it nonetheless serves as a useful confirmation device. (Because of the limited number of valid actions available to agents in the double auction, each valid action, **bid, offer, takebid,** or **takeoff,** is given its own predicate rather than using a more general **action** predicate.)

The above six predicates completely describe the state of the market, abstracting away from any time considerations. The auction rules determine when bids and offers are valid, in the sense that they then become the open bid or offer, and when the taking of bids and offers is valid.

The state of the market changes when either a bid or offer is taken, completing a trade, or the standing bid or offer is superceded. The rules governing these changes in market state are given by the last six clauses in Table I. The tails of each of these clauses can be thought of as consisting of two parts. The first line of the clause contains the condition that determines when the action in the head is to be taken. For example, in the second clause, a trade is made when a Seller takes a bid at the same Price as the standing bid. Without any further action, however, no record of the trade is made, because although **dotrade** is satisfied, it is not added to the database nor are the standing bid and its acceptance removed. Hence, the remainder of the clause does the bookkeeping for the database. The retractions of the bid and its acceptance from the database--they are no longer relevant--occur in the second and third lines of the clause. The fourth line adds the trade as a fact to the database and the final line displays the trade at the standard output of the computer. The third clause functions in an entirely analogous way for the acceptance of offers.

The last four clauses in Table I define procedures for creating a new standing bid or offer. These clauses are structurally similar to those for trades. They start by giving the conditions under which a bid or offer becomes a standing offer--the absence of an standing bid or offer or an improvement upon it--and then make the necessary change to the database. The inelegance of the the numerous assertions and retractions is characteristic of Prolog's implementation of logic programming, and may be avoided under a different implementation. In its purest form the logic program for a market should be entirely declarative and not require the specifications of procedures for altering the database.

V. BUILDING OPTIMALITY INTO A LOGIC PROGRAM

It is tempting to add to a mechanism that has goals "hard-wired" into it the goal of optimality--assuming that optimality can be defined and agreed upon. This section presents a preliminary analysis of what can be done to build optimality into a mechanism using logic.

The "classical" view of economic mechanisms, and the market mechanism in particular, is based on the notion of equilibrium used in physics. Equilibrium is reached when the "forces" of supply and demand, which can be represented by real-valued functions (or correspondences), are in balance in every market. (By contrast, a logic program implementation of a market is in a kind of equilibrium when it has exhausted all possibilities to make inferences.)

The welfare analysis of an equilibrium is based on the properties of the equilibrium for a suitably large domain of preference and production relations. The failure of the market to achieve an optimal allocation because of a mismatch between individual incentives and the social welfare (e.g., externalities, public goods, etc.) can frequently be remedied by altering the way in which prices are set without abandoning the use of the market mechanism. The desirability of these alterations can be confirmed by theoretical means (Clarke taxes, pollution taxes). Frequently, the optimal size of the alteration depends on individual parameters that must be estimated empirically.

Unfortunately, using the axioms for a desirable or optimal mechanism, such as those in Sonnenschein [9], as a logic program will not directly result in the market mechanism: which isthe optimal mechanism as long as convexity prevails, (see Reiter [7]). One reason for this is that the expression of these axioms requires second-order logic; we seek the existence of some predicate (or function) that satisfies certain properties over a specified domain for the predicates (or functions) that determine individuals' choices. Even in stripped-down form, in the tradition of Arrow [1], the logical expression of the axioms requires second-order constructs. (Things may not be as bad as they seem. Because any logic program is itself representable as a set of facts with ":-" considered as a predicate, a second logic program can be used to analyze the logic program for the mechanism. Cf. Bowen and Kowalski [2]).

Even without considerations of second-order logic, the inference mechanisms that form the basis of logic programming operate only on individual instances of a variable. A database with the rules

primate(X) :- human (X).

and

mammal(X) :- primate(X).

will for any instance of a human be able to conclude that the human in question is a mammal. However, it will not be able to derive the general theorem:

mammal(X) :- human(X).

for inclusion in its database. Hence, the logic program cannot derive theorems by the traditional theoretical means.

There are two general situations where optimality can be built into a logic-based mechanism. The first situation is when a simple rule would readily appear to characterize some element of market optimality. For example, with multiple, related markets, the opportunity for profitable, risk-free arbitrage may exist away from equilibrium. The market could have a rule that prevents such a situation from ever occurring, by making itself self-arbitraging. Of course, in the process of doing so it must appropriate for itself some of the implicitly created options (which Smith [8] calls property rights) that formerly belonged to market participants. The advantage of building arbitrage into the market is that the effort that market participants had formerly taken (and for which they had to be rewarded) to sustain equilibrium across assets is now handled by the market mechanism itself.

The second situation is when the market is not public, but is used for the internal allocation of resources by a corporation, for example. In this case, the mechanism need only be optimal for the particular situation faced by the corporation and not over a broad domain of possible situations. However, logic programs are only likely to be of use for mechanisms with modest computational demands. Problems in operations research that are characterized by "combinatorial explosion" tend to become even more "explosive" when computations are made directly from the logical specification of the problem.

VI. CONCLUSION

This paper has demonstrated how the operations of a market mechanism can be based on logical inference. Although logic programming has been used as a convenient way to represent the logical structure of markets, this representation can easily be adapted to other inference mechanisms such as a forward chaining production system.

The discussion of markets as logic programs given here has just scratched the surface of the potential benefits of this approach as well as some of its limitations. In the case of the double auction, there is no need to restrict the actions of agents to predicates; actions could be rules that describe the contingencies under which a bid/offer is to be placed or taken. The drawback of such an extension of the action space is that it becomes possible for the agents' contingencies to be logically inconsistent and thereby deadlock the market. Preventation or detection of deadlocks in this framework may be difficult.

REFERENCES

[1] Arrow, Kenneth, Social Choice and Individual Values, 2nd ed. (Wiley, New York, 1963).

[2] Bowen, K.A. and Kowalski R.A., Amalgamating Language and Metalanguage in Logic Programming, in Clark, K.L. and Tarnlund, S.-A. (eds.), Logic Programming (Academic Press, London, 1982).

[3] Clocksin, W.F. and Mellish, C.S., Programming in Prolog (Springer-Verlag, New York, 1981).

[4] Kowalski, Robert, Logic for Problem Solving (North-Holland, New York, 1979).

[5] Leffler, George and Farwell, C. Loring, The Stock Market (Ronald, New York, 1963).

[6] Lloyd, J.W., Foundations of Logic Programming (Springer-Verlag, Berlin, 1984).

[7] Reiter, Stanley, Information and Performance in the $(New)^2$ Welfare Economics, Proceedings of the American Economic Association, 67 (1977) 226-234.

[8] Smith, Vernon L., Microeconomic Systems as an Experimental Science, American Economic Review, 72 (1982) 923-955.

[9] Sonnenschein, Hugo, An Axiomatic Characterization of the Price Mechanism, Econometrica, 42 (1974) 425-433.

Artificial Intelligence in Economics and Management
L.F. Pau (Editor)

P/G% ANALYSIS: A DECISION-AIDING PROGRAM

Stuart Nagel
Political Science Department
University of Illinois
Urbana, Illinois, U.S.A.

John Long
Director of Marketing
Computer Teaching Corporation
Champaign, Illinois, U.S.A.

Microcomputers are increasingly being used to aid program evaluators in their word processing, data retrieval, and statistical/mathematical calculations. A new development is the use of microcomputers to process information concerning alternative programs, policies, decisions, or other options in order to aid in deciding which option or combination is the best. Using microcomputers in this way enables one (1) to avoid the drudgery of the arithmetic, (2) to be prompted into clarifying goals, alternatives, and relations, (3) to try numerous changes to see their effects, and (4) to have one's creativity stimulated in developing better program evaluation.

THE PROGRAM IN GENERAL

This short article briefly describes a new microcomputer program called Policy/Goal Percentaging Analysis. The program is designed to process a set of (1) goals to be achieved, (2) alternatives for achieving the goals, and (3) relations between goals and alternatives in order to choose the best alternative or combination for maximizing benefits minus costs.

The program is called Policy/Goal Percentaging Analysis because it relates alternative policies to goals, and it makes use of part/whole percentages in order to handle the problem of goals being measured on different dimensions. The measurement units are converted into a system of percentages showing relative achievement of each policy on each goal, rather than a system of inches, dollars, apples, days, or other measurement scores. The abbreviated name of the program is P/G%.

To facilitate applications of part/whole percentaging, an appropriate microcomputer program has been developed. It can be applied to any problem involving one or more policies and one or more goals. The program is especially useful when one is working with many policies, many goals, various measurement units, and other constraints and conditions. The program can run on an IBM PC or an IBM-compatible microcomputer. The program is written in the TenCore language. That is the IBM PC version of the PLATO language developed at the University of Illinois for use in interactive teaching. There are also less versatile versions of the program written in IBM BASIC and Apple BASIC.

COMPONENTS OF THE PROGRAM

The program can perform a variety of useful decision-making analyses such as:

1. Choosing, ranking, or allocating to alternative categories.
2. Working with goals that have a common measurement unit or that are multidimensional.
3. Doing what-if variations on the goals, alternatives, and relations.

4. Doing a threshold or convergence analysis to indicate the scores on the goals, alternatives, or relations that will make a difference in the winning alternative or how resources are allocated.
5. Adjusting results for minimums, maximums, and other constraints.
6. Comparing optimum choices with actual choices in order to reduce the gap between the actual and the optimum.

The decision-aiding system involves basically the following steps:

1. Listing the alternatives from which a choice needs to be made, or to which an allocation needs to be made.
2. Listing the criteria or goals which one wants to achieve and their relative importance.
3. Scoring each alternative on each criterion with as precise or as rough a relation score as is available.
4. Converting the scores into part/whole percentages or other scores that can show the relative relations of the alternatives on each criterion.
5. Aggregating the relative scores for each alternative across the criteria in order to arrive at an overall score or allocation coefficient for each alternative.
6. Drawing a conclusion as to which alternative or combination is best, or how much of a budget or a set of scarce resources should be allocated to each alternative.
7. Changing the alternatives, criteria, relations, and other inputs to see how such changes affect the conclusion.

The computer program is divided into five parts or options covering the following:

1. Accessing, creating, or deleting a datafile of information relevant to resolving a decision problem.
2. Inserting or changing the inputs regarding the alternatives, goals, relations, or amount of scarce resources to be allocated.
3. The initial results based on the alternatives, goals, and relations.
4. The post facto analyses, which include threshold analysis and convergence analysis.
5. A provision for saving and storing datafiles that one might want to refer to in the future.

The post facto analyses are especially useful to aid in resolving disputes as to what the weights or relation-scores should be. Threshold analysis is one option, whereby the computer shows what it would take in changing the goals-weights or the relation scores to bring the second place alternative up to first place or any alternative up to any other alternative. For example, if there is a dispute as to whether a relation-score is a 2 or an 8, and the threshold value is a 10, then there should be no need to dispute the matter further since neither a 2 nor an 8 will make any difference in terms of the second place alternative moving to first place. Convergence analysis is another option whereby the computer shows at what level the weight for a goal becomes high enough to produce results that are quite close to the results that would occur if that goal were the only goal. For example, if there is a dispute as to whether a goal weight is a 5 or a 10 and the convergence value is a 3, then there should be no need to dispute that matter further.

GENERAL APPLICATIONS

The P/G% approach differs from other decision-aiding approaches by virtue of being able to deal meaningfully with all of the following decision-making situations:

1. Multi-dimensional goals.
2. Choosing the one best alternative.
3. Choosing the best combination of alternatives.
4. Making choices where risks and probabilities are involved.
5. Making choices where doing too much or too little is undesirable.
6. Allocating scarce resources, even where there are millions of alternative ways of allocating a given budget to a set of budget categories.
7. Situations with multiple missing information.
8. Situations involving public policy, law, business, medicine, or personal decision-making.
9. Situations where all the goals are measured on the same dimension.
10. Situations involving prediction as well as prescription.
11. Minimums or maximums on the alternatives, goals or other constraints.

The approach also differs from other approaches by virtue of having the following characteristics:

1. P/G% can easily go from alternatives, goals, and relations to drawing a conclusion.
2. It has been translated into a highly user-friendly microcomputer program.
3. It is based on mathematical justifications that relate to classical calculus optimization, especially if one views the part/whole percentages as proxies for non-linear regression coefficients.
4. It comes with lots of illustrative applications and years of relevant experience.
5. It is analogous to mathematical programming procedures such as linear, non-linear, integer, goal, and multi-objective programming, but without the complexity and unrealistic assumptions.
6. The program can systematically compare optimum choices or allocations in order to bring the optimum closer to the actual and vice versa.

Along with the program, there are a variety of demonstration datafiles. They include applications from the fields of law, public policy, health care, and personal decision-making. They also include applications that involve predicting decisions as well as prescribing decisions. One can easily create new applications by inserting a set of tentative alternatives, goals, and relations for various problems.

CHOOSING TO GET MARRIED

Table A applies the methodology to an especially simple example. The example is simple in the sense that (1) there are only two alternatives and two goals, (2) both goals are measured on the same 0-10 scale, (3) both goals are tentatively given equal weight, (4) there is no missing information on the relations, and (5) there are no constraints. The basic alternatives are to get married or to stay single. The basic goals are companionship and privacy.

On a 0-10 scale, getting married scores a 7 on companionship, but only a 3 on privacy in the eyes of the relevant decision-maker. On the other hand, staying single scores only 4 on companionship, but an 8 on privacy. If one gives equal weight to companionship and privacy, then the sum of 7 plus 3 on getting married adds to 10. The sum of 4 plus 8 on staying single adds to 12. Thus, staying single outscores getting married in the initial results by 2 points. There would be a tie if getting married could move up from a 7 to a 9 on companionship, or from a 3 to a 5 on privacy. Likewise, there would be a tie if staying single were considered only a 2 on companionship rather than a 4, or only worth a 6 on privacy rather than an 8.

The threshold analysis says that if companionship is given a weight of 1.67 then there will be a tie. It also says that if privacy is given a weight of .60 when companionship has a weight of 1, then there will be a tie. Thus, if companionship is only as valuable as privacy, then the decision maker should stay single. On the other hand, if companionship is worth at least twice as much as privacy, (rounding to the nearest whole number), then he or she is better off getting married in view of the goals to be achieved, the alternatives available, and the relations between the alternatives and the goals.

Even in this simple example, one can see that the computer program can be helpful in various ways such as (1) organizing one's ideas in terms of alternatives, goals, and relations, (2) scoring the relations so as to provide consistency on each goal, (3) enabling one to see quickly the summation score for each alternative, (4) revealing the threshold value for each relation and each weight, and (5) enabling the user to make changes in the relations and weights to see how sensitive the initial conclusion is to input changes.

TABLE A. DECIDING WHETHER TO GET MARRIED

Goals / Alternatives	Companionship	Privacy	Sum of Raw Scores
Getting Married	7 (9)	3 (5)	10
Stay Single	4 (2)	8 (6)	12
Weights	1.00 (1.67)	1.00 (.60)	

Notes:

1. The numbers not in parentheses are raw scores on a 0-10 scale for companionship and a 0-10 scale for privacy.
2. The initial weights are 1.00 for both goals.
3. The numbers in parentheses are the threshold values which will cause getting married to be of equal satisfaction with staying single. They each involve adding or subtracting 2 from the raw scores since 2 is the threshold difference when summing the raw scores for both alternatives.
4. Since it may be difficult to improve on the companionship and privacy of getting married by 2 points, and it may be difficult to recalculate companionship and privacy on staying single by 2 points, the program reduces to whether the weight of companionship is more than the weight of privacy or is only as much.
5. Getting married in this context could refer to a specific person or just to the abstract idea.

AN ALLOCATION EXAMPLE

Tables 1 through 6 clarify further what the program involves. Table 1 provides the raw data for the problem of choosing between trials and plea bargains as the better method of resolving criminal cases. Table 2 shows how the raw data is converted into weighted part/whole percentages in order to deal with the problem of the delay criterion being measured in years and the respect criterion being measured on a 0-10 attitude scale. Table 3 shows that the optimum allocation of cases is 70% to trials and 30% to pleas in light of the raw data and giving respect twice the importance of delay. Table 3 also shows the discrepancies between the optimum allocations and the actual allocations.

Table 4 shows how those optimum allocations would change if there were minimum and /or maximum constraints on the extent to which certain goals or alternatives have to be provided for. Table 5 shows what it would take in terms of changing the input relations and the goal-weights to enable plea bargaining to become the preferred alternative. Table 6 shows that the weights of the goals converge to the equivalent of infinitely large weights when the weights are only 2, given the other data in the example. Tables 5 and 6 are especially helpful in showing that many disputes over the size of relations and weights are unnecessary because all magnitudes above a threshold or convergence point produce virtually the same results.

The program can also perform a convergence analysis which is another form of sensitivity analysis. It involves determining how much weight a goal needs to be given in order for the allocations to be within 5 percentage points of what they would be if that were the only goal. For example, if respect were the only goal, then 75% of the cases would be allocated to trials and 25% to pleas. That effect is virtually achieved by just giving respect a weight of 2 when delay has a weight of -1 because the allocations then become 70% to trials and 30% to pleas. Likewise, when respect has a weight of 1, delay takes over if it is given a weight of 2 because the allocations then become 15% to trials and 85% to pleas. Those allocations are within 5 percentage points of the 20% and 80% that would prevail if delay were the only goal.

The program can also perform a residual analysis. Suppose, for example, the actual allocation to trials is 20% and 80% for pleas. That means there is a -50 residual for trials since the optimum is 70%, and a +50 residual for pleas since that optimum is 30%. Those residuals are helpful in indicating that the actual decision-makers and/or the researchers may be misperceiving relations or wrongly weighting goals. The program can also perform a constraint analysis. Suppose, for example, there is a constraint that says at least 10% of the cases must go to trial as a matter of basic fairness, and at least 50% must be settled through pleas in order to avoid the expense of trials. If the optimum is 70% and 30%, then the first constraint is satisfied. To satisfy the second constraint, 20 percentage points must be taken from the 70% and given to the 30%. That means the optimum constrained allocation is 50% and 50%.

IMPROVEMENT FOR SPREADSHEETS

The program has the potential for out-performing spreadsheet programs like Lotus 1-2-3. Lotus does "what-if" analysis whereby one asks what would be the effect of a cell change on a row total, column total or grand total. That is highly cumbersome if one has 100 cells (as one does with a 10 x 10 matrix), and each cell is reasonably capable of taking five different values. P/G% analysis instantly tells the user the threshold values for all 100 cells. For example, if the cell on row 4, column 6 has a threshold value of 89, that means any number greater than 89 will result in alternative 5 being the winner, and any number less than 89 will result in alternative 7 being the winner. One thus does not have to experiment with what would happen with a score of 95, 117, 43, or 11.

P/G% is also specifically geared toward aiding in making decisions, whereas Lotus 1-2-3 amounts to little more than a combination of columnar paper and a calculator. P/G% can be used by housewives and others on home computers, not just by business people. It can be used where columns are measured on different dimensions and with different constraints and conditions. It is both prescriptive and predictive. It clearly goes beyond spreadsheet analysis in the next generation of useful computer software.

RELATIONS TO ARTIFICIAL INTELLIGENCE

The P/G% program involves a deductive reasoning process whereby a computer deduces a prescriptive conclusion from premises that relate to goals to be achieved, alternatives for achieving them, and relations between goals and alternatives. There is, however, more intelligence on the part of the program user in deciding on the goals, the available alternatives, and the relations. The P/G% program also involves deductive reasoning in indicating the threshold or tie-causing values for each input item. That in effect involves solving an algebra problem to calculate each threshold value. There is, however, also probably more intelligence on the part of the program user in deciding how to use the information provided, such as whether to accept the best alternative or a combination, and whether to consider the best alternative as firmly the best or as being highly vulnerable.

LIMITATIONS

A limitation which the program currently has is the requirement that one have access to an IBM-compatible microcomputer with 192K of memory and a graphics adapter. The program is, however, being developed for running on other microcomputers. A body of experience is also being developed which will be incorporated into a booklength manual consisting mainly of various applications entitled Better Decision-Making: Relating Options to Goals. Those applications are also leading to further improvements in the versatility of the program. The program is mainly limited by the fact that the real world involves multi-dimensional goals, missing information, complex constraints, and other problems, but the program seeks to handle those problems as well as can be done.

RELATED LITERATURE

This program is related to the field of multi-criteria decision-making. That field includes such literature as Edwards and Newman (1982), Saaty (1980), and Zeleny (1982). In comparison to those methods, the P/G% program is both simpler to use and more realistic in its procedures. The program is also related to spreadsheet analysis, but it is more focused on evaluating alternatives and informing the user as to what changes will make a difference as well as what differences they will make. See Henderson (1983).

FURTHER INFORMATION

For further information concerning this multi-criteria decision-aiding tool, write or phone Stuart Nagel, 361 Lincoln Hall, University of Illinois, Urbana, Illinois, 61801, (217) 359-8541. The microcomputer program is based on Nagel (1984). A copy of the program, the present manual, and the periodic updates can be obtained for experimental purposes for only $20 to cover the cost of a floppy disk, photocopying, postage, and handling. A copy of the current manuscript for the relevant book entitled Better Decision Making: Relating Options to Goals is also available for an additional $15.

REFERENCES

EDWARDS, W. and R. NEWMAN (1982) Multi-Attribute Evaluation. Beverly Hills, Calif.: Sage Publications

HENDERSON, T. (1983) Spreadsheet Software: From VisiCalc to 1-2-3. Indianapolis: Que.

NAGEL, S. (1984) "Multiple Goals and Multiple Policies". Public Policy: Goals, Means, and Methods New York: St. Martin's.

SAATY, T. (1980) The Analytic Hierarchy Process: Planning, Priority Setting, Resource Allocation. New York: McGraw-Hill.

ZELENY, M. (1982) Multiple Criteria Decision Making. New York: McGraw-Hill.

ILLUSTRATIVE DISPLAYS

TABLE 1. RAW DATA FOR CHOOSING BETWEEN TWO POLICY ALTERNATIVES

ALTERNATIVE / CRITERIA SCORING

	delay	respect
trials	120.00	6.00
pleas	30.00	2.00

NOTES:

1. Trials does better on respect than pleas with a score of 6 versus 2 on a 0-10 attitude scale. Pleas does better on delay than trials with a score of 30 days versus 120 days.
2. One cannot simply add -120 to +6 to obtain an overall score for trials to compare with -30 added to +2 to obtain an overall score for pleas.
3. One can, however, note that trials receives 75% of the sum of the 6 plus 2 scores on respect, and pleas receives only 25%. On the other hand, trials receives 80% of the 120 plus 30 scores on delay, whereas pleas receives only 20%.
4. One can more meaningfully add and subtract such part/whole percentages than one can add and subtract the raw scores, especially if one indicates how much more valuable a 1% increase is worth on one criterion versus another.
5. Thus, pleas is a better alternative than trials since it has a higher net part/whole percentage of plus +5% as compared to the -5% of trials. Trials, however, is a better alternative if respect is considered at least twice as important as delay.
6. Part/whole percentaging is thus a useful tool for dealing with the problem of delay, respect, or other goals being measured on two or more different dimensions.

TABLE 2. TRANSFORMED DATA FOR DEALING WITH MULTIDIMENSIONAL GOALS

WEIGHTED PART / WHOLE %

	delay	respect
trials	-80.00	150.00
pleas	-20.00	50.00

NOTES:

1. The above table converts the raw scores of Table 1 into weighted part/whole percentages.

2. The original raw scores on delay were 120 and 30. They convert into part/whole percentages equal to 120/150 or 80%, and to 30/150 or 20%. Those p/w%'s are then multiplied by the weight of -1 for delay yielding -80% and -20%. The original raw scores on respect were 6 and 2. They convert into p/w%'s equal to 6/8 or 75%, and to 2/8 or 25%. Those p/w%'s are then multiplied by the weight of 2 for respect yielding 150% and 50%.

3. Adding -80% to 150% gives an allocation percentage of 70%. Adding -20% to 50% gives an allocation percentage of 30%. This indicates that with the raw data from Table 1, and respect having twice the weight of delay, then the optimum allocation of cases between trials and pleas is 70% trials and 30% pleas.

4. Part/whole percentaging is thus a useful tool for dealing with the problem of multiple alternatives. There are at least 101 alternative ways cases could be allocated to trials and pleas. One could give 100% to trials and 0% to pleas, 99% to trials and 1% to pleas, and so on to 0% to trials and 100% to pleas. There are an infinite number of alternatives if one deals with the decimal percentages and not just integer percentages. Part/whole percentaging, however, makes the allocation process quite simple and meaningful, even though the number of alternatives is indefinite.

TABLE 3. INITIAL RESULTS AND HOW THEY DIFFER FROM PREVAILING PRACTICE

Total Resources = 100.00

Alternative	Actual	Alloc.	Resi(
1trials	20.00	70.00	-50.0(
2pleas	80.00	30.00	50.0(

NOTES:

1. Table 3 shows that the optimum allocation is 70% of the cases to trials and 30% of the cases to pleas, given the relations of Table 1 and the weights of Table 2.

2. In addition to showing those primary results, Table 3 also shows that about 20% or less of all cases actually go to trial, and about 80% or more of all cases are settled through plea bargains.

3. Thus trials are operating 50 percentage points below their optimum, and pleas are operating 50 percentage points above their optimum.

4. Knowing those residuals, or the difference between the actuals and the optimums is helpful in determining how the actuals can be improved and/or in determining how the optimums possibly need redefining.

5. This kind of primary results leads one to experimenting with adding, subtracting, or otherwise changing the alternatives, criteria, relations, measurement units, or weights in order to decrease the residuals between the actual scores and the optimum scores, or to find better alternatives.

TABLE 5. THRESHOLD VALUES NEEDED TO BRING THE SECOND-PLACE ALTERNATIVE UP TO FIRST PLACE

THRESHOLD ANALYSIS

	delay	respect
trial	????	3.71
pleas	0.00	3.23
Weight	-1.667	1.200

NOTES:

1. The above threshold analysis indicates what the original scores have to change to in order to bring the second place alternative up to a tie with the first place alternative.

2. The original scores are 120 days and 30 days on delay for trials and pleas, 6 and 2 on respect for trials and pleas, and a weight of 2 for the relative value of respect over delay. With the original analysis, trials gets a score of 70 and pleas gets a score of 30 in terms of the weighted part/whole percentages, as is shown in Table 2.

3. The threshold analysis says that the scores will become 50 and 50 if trials goes down to 3.71 on respect or pleas goes up to 3.23. The analysis also says that there is no quantity of delay to which trials can increase which will generate a tie so long as respect is twice as important as delay and given the other numbers. The analysis also says that if pleas can go down to zero days from arrest to disposition, then there will be an overall tie.

4. The most useful part of most threshold analyses is the threshold weights since the weights are more subjective than the relations between the alternatives and the criteria. This analysis says that if the relative weight of respect goes down from 2 to 1.2, there will be a tie. Likewise, if the weight of delay goes up from 1 to 1.667, there will be a tie

5. Any one of those six threshold values can be tested by inserting any one of the threshold relations back into the relations table (see Table 1) and asking for the new results, or by inserting any one of the threshold weights.

6. Threshold analysis is thus a useful tool for dealing with the problem of missing information in making decisions. It tells us that if we are concerned with what it would take to bring the second-place alternative up to the level of the first-place alternative, then we should not bother trying to determine the exact score of trial delay because no change on that score will bring pleas up to first place. Likewise, we need not be concerned if we cannot decide whether the trial respect score is 4, 5, 7, or 9, since any figure above 3.71 will make trials a winner. In other words, if any of the six inputs are missing or unclear, the only clarity we need to provide is whether the input is above or below its threshold value.

Artificial Intelligence in Economics and Management
L.F. Pau (Editor)

DYNAMIC POLICY GAMES AND THE GAINS FROM COOPERATION IN INTERDEPENDENT ECONOMIES: AN EXAMPLE FROM US-EEC POLICY MAKING

A.J. Hughes Hallett

Department of Economics
University of Newcastle
Newcastle-upon-Tyne
England

The economic recessions since 1973 have emphasised the interdependence of the major economies and their policy choices. This paper examines whether decentralised control of the world economy effectively limits our ability to steer individual economies. It is well known that noncooperative policies are Pareto inefficient; but there is, as yet, no empirical evidence on the costs of uncoordinated policies, nor on the potential gains from cooperation. In contrast to recent theoretical work in the area, this paper uses an estimated multicountry model in a finite dynamic game framework to estimate those costs and benefits. Successful coordination depends on anticipations, and on timing the fiscal and monetary policy impacts. The gains are relatively small and favour Europe.

INTRODUCTION

One of the most difficult problems of economic policy is being able to anticipate the actions of other decision makers who can affect the course of the economy. One area where this kind of policy interaction has become particularly important is in designing policies for the industrialised countries. The average OECD country now exports about 30% of its GNP, so the policy "spillover" effects from one country to another (and back again) can be very powerful. In such a world rational policy makers must condition their decisions on the policies expected abroad, and they must expect that foreign policy makers will make their decisions on the same basis. Policy selection therefore inevitably takes the form of a dynamic game. The recessions since 1974, and the subsequent debt crisis, have made policy makers acutely aware of the links between their economies and that trade and capital movements increase the interdependence of their policy choices. How should policies be designed under these circumstances, and would internationally coordinated policies lead to better results?

This paper is directly concerned with artificial intelligence in that it shows how a decision maker can develop a model which anticipates rational decisions by other decision makers and then incorporate those anticipations into his own optimal policy selections. Decisions of that type can be used as a benchmark to contrast the losses from decisions which ignore interdependence (i.e. where there is no artificial intelligence) and the gains from explicitly cooperative decisions (i.e. where there is intelligence, but it is no longer artificial). These techniques are used here to compute policies for the US and EEC economies following the 1973 oil price shock using a working econometric model. This is in contrast to previous studies which have used static decision procedures and/or simple analytic models of identically symmetric economies (e.g. Canzoneri and Gray (1985), Oudiz and Sachs (1984), Miller and Salmon (1985)).

OPTIMAL NONCOOPERATIVE DECISIONS

Consider the policy problem facing sovereign governments in two trading economies. Each economy has m_i domestic targets, $y_t^{(i)}$, n_i policy instruments, $x_t^{(i)}$, and is subject to noncontrollable (random) events $s_t^{(i)}$. Consider a finite number of decision periods, t=1...T. The policy variables are $y^{(i)'} = (y_1^{(i)'} \dots y_T^{(i)'})$ and $x^{(i)'}=(x_1^{(i)'} \dots x_T^{(i)'})$ for i=1,2, while $s^{(i)'}= (s_1^{(i)'} \dots s_T^{(i)'})$ represent external shocks. Suppose each economy aims for the ideal values $y^{(i)d}$ and $x^{(i)d}$, so that $\tilde{y}^{(i)}=y^{(i)}-y^{(i)d}$ and $\tilde{x}^{(i)}=x^{(i)}-x^{(i)d}$ define its decision "failures". The objectives of each country can be represented by the loss functions:

$$w^{(i)} = \tfrac{1}{2}[\tilde{y}^{(i)'}B^{(i)}\tilde{y}^{(i)}+\tilde{x}^{(i)'}A^{(i)}\tilde{x}^{(i)}] \qquad i=1,2 \qquad (1)$$

where $B^{(i)}$ and $A^{(i)}$ are positive definite and symmetric matrices. Suppose also that the economies are linked through a dynamic "world" economy

$$y_t = f(y_t,\ y_{t-1},\ x_t^{(1)},\ x_t^{(2)},\ e_t) \qquad (2)$$

where e_t represents any noncontrollable variables. The constraints on the targets in each loss function can be condensed to

$$y^{(i)} = R^{(i,1)}x^{(1)} + R^{(i,2)}x^{(2)} + s^{(i)} \qquad i=1,2 \qquad (3)$$

where $R^{(i,j)}$, j=1,2, are $(m_iT \times n_jT)$ matrices containing submatrices of dynamic multipliers $R_{tk}^{(i,j)} = \partial y_t^{(i)}/\partial x_k^{(j)}$ if $t \geq k$, and zeros elsewhere. Thus $R^{(i,i)}$ measures the responses of country i's targets to its own instruments, and $R^{(i,j)}$ the "spillover" effects from country j's decisions. In practice these multiplier matrices will be evaluated numerically along suitable reference paths, or projections, for $x_t^{(1)}$, $x_t^{(2)}$ and e_t.

Each policy maker will find his own variables constrained by

$$\tilde{y}^{(i)} = R^{(i,i)}\tilde{x}^{(i)} + b^{(i)} \qquad i=1,2 \qquad (4)$$

The vector $b^{(i)} = R^{(i,j)}\tilde{x}^{(j)}+c^{(i)}$, where $c^{(i)} = s^{(i)}-y^{(i)d}+\Sigma_j R^{(i,j)}x^{(j)d}$, defines the information needed by country i in order to make its decision. Each country's optimal strategy therefore depends on, and must be determined simultaneously with, the decisions to be expected abroad. In the absence of cooperation, the optimal decisions $(x^{(1)*},\ x^{(2)*})$ will satisfy $w^{(i)}(x^{(i)*},x^{(j)*}) \leq w^{(i)}(x^{(i)},x^{(j)*})$ for i=1 and 2 and all feasible $x^{(i)} \neq x^{(i)*}$. This equilibrium holds only when both countries perceive that no further gains can be made by varying their reactions to the decisions currently expected from their rival, because to do so would trigger counter-reactions (in the rival's interest) which eliminate any gains made by the first country. However rational decision makers will adjust their reactions whenever they can make gains which would not be completely offset by foreign responses; but they must also expect their rivals to exploit any such opportunities in the same way. Thus, in addition to being conditioned on expected foreign actions, the decision rule for $x^{(1)}$ must allow for the (conjectured) foreign responses, $\partial x^{(2)}/\partial x^{(1)}$, which any changes in $x^{(1)}$ would induce. Then that decision rule must be solved simultaneously with the corresponding rule for $x^{(2)}$, so that the conjectured responses and the decision values are all mutually dependent. Hence the necessary conditions for jointly optimal decisions are:

$$\partial w^{(i)}/\partial x^{(i)}+[(\partial y^{(i)}/\partial x^{(j)})\partial x^{(j)}/\partial x^{(i)}+\partial y^{(i)}/\partial x^{(i)}]'\,\partial w^{(i)}/\partial y^{(i)} = 0 \qquad (5)$$

for i=1 and 2. Unlike conventional solutions which optimise conditional on fixed reactions by the opponent ("if he does that, what should I do?"), the conjectures allow for the opponent's anticipated responses ("if I do this, how will he react and how should I counter that, ... etc.?"). Policy makers evidently expect conjectures to play a role. The OECD, for instance, argues that a "locomotive" policy regime implies positive spillovers and that those spillovers release the balance of payments constraints so that governments will, in anticipation, support higher demand levels than otherwise (OECD Outlook, 23, v-xv).

Excepting the conjectured responses, $\partial x^{(j)}/\partial x^{(i)} - D^{(i)}$, all the partial derivatives required to evaluate (6) are given by (1) and (4). If $D^{(j)}$ were known for j=1 and 2, we could solve (5) to obtain

$$\begin{bmatrix} \tilde{x}^{(1)*} \\ \tilde{x}^{(2)*} \end{bmatrix} = -\begin{bmatrix} G^{(1)'}B^{(1)}R^{(1,1)}+A^{(1)} & G^{(1)'}B^{(1)}R^{(1,2)} \\ G^{(2)'}B^{(2)}R^{(2,1)} & G^{(2)'}B^{(2)}R^{(2,2)}+A^{(2)} \end{bmatrix}^{-1} \begin{bmatrix} G^{(1)'}B^{(1)}c^{(1)} \\ G^{(2)'}B^{(2)}c^{(2)} \end{bmatrix} \quad (6)$$

where $G^{(i)}=R^{(i,i)}+R^{(i,j)}D^{(j)}$. If $D^{(1)}$ and $D^{(2)}$ are unknown then inserting trial values $(D_s^{(1)}, D_s^{(2)})$ into (5) automatically generates the iterations:

$$\begin{bmatrix} I & -D_{s+1}^{(1)} \\ -D_{s+1}^{(2)} & I \end{bmatrix} \begin{bmatrix} \tilde{x}_{s+1}^{(1)} \\ \tilde{x}_{s+1}^{(2)} \end{bmatrix} = \begin{bmatrix} F_{s+1}^{(1)}c^{(1)} \\ F_{s+1}^{(2)}c^{(2)} \end{bmatrix} \quad (7)$$

where $F_{s+1}^{(i)} = -(G_s^{(i)'}B^{(i)}R^{(i,i)}+A^{(i)})^{-1}G_s^{(i)'}B^{(i)}$ with $G_s^{(i)}=R^{(i,i)}+R^{(i,j)}D_s^{(j)}$, and where

$$D_{s+1}^{(i)} = F_{s+1}^{(i)} R^{(i,j)} \neq D_s^{(i)}. \qquad i=1,2 \text{ and } j\neq i \quad (8)$$

An equilibrium $(D_*^{(1)}, D_*^{(2)})$ and $(x^{(1)*}, x^{(2)*})$ exists for (7) since a zero conjectures (open loop Nash) solution exists for every nonzero sum game with convex objectives and strategy sets (Aubin (1979)). If that solution exists, then one also exists for this conjectural equilibrium provided the latter is used only when it implies objective function values which are better for one or both of the players. To do that we can modify (8) by replacing $D_{s+1}^{(i)}$ with $\gamma_i D_{s+1}^{(i)}+(1-\gamma_i)D_s^{(i)}$, where $0\leq\gamma_i\leq 1$ is chosen (at each step) to force $x_{s+1}^{(1)}$ and $x_{s+1}^{(2)}$ "downhill" (i.e. such that $w^{(i)}(\tilde{x}_{s+1}^{(1)},\tilde{x}_{s+1}^{(2)}) \leq w^{(i)}(\tilde{x}_s^{(1)}, \tilde{x}_s^{(2)})$ for i=1 and 2). That implies a search among those conjectural variations which still offer improvements at each stage, and an exhaustive search will ultimately identify $(x^{(1)*}, x^{(2)*})$.

Hence the existence and uniqueness of this equilibrium must be distinguished from the question of whether (8) converges to a unique solution. In general (8) will yield many solutions, and in order to satisfy the joint minimum defined following (4) we must pick that solution which gives the best objective function values for both countries simultaneously. Another justification for the "downhill" property is that it is only sensible to vary one's conjectures in a way that is Pareto improving for both players, since otherwise they simply will not react in the way conjectured. One cannot expect other countries to adjust their reponses unilaterally against their own interests, since that would involve making inter-country comparisons. Finally, (8) is introduced to eliminate inconsistencies between the conjectured responses, $D_s^{(j)}$, and the associated reactions, $D_{s+1}^{(j)}$, induced by rational decision making. Basar (1985) shows that that kind of consistency with real valued policy reactions may not always be possible. Nevertheless, the "downhill" property will continue to eliminate surprises, and any incentive to deviate unilaterally, by picking the best of the real valued solutions without resolving any externalities or making inter-country comparisons.

Country i may now eliminate $\tilde{x}_{s+1}^{(j)}$ from (7) by inverting the partitioned matrix and rearranging terms. In fact the optimal decisions generated by a downhill search yielding $(D_*^{(1)}, D_*^{(2)})$ equal those from the two single player problems: minimise

$w^{(i)}$ subject to

$$\tilde{y}^{(i)} = [R^{(i,i)} + R^{(i,j)}D_*^{(j)}]\tilde{x}^{(i)} + d_*^{(i)} \qquad i=1,2 \qquad (9)$$

where $d_*^{(i)} = c^{(i)} + R^{(i,j)}F_*^{(j)}c^{(j)}$ and $F_*^{(j)}$ is defined by (7) but evaluated using $D_*^{(j)}$; Hughes Hallett (1984). Hence, applying certainty equivalence,

$$\tilde{x}^{(i)*} = -[G_*^{(i)'}B^{(i)}G_*^{(i)} + A^{(i)}]^{-1}G_*^{(i)'}B^{(i)}E_{1i}(d_*^{(i)}) \qquad (10)$$

for i=1,2 and $G_*^{(i)} = R^{(i,i)} + R^{(i,j)}D_*^{(j)}$, where $E_{ti}(\cdot) = E(\cdot|\Omega_{ti})$ denotes an expectation conditional on country i's information at t. These decisions would subsequently be revised by reoptimising them conditional on later information sets (for t=2...T, and i=1 or 2). The computed decisions are therefore always conditioned on a single information set representing either one or the other government's view of the past and future at a given moment.

Three characteristics of these decisions should be mentioned. First, they encompass most standard decision rules because each player anticipates his opponent's reactions, and plans counterreactions assuming that the opponent will be doing the same. In fact, open loop and feedback Nash or Stackelberg solutions are special cases in which $D^{(1)}$ and/or $D^{(2)}$ are restricted to certain preassigned values (Brandsma and Hughes Hallett (1984)). Second, (9) allows for the "noncausal" effects of anticipating the opponent's decisions and their outcomes; i.e. $\partial y_t^{(i)}/\partial x_{t+k}^{(i)} \neq 0$, for $k \geq 1$, since $D_*^{(j)}$ is not block triangular. Hence each decision in (10) reacts to responses conjectured for the future, as well as to contemporaneous responses and the consequences of responses conjectured for earlier periods. Third, reoptimisation with respect to $E_{ti}(w^{(i)})$ maintains optimal and time-consistent decisions (i.e. the revised decisions will be identical to those expected earlier if there is no change in the information sets). Time consistency holds because the optimisation is (a) not dependent on a time-recursive objective function structure, and (b) the reoptimisations using Ω_{ti}, $t \geq 2$, preserve the necessary Markov property for the forward steps of the revision process (Bellman (1961)).

COOPERATIVE DECISION MAKING

Noncooperative decisions are well known to be socially inefficient in the absence of side payments. Da Cuhna and Polak (1967), for example, showed that the entire set of nondominated (or Pareto efficient) decisions may be generated by minimising

$$w = \alpha w^{(1)} + (1-\alpha)w^{(2)} \qquad 0<\alpha<1 \qquad (11)$$

subject to (3). Hence, once a collective objective (or α value) is agreed, both countries could gain by solving this "world" planning problem. But whether those gains would be worthwhile compared to the loss of individual sovereignty, or the difficulty of reaching an agreement, is an issue for which evidence has yet to be produced. Moreover, cooperation may entail redistributing the policy gains in a way which agrees poorly with national priorities or with national bargaining power. It is therefore important to estimate the size and distribution of the gains from cooperation, compared to those of a noncooperative strategy, in order to say anything about the value and sustainability of cooperation in practice.

THE MODEL AND ITS ASYMMETRIC POLICY RESPONSES

The policy dependence between the US and EEC economies has been explored using a version of the COMET multi-country econometric model (Barten, d'Alcantara, Carrin (1976)). The COMET model is typical of the empirical models which are currently used for analysing economic interdependence. It describes the economies of the EEC countries, the US, the remaining OECD countries, OPEC, the Socialist and developing countries. The version used here contains the following changes: (a) aggregation into three economic blocks, to give a systematic specification across the US and EEC economies; (b) consistent accounts for the Rest of the World; (c) the introduction of financial sectors, international capital movements, and endogenous exchange rates.

The US and EEC blocks, some 200 equations in total, form the backbone of the model. The two real sectors have similar structures, based on a conventional Keynesian demand system covering consumption, investment, and foreign trade. Cobb-Douglas production functions determine labour demand and investment. The supply sides of both blocks are modelled by similarly specified potential output functions; potential and actual outputs are reconciled by a capacity utilisation index. In each sector prices are related to import prices and the GDP deflator. The GDP deflator, in its turn, depends on unit labour and capital costs and the utilisation index, while wages are a function of consumption prices, productivity, unemployment, taxes and social security contributions. Finally a rudimentary macro-system explains how revenues in the Rest of the World are devoted to increasing international reserves, lent to one of the other two regions, or spent on imports. The importance of having a rest of the world block is that one country's trade deficit is not automatically the other country's surplus. One can see if policy improvements are obtained at the expense of the remaining countries.

Each monetary sector describes the financial relations between the central bank, commercial banks, the government, the private sector, and the foreign sector. Private and government financial surpluses are the main input from the real sector. Interest rates, which in turn affect both real spending and international borrowing, are determined by those surpluses and by the behaviour of the banks.

Analysis of the model's dynamic properties showed that policy changes lead to quicker and stronger responses in the US than in the EEC. This stems from reactions of the real quantities to price and interest changes, which are both larger and faster in the US structural equations. The effects of these reactions then spread rapidly to other variables because the real and monetary sectors are more closely integrated. The consequences of greater market flexibility in the US show up in more powerful short run policy multipliers (which appear in the diagonal blocks of $R^{(i,i)}$), but less powerful longer run multipliers (which appear in the bottom left submatrices of $R^{(i,i)}$), compared to those for the EEC.

In our policy exercise the US and EEC are assumed to aim at the same targets, but with priorities which differ. These exercises seek policy improvements in response to the oil price rise of 1973, which was an unanticipated shock to both economies. The targets are assumed to be short term stabilisation objectives combined with indicators of the longer run supply position. The policy goals are set out in Table 1. The policy instruments have been selected from those actually used during the period. Social security premiums do not constitute an independent instrument since they are tied to the outlays in order to balance the social security budget. All instruments are treated here as discretionary adjustments to the historically chosen policies. The instruments are all expressed in terms of annual growth rates, except for the discount rate for which the multipliers were based on changes in levels.

TABLE 1: The Objectives of Economic Policy 1974-78

	US		EEC			
	Ideal	Priority	Ideal	Priority	Symbol	Units
Targets:						
Inflation	- 3%	4	- 3%	1	P	% annual growth
Output	3%	4	3%	4	C	% annual growth
Balance of trade	1%	1	1%	4	B	% of GNP
Employment	1½%	1	1½%	1	E	% of labour force
Investment ratio	3%	1	3%	1	IR	% of GNP
Profit ratio	3%	1	3%	1	PR	% of GNP
Instruments:						
Government expenditure	2%	1	4%	1	G	% annual growth
Social Security Outlays	15%	1	16%	1	S	% annual growth
Direct tax, households	10%	1	17%	1	TH	% annual growth
Direct tax, companies	9%	1	14%	1	TC	% annual growth
Discount rate	0.4%	1	-¼%	1	R	Level changes
Central bank loans	5%	1	19%	1	LC	% annual growth
Commercial bank loans	5%	1	19%	1	LB	% annual growth

Note: All variables are measured as deviations from their simulated historical paths based on the initial (1974) information set.

EMPIRICAL RESULTS

Table 2 presents instrument values (averaged over the period 1974-78) for the US and the EEC under three different strategies: (i) Isolationist policies which ignore interdependence (by (6) with $R^{(i,j)}=0$, $i\neq j$); (ii) Noncooperative policies, including anticipations effects, by (10); and (iii) Cooperative (Pareto efficient) decisions from minimising (11) subject to (3) and $\alpha=\frac{1}{2}$.

These three strategies represent the fundamental choice facing the policy makers at the start of the exercise; they can ignore interdependence, set their policies competitively, or pick an equitable compromise by cooperation. Hence all the decision values are computed using the initial (1974) information set.

TABLE 2: Mean Policy Adjustments under Isolationist, Optimal Noncooperative, and Cooperative Strategies (measured as deviations from the simulated historical values, and conditioned on the 1974 information set).

	Isolationist		Noncooperative		Cooperative ($\alpha=\frac{1}{2}$)	
	US	EEC	US	EEC	US	EEC
Instruments						
G	-.96	+.52	+.18	+.68	+.23	+1.01
S	-2.38	+.26	-1.11	+.13	-.61	+.32
TH	-.73	+.41	-.67	-.62	-.40	-.59
TC	-.44	-.03	-.23	-.10	-.14	-.06
R	-.21	-.81	-.49	-.51	-.43	-.15
LC	+.10	+.01	-.05	+.03	+.03	.00
LB	-.24	-.18	-.72	-.04	-.27	-.19
Targets (expected values)						
P	-1.6	-2.2	-2.2	-2.3	-2.3	-2.1
X	+1.9	+2.4	+2.3	+2.3	+2.7	+2.4
B	-2.1	-0.1	-0.5	+0.3	-0.2	+0.4
E	+0.9	+0.8	+1.2	+0.8	+1.2	+0.9
IR	+1.5	+3.8	+1.8	+3.3	+2.0	+3.7
PR	+1.2	+3.4	+1.5	+3.6	+1.3	+3.6

(i) Optimal policies ignoring interdependence:

Isolationist policies for the US call for a cut of 1% p.a. in government expenditures, and of 2½% p.a. in social security payments, while both quantities rise in the EEC. The US fiscal contraction is matched by tax cuts. These fiscal changes mainly affect the household sector in both the US and EEC; and the fact that social security cuts are more intensively used in the US is the product of real wage rigidity found in the US economy compared to the real disposable wage rigidity of the European economies (Branson and Rotemberg, 1980). Hence real wage flexibility is crucial for analysing not only an economy's responses to shocks from abroad, but also for determining what kind of policies are appropriate.

The monetary variables show that the change in European budgets is not financed by loans from the central banks (LC) and that the loans from commercial banks (LB) cause no extra money creation. The main European instrument, the discount rate (R), is lowered throughout the period. In the US, the dependence of budget financing on savings requires a more sophisticated strategy. First a lowering of the discount rate has to induce a fall in interest changes to stimulate economic activity. A rise of the discount rate is then used to acquire savings.

The basic position is therefore one of standard Keynesian deficit financing in Europe, to stimulate aggregate demand and output, with monetary control and falling interest rates to reduce inflation. Meanwhile policies which have come to be associated with "supply side" economics operate in the US; a reduction in government intervention, especially in social security outlays and taxes, is coupled with a tight monetary policy.

(ii) Optimal Noncooperative Strategies:

Here both economies experience rising government expenditures. The US social security cuts are halved, and in Europe they turn positive in 1975-1977. Once again tax cuts appear in both economies, although they are more variable than in the previous case. The US fiscal position is now broadly neutral with reduced, but more flexible, interest rates to offset any crowding out of the expansionary impulse. The EEC, on the other hand, switches to fiscal expansion with an accommodating monetary policy.

The changes in monetary policy are more complicated. A rise in European discount rates initially attracts American capital. The US then has to resort to reductions in the interest rate, which in turn leads to larger adjustments in both monetary and fiscal policy in Europe. Indeed Table 2 shows that the main changes here are in the monetary variables; the US follows a more restrictive supply policy but reduces interest rates, while the EEC now intervenes more actively both with loans and the discount rate.

Finally recognising interdependence has had a greater effect on the US policies than on the EEC policies. The US fiscal disengagement is halved while its monetary policy more than doubles in overall impact. Meanwhile monetary expansion is reduced in the EEC and fiscal neutrality becomes fiscal expansion. Thus policy interactions have led to some convergence in the national policies.

(iii) Optimal Cooperative Strategies:

Cooperation between the US and the EEC takes the optimal policies a step further towards convergence. Government expenditures rise rather faster in both economies, and the US social security cuts are halved once again. Tax cuts are still in evidence, although less prominent in the US. The activism of monetary policy has vanished - particularly the sharp restrictions of money supply and interest rates which appeared in the noncooperative solution. In fact both loans to the government and the discount rates now follow constant or steadily changing paths. This suggests that it may be important to coordinate the timing of monetary policies, and the gains to cooperation might be significant only when that is done.

Overall the cooperative policies call for reduced intervention in the US, and for more stable policies in both economies, compared to the noncooperative strategies. The induced stability provides the opportunity to follow more consistent aggregate demand policies in the EEC. In their turn, higher government expenditures in the EEC are beneficial for the American economy.

THE INCENTIVES TO COOPERATE

Table 2 also shows the average expected changes in the target variables compared to the values obtained by simulating the historical instrument choices. These expected changes are favourable for all variables in both economies, excepting the US balance of trade. However the EEC does relatively badly with the employment target, indicating that European unemployment will be hard to eliminate. Given recent history, it is interesting to note that the cooperative strategy is the only one which has succeeded in reducing both the vigour of monetary policy and the high US interest rates.

Overall the US targets improve as we move from the isolationist to the cooperative solution (especially for production, balance of trade, and investment), but the EEC targets are not much affected by the type of strategy. The gains from cooperation therefore take the form of smaller interventions and improved expected target outcomes in the US, while the EEC enjoys a reduction in intervention effort rather than improved target outcomes. Improvements in the US economy would enable the EEC to reach the same target values with less effort under cooperative policies - both because the favourable spillovers are enhanced and because the adverse spillovers are reduced. On the other hand, an improved EEC economy means that the US needs to intervene less strongly to start a recovery following the oil price shock, and cooperation permits the elimination of conflicts caused by the self-protective EEC measures present in the noncooperative strategies.

The objective function evaluations in table 3 show that the US has twice as much to gain as the EEC by playing noncooperative strategies (72% vs. 39%) whereas the subsequent gains from cooperation are smaller (9% vs. 33%) and favour the EEC by 3 to 1. The incentive for the US to enter a cooperative agreement is therefore not large, and that may be an important reason why the US has favoured a full exchange of information but without cooperative decision making (Feldstein (1983)).

TABLE 3: The Performance Indicators

Strategy	Isolationist	Noncooperative	Cooperative ($\alpha=\frac{1}{2}$)
US objectives: w^*_{US}	188.9	52.2	47.5
EEC objectives: w^*_{EEC}	66.9	40.7	27.2

Note: The simulated historical policies yielded objective function values of 233.1 and 173.1 for the US and EEC respectively.

The incentives to cooperate can be illustrated in a way which is not dependent on comparisons with one particular cooperative solution. The set of socially efficient solutions is generated by minimising $w = \alpha w_{US} + (1-\alpha)w_{EEC}$ for all values of $\alpha\varepsilon[0,1]$. The national objective function values, w_{US} and w_{EEC}, which are implied by that set of solutions are plotted in Figure 1, together with the optimal non-cooperative outcome N. The shaded segment of LL' represents the only set of cooperative solutions which dominate non-cooperation, so that the distances marked BN and AN indicate the maximum gains each country could make before triggering noncooperative reactions from abroad. In this case, AN=11.25

and BN=15.5. If we compute the annual rate of GNP growth, all other variables unchanged, which would yield the same objective function gains, we find that cooperation is "worth" at most an extra 1.1% extra annual GNP growth in the US and 1.5% in the EEC. Therefore none of the dominant cooperative solutions offer very large incentives to cooperate. Moreover, in contrast to the policy improvements from anticipating foreign policy changes in a noncooperative framework, the gains from cooperation always favour the EEC.

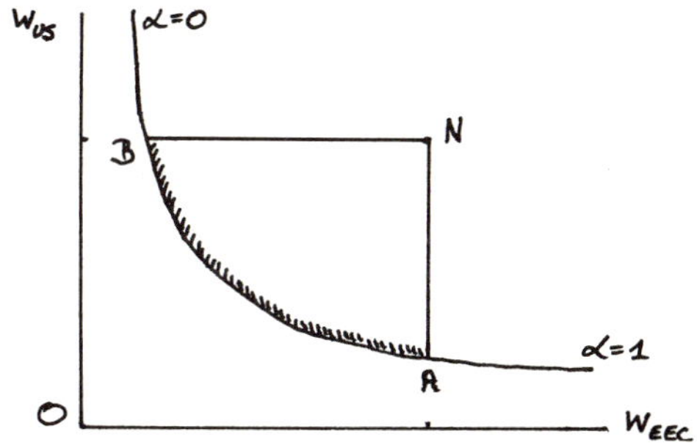

Figure 1: The Gains from Cooperation between the US and EEC

CONCLUSIONS

. Interdependence affects policy design significantly, and in an asymmetric way. Here the US can make greater gains by competitive decision making, while the EEC gains move from cooperative policies.

. Cooperation leads to some harmonisation of national policies, but not to the extent that both countries adopt parallel strategies.

. The US economy should act as a locomotive for economic recovery. International cooperation then allows recovery to be achieved with less effort.

REFERENCES

[1] Aubin, J.P. "Mathematical Methods of Game and Economic Theory", (North Holland, Amsterdam, 1979).

[2] Basar, T. "A Tutorial on Dynamic and Differential Games", paper presented to the Society for Economic Dynamics and Control, London, June 1985, (Coordinated Science Laboratory, University of Illinois, Champaign, Ill., 1985).

[3] Bellman, R. "Adaptive Control Processes: a guided tour" (Princeton University Press, Princeton, N.J., 1961).

[4] Brandsma, A.S. and Hughes Hallett, A.J. "Economic Conflict and the Solution of Dynamic Games" European Economic Review, 26 (1984), 13-32.

[5] Branson, W.H. and Rotemberg, J. "International Adjustments with Wage Rigidity" European Economic Review, 13 (1980), 309-32.

[6] Canzoneri, M. and Gray, J.A. "Monetary Policy Games and the Consequences of Noncooperative Behaviour" International Economic Review (forthcoming, 1985).

[7] Da Cuhna, N. and Polak, E. "Constrained Minimisation of Vector-Valued Criteria in Finite Dimensional Spaces", Journal of Mathematical Analysis and Applications, 19 (1967), 103-24.

[8] Feldstein, M. "The World Economy Today", Economist, June 11, 1983.

[9] Hughes Hallett, A.J. "Noncooperative Strategies for Dynamic Policy Games and the Problem of Time Inconsistency", Oxford Economic Papers, 36 (1984), 381-99.

[10] Miller, M. and Salmon, M. "Policy Coordination and the Time Inconsistency of Optimal Policy in Open Economies", Economic Journal (supplement, 1985).

[11] Oudiz, G. and Sachs, J. "Policy Coordination in Industrialised Countries", Brookings Economic Papers, 1 (1984), 1-64.

Artificial Intelligence in Economics and Management
L.F. Pau (Editor)

MULTIOBJECTIVE DECISION METHOD USING HEURISTIC RULES

Nakaji HONDA and Tadashi MIMAKI

Department of Communication Systems
University of Electro-Communication
Chofu-shi, Tokyo 182, JAPAN

This paper proposes a multiobjective decision method employing a production system. Some heuristic rules included in the production system are derived from a decision maker as his policy, so that these can reduce his burden of judgement in the process of obtaining a solution in multiobjective decision problem. The method can effectively be applied to solve the problem formulated by nonlinear programming, using successive linear programming. The efficiency of the method is tested in the practical example of a multiobjective decision problem.

INTRODUCTION

Multiobjective optimization (MOO) - optimization problem with multiple objective functions - is important problem to be solved in the fields of large system planning, design, management and so on (Cochrane (1973), Carlsson (1983)), which is generally formulated in the form of mathematical programming, especially nonlinear programming (NLP). In many cases, the solution of it is not unique and a set of the candidates of the solution is obtained.

To solve the MOO problem, various multiobjective decision (MOD) methods have recently be developed, e.g., Surrogate Worth Tradoff (SWT) method (Haimes (1975)), Interactive Frank-Wolf (IFW) method (Geoffrion (1972)), etc.. In these methods, the candidates of solution are obtained by using NLP method, from which a preferred solution is chosen by the decision maker (DM) through the interaction with the computer based on his judgement. Therefore, the appropriateness of the final solution might strongly depend on the DM's judgement, that is, his preference. Consequently, if the consistency of the DM's judgement through the iterative process of the interaction can not be maintained due to his arbitrariness, the reliability of the final solution might be poor.

To overcome the forementioned difficulty, a new multiobjective decision method is proposed, wherein the numerical processing is combined with the symbolic processing, with the result that the fluctuation of the decision process due to the DM' arbitrariness is minimized. In other words, some heuristic rules having the form of production system - one of artificial intelligence methodologies (Newell (1972)) - are introduced into the process of choosing a preferred solution from the candidates so as to dispense with some of the DM's judgements. These rules reduce the physical and psychological burden of the DM, because the number of DM's judgements decreases. Moreover, successive linear programming (SLP) (Palacios (1982)) is also employed in this method, whereby the MOO problem in the form of NLP can effectively be solved by linearizing the problem. Finally, in the course of choosing a preferred solution by the DM, the graphical representation of the candidates is used, so that the DM can easily make his judgement.

The second section of this paper deals with the mathematical formulation and algorithm of the proposed method. In the third section, the method is applied to a practical example of housing problem to show the efficiency of the method.

PROPOSED METHOD OF MULTIOBJECTIVE DECISION PROBLEM

Formulation by Using Successive Linear Programming

Multiobjective optimization (MOO) problem is defined as a problem of finding solution $\hat{\mathbf{x}}$ which optimizes a vector objective function $\mathbf{f}(\mathbf{x})$ as follows,

$$\min_{\hat{\mathbf{x}}} [f_1(x), - - , f_n(\mathbf{x})] = \min_{\hat{\mathbf{x}}} \mathbf{f}(\mathbf{x}), \tag{1}$$

$$\text{subject to } \mathbf{g}(\mathbf{x}) \leq \mathbf{0}, \tag{2}$$

where $\mathbf{x}$ is decision variable and $\mathbf{g}(\mathbf{x})$ is constraint. The solution $\hat{\mathbf{x}}$ is obtained in the form of a set, namely, noninferior solution set X_n. Further, multiobjective decision (MOD) problem involving the above MOO problem is also defined to obtain a preferred solution $\mathbf{x}_p$ by assuming a preference function Φ as follows,

$$\min_{\mathbf{x}_p} \Phi [\mathbf{f}(\hat{x})], \tag{3}$$

$$\text{subject to } \mathbf{f}(\hat{\mathbf{x}}) = \min_{\mathbf{x}} \mathbf{f}(\mathbf{x}), \tag{4}$$

$$\text{subject to } \mathbf{g}(\mathbf{x}) \leq \mathbf{0}, \tag{5}$$

where Φ denotes DM's preference characteristics and is not explicitly given as a functional form. In the MOD problem, a preferred solution $\mathbf{x}_p$ is chosen from a solution set X_n which is obtained from Eqs.(4) and (5), based on DM's preference through interaction of the DM with computer without using any numerical functional form.

On the other hand, nonlinear programming (NLP) with objective function $h(\mathbf{x},\mathbf{y})$ can be generally formulated as follows,

$$\min_{\mathbf{x},\mathbf{y}} h(\mathbf{x},\mathbf{y}) = \min_{\mathbf{x},\mathbf{y}} [p(\mathbf{x}) + \mathbf{a}_0\mathbf{y}], \tag{6}$$

$$\text{subject to } \mathbf{w}(\mathbf{x}) + \mathbf{A}_1\mathbf{y} = \mathbf{b}_1, \tag{7}$$

$$\mathbf{A}_2\mathbf{x} + \mathbf{A}_3\mathbf{y} = \mathbf{b}_2, \tag{8}$$

$$\mathbf{l}_1 \leq \mathbf{x} \leq \mathbf{u}_1 \ , \ \mathbf{l}_2 \leq \mathbf{y} \leq \mathbf{u}_2, \tag{9}$$

where $\mathbf{x}$ and $\mathbf{y}$ are n_1- and n_2-dimensional variables for nonlinear and linear parts of the objective function, respectively, and Eqs.(7), (8) and (9) are constraints. $p(\mathbf{x})$ and $\mathbf{w}(\mathbf{x})$ are nonlinear portions of objective function and constraints, respectively, and $\mathbf{A}_1$, $\mathbf{A}_2$ and $\mathbf{A}_3$ are matrices. $\mathbf{l}_1$ and $\mathbf{l}_2$ are the lower limit values of $\mathbf{x}$ and $\mathbf{y}$, respectively, and $\mathbf{u}_1$ and $\mathbf{u}_2$ the upper limits. $\mathbf{w}(\mathbf{x})$ and $p(\mathbf{x})$ can be approximated by means of Taylor expansion around an arbitary point $\bar{\mathbf{x}}$ as follows,

$$\mathbf{w}(\mathbf{x}) = \mathbf{w}(\bar{\mathbf{x}}) + J(\bar{\mathbf{x}})\mathbf{d}, \tag{10}$$

and

$$p(\mathbf{x}) = p(\bar{\mathbf{x}}) + \nabla_p(\bar{\mathbf{x}})\mathbf{d}, \tag{11}$$

where $J(\mathbf{x})$ denotes Jacobian of $\mathbf{w}(\mathbf{x})$, i.e., $J(\mathbf{x}) = (\partial w_i/\partial x_i)$, and $\mathbf{d} = \mathbf{x}-\bar{\mathbf{x}}$. Using Eqs.(10) and (11), NLP of Eqs.(6) - (9) can be

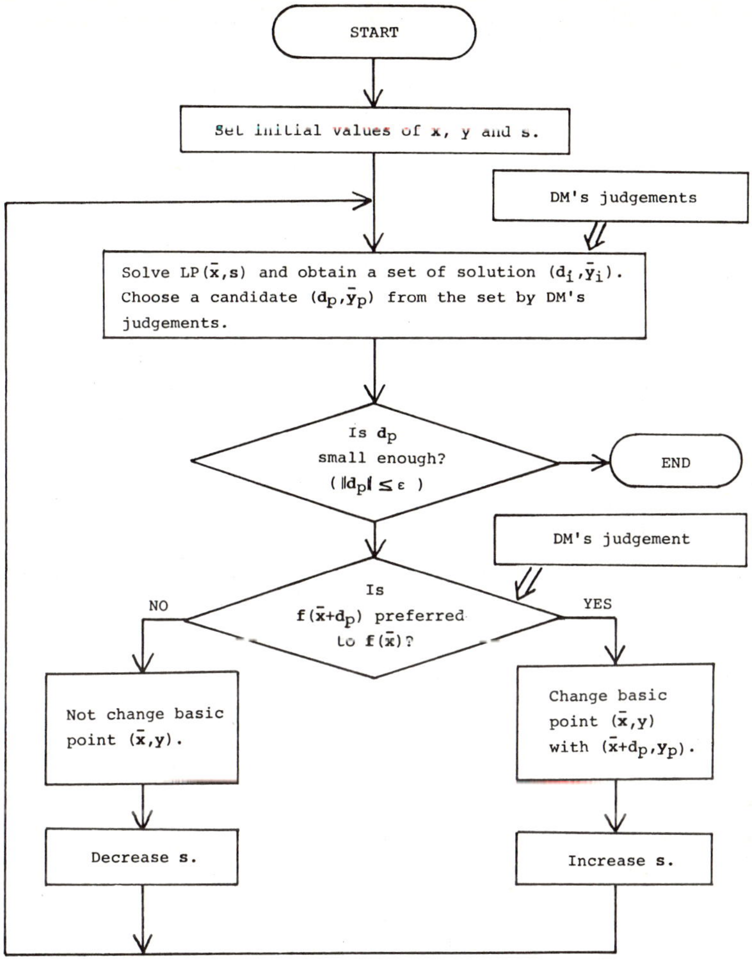

Fig. 1 Procedures of successive linear programming

expressed by the following equations,

$$\min_{\mathbf{d},\mathbf{y}} \; [p(\mathbf{x})\mathbf{d} + \mathbf{a}_0\mathbf{y}], \tag{12}$$

$$\text{subject to } J(\bar{\mathbf{x}})\mathbf{d} + \mathbf{A}_1\mathbf{y} = \mathbf{b}_1 - \mathbf{w}(\bar{\mathbf{x}}), \tag{13}$$

$$\mathbf{A}_2\mathbf{d} + \mathbf{A}_3\mathbf{y} = \mathbf{b}_2 - \mathbf{A}_3\bar{\mathbf{x}}, \tag{14}$$

$$\max(\mathbf{l}_1-\bar{\mathbf{x}},-\mathbf{s}) \leq \mathbf{d} \leq \min(\mathbf{u}_1-\bar{\mathbf{x}},\mathbf{s}),$$

$$\mathbf{l}_2 \leq \mathbf{y} \leq \mathbf{u}_2, \tag{15}$$

where $\mathbf{s}$ is step bounds and $-\mathbf{s} \leq \mathbf{d} \leq \mathbf{s}$. Linear approximation of Eqs. (12) and (13) is valid only in the neighbourhood of $\bar{\mathbf{x}}$ and can be considered as a linear programming (LP) problem denoted by LP($\bar{\mathbf{x}}$,$\mathbf{s}$).

The MOD problem can be reformulated by applying the above linear approximation as follows,

$$\min_{\mathbf{d},\mathbf{y}} \nabla_x \Phi[f(\bar{x})]d, \tag{16}$$

$$\text{subject to } J(\bar{x})d + A_1 y = b_1 - w(\bar{x}), \tag{17}$$

$$A_2 d + A_3 y = b_2 - A_3 \bar{x} \tag{18}$$

$$\max(l_1 - \bar{x}, s) \leq d \leq \min(u_1 - \bar{x}, s),$$

$$l_2 \leq y \leq u_2, \tag{19}$$

where $\mathbf{a}_0 = 0$ of Eq.(12). By introducing SLP, the MOD problem can efficiently be solved by using Simplex Method which is the most popular and basic method for solving LP problem.

Procedures of SLP for solving the MOD problem are shown in Fig. 1 and are briefly described below. At first, initial values of x, y and **s** are given and the LP problem around basic point $(\bar{x},y)$, that is, LP($\bar{x}$,**s**) is then solved to obtain a set of basic feasible solution (d_1,y_1), (d_2,y_2), - -, (d_k,y_k) by using Simplex Method. Subsequently, the most preferable solution (d_p,y_p) is chosen from the set by DM's judgements for paired comparisons among $f(x+d_1)$, $f(x+d_2)$, - - , $f(x+d_k)$. Next, it is checked whether the obtained d_p is small enough, and if so, the procedures are considered to attain a complete convergence and terminated. If not so, the procedures are proceeded to the succeeding step. In the following procedure, it is also investigated whether the candidate of solution $(x+d_p,y_p)$ is suitable for a new basic point of the next iteration, which is determined by comparing $f(x+d_p)$ with $f(x)$ based on the DM's judgement. If suitable, the present basic point (x,y) is changed with the new one $(x+d_p,y_p)$ and step bounds **s** are increased to **s'**, and then LP($x+d_p$,**s'**) is solved to obtain a set of feasible basic solutions of the new iteration. If not suitable, LP(x,s") is again solved with the basic point (x,y) under the decreased condition s". The above procedures are iteratively applied to attain a convergence, namely, to obtain a final preferred solution.

Multiobjective Decision Method Using Heuristic Rules

The MOD problem formulated by SLP involving the DM's judgements can be solved to obtain a preferred solution according to the procedures of Fig. 1. Here, preference function of Eq. (3) is based on the DM's judgements at each required step, as it can not explicitly be defined as a functional form. The judgement which is performed through interaction of the DM with computer, consists of the two parts; the first one is the comparison of performance among $f(x+d_i)$, (i = 1, - -, k), and the other is the comparison between $f(x+d_p)$ and $f(x)$. It is however difficult to keep the consistency of these judgements through the several iterations of SLP procedures.

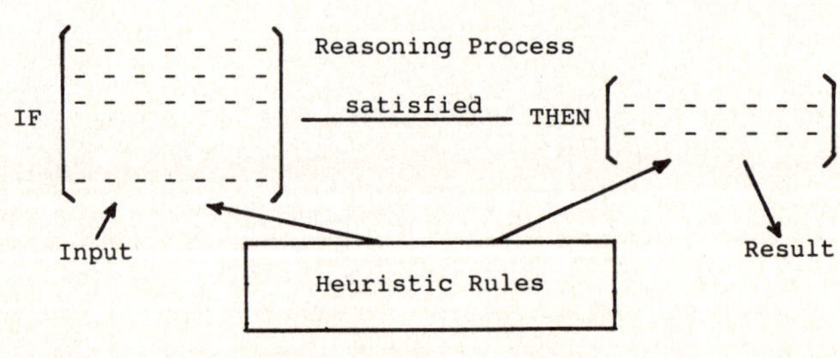

Fig. 2 Diagram of production system

In the present method, production system, which is a methodology of expressing human reasoning process in artificial intelligence, is introduced to some part of the DM's judgements. In the production system, the reasoning process is represented in the form of "if - -, then - -.", which is regarded as a rule. The "if - -" part corresponds to a condition for determining whether an input is satisfied with it, and the "then - -" part corresponds to the conclusion deduced from the satisfied condition as shown in Fig. 2. The rules would work as heuristics in the method, with the result that the number of DM's judgement decreases, and these can reduce the physical and psychological burden of the DM.

The heuristic rules involved in the production system can be derived in advance from answers of the DM for some questionaires which are previously provided from the consideration of the various cases in

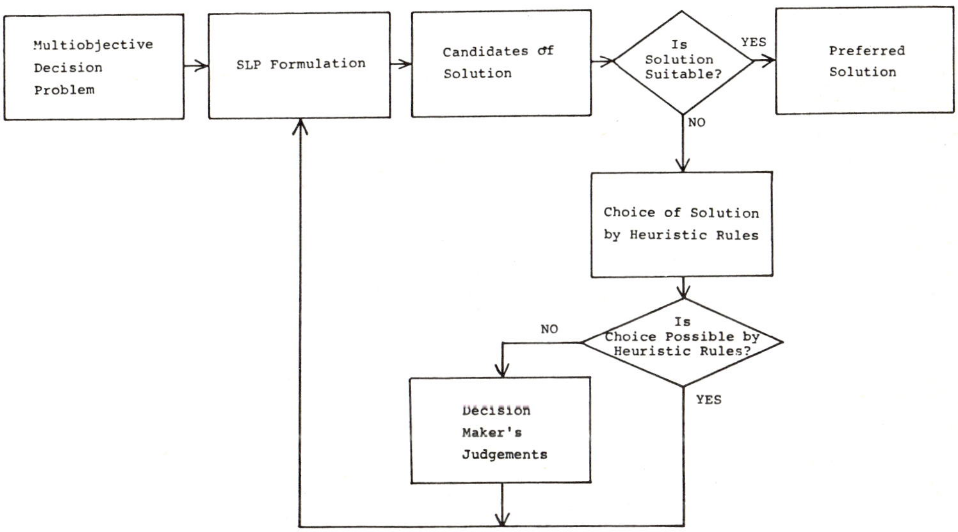

Fig. 3 Algorithm of the proposed method

*** OBJECTIVE FUNCTIONS ***

A		B
36.00	F(1)	26.00
40.00	F(2)	50.00
25.00	F(3)	41.00

WHICH DO YOU PREFER? (A/B)

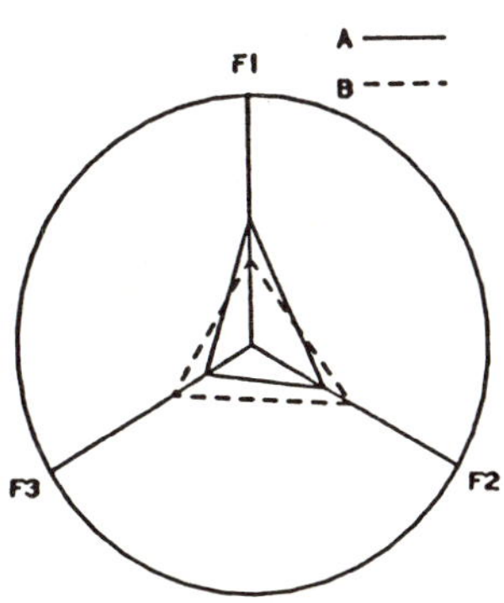

Fig. 4 graphical representation of objective functions for supporting DM's judgement the decision making problem. The obtained rules reflect a policy of the DM for his preference. As an example of rule in MOD problem with 3 dimensional objective function, it is shown that "IF $f_1(\mathbf{x}_a) \leq f_1(\mathbf{x}_b)$ and $f_2(\mathbf{x}_a) \leq f_2(\mathbf{x}_b)$ are satisfied, THEN choose $\mathbf{f}(\mathbf{x}_a)$, that is, $\mathbf{x}_a$ regardless of f_3.". This rule means that the DM attaches more importance to f_1 and f_2 than to f_3 as his policy.

Fig. 3 shows the general flow chart of the method. In the iterative process of solving LP problem by SLP, if the heuristic rule is not available, choice of a solution from the candidates must of course be made depending on the DM's judgements. In the method, graphical representation of the candidates can be used to make the DM's judgement easier. Two paired polygon graphs of multiobjective function are displayed on CRT with the functional values, as shown in Fig. 4.

APPLICATION OF THE METHOD TO A HOUSING PROBLEM

Housing Problem

The proposed method is applied to a decision problem which is to find a house in some place nearby a railway station in Tokyo as shown in Fig. 5. The problem includes 3 dimensional decision variable $\mathbf{x}$ as follows:

- x_1 : distance from the central portion of Tokyo to the nearest railway station (km);
- x_2 : distance from the nearest railway station to the house (km);
- x_3 : area of site for the house (m^2).

The multiobjective function $\mathbf{f}$ of the problem with 3 dimensions is given by,

- f_1 : price of the house (million yen);
- f_2 : time taken for the transportation (minutes);
- f_3 : comfortable and environmental conditions of the house (arbitrary unit).

Their functional forms are defined respectively as follows,

$$f_1 = (x_1 - 80)^2(1 - 0.05x_2)x_3/10^4,$$
$$f_2 = x_1 + 3x_2,$$
and
$$f_3 = -x_2^2 x_3/10^3.$$

Here, smaller the values for f_1, f_2 and f_3, the results will be more optimized. The minus sign of f_3 indicates that for higher value of f_3, the conditions will be better. On the other hand, each component of the constraint $\mathbf{g}$ in the problem is as follows:

$$1 \leq x_1 \leq 50,$$
$$1 \leq x_2 \leq 10,$$
$$100 \leq x_3 \leq 1000,$$
$$x_3 \leq 20x_1 + 100.$$

In this example, the multiobjective function $\mathbf{f}$ is nonlinear, and the constraint $\mathbf{g}$ is linear as shown in the above equations.

Application of the Method

The method proposed in the second section is applied to the example described above, wherein two policies of DM are used to investigate the effectiveness of the method. The first policy employs the price of the house f_1 as the most important criterion in DM's judgements. The second policy employs the comfortable and environmental conditions of the house f_3. A set of rules for each policy is derived from

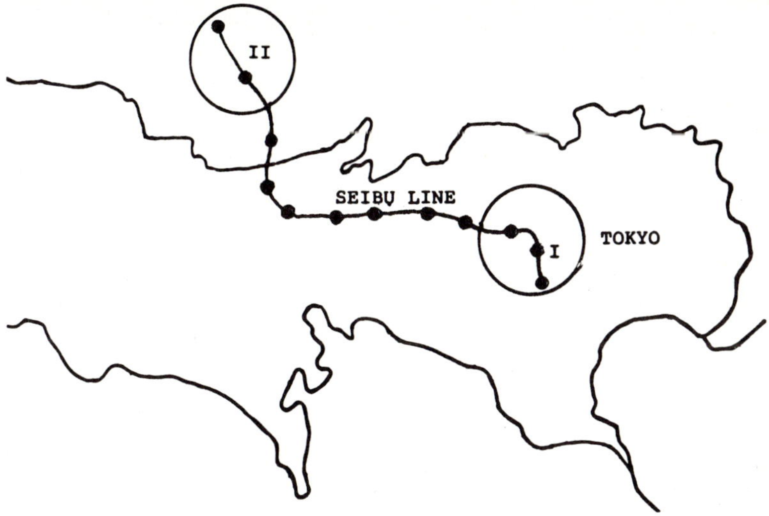

Fig. 5 Decision problem of a house in Tokyo
(I:policy 1 and II:policy 2)

the answers of questionaires for the DM as shown below. Then, the rules themselves choose the appropriate one from the alternatives $\mathbf{x}_a$ and $\mathbf{x}_b$ of decision variable.

[Rules for policy 1]

(1) IF $25 \leq f_1(\mathbf{x}_a) \leq 40$, and $f_1(\mathbf{x}_b) < 25$ or $f_1(\mathbf{x}_b) > 40$,
THEN choose $\mathbf{x}_a$.

(2) IF $f_1(\mathbf{x}_a) < 25$, and $f_1(\mathbf{x}_b) > 40$,
THEN choose $\mathbf{x}_a$.

(3) IF $10 \leq f_1(\mathbf{x}_a)$ and $f_1(\mathbf{x}_b) \leq 25$, and
  (a) IF $f_2(\mathbf{x}_a)$ and $f_2(\mathbf{x}_b) > 45$,
  THEN choose the one with smaller value of f_2.
  (b) IF $f_2(\mathbf{x}_a)$ and $f_2(\mathbf{x}_b) \leq 45$,
  THEN choose the one with smaller value of f_3.

(4) IF $40 \leq f_1(\mathbf{x}_a)$ and $f_1(\mathbf{x}_b) \leq 150$, and
  (a) IF $f_2(\mathbf{x}_a)$ and $f_2(\mathbf{x}_b) \leq 25$,
  THEN choose the one with smaller value of f_3.
  (b) IF $f_2(\mathbf{x}_a)$ and $f_2(\mathbf{x}_b) > 25$,
  THEN choose the one with smaller value of f_1.

[Rules for policy 2]

(1) IF $f_3(\mathbf{x}_a) \geq 60$, and $f_3(\mathbf{x}_b) < 60$,
THEN choose $\mathbf{x}_a$.

(2) IF $f_3(\mathbf{x}_a) > 20$, and $f_3(\mathbf{x}_b) < 20$,
THEN choose $\mathbf{x}_a$.

(3) IF $20 \leq f_3(\mathbf{x}_a)$ and $f_3(\mathbf{x}_b) \leq 60$, and
  (a) IF $f_2(\mathbf{x}_a)$ and $f_2(\mathbf{x}_b) > 60$,
  THEN choose the one with smaller value of f_2.
  (b) IF $f_2(\mathbf{x}_a)$ and $f_2(\mathbf{x}_b) \leq 60$,
  THEN choose the one with smaller value of f_3.

(4) IF $f_3(\mathbf{x}_a)$ and $f_3(\mathbf{x}_b) < 20$, and
  (a) IF $f_2(\mathbf{x}_a)$ and $f_2(\mathbf{x}_b) > 40$,
  THEN choose the one with smaller value of f_2.

(b) <u>IF</u> $f_2(\mathbf{x}_a)$ and $f_2(\mathbf{x}_b) \leq 40$,
<u>THEN</u> choose the one with smaller value of f_1.

DM must choose the one from the alternatives $\mathbf{x}_a$ and $\mathbf{x}_b$ based on his judgement in case that the above rules can not be applied.

Three experiments were undertaken using the above rules.

Experiment 1 -- Using rules for policy 1 and setting initial value $\bar{\mathbf{x}}_0 = (20,5,300)^t$ and step bounds $\mathbf{s} = (0.5,0.5,5)^t$, a preferred solution $\mathbf{x}_p = (1,10,100)^t$ with objective function value $\mathbf{f} = (31,31,10)$ was obtained by employing 17 judgements of DM. In the above initial conditions, 52 judgements were required for obtaining the same result without the rules. Thus the number of judgements decreases by 35 (see Fig. 6(a)).

Experiment 2 -- Changing the initial value of the experiment 1 with initial value $\bar{\mathbf{x}}_0 = (5,8,200)^t$, one could obtain the same solution with 13 judgements using the rules and 36 without the rules (see Fig. 6(b)).

Experiment 3 -- The same experiment was undertaken using rules for policy 2, and a preferred solution $\mathbf{x}_p = (50,10,1000)^t$ with $\mathbf{f} = (45,80,100)^t$ was obtained by applying 25 judgements, where initial value $\bar{\mathbf{x}}_0 = (5,8,200)^t$. The number of judgement was 60 in case of not using the rules (see Fig. 6(c)).

The above experimental results indicate that the heuristic rules can fairly reduce the number of judgements. The DM using the policy 1 made a decision of choosing the housing region nearby the central

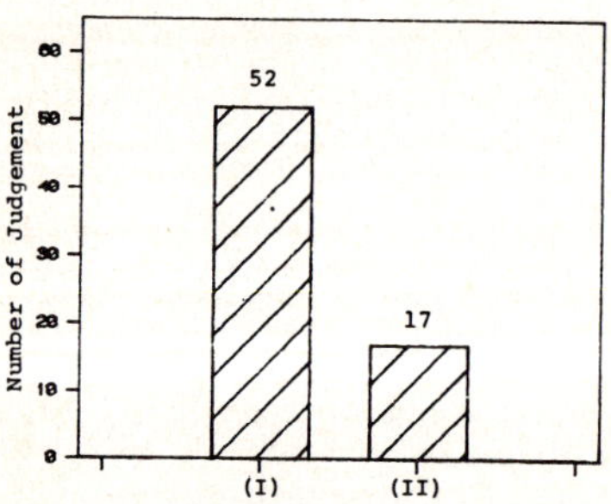

(a) Experiment 1

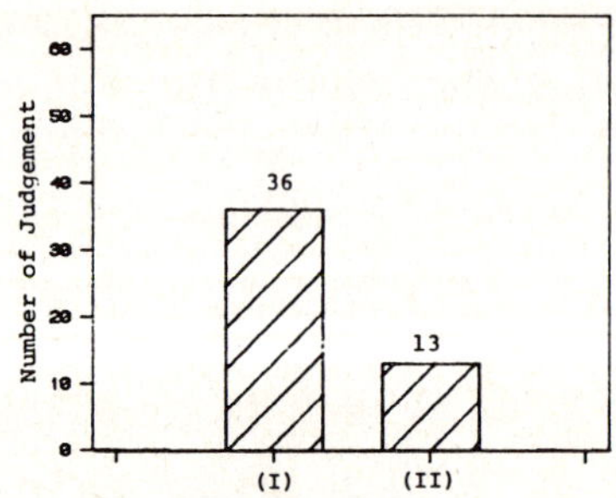

(b) Experiment 2

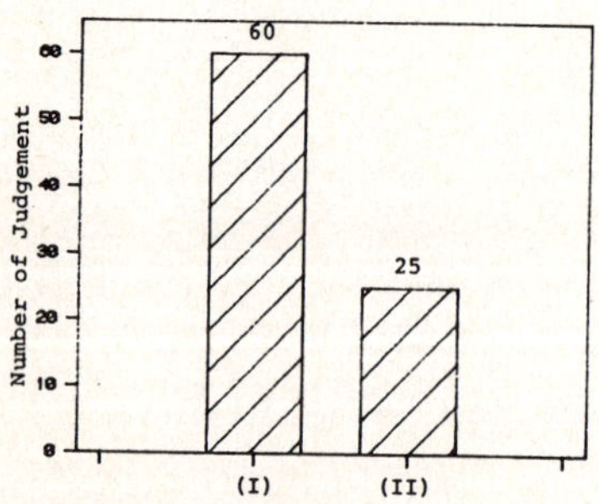

(c) Experiment 3

Fig. 6 Number of DM's judgement in the three exoeriments (I:without rules and II:using rules)

portion of Tokyo, while the DM using the policy 2 chose the suburbs of Tokyo, as shown in Fig. 5.

CONCLUSION

A new multiobjective decision method is proposed in which a production system including heuristic rules is employed. Due to the reduction of the number of DM's judgements, the final decision becomes more appropriate, and the physical and psychological burden of the DM is reduced. The effectiveness of the method is shown by applying it to the practical problems. Generally the data in the MOO problem are not necessarily quantitative, and they may be given even by a set of declaratory sentences, so that the data may contain a lot of ambiguities. Therefore, the future MOD method has to employ a formulation including the DM's qualitative knowledge. Furthermore, the heuristic rules used in the decision process should be generated automatically by learning process.

REFERENCES

(1) J. L. Cochrane and M. Zeleny (eds.): Multiple Criteria Decision Making (South Carolina Press, South Carolina, 1973).

(2) C. Carlsson and Y. Kochetkov (eds.), Theory and Practice of Multiple Criteria Decision Making (North-Holland, Amsterdom, 1983).

(3) Y. Y. Haimes, et al.: Multiobjective Optimization in Water Recouces System, The Surrogate Worth Trade-off Method (Elsevier Scientific Publishing Company, New York, 1975).

(4) A. Geoffrion, et al., An Interactive Approach for Multi-Criterion Optimization, with an Application to the Operation of an Academic Department, Management Science, 19-4 (1972) 357-368.

(5) A. Newell and H. Simon: Human Problem Solving (Prentice-Hall, New York, 1972).

(6) F. Palacios-Gomez, et al., Nonlinear Optimization by Successive Linear Programming, Management Science, 28-10 (1982) 1106-1120.

Artificial Intelligence in Economics and Management
L.F. Pau (Editor)

ON PATTERN RECOGNITION METHODS IN ECONOMETRIC REGRESSION MODEL

Krzysztof Jajuga

Economic Cybernetics Institute
Academy of Economics
Wrocław
POLAND

Two-stage procedure of econometric model evaluation in the case of heterogeneity of a set of observations is proposed. Two approaches, stochastic and distribution-free, are described. There, statistical pattern recognition methods are used to determine homogenous classes of observations. Then the generalized version of least squares method for econometric model evaluation in the distribution-free approach is discussed.

INTRODUCTION.

In the paper we discuss some problems of the use of statistical pattern recognition methods, namely classification methods, in econometric regression model.
Econometric regression model (e.g.([5], [8], [12])) is undoubtedly the most often used statistical tool in economic studies. Its goal is the identification of the existing relationship (or dependence) of a certain economic variable, called endogenous (or dependent) variable, on the set of other variables, called explanatory (or exogenous) variables. If the exogenous variables are influenced by the decision-maker, the econometric model evaluation may support decision-making process.

To describe the relationship between variables, the regression equation is used. Due to its simplicity and relatively clear interpretation, linear regression model is preferred. It has the following form:

$$Y = a_1 X_1 + a_2 X_2 + \dots + a_m X_m + a_0 + e \qquad (1)$$

where:
Y - dependent variable,
$X_1, X_2, \dots, X_m$ - explanatory variables,
$a_1, a_2, \dots, a_m, a_0$ - regression coefficients,
e - error.

In all economic studies, where statistical methods are used, one of two approaches may be assumed. The first one is the stochastic approach, when the data set, that is, the set of observations, is treated as a random sample drawn from a population with a certain probability distribution. The other one is called the deterministic or distribution-free approach. It is to be used when the set of observations may be regarded as a whole population.

Using the regression model, it is necessary to assume, that the set of observations, for which the econometric regression model is evaluated, is homogenous set. When the stochastic approach in economic studies is accepted, the homogeneity means, that the observations constitute a sample from one population with a certain distribution of a random vector $\underline{Z} = [Y, X_1, X_2, \dots, X_m]^T$.

It is usually assumed, that this random vector has multinormal distribution. Then the set of observations, for which the regression model is evaluated, is of hyperellipsoidal shape, and the model is linear one. For m=1, this case may be presented in the Figure 1.

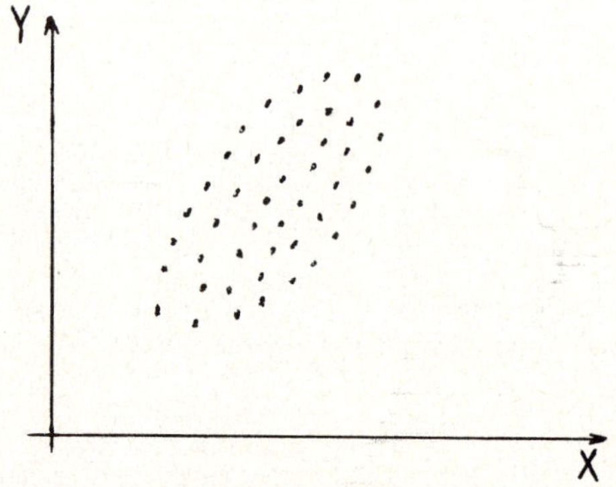

Figure 1
Homogeneity of a set of observations

However, in economic studies this requirement is often not met, particularly, when the observations are given as cross-sectional data. Then the set of observations may be a heterogenous set and may consists of several homogenous subsets. Thus the form of the dependence described by the regression equation may differ significantly for these subsets of observations. In all such cases, it makes sense to study the dependence of Y on $X_1, X_2, \dots, X_m$ for each homogenous subset separately.

For m=1, the case of heterogeneity is presented in the Figure 2.

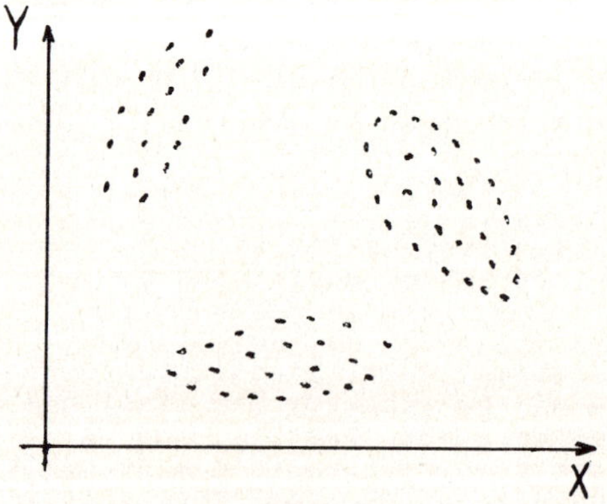

Figure 2
Heterogeneity of a set of observations

To study the dependence by means of econometric regression model in the case of heterogeneity of the set of observations, we propose the following two-stage procedure.

In the first stage, using the (m+1)-dimensional observations:

$$\underline{z}_i = \left[y_i, x_{i1}, x_{i2}, \ldots, x_{im}\right]^T, \quad i=1,\ldots,n,$$

the homogenous classes of observations are determined. These classes have hyperellipsoidal shape. Here:
y_i - ith observation of the variable Y,
x_{ij} - ith observation of the variable X_j,
n - number of observations.

Then, in the second stage, for each homogenous class the regression model is evaluated.

APPLICATION OF STATISTICAL PATTERN RECOGNITION METHODS TO THE DETERMINATION OF HOMOGENOUS CLASSES

The determination of homogenous classes occurring in the set of observations may be considered as a pattern recognition problem. When the stochastic approach is accepted, we may assume that the heterogenous set of observations is a sample from the population, where a random vector $\underline{Z}$ has a distribution being a mixture of K multivariate distributions, for example, multinormal distributions. Thus the density for the observations is given by the formula:

$$f(\underline{z}) = (2\pi)^{-0.5(m+1)} \sum_{i=1}^{K}\left\{P_i|\underline{\Sigma}_i|^{-0.5} \exp\left[-0.5(\underline{z}-\underline{\mu}_i)^T \underline{\Sigma}_i^{-1}(\underline{z}-\underline{\mu}_i)\right]\right\} \quad (2)$$

where:
$\underline{\mu}_i$ - mean vector of ith component distribution,
$\underline{\Sigma}_i$ - covariance matrix of ith component distribution,
P_i - ith mixing parameter.

So each homogenous class of observations is described by $\underline{\mu}_i$, $\underline{\Sigma}_i$, and in addition, by its contribution to the whole set of observations, P_i. Thus we have the classical problem of unsupervised pattern recognition. Using a sample, we have to estimate the parameters of a mixture. Strictly speaking, the number of parameters to estimate is equal to:

$$K\left[m+1+m+1+0.5m(m+1)+1\right]-1 = 0.5K(m^2+5m+6)-1$$

To estimate these parameters, the maximum likelihood method may be used. Due to the large number of parameters and the complicated form of the likelihood function, the analytical evaluation of maximum likelihood estimates is not possible. Instead, numerical methods should be used. We propose to apply the iterative algorithm presented by Bezdek and Dunn (1975).

The algorithm starts from the initial values of estimates. The algorithm is robust with respect to these values, so they can be fixed in any way. Then, in each iteration, a posterior probabilities of belonging are obtained according to Bayes formula. These probabilities are used to calculate new values of estimates. The iterative process is continued till the convergence is achieved.

Then, using obtained in the last iteration estimates:

$$\hat{\underline{\mu}}_j, \hat{\underline{\Sigma}}_j, \hat{P}_j \quad j=1,\ldots,K$$

and the probabilities of belonging:

$$\hat{P}(j|\underline{z}_i) \qquad j=1,\ldots,K \qquad i=1,\ldots,n,$$

the assignment of all observations to the classes is performed. Here, $\hat{P}(j|\underline{z}_i)$ denotes the posterior probability that the observation $\underline{z}_i$ belongs to the jth class.

To solve the assignment problem, Bayes classification rule is used (e.g. [3], [4], [10], [13]). Thus the observation $\underline{z}_i$ is assigned to the jth class, if:

$$\hat{P}(j|\underline{z}_i) = \max_{l} \hat{P}(l|\underline{z}_i) \tag{3}$$

So the set of observations is divided into K disjoint subsets, called classes. Each class, say the ith one, corresponds to particular component of a mixture and may be considered as a sample from multinormal distribution with mean vector $\hat{\underline{\mu}}_i$ and covariance matrix $\hat{\underline{\Sigma}}_i$.

Thus for each class the linear model may be assumed (since for multinormal distribution the regression function is linear) and classical regression methods, for example ordinary least squares (e.g. [2], [9]) are to be applied.

Very often, however, it happens that the deterministic (distribution-free) approach should be assumed. To determine homogenous classes of hyperellipsoidal shape, other statistical pattern recognition methods can be considered. It seems that fuzzy classification methods may be of real usefulness, especially for cases of not well-separated classes. Such cases occur very often in real applications.

To solve the described problem, we propose to use some version of fuzzy ISODATA algorithm, presented by Gustafson and Kessel (1979). This method is based on the minimization of the following function:

$$L = \sum_{i=1}^{n} \sum_{j=1}^{K} f_{ij}^{2} d_{ij} \tag{4}$$

where:

f_{ij} - degree of belongingness of the ith observation to the jth fuzzy class,

d_{ij} - distance of the ith observation to the jth fuzzy class.

So this method gives the homogenous classes of observations, which are fuzzy sets. Also this method is implemented by an iterative algorithm. Each class obtained by this algorithm has hyperellipsoidal shape and is described by the degrees of belongingness of each observation. The hyperellipsoidal shape justifies the linearity of the regression model.

REGRESSION MODEL EVALUATION FOR DISTRIBUTION-FREE APPROACH

The classes obtained by means of fuzzy ISODATA method are fuzzy sets, so each observation has different degree of belongingness to particular class. Thus the use of classical regression methods, for example, ordinary least squares, is not recommended. Instead, we propose the generalized version of least squares method.

Let $\underline{y}$ denote the n x 1 vector of observations of dependent variable and let $\underline{X}$ denote the n x (m+1) matrix of observations of exogenous variables.

The proposed method of linear regression model evaluation for the jth fuzzy class $(j=1,\ldots,K)$ consists in the minimization of the weighted sum of squared residuals, the degrees of belongingness to the jth class being the weights. Applying similar procedure as for ordinary least squares method (e.g. [2], [11], [12]) we get the vector of linear regression coefficients for the jth fuzzy class:

$$\underline{a}_j = (\underline{X}^T \underline{F}_j \underline{X})^{-1} \underline{X}^T \underline{F}_j \underline{y} \qquad (5)$$

where:

$\underline{a}_j$ - $(m+1) \times 1$ vector of regression coefficients for the jth fuzzy class,

$\underline{F}_j$ - diagonal $n \times n$ matrix with $f_{1j}, f_{2j}, \ldots, f_{nj}$ in the main diagonal.

So the regression model is evaluated separately for each fuzzy class, and an account is taken of degrees of belongingness of observations to this fuzzy class.

Jajuga (1985) discusses some basic properties of this method. These properties are analogous to the properties of classical regression metods. Some numerical experiments proved that the use of the presented pattern recognition methods and then the evaluation of regression coefficients for each class, fuzzy or nonfuzzy, lead to econometric model with better fit.

REFERENCES:

1 Bezdek, J.C. and Dunn, J.C., Optimal fuzzy partitions: a heuristic for estimating the parameters in a mixture of normal distributions, IEEE Transactions on Computers 24 (1975), 835-838.

2 Draper, N.R. and Smith, H., Applied Regression Analysis (Wiley, New York, 1966).

3 Duda, R.O. and Hart, P.E., Pattern Classification and Scene Analysis (Wiley, New York, 1973).

4 Fukunaga, K., Introduction to Statistical Pattern Recognition (Academic Press, New York, 1972).

5 Goldberger, A.S., Econometric Theory (Wiley, New York, 1964).

6 Gustafson, D.E. and Kessel, W.C., Fuzzy clustering with a fuzzy covariance matrix, in: Gupta, M.M., Ragade, R.K. and Yager, R.R. (eds.), Advances in Fuzzy Set Theory and Applications (North-Holland, Amsterdam, 1979).

7 Jajuga, K., Linear Fuzzy Regression, submitted to Fuzzy Sets and Systems (1985).

8 Johnston, J., Econometric Methods (McGraw-Hill, New York, 1963).

9 Morrison, D.F., Multivariate Statistical Methods (McGraw-Hill, New York, 1976).

10 Nilsson, N.J., Learning Machines (McGraw-Hill, New York, 1965).

11 Press, S.J., Applied Multivariate Analysis (Holt,Rinehart and Winston, New York, 1972).

12 Theil, H., Principles of Econometrics (Wiley, New York, 1971).

13 Tou, J.T. and Gonzalez, R.C., Pattern Recognition Principles (Addison-Wesley, Reading, 1974).

Artificial Intelligence in Economics and Management
L.F. Pau (Editor)

INFERENCE OF FUNCTIONAL ECONOMIC MODEL RELATIONS FROM NATURAL LANGUAGE ANALYSIS

L. Pau

Battelle Geneva Research Centres
7, route de Drize
1227 Carouge/Geneva
Switzerland

Abstract. This paper introduces a tool for qualitative model building, based on the semi-automatic inference of the structure of a specified economic reasoning by natural language analysis of descriptive texts (policy statements, articles). The applications are: assessment of the consistency of several economic analyses, construction of the structure of an econometric model. This work has being using the LISP programming language.

Keywords. Economics, Artificial intelligence, Natural language analysis, Modelling, Decision theory.

1. INTRODUCTION

Quantitative econometric methods (estimation, regression, control) tend to be restricted to rather short planning horizons in terms of forecasting or decision-making, because of model structure restrictions, besides data limitations. As a result, the range of possible methods, and the range of possible economic policies which can be modeled (control) or inferred (estimation), tend also to be limited. Because of the complexity of inverse control algorithms, goal estimation is very poor.

This paper deals with how judgmental macro-economic knowledge can be acquired from descriptive text (policy statements, articles, speeches, analyses) through syntactic "scripts", in order to infer semi-automatically the functional structure of this specific judgmental reasoning. This structure is represented as a causal semantic network, or formal grammar, the nodes/terminals of which are the economic policy words (aggregates, exogeneous variables), attribute comparison and trend terms (larger, smaller, increasing, etc.), and the qualitative goals (reduce, stabilize, etc.). The causality labels in the network specify how the economic aggregates are influenced, as resulting from the descriptive text. One specific judgmental reasoning is then displayed as a path in this graph; this shows very clearly distributed feedback effects, open-loop policies, disjoint cut sets. The graph can be edited through a lightpen control on a raster display device.

The results of the analysis are:

(1) for each set of aggregates and goals, the derivation of all up-stream nodes and relations causing this state; this corresponds exactly to specifying the right-hand sides in econometric relations, and the set of endogeneous relations;

(2) feeding automatically the results of (1) into the time-series of econometric estimation packages of the econometric models; these results are the functional form of the equations;

(3) providing a natural language explanation, with a graph representation for editing purposes, of forecasting errors and revisions;

(4) allow for judgmental forecasting procedures, by specifying a set of judgmental exogeneous inputs, and applying the formal grammar to rewrite the resulting economic forecast in clear language.

Whereas recently a number of works have been dealing with natural language understanding in general (Bobrow, 1975; Hayes, 1979; Charniak, 1976; Marcus, 1980; Rescher, 1976; Winograd, 1972), with language query systems, or with compilers for econometric model building, there is no known reference dealing with economic applications as described above and in (Pau, 1981). Our approach is also different from algebraic symbol manipulations, and from the extraction of predetermined terms in econometric equations represented by a tree (NG, 1979; Steward, 1965).

It must be stressed that more evolved and complex natural language analysis schemes are known today (ACL, Bara (1984), Cercone (1983), Siekmann (1983)). The primary emphasis of this paper is however to define a problem, and describe a solution which, although semi-automatic and imperfect, is quite useful even for large texts (see Section 7). The same point of view has been used by Johnson (1982), Rowley (1982) in other application areas.

Sections 2 and 3 deal with a brief introduction to formal languages and their inference, as applied to econometric models. The way in which the economic reasoning language is specified is described in Section 4. The semi-automatic inference algorithm is presented in Section 5, with an example in Section 6. The implementation and applications of this approach are reviewed in Section 7 and 8 respectively.

2. INFERENCE OF THE ECONOMETRIC MODEL STRUCTURE

2.1 Econometric model

If we define:

$X \triangleq$ exogeneous variables

$Y \triangleq$ endogeneous variables (state variables, simultaneous variables)

$U \triangleq$ instrument variables

$\theta \triangleq$ model parameters

the simplest econometric model is represented by:

i.	Criterion	$\text{Max } J(Y, U)$
ii.	Model	$F(X, Y, U, \theta) = 0$ or ε
iii.	Measurement equation	$Y = H(X, \theta)$
iv.	Feedback policy	$U = P(Y, \theta)$
v.	Constraints	$(Y, U) \in IK$

2.2 Qualitative model

The qualitative model will be defined in terms of a sequence of causality relations (with feedbacks) between the notions X, Y, U, merged into states $S \triangleq (X, Y, U)$. A state S is either one of the notions X, Y, U or an attributed syntatic expression of these; a causality relation => signifies that the second state S_j is a consequence of the first state S_i:

$$S_i \Rightarrow S_j \qquad (1)$$

2.3 Inference of the model structure

The purpose of this inference is to identify the structures of the criterion J, of the model F, of the measurement H, and of the feedback policy P. By this identification, we express the fact that J, F, H, P do not imply quantitatively any causality relation between states S which is not already in the qualitative model derived from the original text used as learning.

3. FORMAL LANGUAGES

The theory of formal languages is used here to manipulate the symbols representing the states S (Fu, 1975; Hays-Roth, 1978; Shortliffe, 1976; Woods, 1970). The language L(G) is defined by:

i. a terminal vocabulary

$$V_T \triangleq (S_1, S_2, \ldots)$$

ii. a non-terminal vocabulary

$$V_N \triangleq (A_1, A, \ldots\ldots, A_n)$$

iii. an initial symbol σ

iv. a grammar G represented by a set of production rules, by which the string of concatenated symbols on the left is rewritten into the string on the right:

$\alpha \overset{Zj}{\to} \beta$ (also noted $\alpha \overset{j}{\to} \beta$)

$\alpha, \beta \in (V_T \cup V_N)^*$ (set of mixed strings of symbols from V_T and V_N)

Because the terminal vocabulary V_T is in our application a set of economic states, the production rules will specify exactly the causality relations (1) between these states.

The language L(G) is then the set of strings $x \in V_T^*$ of terminal symbols, derived from σ by a sequence of production rules:

$$L(G) = (x \in V_T^*, \sigma \xrightarrow{Z_1, Z_2 \ldots, Z_p} x)$$

L(G) is said to be regular iff all production rules Z are of the type:

$$A_1 \overset{Z}{\to} S_2 A_3 \text{ or } A_1 \overset{Z}{\to} S_2$$

The language is context-free if all production rules are of the type:

$$A_1 \overset{Z}{\to} \alpha \in (V_T \cup V_N)^*$$

The inference of G then consists in, for given V_T, V_N, σ, and within a family of feasible grammars, to infer all production rules of G from a set of learning sentences Δ (natural text after abstraction) assumed to belong to L(G). The results are:

i. the production rules $Z_1, \ldots, Z_n$ representing G

ii. the sequences of production rules leading from σ to each learning sentence in Δ; these sequences of production rules express jointly the causality relations representing the economic reasoning underlying Δ.

4. SPECIFICATION OF THE ECONOMIC REASONING LANGUAGE L(G)

4.1 Non-terminal vocabulary V_N

A finite number m of non-terminal symbols, $A_1, \ldots, A_m$ is specified as needed.

4.2 Terminal vocabulary V_T

An automatic lexical analysis of the learning text is first carried out to estimate the frequencies of occurence and co-occurence of of the words in Δ. The least frequent words or word co-occurences may have to be discarded. Next, the remaining words are classified into various classes of a lexicon/thesaurus representing a relational abstraction (Charniak, 1976; Iversen, 1980; Winograd, 1972; Woods, 1970):

4.2.1 Logical symbols

1. Quantifiers (all, set of, the, some, ...)
2. Truth functions (or, and, not, if, else, then...)
3. Punctuation (.,;)
4. Explicit causality relations:

   <= (reflects, is due to), => (implies,
   effect on,
   results in)

4.2.2 Uninterpreted symbols

They are all problem dependent; all pronoums are replaced by variables:

1. Constants (2-5‰, 2.03 \$, > 8%, n-th quarter, high, low, stable, increasing, decreasing,...)

2. Variables: - all endogeneous variables Y
   - all exogeneous variables X
   - all instrument variables U

   or logical states S_i obtained by logical combination hereof. Since all variables are treated equally, the inference system will not make any difference; the manual abstracting procedure may however add a suffix Y, X or U to indicate the type considered.
3. Relations (equal to, greater than, indexed to)
4. Functions (plus, merger with, ...)
5. Relational applications (greater than, extreme, lagged value, forecasted value, positive impact, maximum)

4.3 Grammar

Described here in an unformal way, all production rules considered are of the following types:

Expression → Constant/Variable
Variables → Variables/Variable
Relational expression → Expression
Functional expression → "

Truth expression → "
Causality expression → "
Quantifier-Variables → Quantifier-Variables/ Variables
Constant/Relation-Expression → Expression

The grammar G of the language L(G) will be represented in a graph-like structure. The arcs of the graph are the production rules, with as nodes the legal strings from $(V_T \cup V_N)^*$. The vocabulary V_T and grammar G may be specified in a high level language if a compiler and parser is available (INTER-LISP, PROLOG, ATN) (see e.g. (Roos, 1983)).

5. INFERENCE ALGORITHMS

As indicated in the Introduction, the proposed procedure is semi-automatic, as currently implemented.

5.1 Manual coding into terminal vocabulary

Using a text editing system of a commercial word processor, each word in the learning text $\Delta = (x)$ is first reduced if necessary (articles, pronouns, etc.), and then codified into one of the classes of symbols in the terminal vocabulary V_T as listed in Section 4.2. The easiest coding system is to add a suffix index if needed. Punctuation is accounted for, because the inference algorithm will only operate on one sentence $x \varepsilon \Delta$ at the time. This manual phase is quite fast on a word processor (e.g. 10 words/minute).

5.2 Automatic inference algorithm

The inference problem is in general quite difficult, but a few simple algorithms can be tested (Fu, 1975; Hays-Roth, 1978). If unsuccessfull, exhaustive search is possible, especially as the library of economic causal relations is not so large (e.g. 1000 production rules). The algorithm used is described in Appendix. It has been programmed in LISP A.I. language.

5.3 Graph representation

The inferred grammar G is represented by a graph, including its state S_i as nodes, and where the arcs are the production rules; the bottom node is the entire learning text Δ.

6. EXAMPLE

This small example is given for illustrative purpose only; the inference step will not be discussed, and only the result will be given.

6.1 Text

The sentence $x = \Delta$ is: "A decline in factory orders reflects negative impact of high interest rates on the second quarter business activity".

6.2 Terminal vocabulary V_T

.	: then
+	: and/also
<=	: reflects, is due to
=>	: implies, results in
2-5	: 2-5%
< 8	: < 8%
> 15	: > 15%

Trend	$\searrow$	: decreasing
	$\nearrow$	: increasing
	$=$	: equal, stable
	$\overline{\wedge}$	: high
	$\underline{\vee}$	: low
Judgment	$\oplus$	: positive impact
	$\ominus$	: negative impact
fY		: factory orders (Y)
iX		: interest rates (X)
bY		: business activity (Y)
Q_n		: n-th quarter

6.3 Non-terminal vocabulary V_N: A_1 - A_9

6.4 Maximal grammar G

$\sigma \xrightarrow{1} A_1.\text{ix} \Rightarrow A_2$ $\qquad$ 1 ~ 1'

$\sigma \xrightarrow{1'} A_2 \Leftarrow A_1.\text{iX}$

$A_2 \xrightarrow{5} \ominus\ A_3\ \text{bY}\ A_4$

$\quad \xrightarrow{6} \oplus\ A_3\ \text{bY}\ A_5$

$\quad \xrightarrow{7} =\ A_3\ \text{bY}\ A_6$

$A_4 \xrightarrow{8} \Rightarrow A_7.\text{fY}$

$A_5 \xrightarrow{9} \Rightarrow A_8.\text{fY}$

$A_6 \xrightarrow{10} \Rightarrow A_9.\text{fY}$

$A_1 \xrightarrow{2} \overline{\wedge}$

$\quad \xrightarrow{3} =$

$\quad \xrightarrow{4} \underline{\vee}$

$A_7 \xrightarrow{11} \searrow$

$\quad \xrightarrow{12} A_1$

$\quad \xrightarrow{13} \nearrow$

$A_3 \xrightarrow{16} Q_1$

$\quad \xrightarrow{17} Q_2$

$\quad \xrightarrow{18} Q_3$

$\quad \xrightarrow{19} Q_4$

$A_8 \xrightarrow{14} A_7$

$A_9 \xrightarrow{15} A_7$

Table 1 - Grammar G

This grammar G includes more causality relations than present in Δ. It is maximal in the sense of including, for given V_T, all rules acceptable in terms of the economic language family (Section 4.3).

6.5 Inference

The learning sentence has been coded into:

$$x = \searrow fY \Leftarrow (\barwedge iX \Rightarrow \ominus Q2.bY)$$

or $(\barwedge iX \Rightarrow \ominus Q2.bY) \Rightarrow \searrow fY$

The inference yields:

$$\sigma \xrightarrow{1\ .\ (2\ +\ 5\ .\ (17\ +\ 8\ .\ 11))} x$$

represented by the parsing graph, or sequence of production rules, which illustrates very clearly the causality relations in this economic reasoning:

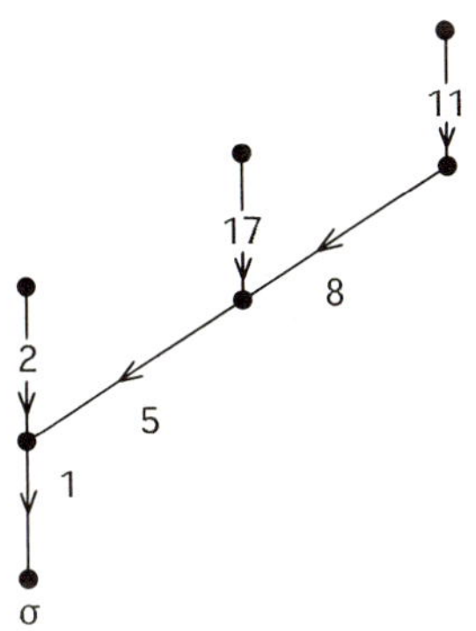

Trend
↓
Factory orders
↓
Date → Business activity
↓
Level → Interest rates
↓
σ

7. LISP IMPLEMENTATION

The LISP implementation consists in:

(A) a manual procedure, on a word processor, whereby the descriptive text is "abstracted" into the terminal and non-terminal symbols of the formal grammar (see 5.1);

(B) an automatic parsing of the concatenated strings of symbols;

(C) an automatic inference algorithm (assuming a regular grammar), which will create the production rules involved, and show how they were linked together via non-primitive terms (see 5.2 and Appendix);

(D) a display of the causal semantic network, for the editing of the nodes, edges, and labels, as well as for specifying a judgmental forecast (see 5.3);

(E) an interface to the estimation algorithm which generates all allowed paths between two specified sets of nodes.

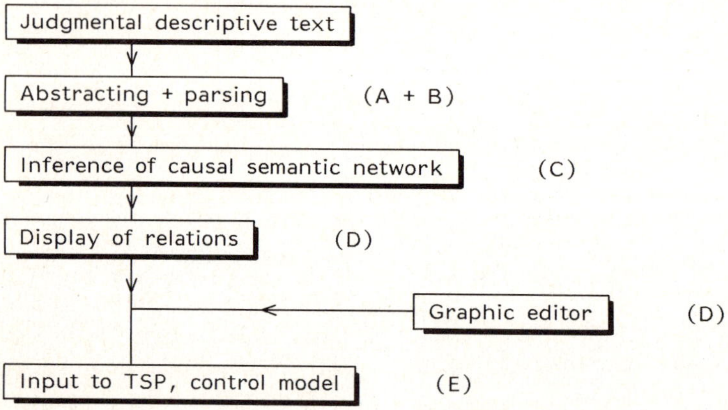

8. APPLICATIONS OF INFERENCE OF THE FUNCTIONAL RELATIONS IN ECONOMIC MODELS

8.1 Structure of an econometric model

(a) In terms of the classification between exogeneous/instrument variables and endogeneous variables, which is often very subjective, the graph representation (Sections 5.3, 6.5) of the inferred grammar G leads to the following logical rules:

- i exogeneous/instrument variables can only be those states S_i represented by leaves (branch terminations) of the graph, or be those states S_j which are connected along one open path to other exogeneous/instrument variables;
- ii endogeneous variables are those states S_k included in closed cycles within the graph, or which are connected along one open path to at least one exogeneous/instrument variable.

(b) The criteria or goals are those endogeneous states to which a relational application is attached (Section 4.2.2.5).

(c) One can also infer the structure of a control low P, by e.g. finding out which endogeneous variables explain (i.e. are cause of) the minimum lending rate. This is obvious from the graph, and the distinction is then very clear between monetarist rules, supply oriented rules, Keyniesian rules and their variants.

8.2 Consistency of an economic reasoning

If two texts Δ_1, Δ_2 discuss the same issue, and must be consistent, this consistency can easily be checked by analyzing and matching the corresponding graphs. An example hereof is the preparation of position papers or in negociations. Tests were carried out on texts of up to 900 words, with automatic graph matching computation.

8.3 Comparison of two economic reasonings

If two texts Δ_1, Δ_2 use the same terminal vocabulary and class of grammar, but are written by two different experts, one can through the corresponding graphs compare the structure of their reasonings in an almost visual way. Such a test has been conducted on four texts of 3000 words about monetary policy.

8.4 Forecasting

Assuming now consistency in the reasoning, the graph may help synthesize economic analyses for various assumptions on the exogeneous and instrument variables. This has been tested on a learning text of 4000 words with 550 production rules, dealing with relative currency adjustments.

CONCLUSION

This research is based on two essential remarks. First, language is an instrument of human reason, and not merely a medium for the expression of thought.

Next, qualitative/"verbal" economic reasoning is often more convincing to decision makers than uncertain numerical forecasts or computations, especially when medium/ long term actions are debated. Maybe econometric models reinforce the relative weight of short term decisions, while qualitative analyses help preparing longer term decisions.

At the same time, these qualitative reasonings/ analyses tend to be inconsistent, and sometimes subjective. Thus the need for an analysis tool to discriminate subjective evaluation elements from quantified objective factors (Jensen, 1982), while relating the two. This is what this paper hopes to contribute to.

APPENDIX

INFERENCE ALGORITHM

1 Regular grammar

If G is regular of type 3 (see Section 3), three algorithms are available; they are based on the theorems of Kleene and l'Etoile, which state that there is an integer N such that for all $x \varepsilon L(G)$ $|x| > N$, x can be decomposed into $x = uvw$ with $uv^kw \varepsilon L(G)$ $k \not\in I_N^N$.

1. <u>Algorithm 1</u>: <u>i</u> Find subsequences v such that $x = uv^kw$, $k \geq 2$ for all sentences x in Δ.

   <u>ii</u> Repeat <u>i</u> for various decompositions of u, w in x.

2. <u>Algorithm 2</u>: compute for increasing values of k, the maximal canonic language; compute the equivalence classes, until all sentences x are produced by such a grammar.

3. <u>Algorithm 3</u>: If there are variable repetitions of the same sub-sequence v in the learning string $x\varepsilon\Delta$, then the following procedure is proposed instead of Algorithm 1. It is based on the concept of successor of different symbols which appear in the strings of Δ.

Let us consider the set $M \triangleq (V_T \cup (\lambda))$, λ being a symbol whose length is null, and define a set Q from a bijective mapping γ from M into Q:

$$q_i \triangleq \gamma(a_i) \quad q_i \varepsilon Q,\ a_i \varepsilon M$$

For each element $q_i \varepsilon Q$, a set Sq_i is defined such as:

$$Sqi \triangleq (a \varepsilon M | \exists\delta,\ \Omega \varepsilon V_T^*,\ \delta\ a_i\ a\ \Omega \varepsilon \Delta)$$

Sq_i is the set of element of M which are the successors of a_i in the strings of Δ. Two states q_i and q_j are said equivalent if:

$$Sq_i = Sq_j.$$

Let Q' be the set of equivalence classes q'_i of Q. For each element $q'_i \in Q'$, a set Tq'_i is defined such as:

$$Tq'_i \triangleq (a \in M \mid a = \gamma^{-1}(q_j),\ \forall q_j \in q'_i)$$

Tq'_j is the set of elements of M which are the antecedents of the elements a ε $Sq'_i \triangleq (U_k\ (Sq_k),\ q_k \in q'_i)$. Then, η, R and q'_o are defined as follows:

i $\quad \eta: Q' \times V_T \rightarrow Q'$

$\quad \eta\ (q'_i,\ \alpha \in Sq'_i) \triangleq (q'_j \mid \alpha \in Tq'_j)$

$\quad \eta\ (q'_i,\ \alpha \notin Sq'_i) \triangleq q_\emptyset$ (trap state)

ii $\quad R \triangleq (q'_i \mid \lambda \in Sq'_i)$

iii $\quad q'_o = (q'_j \mid \lambda \in Tq'_j)$

The inferred automaton is (Q', V_T, η, q'_o, R); it is deterministic and minimal and Card $(Q') \leq$ (Card (V_T) + 1).

2 Non-regular grammars

The parsing must then use an exhaustive search in the language L, with reduction based on the structure outlined in Section 4.3 and on the preliminary remark in this section. In such a case, and if available, one can also use one of the simple inference algorithms for augmented transition networks (ATN) (Woods, 1970).

REFERENCES

ACL: Association for computational linguistics (ACL) annual meetings.

Bara, B.G. (Ed) (1984), Natural language processing, North Holland, Amsterdam.

Bobrow, D, and Collins, A (1975). Repre-sentation and understanding. Academic press, NY.

Burton, R. (1976). Semantic grammars, PhD thesis, UC Irvine.

Cercone, N. (Ed), (1983) Computational linguistics, Pergamon Press, Amsterdam.

Charniak, E., and Wilks, Y. (1976). Computational semantics, North Holland, Amsterdam.

Fu, K.S., and Booth, R. (1975). Grammatical inference. IEEE Trans., Vol. SMC-5, Part 1 (Jan. 1975), Part 2 (July 1975).

Hays-Roth, F. (1978). Pattern directed inference. Academic Press, N.Y.

Hayes, J.E., Michie, D., and Mikulich, L.I. (Ed.) (1979). Machine intelligence. Wiley, NY.

Iversen, K.E. (1980). Notation as a tool of thought. Comm. ACM, vol. 23, No 8, Aug. 1980, pp. 444.

Johnson, W. (1982). The role of prior knowledge in the comprehension of simple technical text, NTIS, AD-A-115638.

Jensen, A. (1982). Personal communication about Johan Voght-Norway.

Marcus, M.P. (July 1979). An overview of a theory of syntactic recognition for natural language. AI Memo 531, MIT.

Marcus, M.P. (1980). A theory of syntactic recognition for natural languages. MIT Press, Cambridge (Parsifal parsing).

NG, E.W. (Ed.) (1979). Symbolic and algebraic computation. EUROSAM-79, Springer, Berlin.

Pau. L.F. (1981). Inference of the structure of economic reasoning from natural language analysis. 1981 Meeting, Society for economic dynamics and control, Copenhagen, June 1981.

Rescher, N. (1976). Plausible reasoning. Van Gorcum Publ., Amsterdam.

Roos, J.L. (1982). Semantic recognition of econometric models with syntactic automata. Proc. COMPSTAT 1982, Part II (Short papers), Physica Verlag, Wien.

Roos, J.L. (1983). Les automates formels appliqués à l'étude et à la classification des modèles économétriques. RAIRO, vol. 17, No 2.

Rowley, M.B. (1982), Foundations for the development of a single natural language Interface, NTIS, AD-A-112866.

Siekmann, J. (Ed) (1983), Automation of reasoning, Springer, Berlin.

Shortliffe, E., (1976) MYCIN. American Elsevier, NY.

Steward, D.W. (1965). Partitioning and tearing systems of equations. Siam, J. Numerical analysis, Vol. 2.

Winograd, T. (1972). Understanding Natural language. Academic Press.

Artificial Intelligence in Economics and Management
L.F. Pau (Editor)

COMPUTER AIDED LEARNING IN A TWO-LEVEL ECONOMY WITH NONLINEAR ECONOMIC REGULATORS

A. Straszak, J. Stefański, A. Ziółkowski, W. Cichocki

Systems Research Institute, Polish Academy of Sciences
Newelska 6, 01-447 Warszawa
Poland

The paper presents a system for computer aided learning which can help managers to adapt to changing environment. The essentials of the approach are: the use of graphical presentation of the results, the possibility of changing model structure by the user, and emphasis laid upon understandable and convenient man-machine dialogue. Application to the analysis of situation of a typical small enterprise in Poland is also discussed.

INTRODUCTION

Many early artificial intelligence programs aimed at problem solving were based on formal reasoning methods which help to reduce the search for a solution. On the other hand most expert systems which appeared to be very successful during the last decade are typically based on knowledge provided by human experts in the form of if-then rules of thumb. This is because researchers became aware that real-life problem solving tasks require a tremendous amount of knowledge. It seems however that the most fruitful way is to combine these two approaches [4]. If programs were able to expand their knowledge base by learning from experience, drawing analogy, and obtaining new heuristics by reasoning, they would be likely in a position to replace a human decision maker in specific situations. However, the human ability should not be neglected because probably there will be always situations in which a man will be necessary. It is doubtful, for instance, that a manager who runs a firm could be replaced by an intelligent computer program. It ought to be emphasized however that a specially designed program can effectively increase the user's ability [10]. And here we have come to a motivation for developing the computer system outlined in this paper. The system has been designed as a learning aid for managers and has been inspired by a specific economic situation in Poland.

Let us consider an economic system outlined in Fig. 1. Due to the new economic reform which has been introduced in Poland, the new rules of economic games between central governmental agencies and enterprises, and within the firms, rapidly increase demand for computer aided learning and analysis of the economic partners' behaviour. A nonlinear and incremental character of the central wage regulator as well as other modifications radically change the enterprises' behaviour and certain processes within the whole economy. Previous experience and knowledge dramatically loose their value. As a result the firms (and their managers) are faced with the problem of learning best behavioural rules according to the new situation. Three main reasons for the increase of demand for computer aided

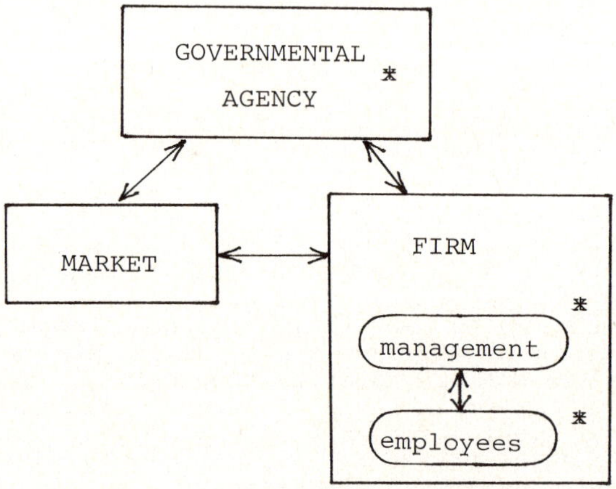

Figure 1
An economic system with three distinguished decision-makers

learning can be distinguished:

(1) rapid environmental changes, especially tax regulations (which may change even twice a year),

(2) an artificial character of some constraints the firms face. By artificial we mean here that they are caused by the legislative framework the firms are free to act within. Such a framework is designed by governmental institutions and often has nothing in common with the managers' past experience,

(3) disagreement of interests among various decision-makers influencing the firm's activity, which transforms one-agent optimization problem into a multi-actor game. Solution of the game is bound up with conjectures about the behaviour of the other partners.

In the sequel characteristic features of the system under consideration are described and an example illustrating its application is outlined.

OUTLINE OF THE SYSTEM

At the time of rapid environmental changes managers are faced with the problem of learning new behavioural rules. The ability to adapt to a changing environment demands intelligence. The aim of the system under consideration is not to replace a manager but to help him, to support the learning process, and therefore it is relevant to Intelligent Tutoring Systems [7]. As a result the system combines human intelligence with the ability of a computer. Such an approach appears to be effective in management since there are many situations in which human abilities cannot so far be replaced by artificial intelligence.

The nature of the human learning process is little understood but we know that the result of learning is not a collection of particular facts or even rules, but rather a sophisticated system of associations among remembered propositions [3]. It seems that in building such a network an important role is played by understanding the nature of facts [5], [2]. And this is probably one of the most powerful learning techniques available to human beings. Therefore the system under consideration helps the user to understand the nature of a particular economic system and their relevant optimization problems. In other words the system enables to look at the problems from different perspectives, to test conjectures and to discover new information by associating facts and drawing analogies. As a result the user can enrich his "knowledge base" and use the system as a tool for developing his reasoning ability. When talking about knowledge we have in mind not only the "simple" knowledge, i.e. the rules in the form of associations of facts, but also the "deeper layers" of knowledge which can explain these associations.

The essentials of the approach are: the use of a graphical presentation of the results, a special non-procedural language facilitating the man-computer dialogue, automatic analysis of the model's structure, possibilities of changing the structure of the model, extended possibilities of manipulating the model's variables as well as automatic minimization of computational effort. We will shortly comment on these properties.

Special language. This is a relatively simple user-oriented easy-to-learn language. Its first function is to describe and then to modify the structure of the investigated model. The sentences used to accomplish this are similar to those in Basic but the difference is that this language is non-procedural by which we mean that the order of putting the formulas in is not important. The second function of the language under consideration is to operate the computer system using simple sentences facilitating the dialogue. For example, if the user wants to find out in what way a variable u depends on the variable v subject to the constraint that another variable w equals 500, he can ask the program to draw the relevant figure writing simply

draw isoquant: w = 500, X = v, Y = u

or

DI: w = 500, X = v, Y = u

Minimization of computational effort. This means that the program analyses interdependences among variables and executes those formulas only which are necessary at the moment (e.g. necessary to calculate the values of v, u and w in the above example; in other words, if neither v, u nor w depend on a certain variable t, its value will not be calculated when executing the above instruction).

Manipulating the model's variables. At any moment the user can define a new variable in a way he likes. It can be an arithmetic formula depending on other variables or it can be a derivative of any variable with respect to any other. This possibility combined with the ability to associate the model's variables in various ways using graphics enables the user to study almost every aspect of the economic system's behaviour.

Analysis of the structure of the model. The two above mentioned features are attractive because the user need not bother about the place in the description of the model in which the change ought to be made. The program analyses interconnections among the model's variables, i.e. the structure of the model, and on this basis automatically determines the order in which all the formulas should be calculated. All contradictions are detected. After carrying the analysis out the model's structure is displayed to the user in the form of a chart. Next the user is asked if he wants to make any change in the structure.

Changing the structure of the model. This feature enables the user to analyse particular aspects of the influence of the structure of the model.

Graphical presentation. As already mentioned the main aim of the system under consideration is to support the human learning process by providing insights into the nature of an investigated economic system. An important role in this process is played by the man-machine communication conventions. We distinguish here two directions of an information flow, namely user-computer and computer-user. In the first case the special, outlined earlier language is used. In the latter case the nature of information is more sophisticated, therefore another way of representation of facts and knowledge had to be chosen. It seems that a graphical representation is much more appropriate for human beings than mathematical expressions, equations or tables. The advantage of such a representation is that it is natural and concise and, as a result, information and knowledge are relatively easy to acquire. Besides, the representation of knowledge can itself be a source of power. The user has a free choice of organizing a figure in order to highlight any aspect he wants to. He can choose one of three types of curves, i.e. ordinary form, parametric form, or isoquants, as well as of sets (in the form $A = \{(x,y)|L(x,y)\}$, where L is a logical expression which depends on the variables x,y). He can associate any variables or model's parameters in a figure and combine figures in a way he likes as well as augment any part of a figure. Those possibilities become more meaningful if we take into account the fact that the user can modify the model's structure and define new variables in various ways.

An important design consideration was to make the program capable of running on a microcomputer. The program is written in FORTRAN with some procedures written in ASSEMBLER (in order to reduce computational time) and implemented on ComPAN microcomputer with graphic devices. Currently the system is being tested on real life problems the firms' managers face.

LEARNING BEHAVIOURAL RULES IN AN ECONOMIC SYSTEM

The outlined system has been designed as a learning aid for actors taking part in an economic game - an application of this kind, in which the system appeared to be especially useful, will be briefly considered in this section. Let us take into account a firm operating in a market and being under the influence of a governmental agency which tries to control the firm's behaviour through tax regulations. Obviously the interests of the firm and the agency do not coincide. On the other hand the nature of the behaviour of a firm can be satisfactorily explained if we take into account the fact that the managers and the employees have different goals. Three types of decisions will be distinguished: tax regulations T connected with the wage and the bonus funds (they can be relatively often changed), a wage fund w and a production q. The employees, treated here as a group represented by a union, want to maximize the net income

$$J_2(T,w,q) = w + B(T,w,q), \tag{1}$$

where $B(\cdot)$ is the bonus bound up with the attained profit $\Pi(w,q)$ which, in turn, together with production q forms the management's objective:

$$J_1(w,q) = \alpha_1 \Pi(w,q) + \alpha_2 q, \quad \alpha_1,\alpha_2 \geq 0. \tag{2}$$

It is assumed that the governmental agency wants to maximize the tax revenue and to reduce inflation, what can be combined in a utility function in the form of a linear combination of these two goals:

$$J_o(T,w,q) = \beta_1 [t_R R(q)+t_p \Pi(w,q)+t_w w]-\beta_2 J_2(T,w,q)/q, \quad \beta_1,\beta_2 \geq 0 \tag{3}$$

where t_R, t_p, t_w are the tax rates connected with the revenue R, profit Π and wages w (the revenues connected with T are not incorporated here because in Poland they are reserved for special purposes).

Let us now focus on the behaviour of the above mentioned three parties taking part in the game. For clarity of considerations we will restrict our attention to the case of the following decision sequence: the agency announces tax regulations T first, then the management determines the wage fund w and then the employees work with the chosen productivity which means that they determine the production q in such a way as to maximize income:

$$q^R(T,w) = \arg \max_{q \in \psi(T,w)} J_2(T,w,q), \tag{4}$$

where the mapping $\psi: R \to 2^R$ describes conditions connected with the motivation to work (they can be defined in various ways - see [8] for an example). The management takes the worker's reaction into account and chooses its decision in the following way:

$$w^R(T) = \arg \max_{w \in \Omega(T)} J_1(w,q^R(T,w)), \tag{5}$$

where $\Omega(\cdot)$ is the set of admissible management's decisions [8]. The problem of the optimization of tax regulations can be also formulated [9]:

$$T^* = \arg \max_{T \in \Theta} J_o(T,w^R(T),q^R(T,w^R(T))), \tag{6}$$

where Θ restricts the forms of tax functions (e.g. in order to eliminate threat strategies).

Let us look at the roughly described economic system from the point of view of the managers of the firm. They want to run the firm successfully in various conditions and therefore they must fully understand the behaviour of the other decision-makers as well as the nature of the relevant optimization problems. Take the question concerning adaptation to changes in tax regulations T as an example. The management's objective (2) does not depend directly on T, but T ought to be taken into account by managers when determining their decision - see (5) (problem (5) cannot be solved analytically). Note, that the influence of T in this case is twofold, first, through the change of the employees' behaviour $q^R(\cdot)$ and second, through the change of the shape of the set of admissible decisions $\Omega(\cdot)$. Those dependencies, especially when combined together, are rather complex - it appears that the managers have no intuition about them and the computer system under consideration ought to help in the reasoning process. And here the problem of representation of complex ideas in a man-machine communication arises. Although there are many ways of knowledge representation [6] the problem we were facing here is specific in the sense that the more sophisticated information is transmitted from the computer to the user. In the reversed information flow an earlier mentioned special language is used but the program should express information in a more concise, suitable for the user way. A graphical representation turns to be such a powerful intuitive device. Using the various possibilities the system offers, the managers can obtain insight into the nature of the problem (5) and the sensitivity of its solution to changes in tax regulations.

Another example of a question the managers are interested in is the nature of dependence of the employees' reaction function q^R on the wage fund w. In this case, like in most of the other cases, an analytical solution is impossible. Obviously, using our system, the managers can easily obtain this dependence in a graphical form (or in the form of a table of values) but it does not explain why, in fact, the employees tend to react in such a way. In the case of considering the sensitivity of q^R to changes in real valued parameters the situation is relatively simple, it becomes more complicated if we want, for instance, to investigate the dependence on the shape of a certain set. In solving (4) an important role is played by the set $A_\psi=\{(w,q)|q\in\psi(T,w)\}$, i.e. the set of the decisions, taken inside a firm, for which motivational conditions (given by the mapping ψ which appears in (4)) are satisfied. This is, in turn, connected with the definition of the mapping ψ which, in fact, is always only a conjecture. The need to incorporate the mapping ψ may be illustrated by the following simple example. Let us suppose that in a certain situation the employees are in a position to increase their net income by 0.1% (which makes, for instance, 1 $ per person) if they increase their effort by 20%. It is clear that, from the practical point of view, the incentive to increase effort is not sufficient although theoretically it exists. If we accepted such a "theoretical" behaviour, the mapping ψ would not be taken into account (to be precise: $\psi(T,w)=[0,\infty)$). But if we want to incorporate the above mentioned phenomena we must make a certain conjecture about the nature of ψ (an example is given in [8]). The extensive possibilities of the computer system under consideration greatly facilitate arriving at the appropriate definition of ψ. Note that questions of this kind often face us when considering decision problems involving several decision-makers. In such cases we should take into account psychological phenomena and the other partners' subjective perceptions of the conflict [1].

Using examples connected with the above outlined economic system we merely tried to point out that for a manager who wants to act successfully in a changing and involving other partners environment there is no other way out but to understand the nature of the behaviour of the system. And the computer system under consideration greatly facilitates this process.

CONCLUDING REMARKS

The basic idea behind the development of the computer system outlined in this paper was to support the learning process, to facilitate the understanding of the economic system's behaviour. Behaviour of such a system as a whole results from interactions of several decision makers who are free to act within some specified boundaries. Providing ready-to-accept solutions to the relevant optimization problems is not sufficient in such a case and therefore our system tries to enable the user to explain the nature of the results and, using various means, to develop the user's reasoning ability and his "knowledge base". In the man-machine communication a special language is used and a graphical representation has been emphasized. The program analyses data describing the investigated model and automatically determines the order in which all the formulas should be executed. The computational effort is also automatically minimized.

Certainly the computer system under consideration is not in a position to help solve all the problems the managers and other decision-makers are facing. But even if certain problems cannot be satisfactorily dealt with, their existence can, and should be, recognized.

REFERENCES

1. Bryant J., Modelling Alternative Realities in Conflict and Negotiation, J. Operational Research Society, vol. 35, no. 11, (1984) 985-993.
2. De Kleer J., Brown J.S., A Qualitative Physics Based on Confluences, Artificial Intelligence, vol. 24 (1984) 7-83.
3. Estes W.K., Human Learning and Memory, in: Morler P., Terrace H.S. (eds.), The Biology of Learning (Springer Verlag, 1984).
4. Kastner J.K., Hang S.J., A Review of Expert Systems, Europ. J. of Operational Research 18, (1984) 285-292.
5. Kuipers B., Commonsense Reasoning about Causality: Deriving Behavior from Structure, Artificial Intelligence, vol. 24 (1984) 169-203.
6. Sage A.P., Models for Knowledge Representation and Cognitive Effort in Human Problem Solving, 9th IFAC World Congress, Budapest, Hungary 1984. Prepints, vol. VI, 216-221.
7. Sleeman D., Brown J.S., Intelligent Tutoring Systems (Academic Press, New York, 1982).
8. Stefański J., A Game Theory Model of Labor-Management Conflict and Compromise, in: Brandstaetter H., Kirchler E. (eds.), Economic Psychology (Trauner Verlag, Linz 1985).
9. Stefański J., Cichocki W., Tax Regulation Design as a Strategy Selection in a System with Conflicting Goals, Int. Symp. on Systems Analysis and Simulation, Berlin, GDR, 1985, Proc., 155-153.
10. Su Shi-quan, A Structure for Flexible Interactive Decision--Making, 9th IFAC World Congress, Budapest, Hungary 1984. Preprints, vol. VI, 228-233.

Artificial Intelligence in Economics and Management
L.F. Pau (Editor)
Elsevier Science Publishers B.V. (North-Holland), 1986

USER CONTROL KNOWLEDGE IN A TAX CONSULTING SYSTEM

by C. Duncan MacRae*
U.S. Department of Housing and Urban Development
7th and "D" Sts., S.W., Room 8204
Washington, DC 20410

Abstract

The purpose of this paper is to demonstrate the utility of including knowledge possessed by the user in developing a control strategy for an expert consulting system. Acquiring declarative knowledge imposes a burden on the user in terms of responding to the queries for facts as the system uses its control knowledge in an attempt to apply its procedural knowledge. Allowing the user to participate in the control strategy reduces this burden by reducing the number of unnecessary queries for facts. In this paper the input of control knowledge possessed by the user is illustrated in the context of a consulting system for problem solving in the domain of the Federal income tax law. This system is intended to be used by an accountant or lawyer who formulates a question of tax research and provides facts regarding a specific taxpayer to answer the question. The system is implemented in the logic programming language Prolog.

*The research forming the basis for this paper was performed while the author was with the U.S. Department of the Treasury. Opinions expressed are those of the author and do not necessarily represent the views of the Department of Housing and Urban Development or the views of the Department of the Treasury.

USER CONTROL KNOWLEDGE IN A TAX CONSULTING SYSTEM

by C. Duncan MacRae
U.S. Department of Housing and Urban Development

It is common to divide the knowledge needed by an expert consulting system into three categories: declarative knowledge, procedural knowledge and control knowledge [Nilsson, 1980]. Declarative knowledge consists of a data base of facts specific to an individual user of the consulting system. Procedural knowledge is knowledge regarding a specific domain of expertise, e.g., medicine or law, represented in the form of if-then statements or production rules. Control knowledge is the knowledge about desirable strategies for selecting the rules to solve the problem addressed by the system.

Declarative knowledge is provided by the user typically in response to queries by the expert consulting system, as it attempts to match antecedents of rules to the facts in order to infer the consequents of the rules [Sergot, 1983]. The procedural knowledge is obtained from the expert in the domain to which the system is applied. Control knowledge is then typically provided by an AI expert, although increasing attention is being devoted to acquiring some control knowledge from the domain expert [Davis, 1980].

The purpose of this paper is to demonstrate the utility of including knowledge possessed by the user in developing a control strategy for an expert consulting system. Acquiring declarative knowledge imposes a burden on the user in terms of responding to the queries for facts as the system uses its control knowledge in an attempt to apply its procedural knowledge. Allowing the user to participate in the control strategy reduces this burden by reducing the number of unnecessary queries for facts.

In this paper the input of control knowledge possessed by the user is illustrated in the context of a consulting system for problem solving in the domain of the Federal income tax law.[1] This system, which is currently under development, is intended to be used by an accountant or lawyer who formulates a question of tax research and provides facts regarding a specific taxpayer to answer the question.[2] The system is currently implemented in the logic programming language Prolog [Pereira, 1983].[3]

Following this introductory section the declarative knowledge or data base of tax facts for a specific taxpayer in the current version of the tax consulting system is briefly described. Next the procedural knowledge or rule base of income tax law in the consulting system is presented. Then the control system or inference engine employed in the system is discussed. The paper concludes with a summary of results.

---

1 For an exposition in the context of tax problem solving of the concepts employed in a rule-based consulting system, see MacRae [1985].

2 For a review of the application of computer-assisted analysis techniques to taxation, see Kovach [1982].

3 The Micro-PLANNER programming language employed by McCarty [1977] may be viewed as a precursor of Prolog.

I. DECLARATIVE KNOWLEDGE

The declarative knowledge relevant to tax problem solving is represented in a global data base, which consists of tax facts for a specific taxpayer. A fact, i.e., a proposition, is represented in the current version of the tax consulting system as a Prolog structure.

For example, the fact that the 'Megabucks lottery prize' is compensation for services income for 'Jane Doe' is represented by the structure

```
fact(['Megabucks lottery prize',is,compensation,
     for,services,income,of,'Jane Doe']),
```

where the argument of the functor "fact" is a Prolog list whose elements are Prolog constants, as indicated by terms beginning with lower-case letters or terms set off in single quotes, e.g., 'Megabucks lottery prize'.

Negation is treated explicitly in this consulting system, rather than as failure, as is common in Prolog-based expert systems [Clark and McCabe, 1982]. For example, the fact that the Megabucks prize is not excludable by law from the gross income of Jane Doe is represented by the structure

```
fact(~['Megabucks lottery prize',is,excludable,
      by,law,from,gross,income,of,'Jane Doe']),
```

where ~ is a defined operator recognized by the system inference engine, which is described below.

II. PROCEDURAL KNOWLEDGE

The procedural knowledge relevant to tax problem solving is represented in the form of if-then statements or production rules describing the income tax law.[4] The law includes not only the Internal Revenue Code and the associated Treasury Regulations but also the rulings of the Internal Revenue Service and the relevant court decisions. In the current version of the tax consulting system the rules are represented as Prolog structures.

For example, the conditions given in Treasury Regulations 1.61-2(a) for determining if any item of compensation for services is income for any taxpayer can be represented by the structure

```
rule('Reg. Sec. 1.61-2(a)',
    ([Item,is,income,of,Taxpayer] if
     [Item,is,compensation,for,services,income,
      of,Taxpayer])),
```

where "if" is a defined operator, recognized by the Prolog-based inference engine, and unquoted terms beginning with upper case letters are Prolog variables.

There are many definitions in the tax law, explicit or implied. Since negation is not treated as failure in the prototype system, the "only if" part of a definition must be treated explicitly [Kowalski, 1979]. In the current version of the tax consulting system, the "if" part of the definition is represented in the form of a rule, as shown above. Then the "only if" part is represented by a second rule formed by negating the consequent and antecedents of the first rule.

For example, the general definition of gross income in Treasury Regulations 1.61-1(a) is given by

---

4 For a discussion of representing the tax law in terms of if-then statements, also see Allen and Orechkoff [1957].

```
rule ('Reg. Sec. 1.61-1(a)',
      ([Item,is,gross,income,of,Taxpayer] if
       [Item,is,income,of,Taxpayer] and
       ~[Item,is,excludable,by,law,from,gross,income,
         of,Taxpayer])).
```

and its converse

```
rule ('Reg. Sec. 1.61-1(a)',
      (~[Item,is,gross,income,of,Taxpayer] if
       ~[Item,is,income,of,Taxpayer] or
       [Item,is,excludable,by,law,from,gross,income,
        of,Taxpayer])).
```

where "and" and "or" are defined operators, interpreted by the inference engine of the tax consulting system.

In addition to tax information, the rules contain some control information. To help guide the inference engine the rules are grouped under headings which are represented by structures. In the current system, the groups correspond to the section of the Internal Revenue Code or Treasury Regulations referenced by the rule. For example, the structure corresponding to Reg. Sec. 1.61-2(a) is

```
heading('Reg. Sec. 1.61-2(a)',
        'Income - compensation for services').
```

As we will see in the next section, these headings are employed by the user to guide the search for an answer to a question posed to the system. The size of the groups, therefore, involves a choice between the user cost of acquiring declarative knowledge and the cost to the user of providing control knowledge. The smaller the size, the smaller the user cost of acquiring facts that might match the antecedents of these rules but the larger the user cost of choosing among rule groups, since there are a greater number of groups.

III. CONTROL KNOWLEDGE

The inference engine or control system of the tax consultant is an interpreter written in Prolog. The control system is currently designed to allow the user to ascertain whether certain tax facts are true or false or can be inferred to be true or false using the tax law as represented by the rules in the knowledge base, given already known facts and answers by the user to questions of fact.

The overriding objective of this consultant system is that the time and effort of the user should be economized rather than time or storage on the computer. Accordingly the user is never asked a question that the computer could derive for itself. Furthermore, to economize on the volume of the questions asked of the user, the user is allowed to direct the search for the answer.

Short of working through the Prolog code for the tax consultant system, the best way to understand how the inference engine works is with an illustration. Let us imagine that Frank Jones is a recipient of the Foo Award for achievement in the field of artificial intelligence. To confirm whether or not the Foo Award is an item of gross income of Frank Jones, we enter in response to the tax consultant system prompt >

```
'Foo Award' is gross income of 'Frank Jones' ?
```

The inference engine first tries to ascertain whether the fact that is queried, or its negation is in the data base, i.e., is already known. If the fact or its negation is not already known, then the system attempts - using goal directed reasoning or backward chaining - to derive the fact from already known facts and available rules but without asking the user for any further facts or guidance in the search. Again the objective is to economize on the user not on the computer. The system will never ask for help doing what it can do for itself.

If the system is not able to confirm or deny the fact that is being queried without further facts from the user, then the user is informed of the class or classes of rules that have the question as a consequent. For example, to the query given above the system would, in the absence of any facts, respond

```
[ Backward chaining]
Foo Award is income of Frank Jones ?
true(t)/false(f)/1.-10./unknown(u)/why(w)
 1:  Income - compensation for services
 2:  Income - derived from business
 3:  Income - gains derived from dealing in property
 4:  Income - interest
 5:  Income - rents and royalties
 6:  Income - dividends
 7:  Income - alimony, ...; annuities; income from life
                insurance ...
 8:  Income - pensions
 9:  Income - income from discharge of indebtedness
10:  Income - ... partnership ...; ... decedent ...;
              ... estate or trust
```

where the classes of rules correspond to groupings of the 15 items of income listed in Section 61 of the Internal Revenue Code. The rules link Section 61 for these items of income to other sections of the Code.

Given the response from the system above, the user may choose any of the classes of rules to explore. The choice does not commit the user to a class of rules. If the class fails to confirm or deny the queried fact, then the list of classes would ultimately be presented again, but minus the class that failed. The user also has the opportunity to answer "true", "false" or "unknown" to the question posed, rather than selecting a class of rules to pursue. This "answer-first" feature will be described below. The system also has an explanatory "why" capability that will be discussed below.

Let us assume that we decide to explore the rules for compensation for services, i.e., answer "1". The system would then respond

```
[Backward chaining]
Foo Award is compensation for services income of Frank Jones ?
true(t)/false(f)/1.-8./unknown(u)/why(w)
1: Compensation for services - distributions from employees' trusts
2: Compensation for services - compensation for child's
                               service
3: Compensation for services - prizes and awards
4: Compensation for services - gifts
5: Compensation for services - compensation for injuries
                               or sickness
6: Compensation for services - accidents and health plans
7: Compensation for services - scholarship and fellowship
                               grants
```

8: Compensation for services - miscellaneous items

to which we readily answer "3".

The system now reports that it is exploring the "Prizes and awards - in general" class.

[Backward chaining]
Prizes and awards - in general

Foo award is received as prize or award to Frank Jones ?
true(t)/false(f)/unknown(u)/why(w)

If for an antecedent of a rule there is no rule with that antecedent as consequent, then the user must be queried regarding the antecedent. For example, the user is queried above regarding whether the Foo Award is a prize or award to Frank Jones, since the rules in the class being considered "Prizes and awards - in general" depend on knowing this fact. The user can answer "true", "false" or "unknown". If the user answers "false", the fact that the Foo Award is not a prize or award to Frank Jones will be added to the database of facts. If the answer is "unknown", no facts will be added to the database but the user will not be queried again for this fact. Hence, all rules that depend on the truth or falsehood of the fact will fail to apply.

Assuming that the user answers "true" to the question above, the system would then ask

Foo Award is Sec. 117 scholarship or fellowship income of Frank Jones ?
false(f)/true(t)/unknown(u)/why(w)

to confirm that the prize or award is covered by Section 74 of the Internal Revenue Code rather than Section 117 on scholarships and fellowships.

Note that the user is prompted first with "false" and then with "true". The first answer in the prompt indicates the answer which would allow the system to confirm the truth of the consequent using the rule under consideration with the queried fact as antecedent. In this way the system provides further information to the user regarding the character of its reasoning process. To confirm this we ask "why", to which the system responds

Sec. 74 implies:
Foo Award is Section 74 prize or award income of Frank Jones
if
Foo Award is received as prize or award to Frank Jones
and
∿ Foo Award is Section 117 scholarship or fellowship grant
income of Frank Jones

Assuming that the user answers false to the question above, the system responds first with

[Forward chaining]
Prizes and awards - in general
Sec. 74 implies:
Foo Award is Sec. 74 prize or award income of Frank Jones !

[Forward chaining]
Income - compensation for services
Reg. Sec. 1.61-2(a) implies:
Foo Award is income of Frank Jones !

As we can see, the system engages in fact-driven reasoning or forward chaining, much in the way a human would. Once a fact has been ascertained either by query or by inference, the system looks to the rules with that fact as an antecedent to see if any of the consequents of these rules can now be inferred given this new fact and the existing facts in the data base. Since the system attempts to forward chain before it returns to backward chaining, inferences are actually made through forward chaining. But the rule choices and queries posed to the user are determined by backward chaining. In this way the reasoning process that the system carries out corresponds to the process that a human would undertake when confronted with a similar problem.

Once the system can no longer engage in forward chaining, it returns to backward chaining to verify the original query

```
[Backward chaining]
Gross income - general definition

[Backward chaining]
Compensation for services, ... - prizes and awards

[Backward chaining]
Foo Award is excludable under Section 74
     from gross income of Frank Jones ?
false(f)/true(t)/1.-3./unknown(u)/why(w)

1: Prizes and awards - From giveaway show; door prize;
                        from employer
2: Prizes and awards - in general
3: Prizes and awards - Nobel prize; Pulitzer prize
```

As mentioned above, whenever there is a choice of which rule class to explore to verify a fact, i.e., item i is excludable under Section 74 from gross income of taxpayer t, the user is given the opportunity of not only choosing a rule class but also choosing to verify the fact directly. This "answer-first" feature allows the user to terminate a line of inquiry which he knows either will be unproductive or is unnecessary.[5] For example, if the user knew Section 74 of the Code sufficiently well that he did not need to be reminded of the law in the area, he could simply state the truth or falsehood of the fact rather than having to answer queries about numerous antecedent facts. In this way the system economizes on the time and effort of the user.

Assuming that the user does not wish to state the fact directly, he must choose which rule class to explore initially. As has already been pointed out, the prompts are ordered, with the first answer indicating the answer which would allow the system to confirm the truth of the consequent using the rule under consideration with the queried fact as antecedent. The classes are ordered in a similar manner, with the first class containing rules (if any) that would allow the system to confirm the truth of the consequent under consideration and the last class containing rules (if any) that would allow the system to confirm the falsehood of the consequent.

For example, the first class above, dealing with giveaway show, door prizes, etc., is a class of examples, in the Treasury Regulations for Section 74, of prizes and awards that are not excludable from gross income. The third class, Pulitzer and Nobel prizes, is a class of examples of prizes and awards that are excluded from gross income. The second class, "Prizes and awards - in general", however, contains provisions from Section 74 that determine in general whether or not an item is excluded from gross income. The prizes and awards dealt with in the first class are examples of prizes or awards that do not meet one or more of the conditions for exclusion from gross

5 The expert consulting system MYCIN [Shortliffe, 1976] popularized the use of what is referred to in this paper as the "answer-first" feature.

income under Section 74(b). The prizes and awards dealt with in the third class are examples of prizes or awards that do meet the conditions in one way or another. But in neither case of examples are there indications in the Regulations which conditions for exclusion were or were not met.

Since the Foo Award does not correspond to one of the examples in the Regulations for Section 74, we choose the second class to which the system asks

```
[Backward chaining]
Foo Award is in one of Section 74 categories of past achievement
     of Frank Jones ?
false(f)/true(t)/1.-4./unknown(u)/why(w)
1:  Prizes and awards - fishing derby
2 : Prizes and awards - sports awards
3:  Prizes and awards - scientific achievement
4:  Prizes and awards - in general
```

where being "in one of Section 74 categories of past achievement" is the first of the three conditions for exclusion from gross income under Section 74. The first three classes of rules correspond to Internal Revenue Service rulings and Federal judicial interpretations dealing with the first condition. The fourth class contains the rules detailing the Section 74 categories of past achievement, as spelled out in the Internal Revenue Code.

Although the Foo Award does not correspond to the first two classes of rules, it might fit a fact pattern in the third class, i.e., scientific achievement. Thus, we choose this class to which the system asks

```
Foo Award is made in recognition of 'Rogallo' scientific
     achievement of Frank Jones ?
true(t)/false(f)/unknown(u)/why(w)
```

Evidentally there is only one "scientific achievement" case dealing with the first condition for exclusion, i.e., the Rogallo case.

In the tax consultant system there is ideally a rule for every case and ruling dealing with the sections of the Internal Revenue Code that are currently covered by the system. In this way the user is put on notice that there are Service positions or Court decisions dealing with the issue about which he is being queried. However, the cases and rulings have not been "briefed," i.e., the holdings of these cases have not been expressed in terms of rules. Therefore, he must perform the tax research necessary to ascertain whether or not his fact pattern fits the pattern of the case or ruling cited.

To get the citation to the Rogallo case we simply ask "why", to which the system responds

```
Rogallo v. U.S., 475 F. 2d 537 (CA4 1973) implies:
Foo Award is in one of Section 74 categories of past achievement
     of Frank Jones
if
Foo Award is made in recognition of Rogallo scientific
     achievement of Frank Jones
```

Assuming the Foo Award does not fit the facts of the Rogallo case, the user would answer "false", to which the system would ask

```
[Backward chaining]
Foo Award is in one of Section 74 categories of past achievement
     of Frank Jones ?
```

```
false(f)/true(t)/1.-3./unknown(u)/why(w)
1:  Prizes and awards - fishing derby
2:  Prizes and awards - sports awards
3:  Prizes and awards - in general
```

indicating that the "scientific achievement" class of rules has been eliminated by the system.

Since we have already eliminated the first two classes of rules, the only choice now is the third class of rules, spelling out the Section 74 categories of past achievement. Therefore, in response to this choice the system first asks

```
Foo Award is made in recognition of religious achievements
     of Frank Jones ?
false(f)/true(t)/unknown(u)/why(w)
```

to which we answer "false". Next the system asks

```
Foo Award is made in recognition of charitable achievements
     of Frank Jones ?
false(f)/true(t)/unknown(u)/why(w)
```

to which we again answer "false". Then the system asks

```
Foo Award is made in recognition of scientific achievements
     of Frank Jones ?
false(f)/true(t)/unknown(u)/why(w)
```

to which we answer "true" so that the system concludes that the first condition for exclusion from gross income under Section 74 is satisfied:

```
[Forward chaining]
Prizes and awards - in general
Sec. 74 implies:
Foo Award is in one of Section 74 categories of past achievement
     of Frank Jones !
```

Note that there were no germane cases or rulings.

The system next turns to the second condition for exclusion from gross income:

```
[Backward chaining]
Gross income - general definition

[Backward chaining]
Compensation for services, ... - prizes and awards

[Backward chaining]
Frank Jones was selected with action on his part to receive
     Foo Award ?
true(t)/false(f)/1.-3./unknown(u)/why(w)
1:  Prizes and awards - civic achievement award
2:  Prizes and awards - participation in contest
3:  Prizes and awards - Rockefeller Public Service Awards
```

where all three classes of rules correspond to cases and rulings on the issue about which we are being queried.

Assuming that we are confident enough to answer "false" without further research into the pertinent cases and rulings, the system then turns to the final condition for exclusion:

```
[Backward chaining]
Frank Jones is required to render substantial future services
    for Foo Award ?
true(t)/false(f)/1.-2./unknown(u)/why(w)
1: Prizes and awards - scientific achievement
2: Prizes and awards - Maria Moore Cabot prize
```

We are prepared to answer with a response of "false"; but since the Foo Award is a scientific achievement, we check out the first class, to which the system asks

```
Foo Award is made in recognition of 'Mueller' scientific
    achievement of Frank Jones ?
true(t)/false(f)/unknown(u)/why(w)
```

After reviewing the Mueller case we can answer "false" to which the system then responds, since there is now only one class,

```
[Backward chaining]
Prizes and awards - Maria Moore Cabot prize

Foo Award is 'Maria Moore Cabot' prize to Frank Jones ?
true(t)/false(f)/unknown(u)/why(w)
```

to which we immediately respond "false".

Now having eliminated the available rule classes, the system once again asks,

```
[Backward chaining]
Frank Jones is required to render substantial future services
    for Foo Award ?
true(t)/false(f)/unknown(u)/why(w)
```

to which we now answer confidently "false". The system then concludes

```
[Forward chaining]
Prizes and awards - in general
Sec. 74 implies:
Foo Award is excludable under Section 74 from gross income of
    Frank Jones !

[Forward chaining]
Compensation for services, ... - prizes and awards
Reg. Sec. 1.61-2(a)(2)(iii) implies:
Foo Award is excludable by law from gross income of Frank Jones !

[Forward chaining]
Gross income - General definition
Reg. Sec. 1.61-1(a) implies:
Foo Award is gross income of Frank Jones !
```

The Foo Award to Frank Jones does indeed satisfy the conditions for exclusion from gross income under Section 74 of the Internal Revenue Code; it is not gross income for him.

IV: CONCLUSIONS

The traditional approach to designing an AI production system is to focus on the computational cost of incorporating knowledge in the system. It is recognized that there is a tradeoff between the control strategy cost of incorporating knowledge and the rule application cost [Nilsson, 1980]. The more "informed" the system, the lower the computational cost of applying the rules but the higher is the computational cost of the control strategy.

This approach ignores, however, the cost to the user in terms of time and effort in responding to queries for facts to allow the rules to be applied. It also ignores the potential for the user to contribute control knowledge to reduce the number and character of requests of the user for declarative knowledge.

In this paper we have seen the utility of incorporating user control knowledge in a tax consulting system, which is intended for use by accountants and lawyers with problems of tax research. In this system, which is currently under development, declarative knowledge, i.e., facts, are represented as Prolog structures, as is procedural knowledge, i.e., rules. The inference engine of the system is a Prolog-based interpreter, which allows the user to respond not only to queries for facts but also to queries for which class of rules to explore in an attempt to resolve the issue of tax research posed. There is an explanatory "why" capability in the system to aid the user in responding to these queries.

We have also seen that there is a tradeoff between the user cost of declarative knowledge and the user cost of control knowledge. The more the user contributes to the control strategy, the lower the user cost of acquiring the facts to apply the rules but the higher the user cost of the control strategy.

REFERENCES

Allen, L. E. and G. Orechkoff, "Toward a More Systematic Drafting and Interpreting of the Internal Revenue Code," University of Chicago Law Review (Autumn 1957), pp. 1-62.

Clark, K. L., "Prolog: A Language for Implementing Expert Systems," in J. E. Hayes et al eds. Machine Intelligence 10 (Ellis Horwood, 1982).

David, R., "Meta-Rules: Reasoning About Control," Artificial Intelligence (1980) pp. 179-222.

Kovach, R. J., "Application of Computer-assisted Analysis Techniques to Taxation," Akron Law Review (Spring 1982).

MacRae, C. D., "Tax Problem Solving with an IF-THEN System," in C. Walter ed. Computing Power and Legal Reasoning (West, 1985).

McCarty, L. T., "Reflections on TAXMAN: An Experiment in Artificial Intelligence and Legal Reasoning," Harvard Law Review (March 1977), pp. 837-893.

Nilsson, N. J., Principles of Artificial Intelligence (Tioga, 1980)

Pereira, F., ed. C-Prolog User's Manual, (Department of Architecture, University of Edinburgh, 1983).

Sergot, M. A., "A Query-the-User Facility for Logic Programming," in P. Degano and E. Sandewall eds. Integrated Interactive Computing Systems (North-Holland, 1983).

Shortliffe, E. H., Computer-based Medical Consultations: MYCIN (American Elsevier, 1967).

Artificial Intelligence in Economics and Management
L.F. Pau (Editor)

AN EXPERT ADVISORY SYSTEM FOR GOVERNMENT REGULATIONS: KNOWLEDGE ACQUISITION METHODOLOGY

B. Tauzovich++, S. Matwin+, F. Oppacher+++, D. Skuce+, S. Szpakowicz+

\+ Dept. of Computer Science, University of Ottawa, Ottawa, Canada
++ Cognos Inc., Ottawa, Canada
+++ School of Computer Science, Carleton University, Ottawa, Canada

A methodology is described for building knowledge base systems that handle the knowledge found in regulations, specifications and other similar documents. The approach involves manually translating the document into a simple, English-like language. which combines a production rule approach with constraints, hierarchies and scripts. Our methodology structures the process of translation and verification using several software tools. The retrieval process is based on various types of deduction and associative indexing of rules and facts. Though our example is travel regulations, the method is general enough to be useful for most technical material, such as software description, design or service specifications, or training manuals.

1. INTRODUCTION AND OVERVIEW

The goal of the research described here is to develop a variety of advisor systems which we term 'Knowledge Source Systems' (KSSs). Such systems are intended to initially augment and eventually replace conventional natural language (NL) documents for storing suitable types of knowledge. Machine understanding of written NL of the kind encountered in these documents is probably one of the most challenging and practically interesting problems for AI. We believe that our approach is an important step toward this goal. The methodology we are proposing will result in computer systems which will eventually replace the following types of documents: rules and regulations of an organization; specifications for the design of some structure or system; documentation on how to use or service some device or system; legal or medical case histories; textbook knowledge, e.g. in medicine, engineering, or computer science.

Virtually all such information is stored at present in printed NL form, which is perhaps machine readable but not machine understandable. When information is expressed in unconstrained NL, retrieval and understanding are subject to all the lexical, syntactic, semantic, logical, and organizational errors and uncertainties that humans can make. To significantly reduce these serious communication errors, computers must participate in formulating, checking and retrieving knowledge in ways far beyond what today's information retrieval (library searching or document retrieval) systems or specialized documentation aids offer. To do so, we believe it is necessary to encode the information in a highly-structured form, following certain principles developed in AI research. When thus encoded, knowledge becomes more interpretable by computers. In addition, people are pleased to find that much of the frustrating vagueness usually found in even the best of NL sources has been eliminated or at least controlled.

In summary, we seek a general methodology for capturing and making easily accessible and understandable, both to humans and to software components, the kinds of knowledge found in applications such as those mentioned above.

There are two main components to such a KSS:

a) an encoding methodology whereby the unconstrained NL of the source text is replaced (manually, with computer assistance) by a logic-based, NL-like text which captures the semantic essence of the source material and eliminates the uncertainties and ambiguities;

b) an interactive retrieval system which enables the user to quickly find relevant knowledge.

In this paper, we attempt to describe and systematize the process that knowledge engineers perform, as an essential first step.

Our approach involves:

* partitioning knowledge into declarative and procedural forms (we deal only with the former in this paper, though we have worked extensively on both);

* partitioning declarative knowledge into several types: lexical knowledge, facts, and rules;

* structuring knowledge into two easy-to-read formats that facilitate both machine and human understanding: one a restricted English, termed ELESK, the other an English-like logical language, termed LESK [8] (a simple mapping exists between the two);

* developing a well-defined methodology for translating the source NL into the formalized formats, together with software tools to facilitate this difficult process.

In this paper we will explain our encoding method using as an example Canadian government travel regulations, which we have selected and studied extensively as typical of institutional regulations. We have attempted to keep our methodology as general as possible, so that most of the knowledge structuring devices we use would be useful in other applications. The question-answering component of our system will not be discussed here. It is reported in another paper [9].

The software tools which assist the translation have been implemented in C-Prolog for the VAX under UNIX.

2. REPRESENTATION OF RULES

2.1 The Four Representational Forms

The basic structure of our representation for a rule is derived from Horn clauses similar to those in PROLOG. When written in a PROLOG-like form, i.e.

$$\text{body} \rightarrow \text{head}$$

we call this the 'internal form'. It means: "any instantiation of the variables which makes the body true makes the head true". Since the internal form is unpleasant to read, we have defined a simple, English-like form we term LESK (Language for Exactly Stating Knowledge) [8]. A straightforward bidirectional translation exists between internal form and LESK, implemented by a compiler written in PROLOG. For example, a (simplified) internal form of a rule might be

```
    claims(Ee, Exp) & has(Ee, Ppay)
  → claims_with(Ee, Exp, Ppay)
```

The corresponding LESK form is

```
if      Employee claims Expense
        Employee has Proof_of_Payment
then    Employee claims Expense with Proof_of_payment
```

We have defined a second version of LESK (ELESK) which eliminates the use of variables and is a restricted subset of English. This is desirable for showing encoded rules to experts for verification of correctness, and also for use as a convenient query language. (Skilled personnel may prefer the LESK form because it is briefer.) LESK and ELESK can be generated from the internal form, and vice versa. We will not discuss ELESK in this paper.

The fourth form is the original English text. Our system stores the internal form and the original text so that a user may always know from where a LESK rule came.

2.2 Knowledge Base Structure

There are two structural dimensions to our knowledge base organization. One, the division of rules and supplementary information into hierarchical units, will be discussed in Section 3. The other, the classification of knowledge types, is summarized in Fig. 1. We have concentrated at present on declarative knowledge; the only procedural knowledge we discuss here (i.e. about sequences of actions) is in elementary scripts, described in Section 3. The fact/rule dichotomy is derived from PROLOG, though we do not treat our rules as procedures in the PROLOG sense, but use them declaratively. A definition is a rule which answers the question 'what is the meaning of ...?'. Regular rules are those derived from source text statements which are not definitions.

Facts are statements used in isolation, i.e. without syntactically attached conditions. Facts and rules use domain-specific predicates, which are derived from nouns, verbs and adjectives in the source text. A fixed set of domain-independent predicates are those useful in all subject areas, and are predefined in LESK.

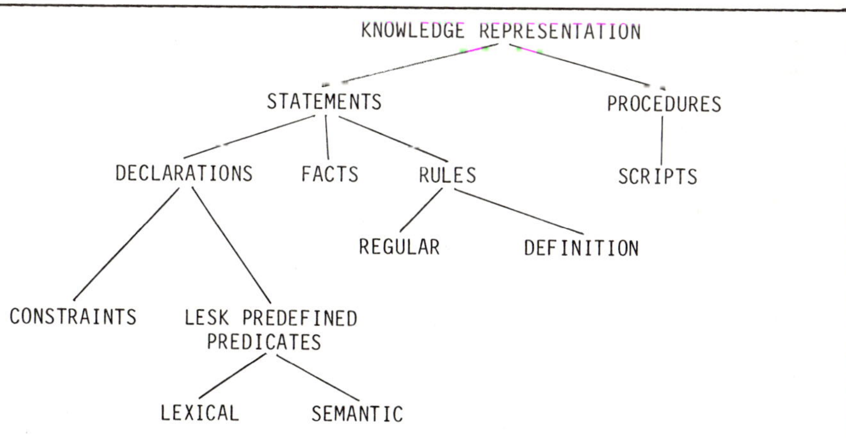

FIGURE 1. KNOWLEDGE REPRESENTATION HIERARCHY

3. METHODOLOGY OF KNOWLEDGE ACQUISITION

3.1 General Organization of the Translation Process

In our system, knowledge acquisition is quite different from the normal approach in expert system development. Rather than interviewing an expert, we rely mainly on the written text of the source document, though one could acquire knowledge verbally using LESK to write it down. The heavily interactive process of extracting knowledge from an expert by means of interviews, combined with disambiguation of that knowledge and attempts to make it more complete, is replaced by careful analysis of the written document which is the authoritative source. Of course, ambiguity and incompleteness of the knowledge source are still an issue, which can only be solved satisfactorily by consulting experts. Access to an expert, who is ready to answer questions, is necessary to have confidence in the correctness of the translation.

Translating a document into LESK is broken into two principal stages: (a) preliminary analysis of the source document; (b) the actual translation.

Each of these stages may be iterated, in combination with a critique of the result by an expert, giving the following overall scheme of the translation methodology shown in Fig. 2.

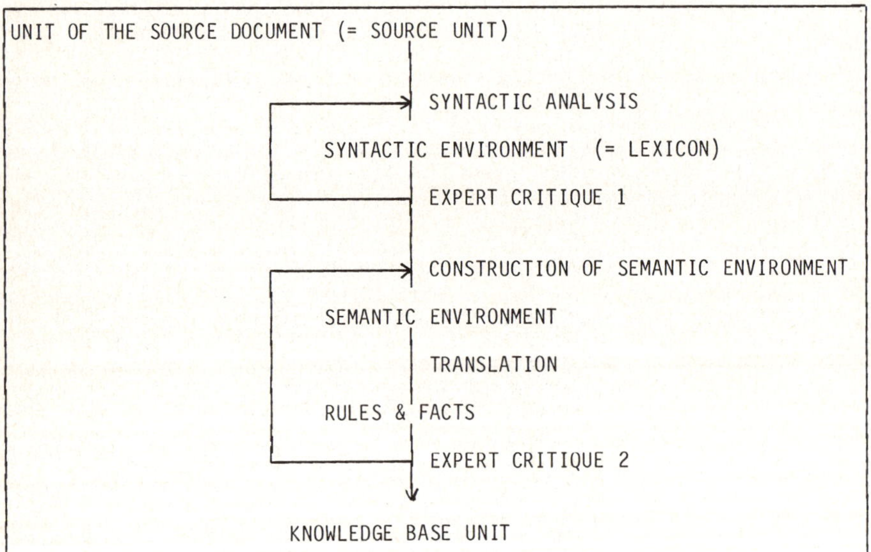

FIGURE 2. BASIC TRANSLATION SCHEME (BTS)

Typically, documents which will be subject to the translation process are structured into source units: chapters, sections, subsections etc. The smallest source unit could be one sentence. In our approach, we proceed incrementally by applying the Basic Translation Scheme (Fig. 2) to source units, one at a time. The corresponding output of each BTS application is called a 'Knowledge Base Unit' and consists of two basic components: the environment and the rules and facts. The syntactic analysis phase provides part of the environment, which is referred to as the syntactic environment. (By lexicon, we mean the syntactic environment.) The translation develops the essential content of the unit, the rules and facts, augmented by the semantic environment, which are other modifying statements that apply to the rules and facts in the unit (see section 3.3.1).

3.2 Syntactic Analysis

The first stage creates a framework which greatly facilitates the translation.

The text of the source document is first made available as a computer file, and basic statistical information (i.e. word count, sentence count) is gathered. Each source unit is assigned a number by which it can be referred to. (UNIX can provide the basic tools, e.g. the 'diction' program, to carry out some of these tasks, but we have built our own software to do this.) Thus we discovered a number of facts about our document, e.g. that the verb 'reimburse' occurs much more often that any other verb, and that the modal 'may' occurs much more often than 'can' (this was not at all obvious by visual inspection of the source document).

The analysis program is controlled by an operator, who need not have much linguistic training nor real understanding of the subject matter of the document. The program reads the source document word by word and the operator assigns one or more grammatical categories (at present, one of: proper noun, count noun, mass noun, adjective, verb, adverb) to each word. Some aspects of morphological analysis are automated, e.g. the program categorizes each standard verb as active, past participle, gerund etc. Words may also be ignored, as not appearing in the LESK translation. If the operator is not sure how to categorize a given word, he/she can have this word displayed in the context of the enclosing sentence and review how it has been used previously. In future versions, we intend to automate the lexical analysis further by using prepared dictionaries.

Once the task of lexicon development is largely completed, the result is reviewed by an expert (the 'expert critique 1' process in Fig. 2). At this stage, the first job of the subject matter expert is to check the word classifications.

3.3 Translation into LESK

3.3.1. Building the Semantic Environment

In the second stage, translation of the regulations into LESK takes place. The translation normally proceeds according to the source unit structure of the document, but one might decide to restructure it completely. As defined in the previous section, each knowledge base unit resulting from the translation may introduce a semantic environment, i.e. a set of definitions and certain conventions necessary to understand the meaning of rules in this unit. Units are nested, analogous to blocks in a computer language. Each unit can begin with its own environment, which applies to it.

The syntactic environment is the lexical information from stage 1. The semantic environment introduces declarations, definitions, constraints, and scripts.

VARIABLES — These are declarations which specify variables by a list of LESK statements; each statement introduces and describes a variable as belonging to a class denoted by a count noun phrase.

HIERARCHY — These are declarations which specify two types of hierarchical relationships between classes of entities:

- KINDS — declarations which unambiguously state that a class is considered partitioned into two or more disjoint subclasses, with common noun phrases given for each.
- IS-A — declarations which specify the subset relationship between classes that is not a partition into subclasses (i.e. 'kinds').

SYNONYMS — These declarations are divided into two groups:

- SYNONYMOUS WORDS — are simply words (or phrases treated as words) which may be substituted one for the other in this unit. For instance, 'trip' and 'journey' are defined as synonyms. In each list of synonyms, one word is flagged as a canonical synonym for all the other words on that list. Only canonical synonyms are used in further translation of the source; other synonyms play an important role in the question answering process.

SYNONYMOUS STATEMENTS — are logically equivalent statements in this unit, e.g.

Employee stays in Accommodation
= Employee uses Accommodation

DEFINITIONS — These are rules which serve to answer 'what is the definition of' questions. They define one word or phrase in terms of others which are assumed known, or defined elsewhere.

CONSTRAINTS — These are domain-derived predicates which must be true if a rule in the unit is to be used, but which one would not want to repeat laboriously in every rule. (For example, Section 5 of the document applies to 'normal travel status', which is up to two months in duration.)

SCRIPT — This is a list of statements about actions, using variables and basic verbs. Our 'basic verbs' roughly correspond to 'primitive acts' in Schank's Conceptual Dependency Theory [7]. As in Schank's approach, a script organizes the temporal and procedural inferences between basic verbs. The main difference is that basic verbs are higher level concepts, derived directly from the source document. The script represents the sequence of events which normally takes place in a particular context (e.g. when accommodation is mentioned in the context of business travel). During translation, scripts are used to fill in gaps in the translation achieved so far. For instance, the regulations determine circumstances in which an employee is reimbursed for the expenses, without mentioning explicitly that before being reimbursed the employee must claim these expenses. The verb 'claim' will therefore appear in the LESK rule since the translator, after having consulted the script, will reconstruct all the actions involved in the rule, either explicitly or implicitly.

3.3.2 Translation of Source Text

The translation process, which yields rules and facts (RFs), must repeatedly choose a part of the text which is to be translated omitting no essential knowledge. It is possible that one sentence will be translated into more than one RF. On the other hand, several sentences may be translated into a single RF.

The person doing the translation (the 'translator') determines first what portion of the source text will be translated into an RF. If the result of translation is to be a rule, the translator first determines the rule head. The main verb of the translated portion of the text (or its synonym) is used as the head predicate. The body of the rule is obtained by translating noun phrases and embedded sentences from the source into LESK. The translator first determines which common nouns are to be mapped into existing variables, and what new variables are to be introduced. Noun phrases corresponding to these variables are then translated into body statements, and the body and the head are assembled into a rule.

In some cases, the translator feels (or learns from the expert) that a rule has to be a necessary and sufficient one. Typically, one of the conditions in the body of the rule gives the entire rule this if-and-only-if meaning, e.g. "An employee, using approved commercial accommodation, is reimbursed for the expenses provided that he presents a proof of payment". It turns out that when the proof of payment is absent, then - even though the accommodation was approved and used - no reimbursement takes place. The approach we have taken is to translate a rule like this into two rules to reflect its necessary and sufficient character:

```
if      Employee uses Commercial-Accommodation
        Commercial-Accommodation is approved

        Expense is an expense for Commercial-Accommodation
        Employee has a proof_of_payment for Expense

then    Employee shall be reimbursed Expense

if      Employee uses Commercial-Accommodation
        Commercial-Accommodation is approved
        Expense is an expense for Commercial-Accommodation
        there is no P such that
          P is a proof_of_payment for Expense

then    Employee shall not be reimbursed Expense
```

4. RELATED WORK

The methodology outlined in the previous sections is meant to guide the early phase of knowledge acquisition, namely the initial structuring and encoding of documents expressed in largely unconstrained natural language. Individual stages of such a process can be partly automated, either now or in the near future, after developing the necessary tools. The existing automated knowledge acquisition tools (e.g. [1], [5], [11]) are concerned with later stages, wherein some formal representation has been achieved.

A system which bears some similarity to our approach has been described in [10]. It accepts input in a small subset of English. New concepts can be defined by paraphrase in restricted English. The system answers questions about the domain under consideration, and also questions about its own knowledge representation.

The system presented in [3] and [4] learns by accepting input, in restricted English, about domains that can be described in logic. Also, the system assists the user in handling generic and procedural knowledge. Our system seems to have greater deductive power but lacks the ability to interface to other software.

Knowledge sources systems have some common properties with deductive data bases with natural language user interfaces (see [2]). However, rather than providing the user with facts relevant to specific domain questions, our system supplies "generic" information, i.e. rules applicable to a given typical situation or a general problem.

5. CONCLUDING REMARKS

This paper has reported the preliminary design of both a KSS and an associated knowledge acquisition methodology which we believe are unique in a significant number of ways. The most important of these are the design and use of LESK to bridge the gap between natural language and the computer's capabilities, and a well-defined methodology for working with a source document to transform it into suitable knowledge structures.

Our approach to knowledge representation shares much with other rule- based systems, particularly those which permit logical variables (e.g. PROLOG-based systems). The use of ELESK and LESK as convenient surface syntax, and the use of units to structure the knowledge base similarly to a document we believe to be valuable extensions to existing rule formats.

A final interesting question is to consider to what degree it might be feasible to process the raw source text in some direct way to yield a knowledge base. Could a machine read the source text and understand it sufficiently well to convert it into clear and simple rules as we have done mentally? We believe that this process would involve all the complexities of machine understanding, and is very similar to the process of totally automatic machine translation, which is still a dream despite many years of research. What we have in mind for the near future, and are indeed beginning to study seriously, is a semi-sutomatic machine translation system, which attempts a translation of a sentence, but which require a knowledgeable operator to help with all the ambiguities and choices that require intelligence and experience. Such a hybrid system should be practical within several years.

BIBLIOGRAPHY

[1] Davis, R., Lenat, D., "Knowledge-based Systems in Artificial Intelligence" (McGraw-Hill, New York, 1980).

[2] Gallaire, H., Minker, J., Nicholas, J.-M., "Logic and Databases: A Deductive Approach" (ACM Computing Surveys, vol. 16, no. 2, 1984).

[3] Haas, N., Hendrix, G., "Learning by Being Told: Acquiring Knowledge for Information Management", in [6], pp. 405-427.

[4] Hendrix, G., "KLAUS: A System for Managing Information and Computational Resources" (Technical Note 230, SRI, Menlo Park, California, 1980).

[5] Michalski, R.S., "A Theory and Methodology of Inductive Learning". In [6].

[6] Michalski, R.S., Carbonell, J.G., Mitchell, T.M., "Machine Learning" (Tioga Publishing Co., Palo Alto, California, 1983).

[7] Schank, N., Riesbeck, C.K., (eds.), "Inside Computer Understanding", (Lawrence Erlbaum Associates, Hillsdale, N.J., 1981).

[8] Skuce, D., "The LESK Tutorial", Department of Computer Science, University of Ottawa, TR-83-03 (July 1983).

[9] Skuce, D., Matwin, S., Tauzovich, B., Szpakowicz, S., Oppacher, F., "A Rule-Oriented Methodology for Constructing a Knowledge-Base from Natural Language Documents" (Proc. Conference on Expert Systems in Government, Washington, D.C., Oct. 1985).

[10] Thompson, B.H. Thompson, F.B., "Introducing ASK, a Simple Knowledgeable System" (Proceedings of the Conference on Applied Natural Language Processing, Santa Monica, California, February 1983).

[11] Winston, P.H., "Learning New Principles from Precedents and Exercices: the Details" (AI Memo 623, MIT, Cambridge, Mass., 1981).

Artificial Intelligence in Economics and Management
L.F. Pau (Editor)

AN EXPERT SYSTEM USED TO PREVENT THE DISCLOSURE OF SENSITIVE INFORMATION AT THE UNITED STATES ENVIRONMENTAL PROTECTION AGENCY

JERALD L. FEINSTEIN

Booz·Allen & Hamilton
4330 East-West Highway
Bethesda, MD 20814
U.S.A.

This paper describes an EXPERT SYSTEM for sensitive data/information disclosure avoidance developed by the author and used at the United States Environmental Protection Agency (EPA).

BACKGROUND

The Toxic Substances Control Act, 15 USC 2620, requires manufacturers, importers, and processors to submit information to the Agency on the tens of thousands of chemical substances in commerce. Much of this data is claimed as confidential by submitters under Section 14 of the Act. The information collected under the Act forms the basis for EPA's evaluation under TSCA of the relative health and environmental risks posed by chemical substances in U.S. commerce.

There are two kinds of information disclosure of concern to the Agency - direct and indirect. Direct disclosure is the release of information that is claimed as confidential by the submitter. A disclosure of this kind would usually be the result of judgemental error, a failure to follow security procedures, or intentional release.

Indirect disclosure occurs when the information released in combination with information already available to the public, can be used to <u>closely estimate</u> other highly sensitive or confidential corporate information. In many instances someone using a computer might be able to use data released by EPA to closely estimate sensitive information describing corporate strategies, research and development plans, or pricing structures.

EPA takes all reasonable measures to prevent the unauthorized disclosure of CBI. This emphasis on protection of sensitive corporate data is mandated by law, but at the same time it is a practical measure to ensure the cooperation and candor of the chemical industry. If chemical companies are not confident that their trade secrets and other sensitive corporate information are properly safeguarded, they will be less likely to cooperate actively in activities under TSCA.

Because of increasing public participation and debate in certain TSCA regulatory areas EPA determined that it also was necessary to attempt to analyze certain types of information before it is publicly released to determine whether it could be used to estimate other information which has been protected as CBI. To attempt such an ambitious goal in a conventional manner would involve many more resources than would be practical. Therefore, the only acceptable way to achieve the desired objective while staying well within the Agency's tight budgetary constraints was to automate the information analysis task by using sophisticated artificial intelligence and knowledge based systems techniques.[1] These techniques are used to emulate the decision making process of an "industry expert" who is trying to evaluate the impact of the public release of information. If the emulated "expert" determines that public disclosure would violate established Agency release criteria, then the information would either be supressed or generalized further to meet release criteria.

JUST WHAT IS AN EXPERT SYSTEM

Simply put, an expert system is a computer program that uses artificial intelligence techniques to emulate a human expert in solving complex problems.[2] More importantly, the system can perform as well as a human expert in specifically defined jobs and serves as a consultant for the non-expert. To do this effectively, the system must interact with the non-technical user and be very easy to use. Further, the expert system must be able to explain why, or list the reasons it chose a particular course of action.

Recent advances in the field of artificial intelligence make possible a new kind of tool to help speed the completion of certain complicated, yet well defined, tasks. These new tools are called knowledge based expert systems--an application of knowledge engineering. Knowledge engineering is the discipline of using artificial intelligence techniques to build a system that is capable of emulating the decision processes of an expert; that is, analyzing and documenting just how an expert uses information to solve problems or to make decisions within some well defined domain of expertise.[3] The important term "knowledge based" is included in the definition because these new systems are distinguished from older decision support systems by the important addition of a knowledge base. Data bases are included in the older, more conventional systems, while both data and knowledge bases form a part of the new "smarter" systems. Knowledge in these new systems is represented by expandable sets of relationships. Just like the human expert, these systems can learn and do a better job by obtaining additional knowledge about the job they are supposed to do. Knowledge relationships may take the form of fixed or variable rules, probalistic relationships among things, as well as more complicated relationships among information elements.

To effectively design an expert system, the knowledge engineer must be able to work closely with the human expert, side by side if possible. During this time the engineer documents the kinds of problems encountered and the way the human expert goes about solving these problems. Engineers at EPA recorded how the expert uses experience and training to follow well defined rules and procedures in analyzing the impact of a planned information release. "Tricks of the trade" were studied, and it was noted that little time was wasted in the trivial pursuit of unneeded information. Necessary information was quickly identified and located. The step-by-step analysis of data, mathematical calculations, the what if? questions--all were efficiently documented in terms of flow diagrams. At the completion, the entire process was rewritten and crystalized in the form of decision tables and rules.

At this point, each task was analyzed to learn what kinds of inference techniques were being used: rule based, Baysian, hypothesis testing, etc. It was found that none of the standard inference mechanisms would, in total, meet the Agency's needs. The "expert" needed to visualize quickly how seemingly unrelated information could be pieced together to develop more refined estimates of unavailable information. In the military intelligence arena, this process is called information fusion. Therefore EPA needed to develop a new and better way to represent knowledge as well as new inference or reasoning algorithms to allow the efficient fusion of information.

SYSTEM COMPONENTS

An expert system typically is composed of six modules. They are: (1) Natural Language Interface, (2) System Editor, (3) Knowledge Base, (4) Data Bases, (5) Inference Machine, and (6) Executive Module to coordinate all internal system activities.[5]

The Natural Language Interface (NLI) enables the user and expert system to communicate easily in a natural English dialog. Using the NLI, screens containing important feedback are generated and presented to the user via the interactive terminal.[6] This simple user interaction is demonstrated in the Sample Session portion of this paper. Another function of the NLI is to translate the English-like user response into code that is meaningful to the system as well as to translate system output code into easy-to-understand conversational English text.

The Executive Module reacts to instructons and questions from the user through the NLI. Its role is similar to that of an orchestra conducter who must guide many activities at nearly the same time. As instructions come in from the user, it coordinates the activities of all parts of the system--which rules to use, what data in which bases need to be accessed, etc. Results are relayed back through the NLI where they are translated into conversational English for the user.

I distinguish the Knowledge Base from the Data Base in that the former contains general rules and relationships about the raw data stored in the bases. The knowledge base can expand and grow, and as it does, additional and sometimes more accurate inferences can be made. The Inference Machine is a collection of different kinds of reasoning algorithms. Depending on the problem or the kinds of questions the user is asking, the Executive Module extracts the required data and identifies the rules and relationships that the Inference Machine will use to generate the answers to the questions asked.

If the user wants to change any system parameter, the System Editor is the proper tool. Rules, data or knowledge elements may be changed by the Editor. In essence, the Editor can function as a manual override, able to get at any part of the system.

THE ALGORITHM

Knowledge can be expressed in a very general manner using concepts borrowed from the theories of linear systems and fuzzy sets. Mathematically, knowledge or information can be represented as n-dimensional arrays where the coordinate frames are defined as information elements. In addition to equality relationships, inequalities and bounds or ranges are permitted to express the more generalized conditions resulting from imprecise descriptions of information elements. Constraint propagation algorithims are used to deal with these kinds of relationships.

The basis for this method of knowledge representation is founded upon the relative or relational structure of knowledge.[4] Of interest are not only the basic elements (information) themselves, but also how these elements are linked (relative to each other). These ideas are implicit in the mathematical reasoning of geometric proofs. Language structure also follows on a similar pattern. The elements (words) are derived (defined) relative to each other and can be linked back to a few shared primitives. In essence, this method of knowledge representation results in an inference mechanism (reasoning technique) that is highly efficient and particularly well suited to tasks requiring information fusion.

This abstract definition of information is brought down to earth when we examine how the disclosure avoidance problem is worked.[7-11] "Known" information can be known exactly or to within some range of values, or may be known only to the extent that it is larger or smaller than some other known or unknown value. Then again, unknown information may be completely or just partially unknown. These highly complex relationships result in nth order interactions that must be evaluated in order to generate accurate estimates of sensitive data.

This abstract definition of information provides the needed framework for generalized disclosure avoidance.[12] Highly complex forms of analysis are possible within this theoretical framework; however, this paper will focus on one of the more simple forms, the linear form. More complicated representations will be topics for future papers.

THE LINEAR FORM

Information can be expressed in terms of sets of generalized linear relationships of the form:

$$Ax_{ij}-b_i \ (\leq\ ,\ \geq\ ,\ =)\ \emptyset$$

over i, j, . . .

where the Xs are information elements

As discussed, in the typical disclosure avoidance problem, some X_{ij}'s . . .

can be completely unknown:
$(-\infty \geq X_{ij} \geq \infty)$

or known only approximately to within some interval:

$$(X_L \leq X_{ij} \leq X_U)$$

where X_L and X_U are lower and upper bounds respectively.

For disclosure analysis, it is significant that sets of information can be represented and unified in this manner, as it opens the door to a number of mathematical programming approaches.[13-15]

Using a mathematical programming approach, it is possible to accurately estimate the targeted information. This is because the relationships are, in effect, related or interlocking linear constraints. Constraint propagation methods can be used to find a maximum and minimum for each of the information elements. It is exactly these maxima and minima that bracket or bound the actual values of the sensitive data. Further, given the data proposed for release, this yields the best possible (L-1 Norm) estimate of the sensitive information.

GEOMETRY OF THE ALGORITHM

The linear information relationships describe a set of hyperplanes that bound a convex polyhedral region in hyper-space.[16] The core algorithm must find the points within the convex polyhedron which achieve a minimum and a maximum value. This is accomplished by using a sequence of objective functions of the form:

$$\text{MAX, MIN } X_0 = X_{ij}$$

subject to all expressed relationships. This guarantees that the unknown or sought after information element is optimally estimated based upon all available knowledge.

In essence, this is accomplished by searching the feasible region for a maximum or minimum in positive and negative directions along the coordinate axes. For each axis, an interval

$$\text{MIN } X_{ij} \leq X_{ij} \leq \text{MAX } X_{ij}$$

is defined.

Thus,

$$\text{MIN } X_{ij} \text{ and MAX } X_{ij}$$

become the bounds of the smallest interval bracketing the unknown value of X_{ij}.

The upper and lower bounds of the estimates that are generated by this method represent the smallest (best) interval estimate that is mathematically consistent with all of the nth order information dependencies and is guaranteed to contain the true value.[17] It is possible to get tighter estimates if the 100% confidence requirement is relaxed.[18] This is, however, a matter of choice and circumstances and will not be addressed in this paper.

SIMPLE EXAMPLE

While the typical information release at EPA may involve a large number of companies, many data elements, and complicated information relationships, it will be instructive to consider two very small, trivial, yet highly representative problems involving only one kind of information - the actual amount of a chemical produced by several companies. This kind of problem is important because the actual amount of a chemical that is either manufactured or imported, in many cases, must be reported to EPA. At the same time, with certain kinds of chemicals, production data is highly sensitive and a closely guarded secret which is almost always claimed as confidential business information. This is the kind of information companies do not want their competitors to obtain, as it is useful in estimating the size of the market, market shares, in developing competitive pricing strategies, and much more.

The Agency often must make public at least summary information such as how much of a certain chemical (the aggregate amount manufactured by all producers) is manufactured or imported in the United States, locations where it is used, etc. This is needed by EPA as well as individual State environmental agencies to estimate national and local chemical exposure levels.

The following simple examples illustrate the principles involved. Let us assume that a would-be intruder (i.e., an individual attempting to use data released by the Agency to estimate the value of sensitive information) is aware of the fact that a particular substance is manufactured by three companies named COA, COB, and COC; EPA has released the information that total annual production of the substance in question is between 1,000,000 kg and 1,500,000 kg. Because COC did not claim its production volume as confidential, it is assumed that the would-be intruder knows COC's annual production, which is 200,000 kg. Furthermore, a well-respected trade journal has just published the information that COA is the largest single producer of the substance.

With this configuration of the knowledge base, the inference mechanism estimates that the true production volume of COA is between 400,000 kg and 1,300,000 kg., and that for COB is between 0 and 650,000 kg.

Another example further illustrates the power of the inference mechanism to generate best estimates of sensitive data. A second hypothetical chemical is known to be produced by six different companies (COA, COB, COC, COD, COE, and COF), and it has been published that 3,600,000 kg were produced in a particular year. COB, COD, and COE did not claim their data as CBI, so it is assumed that their production volumes (300,000 kg, 400,000 kg and 500,000 kg, respectively) are public knowledge. Additionally, a trade journal report has revealed that the COA production volume is larger than COE and that COF accounts for more than half of the annual production of the chemical.

These information relationships are established within the knowledge base. From this knowledge, the inference mechanism indicates that the production volumes of the companies which claimed their information as confidential could be estimated using the informaton released by EPA as follows:

COA between	500,000	and	600,000	kg
COD between	0	and	100,000	kg
COF between	1,800,000	and	1,900,000	kg

These are very close estimates of production volumes. In the event that an estimate comes within a percent range of the true production volume which has been previously established as "too close", than the expert system simply advises the user of this condition and reports that the information may not be released.

References

[1] Hays-Roth, F., Waterman, D., and Lenat, B., Building Expert Systems. Addison-Wesley, 1983.

[2] Weiss, S. and Kulikowski, C., A Practical Guide to Designing Expert Systems. Rowman & Allanheld, 1984.

[3] Barr, A. and Feigenbaum, E., The Handbook of Artificial Intelligence. HeurisTech Press, 1981.

[4] Nilsson, N., Principles of Artificial Intelligence. Tioga, Palo Alto, CA 1980.

[5] Davis, R., "Expert Systems: Where Are We? and Where Do We Go From Here? AI Magazine, Spring 1982, pp. 3-22.

[6] Davis, M. W., Anatomy of Decision Support. Datamation, 201-210, June 15, 1984.

[7] U.S. Department of Commerce, Statistical Policy Working Paper 2: Report on Statistical Disclosure and Disclosure-Avoidance Techniques. Washington, D.C.: U.S. Government Printing Office, 1978.

[8] Dalenius, T., The Notion of Portable Statistical Disclosure Control. Report #4/1 in the Series of: Access to Information Through Censuses and Surveys. Providence, R.I.: Department of Statistics, Brown University, 1981.

[9] Dalenius, T., Confidentiality in Surveys, A Research Program. Report #1 in Series: Confidentiality in Surveys, Stockholm: Department of Statistics, University of Stockholm, 1976.

[10] Cox, L. H. and Sande, G., Techniques for Preserving Statistical Confidentiality. Proceedings of the 42nd International Statistical Institute, 1979.

[11] Cox, L. H., Suppression Methodology and Disclosure Control. Journal of the American Statistical Association, 1980, 75, 377-385.

[12] Bryon, R. P. (1977). Estimation and Inference For Large Econometric Systems. Econometrica, 45, 1499-1516.

[13] Dixon, L. C. (1972). Nonlinear Optimization, pp. 89-93. London: English University Press.

[14] Theil, H. (1961). Economic Forecasts and Policy. Amsterdam: North-Holland.

[15] United Nations (1968). A System of National Accounts, Series F, No. 2, Rev. 3.

[16] Topping, B. J., A Model For Optimum Linkage of Records, Journal of the American Statistical Association, 63 (DEC68) 1321-32.

[17] Zadeh, L. and Fukanaka, K. (editors). Fuzzy Sets and Their Application to Cognitive Decision Processes. Academic Press, New York, 1975.

[18] Duda, R., and Hart, P., Pattern Classification and Scene Analysis. Wiley, New York, 1973.

General Reading

Feinstein, J. L. and Siems, F., EDAAS: an expert system at the U.S. Environmental Protection Agency for avoiding disclosure of confidential business information. Expert Systems - The International Journal of Knowledge Engineering, Vol. 2, No. 2 (APR 1985) P. 72.

RAND, The Rosie Language Reference Manual, 1981.

Bellman, R., Cooke, K., Lockett, J., Algorithms, Graphs, and Computers. Academic Press, New York, 1970.

Berge, C., The Theory of Graphs and Its Applications. Wiley, New York, 1962.

Goldman, S., Information Theory. Prentice-Hall, New York, 1955.

Artificial Intelligence in Economics and Management
L.F. Pau (Editor)

DESIGNING EXPERT SYSTEMS IN A BUSINESS ENVIRONMENT

James Clifford, Matthias Jarke, and Henry C. Lucas, Jr.
Graduate School of Business Administration, New York University
90 Trinity Place, New York, N.Y. 10006, USA

The integration of an ES into a business environment presents a different set of problems to the designer. First, it can be difficult to isolate and draw boundaries around the domain of the business problem. Second, there is often a need to generate a large number of expert decisions in a short period of time. That is, there can be many transactions requiring some expertise to process, such as applications for life insurance. Finally, there may exist a number of computerized transactions processing systems which interact with very large databases and there may be a need to integrate the ES with these existing systems. This paper discusses these general issues involved in developing expert systems for business applications, with particular examples drawn from the domain of insurance underwriting.

1. INTRODUCTION

An expert system (ES) is a computer application that provides decision support similar to that of a human expert in solving a problem. The systems analyst who builds an expert system is called a knowledge engineer; his or her role is to learn the expert's approach to problem solving. Usually the knowledge engineer can formulate the expert's techniques as a series of rules. Then, an Artificial Intelligence language like Prolog can be used to design a computer system that exhibits some of the decision making characteristics of the expert.

Most expert systems to date incorporate knowledge that is primarily scientifically oriented; for example, applications exist in medicine, chemistry and biology [CJV 83]. These systems can be characterized as having a clear task and expertise that is relatively easy to locate. Generally the problems to which these applications are applied require substantial time, such as the diagnosis of a patient's diseases. Frequently, existing ES's are used in environments where there was no previous computer support.

The conditions imposed by a business environment differ from those described above. First there appears to be extensive interaction among different tasks; drawing the boundaries for what the expert does is not easy. Second, there may be substantial expertise required to perform a given task, but the expert is often functioning in a high volume, high pressure environment. He or she often has to generate a large number of expert decisions in a relatively short period of time. Finally, successful business utilization of expert systems technology will require that these systems interact heavily with existing business subsystems, such as transactions processing and database management systems.

This paper reports on the authors' experiences and reflections on the design of an expert system for life insurance underwriting. The particular application is underwriting applications for life insurance for a large insurance company. The problem, as in many ES, is essentially one of classification: determining into which insurance category an applicant falls for insurance purposes. The problem is an important one, and is a routine part of the business. Transactions volumes are high and the underwriter makes use of a large volume of information in coming to a decision. In addition, the underwriter must interpret facts and frequently apply judgment based more on experience or rules of thumb than on clear-cut policies. While insurance firms are some of the largest users of computer-based processing systems, the fact that there are very few systems to aid in the underwriting decision (for an exception, see the CAUSE underwriting system [A 80]) provides evidence that significant human judgment is required for this task.

2. EXPERT SYSTEMS IN THE BUSINESS ENVIRONMENT

One generally accepted macro view of the managerial control processes in an organization defines the structure as consisting of a hierarchy of three distinct but cooperating levels of activity and decision-making [A 65, S 60]. Operational control, the lowest level in the hierarchy, is concerned with all of the details of the individual transactions which constitute the activity of the business. One level higher is the managerial control level, where more summary information about the business is needed in order to support medium-level decisions affecting the management of the business functions. Finally, the top level consists of the strategic planning and policy making function which sets the goals and defines the overall nature of the business organization.

Traditional data processing systems have primarily concerned themselves with the lower two levels of this hierarchy. When one thinks of business processing systems one thinks of such transaction processing systems as order-entry or inventory management, and such managerial reporting systems as accounts receivable and general ledger. More recently, a class of somewhat less-defined systems known as Decision Support Systems are primarily aimed at supporting the kinds of decisions that are required at the higher levels of this hierarchy.

We believe that expert systems and expert systems technology have a role to play at all levels of this organizational hierarchy. The reason for this is that, orthogonal to this hierarchic view of the nature of the business activity is a view of the complexity of the activity being carried on. Accepting this classification of business activities along a complexity scale ranging from "structured" to "semi-structured" to "unstructured", these two parameters, level of activity and complexity of activity, produce a matrix of business activity types. We might view the situation therefore as in Figure 1, and ask ourselves (a) where in this matrix does a particular activity lie, but, more importantly for this discussion, (b) where in this matrix are traditional DP techniques and the newer ES techniques most suited?

Traditional DP techniques will continue to be applied successfully to both transaction and middle-level information systems, but primarily at a routine level of difficulty. What is beginning to happen, however, is that the techniques of ES and DSS technology are being applied at some routine problems at the strategic level, and also at complex problems at all three levels. For the really difficult problems at all three levels, it seems that the jury is still out; we will have to wait both for some more powerful ES/DSS techniques, languages and tools, and also for an evaluation of the success/failure of these techniques at the complex level.

	STRUCTURED	SEMI-STRUCTURED	UNSTRUCTURED
TRANSACTION	DP	ES	ES*
MIDDLE-LVL	DP/DSS	ES/DSS	ES*
STRATEGIC	ES/DSS	ES*	?

ES* = Expert System, Future Technology

Figure 1: Taxonomy of Computer Applications

The vast majority of the ES's that have been built have been intended for an environment in which there was a long interaction between a human and the system in an effort to come to a reasonable decision for a single problem. R1 [M 82] is probably the first ES which moved closer to the transaction processing realm. It also appears to be one of the few expert systems in actual routine use. This system advises systems engineers at Digital Equipment in configuring VAX computers. Although advertised as "the" major success in expert systems to date, it should be noted that its development costs have reportedly far exceeded the current or expected benefits of the system. We can conclude that (a) ways must be found to reduce the costs of building expert systems, and (b) one has to be very careful in selecting an application domain with sufficient potential payback. As noted above, the latter can be achieved by supporting either important single decisions or mass-processing of transaction-like, medium-complexity decisions.

What are some of the characteristics of transaction processing systems? The first is that they must be able to handle a high volume of transactions per unit of time, i.e., they should not spend a long time agonizing over the decision for any particular case. Many people feel that ES's will not be trusted to make decisions unilaterally in complex tasks, but rather will only be effective when built to operate in conjunction with human experts in the domain.

A second issue is that traditional systems typically have a high level of interaction with other systems in the business, e.g. a DBMS, other transaction systems and systems at the middle and strategic levels of the organization. Most ES's to date have been built by systems designers who were free to construct their knowledge base in isolation from any existing organizational databases, policies, or constraints. By contrast, a business ES will undoubtedly have to rely upon an existing DBMS for the major part of its factual knowledge about the enterprise in question, and probably upon existing business subsystems -- transaction systems, mathematical modelling systems, decision support systems, etc. -- for some of the data processing that will be relevant to its proper functioning [JV 84, VCJ 85]. These components of the business system have attained the status of an important corporate resource, and ES technology, if it is to succeed in this environment, will have to accommodate itself to this view and the policies and structures that it has generated.

Finally, a third characteristic is that systems must be able to track transactions through various stages of processing, for example from initial processing through an "awaiting action" state through a "final disposition" state, since in many applications not all transactions can be completely processed in one pass. Each of thes factors should influence the shape of business ES's that might be built for complex problems at the transaction level.

Before discussing some of the more general issues involved in business ES deployment, the next section provides a context by discussing the particular application of insurance underwriting.

3. THE UNDERWRITING EXPERT SYSTEM

An insurance policy transaction begins when the sales representative and the customer complete an application form and forward it to a regional office for underwriting. Here the application is assigned to an underwriter based on the size of the requested insurance policy and the type of medical information provided on the form. At this point the underwriting process begins.

An insurance underwriter is basically charged with determining whether or not the company should accept a customer. This overall task involves examining the potential customer's application and all other accompanying material to determine either (a) accept the customer in such and such a rating category, or (b) reject the customer for such and such reasons, or (c) withhold a final decision pending the acquisition of additional supporting information. In the company cooperating in this research, the type of product involved is life insurance of any kind, term or whole life.

Underwriting is not a single decision at one point in time. Rather, there are two distinct decision styles. The underwriter first makes a decision on what information to request, for example, a medical examination, report from the applicant's personal physician or several other pieces of information. The application is placed in a file pending the arrival of the information needed for underwriting. When all data are complete, the underwriter examines the information and makes a decision that classifies the applicant into one of a number of categories, each having a different price for a given level of insurance coverage.

3.1. The Information-Gathering Decision

Figure 2 shows the different sources of information available to the underwriter. The applicant signs a release giving consent for all of this information to be made available to the company, and for the results of the underwriting process to be reported to a computerized database. Much of this information costs the insurance company money to obtain; in addition, the more information requested, the longer the underwriting process is likely to require, resulting in the potential loss of the customer to the competition.

A check of computerized databases of applicants for insurance for most large carriers in the U.S.
A medical examination by varying levels of medical personnel from a paramedic to a specialist.
A report from the applicant's attending physician.
A mercantile report or credit and community investigation.
A driving report from the Department of Motor Vehicles.
Tax returns and/or a financial statement from the application.

Figure 2: Sources of Underwriting Information

One of the most important sources of information for the underwriting decision is the applicant's previous insurance history. This information can come from two sources. There is an industry-wide database maintained by the major U.S. insurance companies. Each time a company rejects an applicant for insurance, it reports that fact, and the reasons for the rejection, to this shared database. When an individual applies for insurance, an automatic search request is issued to this database in certain instances, for example is the amount of coverage applied for is over a certain threshold, or the applicant is over a certain age. A second source of similar, though more detailed, information is the company's own internal database.

The next information that might be requested is a medical examination. Such factors as the age of the applicant and the amount of insurance requested will determine the scope of a medical examination. In addition, there are questions on the application about medical history. If the applicant reports one or more of a number of conditions, the underwriter will generally ask for a medical examination. This decision is complicated by the fact that there are several types of medical exams; the applicant may need a paramedical exam, a doctor, or a company-appointed specialist.

Certain answers on the application cause the underwriter to ask for a report from the applicant's attending physician. Usually the doctor photocopies the most recent part of the patient's record and sends it to the company. Naturally the complexity of reading a handwritten report, difficult enough for the human "expert," were sufficient to place the examination of these reports outside the scope of the proposed system.

A mercantile report is like a credit investigation. However, it focuses on the behavior of the applicant and may be requested for a number of reasons. Again, a major reason for authorizing this type of report is the face amount of the requested policy. Other triggers include such factors as the occupation of the applicant, a history of motor vehicle problems, or perhaps a medical disability. A mercantile report always includes a query to the department of motor vehicles to determine the applicant's driving record.

Finally, for certain very large policies, the applicant will be requested to submit a financial statement, usually in the form of a copy of a tax return.

3.2. Underwriting Decision

Given the requested information, the underwriter can evaluate the application. The underwriter assigns scores for various conditions and diseases; the more points assigned to an application, the higher the cost of the insurance. There are a number of possible categories into the which the application will be placed, each one representing a different premium schedule. There can be a substantial dollar difference in premiums between the various categories, so the underwriting decision is an important one for the applicant. In addition to the classification, certain medical conditions will warrant a surcharge of so many dollars for every thousand dollars of insurance for a period of years.

Not all risks are additive, as assumed in the scoring system. In such cases, the underwriter applies judgmental rules. For example, an application is rejected if the applicant has a history of mental problems and is unemployed, even though none of these properties have a high score by themselves.

4. KNOWLEDGE ACQUISITION

4.1. General Issues in a Business Environment

Most expert systems have been built in an environment where the expertise of one person was evoked during knowledge acquisition, systematized, and incorporated into the knowledge base. In a business system, the knowledge acquisition process is complicated by the distributed nature of the expertise. Among the possible sources for relevant expertise are existing applications programs and other computerized systems; manuals, rule books, policy statements or other written materials representing compiled expertise of the organization; human experts from various departments or functional areas. Among the problems that this diversity of knowledge sources poses are the following: inconsistency across the sources; incompatibility of the view of the problem space; potential compromising of a human expert who may disagree with a stated policy or rule. The issue of resolving conflicts or disparities among multiple experts is one that will increasingly be an issue in the development of expert systems [H 86].

The security of the organization's rules is an added issue in business ES's. The power and flexibility of the knowledge representation tools used to build ES's, i.e., the ability both to represent rules and policies declaratively and to access and modify these rules during program execution comes with a price. Just as data in a DBMS is seen as a corporate resource which must be protected from mis-use, so too (perhaps even more so?) business policies, strategies and rules encoded into the knowledge base of the expert system must be protected. One offshoot of this necessity to preserve the confidentiality of business rules is the difficulty of publishing results in the area of business expert systems; most of the real progress involves the development of prototype systems in confidential application areas.

4.2. Underwriting System in Particular

The human expert used in the knowledge acquisition and prototyping for this system is a senior lay medical underwriter. He can underwrite policies up to about a quarter of a million dollars, and other underwriters send to him any applications that need some medical judgment. The design team met with the expert for a period of six months prior to writing any code. The meetings began with the expert describing his job and decisions. Soon, the designers asked the expert to bring various applications and talk through his decisions on each one. A protocol analysis of these applications reviews provided enough understanding of the process to involve the expert in design. The designers and human expert worked together to complete Figure 2 and to describe the rules that apply for requesting each type of information.

The system was then developed piece by piece, first designing the data structures needed to represent all of the information relevant to the decision, and then building the rules that determine when a request for individual pieces of additional information are necessary. Moreover, there were rules for developing a composite "score" of the application, which could potentially contribute both to a request for additional information and ultimately to the insurance classification of the application. The development proceeded in the usual ES development mode, namely as a sequence of successive refinements to the quality of the system's decision making. Each meeting we would review the performance of the system on an application with our human expert, and discover where and why it had errors or been incomplete. In the next meeting we would have developed new rules to handle the previously discovered problems, and then proceed to discover new ones.

At this point, an expert system is working for the first underwriting decision, on what information to acquire. In a limited "test" of the system against eight applications chosen by the underwriter to reflect a broad spectrum of application types, the system's performance was comparable to our advisor. In a production environment the system would need substantially more thorough testing, in a carefully planned and controlled test against many more cases and also involving other underwriters. One could eventually envision a series of expert systems, each making extensive use of part of the firm's database. An actuarial expert (cf. [SJ 85]) could be queried by the underwriting expert and could produce a customized risk analysis for each applicant. An overall picture of some of the system interconnections desirable in the insurance company environment is shown in Figure 3.

5. RELATIONSHIP TO TRADITIONAL SYSTEMS ANALYSIS AND DESIGN

To what extent is the design of an expert system different from that of a conventional, computer-based system in a business firm? Table 1 shows the stages in the conventional life cycle for a business information system [L 85].

5.1. Traditional Systems Analysis and Design

Usually someone in the firm has an idea for how a system might improve information processing or solve a problem. The systems staff conducts a feasibility study showing various costs and benefits (including intangible benefits) and management is asked to approve developing the application. During systems analysis a design team of users and analysts document the details of present information processing procedures.

The team creates the design and specifications for a new system. Programmers develop necessary code or modify packages. The team tests the system, trains users and converts to the new application. During maintenance, the information services department makes changes and enhancements to the system, an activity that consumes on the average 50% of the discretionary resources of the department.

5.2. Prototyping

What is different in the development process for an expert system based on the experience with the underwriting expert? A new approach to conventional design called prototyping has received a great deal of recent attention [L 85]. Table 1 shows that a prototype differs significantly from traditional development approaches. Basically, the prototype is a working model of a system or some part of it.

In the conventional approach, the user does not receive feedback until too late in the process; often the user does not understand the system, but yet agrees to its specifications. With a prototype, the user has something concrete to which he or she can respond; the prototyping process also tends to draw the user into the design process. It is hard to avoid user involvement with a prototype.

5.3. Expert Systems Design

The design of an expert system comes closest to the prototyping process. Some of the major differences between prototyping and ES design result from the current R&D nature of expert system development. So few of these systems exist in a business environment that a clear methodology has not emerged for their design. Based on experience with the underwriting expert system, six issues will be addressed, below: reliance on a single expert, staffing, program structuring, user training, implementation, systems maintenance, and accountability.

Based on the experience with the underwriting expert, one significant difference with other design approaches is the reliance on a single expert. ES designers have generally been unanimous that one cannot currently design an expert system if it is necessary to adjudicate among different experts with differing opinions. In conventional design, most organizations try to include as many potential users in the design process as feasible.

An issue of major concern to businesses weighing the potential costs and benefits of pursuing ES technology is one of staffing. DP departments do not currently have staff who are familiar with AI languages or with the process and techniques of knowledge engineering. A commitment to ES development will require substantial investment either in outside consultants, training for current staff members or the hiring of new staff trained in ES development. However, this expertise is itself still rare, making it difficult to locate and then keep a staff of knowledge engineers. A final point is that the maintenance of ES's is more akin to the learning and maturation of a human expert than to the maintenance and enhancement of traditional DP systems. Staffing over the lifetime of the usefulness of an ES, which is assumed to be rather lengthy, poses an additional problem.

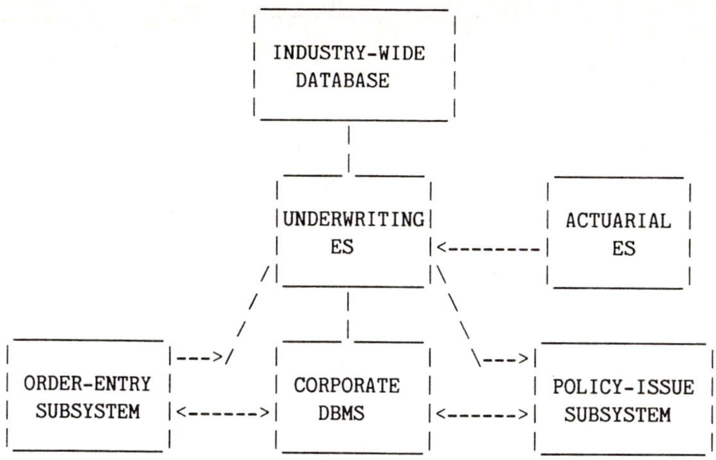

Figure 3: Underwriting System in Context

LIFE CYCLE	TRANSACTION PROCESSING SYSTEM	PROTOTYPE	EXPERT SYSTEM
Inception	Idea for system	Idea for system	Idea for system
Feasibility Study	Cost/Benefit; Mgmt. approval	Working prelim. version	R & D; Set boundaries
Systems Analysis	Details of current procs.	Work with user group	Listen to single expert
Design	Create new system	Iterative enhancement	Begin to code single expert
Specifications	Detailed design	Evolving prototype, or prototype as model for system	Expert critique; new rules added
Programming	Code specs.	Code specs.	Add rules
Testing	Debugging; Acceptance testing	Debugging; Acceptance testing	Continued enhancement; Problems when exposed to others
Training	For users	For users	For non-experts?
Conversion	Scheduled	Gradual evolution	Gradual
Operations	Maintenance & enhancements	Maintenance & enhancements	Evolving expertise

Table 1: System Life Cycle Comparisons

With an ES the designers are using a different type of language than COBOL or even fourth generation, nonprocedural languages. There is relatively little experience with rule-based languages in the business environment. One advantage of these languages is purported to be the ease with which rules can be added as designers acquire new knowledge. Experience with the underwriter shows that some new knowledge can be significant enough to require restructuring of parts of the program even though it is written in Prolog, a rule-based language.

With an ES training is a potential problem; what happens when other experts are asked to evaluate the system? If it was designed with a single expert, will it necessarily be robust enough to pass tests designed by colleagues? How does one approach the training of users? How does the system respond when a nonexpert user presents a situation beyond its domain of expertise? Designers of commercial systems are used to developing applications with extensive error checking, sometimes well over half of the code exists to detect user errors. Will expert systems designers be able to detect and prevent user errors?

Because there are few ES in business, no one has addressed the question of implementation for these systems. In the underwriting environment, many overall implementation questions arise. Will an underwriting expert support or replace the human underwriter? Will it be used for the thousands of policy applications that require modest human expertise, eliminating a layer of underwriters at the level below the senior lay underwriter in this study? These questions will naturally arise in other business areas where ES's are being introduced; they will need to be considered carefully if business is to seriously accept the introduction of this technology.

Maintenance is a major problem in the information processing industry. Expert Systems will add to this problem, not lessen it. New rules will be discovered so there will have to be a staff to tend the system and incorporate new knowledge. The domain and nature of the problem addressed by the ES may change as well. Successful ES's will probably become members of a class of enduring systems, applications so expensive or so complex that one could not envision replacing them completely. Good examples of this type of systems are those used by airlines for making passenger reservations. Two U.S. carriers have invested over $200 million on their systems [GS 84]; it is inconceivable that these systems will ever be totally replaced. Instead, they will grow and be modified over time.

A final issue relates to the notion of auditing and accountability. Expert systems will presumably become more and more involved in making and/or assisting in the making of complex, high-risk decisions. In many applications, e.g. insurance underwriting, drug synthesis, etc., there are corporate and legal responsibilities for maintaining complete records about the decisions made and the environment in which they were made. Increasingly, lawsuits are won (or lost) with the help of such documentation. The recording and maintenance of such information about a decision as when, how, why, and under what assumptions about the "state of the world" was a decision made will increasingly become part and parcel of the expected behavior of expert systems as they begin to become involved in the making of crucial organizational decisions.

6. SUMMARY AND CONCLUSIONS

In summary, the introduction of Expert System technology into a business environment presents new and challenging problems as well as opportunities. Our experience in developing the underwriting expert illustrates both of these facets of this technology transfer. The opportunities involved in computerizing activities that have until now resisted automation, with the potential for an increase in speed, accuracy, and competitive edge, are very real and attractive. The problems are no less real: how to incorporate techniques of knowledge engineering into environments more comfortable with traditional systems analysis and design techniques; how to minimize the cost of the knowledge acquisition and knowledge engineering process; how to integrate ES's into the wide family of cooperating systems that are today the norm in most businesses; how to manage the overall human impact of this technology on the employees and their relationship to their job environment, their colleagues, and their careers. Clearly much more research is needed on the design and implemention of ES's if this technology is to become widely adopted in the business environment.

REFERENCES

[A 80] Alter, S. Decision Support Systems: Current Practices and Continuing Challenges, Addison-Wesley 1980.

[A 65] Anthony, R.N. Planning and Control Systems: A Framework for Analysis, Harvard University GSBA, Studies in Management Control, Cambridge, Mass., 1965.

[CJV 83] Clifford, J., Jarke, M. and Vassiliou, Y. "A Short Introduction to Expert Systems," IEEE Database Engineering, vol. 8, no. 4, December 1983.

[GS 84] Gifford, D. and Spector, A. "The TWA Reservation System," Communications of the ACM, 27,7, July 1984, 650-685.

[H 86] Hewitt, C. "Implications of Open Systems", in M.Jarke (ed.), Managers, Micros, and Mainframes: Integrating Systems for End Users, John Wiley 1986.

[JV 84] Jarke, M. and Vassiliou, Y. "Coupling Expert Systems with Database Management Systems," in W. Reitman (ed.) Artificial Intelligence Applications for Business, Ablex, Norwood, N.J. 1984, pp.65-85.

[L 85] Lucas, H.C., Jr. The Analysis and Design of Information Systems, 2nd ed., McGraw-Hill, 1985.

[M 82] McDermott, J. "R1: A Rule-Based Configurer of Computer Systems", Artificial Intelligence, vol. 19, no. 1, pp.39-88.

[S 60] Simon, H.A. The New Science of Management Decision, Harper & Row, New York, 1960.

[SJ 84] Sivasankaran, T., and Jarke, M. "Logic-Based Formula Management Strategies in an Actuarial Consulting System", Decision Support Systems, vol. 1, no. 3, 1985.

[VCJ 85] Vassiliou, Y., Clifford, J., and Jarke, M. "Access to Specific Declarative Knowledge by Expert Systems: The Impact of Logic Programming," Decision Support Systems, vol. 1, no. 2., 1985.

Artificial Intelligence in Economics and Management
L.F. Pau (Editor)

EXPERT SYSTEMS AND BOARD LEVEL DECISIONS

David G. Demetrius

Unidata Europe Limited
Av. Albert Einstein 11, Bloc 3
B-1348 Louvain-la-Neuve
Belgium

and

School of Industrial & Business Studies
University of Warwick
Coventry CV4 7AL
U.K.

The extent to which board-level decision making may be able to be reduced to rule based procedures is discussed. It is the author's contention that current developments in Expert Systems enable the less structured decision making of top-level management to be approached from a systems viewpoint more readily than was previously possible. Various aspects of Expert Systems are then mapped against board level decisions. Examples from a financial rule base are provided.

INTRODUCTION

An analysis of business systems which have been designed and built in the past would show that there have been a large number of systems built for decision making but that these have largely been aimed at the level of middle management or below. Operational Research in particular has generated many such systems, typical examples being in the areas of production scheduling, stock control, project planning or delivery route optimisation. In AI research, similar examples are also now becoming common.

If, however, one looks at systems which have been built as board-level aids, it will be seen that the vast majority of these are purely information providers rather than decision making tools. The most significant area is of course the financial one where various accounting and financial reports are prepared which, on occasions, deluge the directors with information. Sales summaries, economic forecasts and the like fall into the same category.

The obvious question, therefore, is: "Why have the two categories, decision making systems and board-level systems, not been combined to provide true systems for board-level decision making?"

There are, in the view of the author, two factors which help to explain this lack. The first is the technical difficulty of adequately modelling board decisions and the second is the lack of senior management support for such an approach even if it could be achieved.

The difficulty in modelling is partly genuine and partly imaginary. It is certainly true to say that board decisions are relatively less structured than other management decisions and that this makes the modelling process more complicated. But there is also a perception that such decisions are purely based on subjective judgement and that they therefore are inherently impossible to model. The idea of companies being run by 'rules of thumb' or 'seat of the pants management' is a common misconception.

This view is often shared by the senior managers themselves, thus contributing to their lack of support for the development of decision making systems for their work. There is often a genuine belief on the part of directors that their decisions are unable to be analysed.

There is of course also the argument that this misconception is perhaps promulgated by many senior managers due to a desire to maintain the mystique surrounding their positions.

EXPERT SYSTEMS TO DATE

Turning specifically to the development of Expert Systems, it will be seen that by far the majority of work to date has been in the scientific and technical areas. This is partly due to a historical medical base for Expert Systems from which it is very difficult to break away. Nevertheless, the applications are real and are being used in day-to-day situations. The area of fault diagnosis, for example, has given rise to a number of different applications in widely varied fields.

Some Expert Systems have been built for business applications, but these have tended to be for low level specialist tasks. Examples are given in Table 1.

Table 1.: Examples of Expert Systems in Business Areas

* Fault diagnosis
* Assessment of credit ratings
* Computer sizing
* Taxation
* Insurance broking
* Purchasing

An absence of Expert Systems for senior management decisions at present does not, however, necessarily preclude their development in the future. Hardware and software technology are both developing extremely rapidly and performance, explanation and learning in Expert Systems are all improving. It is reasonable therefore to assume that if systems are theoretically possible now then they will be commercially viable in the not too distant future.

THE APPROPRIATENESS OF EXPERT SYSTEMS

In order to determine the appropriateness of Expert Systems for board level decisions, this paper considers three aspects of such systems. Firstly the types of expert task suitable for such an approach are identified ; secondly the characteristics of problems appropriate to Expert System modelling are listed; finally a number of bi-polar classifications of Expert Systems are enumerated. The major functional areas of companies are then looked at in turn, using each of these aspects to provide an overall classification of board decision making.

Various analyses of the types of expert task have been published in the past. The list provided in Table 2. is a synthesis of such previous efforts in an attempt to provide a comprehensive coverage of the full range of tasks likely to be encountered.

Table 2.: Types of expert task

* Interpretation
* Diagnosis
* Monitoring
* Prediction
* Planning
* Design
* Procedures
* Selection
* Decision making

Similarly, when one considers characteristics of problems suitable for Expert Systems, the literature provides many different check lists. Table 3. is a consolidation of some of these lists into a comprehensive list.

Table 3.: Characteristics of problems suitable for Expert systems

* Narrow specialty area without a lot of commonsense knowledge
* Task is neither too easy nor too difficult for human experts
* Task can be defined clearly
* Knowledge is already available in some written form
* Application area calls for continuous update of logic rules
* System can be developed in a modular way
* Complex and/or large solution search space
* Large amounts of domain specific knowledge
* Heuristic search approach
* User will be able to maintain and improve the knowledge base
* There is a clear incentive for the user to use the system
* Commitment from experts is available

With respect to the third and final aspect, the various ways of classifying Expert Systems, four polarisations are considered relevant to the current study.

Firstly, systems may be either opaque or consultative. The former describes systems which are mathematically correct but do not mirror the system actually employed by experts. Consultative systems on the other hand accurately represent and explain the reasoning of experts.

The second classification concerns whether the search is by forward (data or event driven) or backward (goal driven) chaining. It is suggested that the actual processes of business decision making are often a combination of both. The decision maker normally starts forward from a given situation in which he finds himself until he has identified a set of feasible goals for evaluation and then switches to a backward chaining approach in order to see which of these goals best satisfies his situational criteria.

Thirdly, systems may be classified according to whether the search is by direct analysis to or from the prime goal or whether it is via a series of sub-goals. Both methods can be found in the managerial decision making process.

The last classification considered in this paper concerns whether the system is a pure Expert System or not. Many systems, although having an Expert System as a kernel, have side systems for ancillary calculations, modelling or information storage. These side systems may or may not be written in an AI language.

These four classifications are summarised in Table 4.

Table 4.: Classifications of Expert Systems
* Opaque or consultative
* Forward or backward chaining
* Direct analysis or via sub-goals
* Pure system or with side systems

THE RELEVANCE TO BOARD DECISIONS

Having now described the three aspects of Expert Systems being considered (i.e. types of expert task, appropriate characteristics of problem, classifications of system), it is possible to evaluate the relevance of such systems to board decisions.

In Table 5., each of the major functional areas in board-level decision-making is mapped against the three aspects. The entries in the table are not intended to be exhaustive but rather to indicate the major attributes of decisions in the different functional areas.

A number of entries in this table are worth additional comment. Firstly, all the areas, with the exception of Sales, are considered to show an excellent fit with the characteristics of problems suitable for an Expert System approach. The most notable exception to this is possibly the availability of knowledge in some written form. In addition, as has been stated earlier, obtaining commitment from experts can be a problem. The Sales area, however, shows a poor fit with many of the characteristics, largely due to the highly unstructured and varied nature of the Sales process.

It will also be noted that all the areas have been classified as requiring consultative systems, with Manufacturing also using opaque systems. In general, businessmen are more ready to accept systems which they can understand and which they can see mirror their own approach. They are distrustful of 'black box' systems. The Manufacturing area, however, has a historical base of such opaque systems, notable examples being Linear Programming models for production scheduling or raw material allocation.

Manufacturing, together with Finance, is also an area where the use of side systems is likely. Expert systems in these two areas would need to draw on input not only from the user of the system but also on such other systems as scheduling and inventory models for Manufacturing or accounting systems and ratio analysis for Finance. The Marketing and Sales areas are considered more capable of having the full requirements of the decision model embodied in an Expert System.

Table 5.: Mapping of major functional areas against aspects of Expert Systems

	TYPE OF EXPERT TASK	CHARACTERISTICS OF PROBLEMS	CLASSIFICATIONS OF SYSTEMS
MARKETING	Interpretation Planning Selection Decision-making	Excellent fit with characteristics	Consultative F'ward chaining Via sub-goals Pure systems
MANUFACTURING	Planning Design Selection Decision-making	Excellent fit with characteristics	Opaque & Cons. B'ward chaining Direct Side systems
SALES	Prediction Planning Selection Decision-making	Poor fit with characteristics	Consultative B'ward chaining Via sub-goals Pure systems
FINANCE	Interpretation Planning Procedures Selection Decision-making	Excellent fit with characteristics	Consultative F'ward & B'ward Direct Side systems

With respect to the direction of chaining,although, as stated earlier, business decision makers tend to use a combination of both forward and backward chaining, the different functional areas often show a predominance for one or the other. Decision-making in the Manufacturing and Sales areas tends to be goal driven (i.e. backward chaining) whereas Marketing is more data driven (i.e. forward chaining). Finance usually exhibits a combination of both.

If board decisions are then capable of an Expert Systems approach, what would a typical rule-base look like? The author has looked at each of the major functional areas and developed examples of such rule-bases. These examples have been shown to experts in the various fields who have indicated initial agreement with the logic of the rules. The author is at present building a test vehicle for further feedback.

Examples from a rule-base for evaluating corporate financial structures are shown in Table 6. The goals of such a system would be the alternative financial structures possible.

e.g.: Increase equity by issuing ordinary shares
Increase equity by issuing preference shares
Borrow additional funds using short term loans
Borrow additional funds using long term loans

Table 6.: Typical rules for financial structures Expert System

```
* IF   ( reason for evaluation is routine
       AND ratios are within set tolerances
       AND set tolerances do not need changing )
  THEN ( structure does not need adjusting )

* IF   ( assets are long lived )
  THEN (long term financing is preferred )

* IF   ( future growth rate of sales is high
       AND earnings per share is important
  THEN ( borrowing is be preferred over equity financing )

* IF   ( leverage is beyond industry norms )
  THEN ( availability of loan funds is low )

* IF   ( 'debt ratio' is outside set  tolerances
       OR 'times interest earned' is outside set tolerances
       OR 'fixed charge coverage' is outside set tolerances
  THEN (leverage is beyond industry norms )

* İF   ( a rise in profits is expected
       OR a rise in the general price level is expected
  THEN ( long term debt is preferred )

* IF   ( voting control should not be devolved )
  THEN (preference shares are preferred to ordinary shares
```

Such a system would also rely on input from side systems such as the accounting system, ratio analysis, tables of industry norms and sales and profit forecasting models.

If one addresses the question of which of the many available Expert System tools are most appropriate for board decision systems, it will be seen that the classifications in Table 5. can be used to assist in the selection process. For example, many tools are most appropriate for diagnosis problems whereas diagnosis is not a type of expert task commonly found in board decisions. Systems with good links to external routines (e.g. FORTRAN links) will be useful for those areas with side systems. A similar plus would apply to those with good data-base interaction. In view of the difficulty in gaining the commitment of experts in this area, 'user friendliness' (i.e. good man-machine interfaces) are also an important feature. Good reporting and graphics capabilities fall into this category as does a good explanation facility.

FUTURE DEVELOPMENTS

Finally it is worth noting areas where improvement is needed in Expert Systems if they are to be truly useful in board-level decision-making. The handling of uncertainty is important, approximate rules being commonplace in such decisions. Natural language understanding, or perhaps more accurately commercial language understanding, must also be developed. Thirdly, the general area of interfaces to side systems is one which has received inadequate attention to date. Finally, in view of the inherent difficulty in obtaining time from company directors, knowledge acquisition methods must be improved.

CONCLUSION

In conclusion, the author believes there is a bright future for Expert Systems in the board room, although further developments are required before they they will be commercially viable. Expert Systems provide the opportunity to bridge the gap between systems thinking and management practice.

Before such a bridge becomes a commercial reality, however, it will be necessary for a number of improvements to be made in Expert Systems technology.

REFERENCES

[1] d'Agapeyeff A., Report to the Alvey Directorate on a short survey of expert systems in UK business, Alvey News (IEE, London, 1984).

[2] Barr A. & Feigenbaum E.A., The handbook of artificial intelligence, vols. 1 & 2 (Pitman, London, 1981/2).

[3] Butler Cox Foundation, Expert systems, Report series, No. 37 (1983).

[4] Cohen P.R. & Feigenbaum E.A., The handbook of artificial intelligence, vol. 3 (Pitman, London, 1982).

[5] Feigenbaum E.A. & McCorduck P., The fifth generation : artificial intelligence and Japan's computer challenge to the world (Michael Joseph, London, 1984).

[6] Hayes-Roth F., Waterman D.A. & Lenat D.B., Building expert systems (Addison-Wesley, Reading, Mass., 1984).

[7] Janis I.L. & Mann L., Decision making (Collier-MacMillan, New York, 1977).

[8] Kepner C.H. & Tregoe B.B., The rational manager (McGraw-Hill, New York, 1965).

[9] Waterman D.A. & Hayes-Roth F., eds., Pattern-directed inference systems (Academic Press, New York, 1978).

[10] Winston P.H., Artificial intelligence (Addison-Wesley, Reading, Mass., 1977).

[11] Winston P.H. & Prendergast K.A., The AI business : the commercial uses of artificial intelligence (MIT Press, Cambridge, Mass., 1984).

Artificial Intelligence in Economics and Management
L.F. Pau (Editor)

CAN ARTIFICIAL INTELLIGENCE DO BETTER THAN HUMANS AT LEADERSHIP?

M A P Willmer

Reader in Operational Research
Manchester Business School
Manchester
Great Britain

This paper considers whether it is possible that some form of artificial intelligence could be more successful than humans in controlling and motivating subordinates as well as minimising the effects of distortion in information flows.

Of particular interest are those situations where subordinates have a large measure of influence over information flows and where their superiors need information to make decisions concerning the internal control of the organisation, and strategic policy. Indeed, sometimes one wonders where control in an organisation really lies!

In an attempt to gain insights into leadership problems, a simulation was constructed of a company that produces clunks. Attention was focussed primarily on the decision-making of the Chief Executive and the Managers. The human response characteristics used in the simulation are based on an analysis of the behaviour of production managers attending Operational Management Courses at Manchester Business School. Several artificial intelligence approaches to leadership are considered and the results obtained are compared with those produced by humans in similar circumstances. The results should be of interest to all those concerned with management control in organisations where opportunities for information distortion abound.

INTRODUCTION

Leadership for those brought up on a diet of John Wayne films is represented by a mounted cavalry officer with right arm raised ready to lower it in the direction of the enemy whilst exhorting the troops behind to charge. Leadership of a modern complex organisation, however, is a vastly different matter and over the years much has been written on the question of what makes a good leader. For example, Reeves (1970) noted that the most common attributes of leaders are: intelligence, motivation, decision-making, interpersonal relationships, personal integrity, stamina, conceptual ability, recognition of creativity in others and charisma. Furthermore, styles of leadership may either be democratic, autocratic or laissez-faire.

To be effective the leader of a large organisation has to be more than the man who stands facing the crowd. His task is to inspire and motivate others. As Carlsson and Misshauk (1972) noted: "In the business environment effective implementation usually requires working with other people. Thus, the knowledge that an individual may have is practically useless unless it can be communicated to others. Finally, the action resulting from the communication of ideas must be coordinated in order to achieve a common goal."

In small organisations where the leader and his subordinates operate on the same site people are able to get to know one another reasonably well. For larger organisations especially as they develop and establish branches in many diverse places a leader and his subordinates may know very little about one another as individuals. They may meet only infrequently and subordinates in particular may be very much on their guard, trying to make a good impression. It is only human nature that the more powerful the leader, the more influence he has on the lives of those who work for him and the more they will tend to tell him what they think he wants to hear. Indeed, as so many powerful people have found to their cost, although they may have power the truth is something that often eludes them, see Lucas (1938).

Under these circumstances the leader is faced with many problems associated with the complexities of controlling and motivating staff and with the distortion of information. Of particular interest are those where subordinates have a large measure of influence over the information that is needed by their superiors to make decisions concerning

1. the internal control of the organisation, and
2. strategic policy.

These problems become more acute when there is only infrequent contact between the leader and his subordinates: the scope for frank communications and the establishing of meaningful relationships tends to become restricted. Thus the leader may appear remote to his subordinates and his personal qualities may remain obscure. Previous papers have explored the questions of system uncertainty and leadership, and subordinate behaviour and management control in such situations, see Willmer (1978 & 1980). This paper examines the leadership question in greater depth and considers whether it is possible that some form of artificial intelligence could be more effective as a leader than humans in controlling and motivating subordinates as well as in minimising the effects of distortion in information flows.

Unreliability of Management Control Information

Revans (1969) noted that any information system may suffer from faults of design and operation and he listed those that occur most frequently. Difficulties in human systems arise with respect to the collection and interpretation of data as well as with the transmission of information from one part of the system to another. At each link of the communication process information is received, processed and transmitted and with humans involved there is always a possibility that the message will become lost, distorted or misunderstood. As noted by Miller (1972) distortions occur in command messages flowing downwards and in reports flowing upwards. In connection with the former, Rogers and Agarwala-Rogers (1976) suggest that: "Such distortion seems to have been responsible for the My Lai massacre of Vietnam civilians by American troops in 1968". It would seem that an order "On no occasion must hamlets be burned down" became "Do not burn down any hamlets unless you are absolutely convinced that the Vietcong are in them" to "If you think there are any Vietcong in the hamlet, burn it down" to "Burn down that hamlet" as it passed from divisional headquarters to the troops on duty.

Although much has been learnt about the design of good management information systems, there is no guarantee that the causes of error will be entirely eliminated. Leaders will find it prudent therefore to remember that, since their communication channels are unlikely to be completely reliable, they may be more uncertain about a particular situation than they should be. This increase in uncertainty can be thought of as noise and it has been found convenient to distinguish between two types; (see Willmer, 1970).

a) Internally generated noise which is due to information becoming lost or distorted inside an organisation or because insufficient use is made of information already obtained, and

b) Background noise which is due to the organisation not receiving the appropriate information in the first place.

Similarly, leaders may feel more certain about the true situation than they should be, bearing in mind the data available. This effect can be thought of as "pseudo-certainty".

Distortions may occur accidentally or be caused deliberately especially when there are major differences of objective between people in an organisation. Many instances of errors being deliberately introduced have been noted in the literature. For example, with regard to the budgetary process, Williamson (1964) and Schiff and Lewin (1970) found that managers understated revenues and overstated costs in attempts to obtain slack budgets. Lowe and Shaw (1968) found that line managers introduced bias into their sales forecasts. These examples are characterised by the superior and his subordinates having different objectives, and information being biased by subordinates in order to achieve their own goals, a type of conflict in which the parties develop "ploys" and "counterploys", see Anthony and Herzlinger (1975).

One factor which tends to exacerbate the internal deliberate distortion situation is the assessment of the performance of an individual by the leader using information supplied by the subordinate under review. The leader by rewarding a subordinate inappropriately can affect not only that person's attitude but also the attitude of others. Afterall it is basic human nature that some employees will try to make it look as though they are better performers than their efforts genuinely merit. It should not therefore be thought that this is a contemporary problem brought about by modern management methods and technology. Some fifty years ago that great London detective F.B. Wensley (1931) warned: "there are men ...with a streak of vanity that impels them to adopt a pose at the expense of those who have really done the work. They like to bask in the limelight...As Chief Constable I was always on my guard against this sort of thing and made it my business to see that credit went in the right direction. Unless kept in check it breeds resentment and checks energy".

For many of the leadership situations being considered in this paper, opportunities may arise where the information flows affecting the assessment of subordinates can be manipulated by the subordinates themselves. Where an organisation operates branches in several very different environments and where the managers of each branch know that they are competing with one another for promotion is one example. In circumstances such as these one may wonder where control in the organisation really lies! Is it with those with nominal authority or with those who are able to affect the information that is used in the decision-making process ?

Who controls Whom?

Much of our thinking about management control problems is strongly influenced by the fundamental control model of cybernetics. Essentially the controller has an objective for the system under his command. He also knows the present state of this system and can thus determine an error signal. At his command are a number of options and he can select that option which eliminates or minimises the error. This model of control has its origins in the physical sciences where it has enabled mankind to exert considerable authority over natural systems. However, where human organisations are concerned many of its underlying assumptions are far from valid. Its application to management control systems has been severely criticised by Hofstede (1978): "A distinction is made between routine industrial-type processes for which a homeostatic paradigm is more suitable, and non-routine, non-industrial-type processes, for which a political paradigm is recommended. Attempts at enforcing a cybernetic paradigm on the latter process, like Program-Planning-Budgeting Systems (PPBS) and Management-By-Objectives (MBO) are bound to fail."

The question of who really is in control in those organisations where subordinates have many opportunities for manipulating information flows is a very interesting one. The nominal superior may have all the outward trappings of authority - the thick piled carpet in the large office, the luxurious car and the key to the executive loo. He may be able to call for data and may be the person who formally announces his decisions to the workforce. On the other hand, his subordinate may know how his superior's mind works, his weaknesses and pet theories, and then feeds him the information that ensures a particular decision is made. A leader may set objectives, discuss targets with his subordinates, tell them how they will be rewarded and later give them the rewards he deems appropriate. Nevertheless, when they massage and manipulate information flows, he can have very real problems in making his authority felt and ensuring that he is in command. One well-known way of viewing an organisation is to compare it to the human body, see Beer (1972). However, as Morris has warned: "The Big Toe can think". Clearly, therefore, when subordinates can affect the information flows the usefulness of the cybernetic approach and models derived from it is limited.

The target setting and reward systems found in many budgetary control processes illustrate these limitations well. To avoid causing trouble leaders should be sure whether they are using budgets for planning or for control since trying to use for both purposes can encourage subordinates to play the numbers game, see Churchill (1984). Similarly Carruth and McClendon (1984) warn accountants to be aware of the behavioural implications of using budgets for control and evaluation: "Using budgets as a pressure device by over-emphasizing 'meeting the budget' can limit the autonomous actions necessary for business growth."

For both planning and control purposes, statistics have tended to be relied upon in preference to qualitative information. Perhaps this is because decision-makers, who in the words of Meal (quoted in Brown, 1970), "..want to think of themselves as individuals whose greater grasp of the available information and whose greater insight remove the uncertainty from the situation", have greater faith in numbers than in other data. Afterall, as Rapoport (1965) noted: "Numbers are the simplest and most universal linguistic invariants".

Nor is this belief in the authority of statistics a modern phenomena, brought about by the power of contemporary computers generating an attitude of "what the computer says must be true". Bogdan and Ksander (1980) and Graham (1982) quote Stamp (1929) as saying: "The Government are very keen on amassing statistics - they collect them, add them, raise them to the nth power, take the cube root and prepare wonderful diagrams. But what you must never forget is that every one of these figures comes in the first instance from the....(village watchman), who just puts down what he damn pleases."

Indeed, as has been pointed out by Willmer (1984), some people view numbers not as objective data but as strategic acts used to achieve specific objectives. This reference also outlines the standard techniques of those who use numbers to achieve strategic objectives. An example of their use in practice is given by Lipsey (1985) in relation to the British Government's handling of the unemployment figures. The prudent executive should not forget that, as Graham notes: "data reflect what most people wish was reality or what people want you to believe is reality".

The ingenuity that humans have shown in finding ways of manipulating and massaging data to meet their objectives means that, in most situations involving groups of human beings, the power of the control system is derived from the leadership that executives breathe into it! To explore more thoroughly the question of leadership under these circumstances and to give insights into the different aspects of the superior/subordinate interface and the effects of various methods of performance appraisal on both the motivation of employees and the manipulation of data, a business simulation representing a production situation was created.

So You Think That You Would Make a Managing Director

This simulation represents a large multi-national company whose subsidiaries are engaged in a wide variety of activities and is concerned with the management of people and machines in a production environment. Attention is focussed on one of these subsidiaries called International Castings Ltd. which produces "clunks". This company has two factories both situated a long way from head office in unpleasant surroundings so that it is rarely convenient for top level staff to visit them.

The situation is simplified by assuming that the organisation has two levels of authority. At the superior level there is the leader who has two subordinates each of whom is the manager of a clunk factory reporting directly to him. Participants engage in decision-making at both the subordinate and the superior levels. First, they are asked to imagine that they are the manager of one of the factories. Here their task is to become familiar with the problems of manufacturing clunks and to understand the superior's style of leadership. They have therefore to operate in a socio-technical environment where the technical decisions are concerned with the way in which men, money and machines under their control are used. The factory, its machines and workforce, are described more fully by Willmer (1978). At the social level they have to persuade their superior that they are competent, capable and dependable.

For the guidance of its managers the company has established a number of rules which should theoretically be adhered to in the running of each factory. However, the simulation has been designed so that the subordinate is the main source of information about how his factory is being run and how well it is performing. Thus, as the superior rarely visits the factory, subordinates may violate these rules without fear of immediate exposure. The extent to which production is affected by rule violations depends on which ones are broken and the impact that some violations can have both in the short and long term on the state of the equipment and the morale of the workforce. The information flow within the organisation is illustrated diagrammatically in fig.1.

After a period playing the role of subordinate, participants are promoted to the position of leader. Here their objective is to handle subordinates in such a way that:

(i) output is increased
(ii) the managing director is aware of the way his factories are being managed.

The computer programmes in both parts of the simulation are based partly on assumptions and partly from the analysis of data obtained from the behaviour of managers who have been participants. Most of this behavioural data relates to production managers from multi-national companies who have attended Operational Management Courses at the Manchester Business School. Thus during the first part of the simulation the computer represents the equipment, the workforce and the leader. At the start each subordinate is told that his leader has believed for some time that clunk production is too low, and that the previous manager was sacked for incompetence. However, the simulation has been designed so that the subordinate cannot normally meet the initial aspirations of his boss by totally obeying the rules. Each month starts with the subordinate being told his leader's primary objective. There are three possibilities:

1. to produce as many clunks as possible,
2. to get as close to the agreed target as possible,
3. to be truthful about the number of violations made.

Superior and subordinate then negotiate a target. This is followed by the subordinate being asked to decide upon issues relating to the running of the factory: the levels of overtime for the different types of workers, the number of maintenance men to be put onto production duties, etc. The subordinate has also to decide how many clunks he does not want recorded until the following month and the number of rule violations that he has committed. The recorded production figures and the number of confessions are given to the superior who assesses his subordinate's performance and gives him a rating normally between 50 and 100.

As has been noted earlier, the simulation has been designed so that the subordinate is the main source of information about how a factory is being run and how well it is performing. Thus, the decision about how many rules to confess to having violated, like the reaction to the leader's target proposal and the production not declared each month, may be viewed as essentially tactical depending upon the impression that the subordinate hopes to leave in the mind of the leader about his competence. The simulation shows clearly the fundamental conflict of objectives between the Managing Director and his subordinates. The leader wants the highest possible production and an accurate knowledge of the state of affairs at his factories: the subordinate wants to be thought well of by his boss. As the subordinate has a significant amount of control over the information that his boss needs to assess him, he can if he has the necessary skills manipulate the information flows to improve his boss's perception of his performance. The reaction of managers when faced with this situation is given by Willmer (1980) and a discussion of some of the ethical considerations is given by Willmer and Keiser (1982).

Experience is any human organisation soon reveals examples of people who possess skill at developing a level of appreciation far beyond their actual worth. Similarly there are those who quietly and effectively get on with the job whilst their contribution and competence is doubted by those at a higher level. Examples of such cases are given by the simulation results shown in fig.2. In this figure the actual average score is plotted against the average clunk production for a number of managers. The line NN represents the case of the naive manager who engages in no tactical attempts to modify his boss's perceptions to his own advantage. At the lower end of the production range he breaks no rules and says so. At the higher production levels he breaks rules but honestly admits it. Thus anyone who achieves a result above the line may be viewed as an Appreciation Amplifier whilst those below the line may be called Appreciation Attenuators.

When participants are promoted to the leader's position at Head Office it is their task to set the main objective, to lead the target negotiation process and to reward or punish as appropriate. The computer at this stage acts as two cynical old hands who have heard many fine words in the past from other Managing Directors. Again the programme is based partly on assumptions about human behaviour and partly on the way people have responded when they have acted out the role of boss. Whereas subordinates enjoy considerable freedom to manipulate information to influence their superior's perceptions, participants soon find that the task of motivating and controlling such people is very difficult. Because of the nature of the contact with their subordinates there is no scope for frank and full discussions. They know that their subordinates may be using their power over the information flows tactically - to create a better perception of themselves. To control the situation therefore participants have to rely on their skills at setting main objectives, on the way that they handle the target setting negotiations, and on their ability to reward or punish appropriately. Since the Managing Director communicates with his subordinates using only the briefest of messages and without attempting to get to know them personally, there is no possibility of any human relationship being established. In such circumstances is it feasible that some form of artificial intelligence could be more successful than humans at the art of leadership?

Results: Humans vs. Artificial Intelligence

By Artificial Intelligence I am thinking of a mechanism which, given the information available to the Managing Director, tells a subordinate his rating for the previous month, the main objective for the coming month, the initial target, the agreed target, as well as estimating the number of rule violations committed. The results for several groups attending Operational Management courses at the Manchester Business School are given in figs. (3a) & (3b). In fig.(3a) the variation of production is shown with time and it can be seen that the overall average rises steadily over the year. Also shown are the variations for the top and bottom ten subordinates. The wide spread shows clearly that some subordinates were not being controlled or motivated effectively by their superiors. Fig(3b) shows the error level over the same time period, where

$$\text{error level} = | \text{actual} - \text{perceived number of violations} |$$

The figure shows that for most of the range the bosses in the case of the "bottom ten" appear to have a better appreciation of what is happening in the factory than those in the "top ten" group. However, when the error rate is plotted against production, see fig.(3c), it can be seen that increased production tends to lead to an increased error rate in both cases. When this trend is taken into account it follows that, at a given production level, the error rate for the "bottom ten" is greater than that for the "top ten".

To explore the differences between the performance as the Managing Director of humans with that of some form of Artificial Intelligence, it will be assumed that the boss is programmed to operate according to the following rules:

Strategy A

1) On taking command the work of both subordinates is assessed as satisfactory. Subsequently their assessments will be determined by the rating the boss is given for his own activities, i.e. they are told that, if he does badly, he will reward them badly and vice-versa.
2) Production is always the main objective.
3) The initial target in the first two months is set at 31800 clunks. Thereafter the target is increased by 500 if in two consecutive months the recorded production is within 300 clunks of the agreed target up to a maximum of 35,000 clunks.
4) The agreed target is always midway between the initial target suggested by the boss and the value offered by the subordinate.
5) The subordinate is always believed.

Strategy B

As strategy A except that the boss is assumed to be more of a "hawk". The differences are:

3) The initial target in the first two months is set at 31800 clunks. Thereafter the target is increased by 800 if in two consecutive months the recorded production is within 300 clunks of the agreed target up to a maximum of 36,000 clunks.
4) The agreed target is only reduced by 10% of the difference between the initial target suggested by the boss and the value offered by the subordinate.

The results are shown in figs4(a,b,&c). With regard to production it can be seen from fig.4(a) that strategy A gives a result very close to that of the "Top Ten" - there is a rise from about 30,700 to 33,000 clunks per month. Strategy B on the other hand has a faster rate of growth but peaks at month 6 leading to a steady decline. Fig.4(b) shows the variation of the error level with time and it can be seen that strategy A is less successful than the "Top Ten" over the whole of the year. Strategy B on the other hand is less successful during the early months but later gives a lower error level. When these results are compared on an Error level /Production graph a number of interesting points arise, see fig.4(c). First, the success of the "Top Ten" over both strategies can be clearly seen. Secondly, all curves show a kind of hysteresis effect, i.e. the error level when production is rising tends to be less than that when production is decreasing. This effect is most marked in the case of strategy B. As far as humans are concerned one explanation could be that, when production is increasing the superior feels good and adopts an optimistic view of his subordinates activities. In contrast, when production is falling, he becomes more cynical or realistic. In view of the fact that the phenomena occurs for both the humans and the computer-based strategies it is more likely that it is caused by a change in the attitude of the subordinates to reporting rule violations. Could it be that doing better leads to more information distortion whilst doing worse produces more reliability?

Both strategies A and B assume some knowledge of the maximum number of clunks that can be built each month at the factories regardless of whether rules are violated or not. Determining this limit is a key issue in the control of many managerial problems. When faced with such situations it is helpful to bear in mind two levels of production performance suggested by Beer (1972):

1. the capability level - that which a completely efficient subordinate could achieve with existing resources and operating under existing restraints.
2. the potentiality level - that which could be achieved by fully utilising existing resources and optimally relaxing the restraints.

Thus, if one asks a subordinate to work above the capability level, he must violate the regulations whilst asking someone to exceed the potentiality level is requesting the impossible. In the case of strategy A the target was set at roughly the potentiality level whereas in strategy B it was comfortably exceeded. This explains the failure of this strategy to maintain high production, see fig. 4(a) - the target set is impossible and the subordinate 'switches off'.

To explore the effect of the superior having no prior knowledge of the potentiality level and thus compelling him to estimate it from the data given to him by his subordinate, several further strategies will be considered.

Strategy C1

This is the same as strategy A except that:

3) The initial target in the first two months is set at 31800 clunks. Thereafter the target is increased by 500 if in two consecutive months the recorded production is within 300 clunks of the agreed target. On each month after the first two an additional factor is also added to the initial target. This amount is equal to the mean of the difference between the recorded and the agreed target for the previous two months.

4) The agreed target is only reduced by 10% of the difference between the initial target suggested by the boss and the value offered by the subordinate.

Strategy C2

This strategy is similar to strategy C1 except that the initial target is increased by 1000 instead of 500 when the recorded production is within 300 clunks of the agreed target in the previous two months.

Strategy D1 and D2

Similar to strategy C1 except that only 20% of the mean of the difference between the recorded and the agreed target for the previous two months is added to the initial target.

The results from these strategies are compared with those of the "Top Ten" in figs.5(a&b) and 6(a&b). The variation of production with time is given in figs. 5(a&b) where the sensitivity of strategies C1 and C2 to differences between recorded production and agreed target can be clearly seen. When the smaller basic increment of 500 clunks is in operation production starts to fall off after month 2 but later recovers to reach a level slightly less than that achieved by the "Top Ten". On the other hand, the higher basic increment of 1,000 clunks leads to a smaller initial drop but produces a peak after about six months. This point again corresponds to the subordinate being asked to operate beyond the potentiality level and is followed by a collapse in production as he becomes "switched-off". These effects are not nearly so pronounced in the case of the strategies D1 and D2. Here the tighter control over the way the initial target is modified to take account of deviations from the target in earlier months is evident. The strategies are compared on an error level/Production graph in figs.6(a&b). From fig.6(a) it is interesting to note that the hysteresis effect does not occur for strategies C1 and C2. Indeed the error level tends to rise to a plateau in both cases. However, when tighter control is exercised over the way the initial target is modified (strategies D1 and D2) the hysteresis effect returns, see fig.6(b).

Figs.7(a,b&c) give the results when the reward criterion is changed to put greater emphasis on increased production. Thus strategy C1 is modified as follows:

Strategy E1

1. The subordinate's performance is assessed as satisfactory in the first two months. Thereafter an increase in production of more than 400 is deemed to be good whereas a fall in production is deemed to be poor.

Strategy E2

Similar to strategy E1 except that only 20% of the mean of the difference between the recorded production and the agreed target for the previous two months is added to the initial target.

The figures show that the "Top Ten" still achieves better results although strategy E1 does end up in the same area of the Error level/Production space after 12 months.

In all the above cases it has been assumed that the subordinate will tell the truth about the number of violations of the regulations that he has made. Except for strategies E1 and E2 the hope was that, by making his reward correlation with the superior's score, honesty would be recognised as the best policy. The comparisons noted above indicate that changing the emphasis to production leads to an improvement in some cases. Nevertheless as has already been noted, the "Top Ten" humans seem to do better than all the computer based strategies considered so far.

Strategy F

If the design of the Artificial Intelligence is allowed to include some knowledge of the capability and potentiality levels use can be made of the fact, noted by Willmer and Berry (1976), that the superior's uncertainty about the state of his factory is greatest at these levels and reduces to a minimum in between. To incorporate this finding strategy A will be modified thus:

5. If production is less than 31,800 clunks and the deviation from the target is less than 400, it is assumed that the subordinate has committed one more violation than he admits. If the production is greater than 33,000 clunks, it is again assumed that he has committed an extra violation. Otherwise he is believed.

The results are given in figs.8(a,b&c) where it can be seen that production is less than both strategy A and the "Top Ten". Also the error level is lower than that of strategy A and when plotted on an Error level/Production graph the improvement achieved by strategy F can be clearly observed. However, the"Top Ten" humans were still able to obtain lower error levels over a wider production range than the computer-based strategies.

The results show that humans are able to cope with the problem of distorted information a little more successfully than the Artificial Intelligence models used. Although the development of more sophisticated models may lead to improved performances, it must be remembered that executives have to cope with messy situations. Often the first hurdle that the decision-maker has to overcome is to formulate his problem in a meaningful manner. It is the human mind that creates the basic order. Pym(1984) warns that we should be careful not to abdicate to information technology the responsibility for creating such order and suggests that it could be a liberating force if the part played by the human mind is explicitly recognised. There are already some who feel that the role of Artificial Intelligence is limited. Alexander(1984) quotes an expert as saying that the proper application for expert systems are structured selection problems and expressed the view that: "expert systems that can routinely outperform human experts will be much rarer than the hoopla suggests".

Some thirty years ago Boolean's algebra was the latest tool for solving the problems of managers. However, little is heard of it today. To prevent Artificial Intelligence suffering a similar fate when applied to the broad problems of management, its supporters must not forget that the data on which it has to work are the result of a social process, that humans sometimes do not obey the rules, and that people's personal objectives often differ from those of the organisation and they act accordingly.

REFERENCES

(1) Alexander, T.(1984), "Why Computers can't outthink the Experts", Fortune, Vol.110,No.4.
(2) Anthony, R.N. and Herzlinger, R.(1975), "Management Control in Non-profit Organisations", Homewood, Illinois, R.D. Irwing.
(3) Beer, S.(1972), "The Brain of the Firm", Allen Lane, London.
(4) Bogdan, R. and Ksander, M.(1980), "Policy Data as a Social Process: A Qualitative Approach to Quantitative Data", Human Organisation, Vol.39,No.4.
(5) Brown, R.V.(1970), "Do Managers find Decision Theory useful?", Harvard Business Review, 48, 3.
(6) Carlsson, J.G.H. and Misshauk, M.J. (1972), "Management Decision Simulations: Introduction to Gaming", John Wiley.
(7) Carruth, P.J. and McClendon, T.O. (1984), "How Supervisors react to 'meeting the Budget' Pressure", Management Accounting, November.
(8) Churchill,N.C. (1984), "Budget Choice: Planning vs. Control", Harvard Business Review, July/August, Vol.62, No.4.

(9) Graham, R.J. (1982), "Give the Kid a Number: an Essay on the Folly and Consequences of trusting your Data", Interfaces, June, Vol.12, No.2.

(10) Hofstede, G.H. (1978), "The Poverty of Management Control Philosophy", Academy of Management Review, July.

(11) Lipsey, D. (1985), "Numbers game does not add up", Sunday Times, London, 7th April.

(12) Lowe, E.A. and Shaw, R.W.(1968), "An Analysis of Managerial Biassing; Evidence from a Company's Budgetary Process", Journal of Management Studies, Vol.5, No.3, October.

(13) Lucas, F.L. (1938), "The Delights of Dictatorship", W. Heffer and Sons Ltd., Cambridge.

(14) Miller, J.G. (1972) "Living Systems: The Organization", Behavioural Science, 17.

(15) Morris J. (1983) "The Brain, the Heart and the Big Toe", Creativity and Innovation network, Vol.9, No.1, January.

(16) Pym, D(1984), "Technology and the Illusion of Order", London Business School Journal, Vol.9, No.1.

(17) Rapoport, A. (1965), "Operational Philosophy", John Wiley & Sons, New York.

(18) Rogers E.M. and Agarwala-Rogers R. (1976) "Communication in Organizations", The Free Press, New York.

(19) Reeves, E.T. (1970), "The Dynamics of Group Behaviour", American Management Association, Inc.

(20) Revans, R.W. (1969), "The Structure of Disorder", Survey of Cybernetics, Ed. J. Rose, ILEFFE.

(21) Schoff, M. and Lewin, A.Y. (1970), "The Impact of People on Budgets", The Accounting Review, XLV, April.

(22) Wensley, F.B. (1931), "Detective Days", Cassell and Co., London.

(23) Williamson, D.E.(1964), "The Economics of Discretionary Behaviour: Managerial Objectives on a Theory of a Firm", Prentice Hall.

(24) Willmer, M.A.P. (1970), "Crime and Information Theory", Edinburgh University Press.

(25) Willmer, M.A.P. and Berry, A.J. (1976), "Managerial Performance and System Uncertainty", Third European Meeting on Cybernetics and Systems Research, Vienna, Austria.

(26) Willmer, M.A.P. (1978), "System Uncertainty and Leadership Strategy", Proceedings of the European Meeting of Cybernetics and Systems Research, Linz, 1978, Progress of Cybernetics and Systems Research, Vol.III, Hemisphere Publishing Corporation, Washington D.C.

(27) Willmer, M.A.P. (1980), "Subordinate Behaviour and Management Control", Proceedings of the 5th European Meeting of Cybernetics and Systems Research, Vienna, 1980.

(28) Willmer, M.A.P. and Keiser, J. (1982), "The Ethics of Deviousness", Manchester Business School Review, Vol.6, No.2, Summer/Autumn.

(29) Willmer, M.A.P. (1983) "The Contribution of the Cybernetic Approach to Management Control", New Perspectives in Management Control, Ed. A. Lowe and J.L.J. Machin, Macmillan, 1983.

(30) Willmer, M.A.P. (1984), "Freedom in a Numerate World", Paper presented at the Orwellian Symposium, Baden-Baden, August.

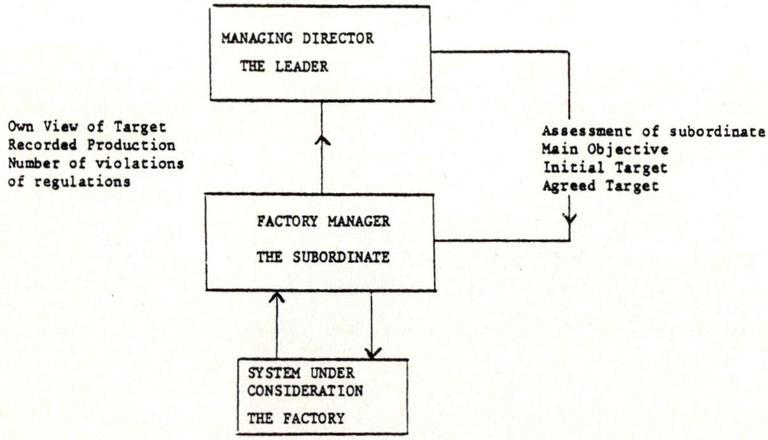

THE INFORMATION LINKS AT INTERNATIONAL CASTINGS LTD

Figure 1

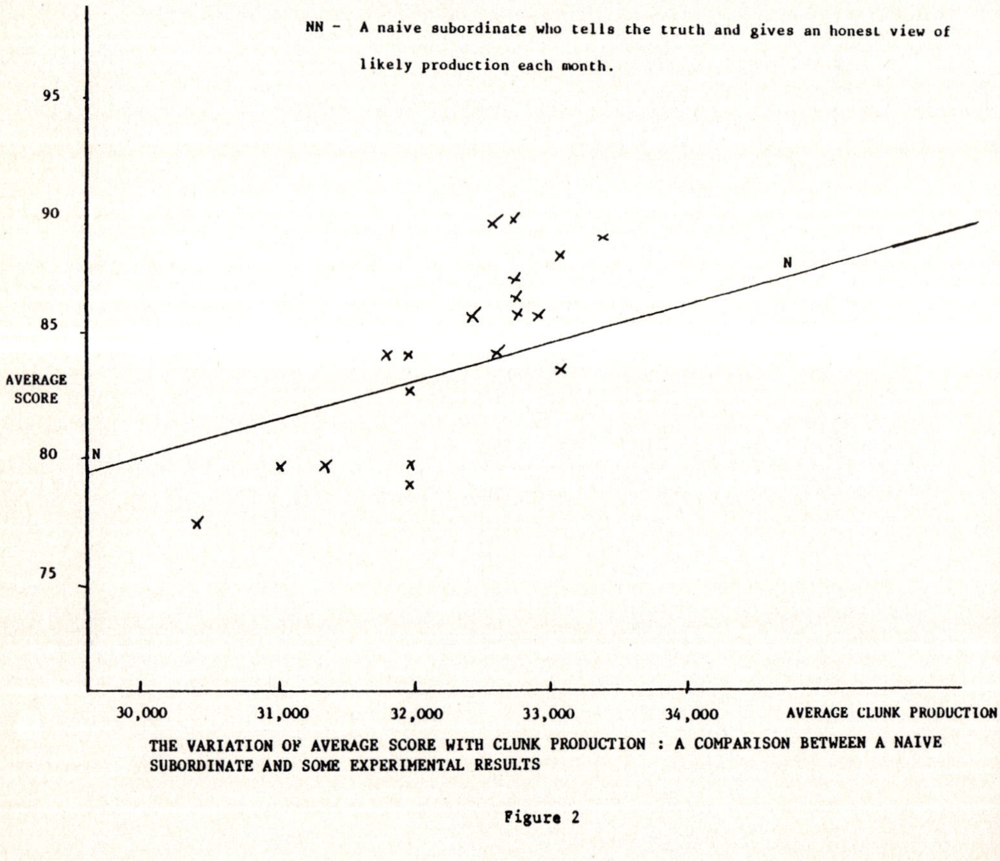

THE VARIATION OF AVERAGE SCORE WITH CLUNK PRODUCTION : A COMPARISON BETWEEN A NAIVE SUBORDINATE AND SOME EXPERIMENTAL RESULTS

Figure 2

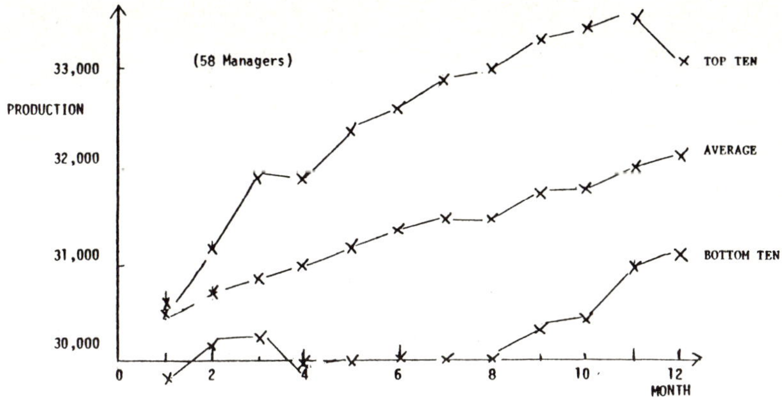

VARIATION OF PRODUCTION WITH TIME

Fig. 3(a)

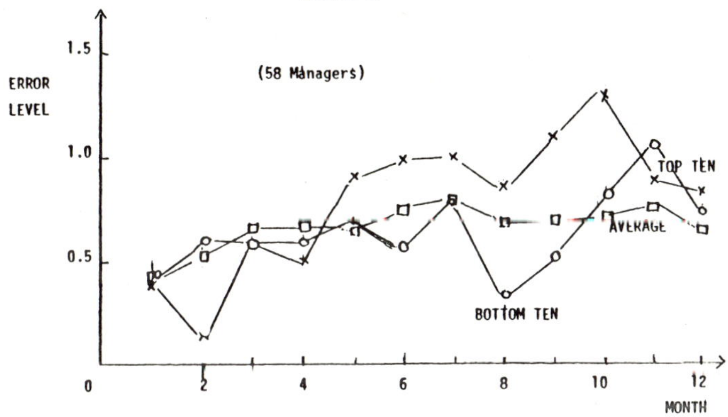

VARIATION OF ERROR LEVEL WITH TIME

Fig. 3(b)

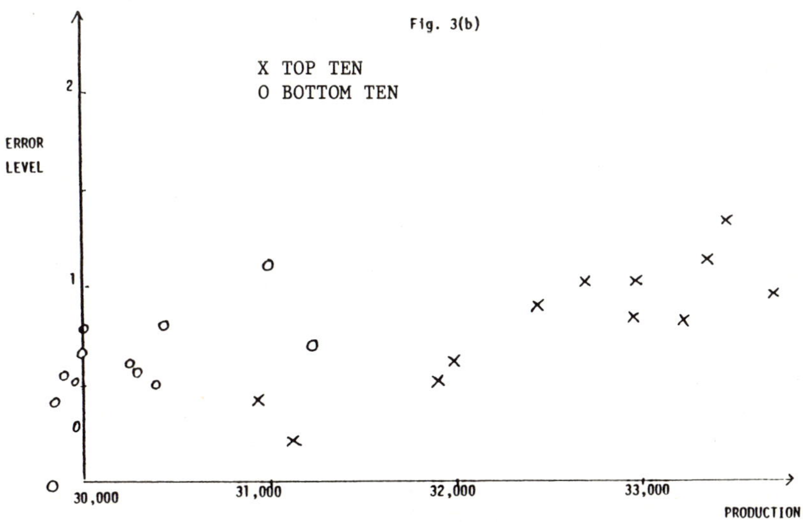

THE VARIATION OF ERROR LEVEL WITH PRODUCTION

Fig. 3(c)

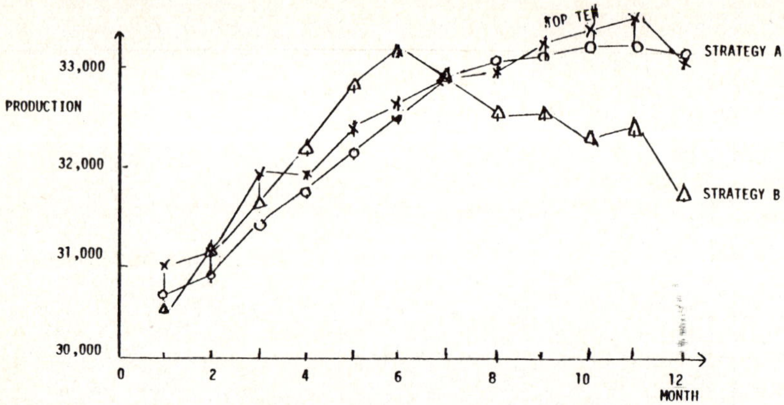

COMPARISON BETWEEN 'TOP TEN' HUMANS AND TWO A.I. STRATEGIES

Fig. 4(a)

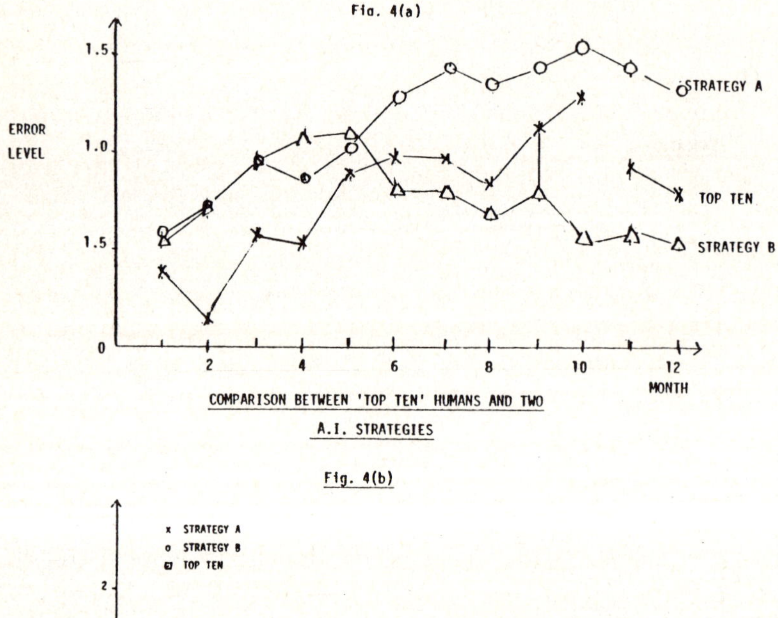

COMPARISON BETWEEN 'TOP TEN' HUMANS AND TWO A.I. STRATEGIES

Fig. 4(b)

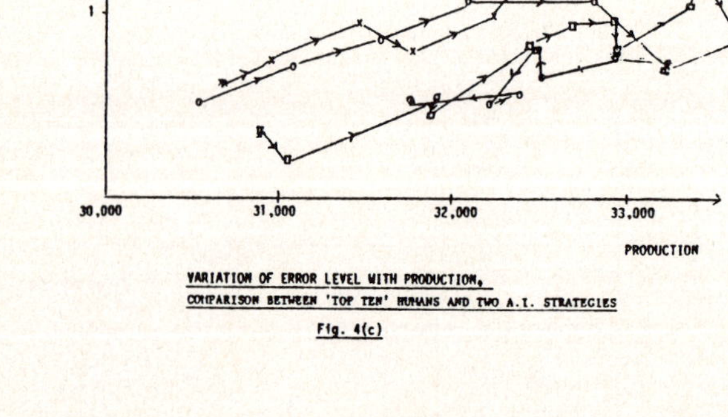

VARIATION OF ERROR LEVEL WITH PRODUCTION,
COMPARISON BETWEEN 'TOP TEN' HUMANS AND TWO A.I. STRATEGIES

Fig. 4(c)

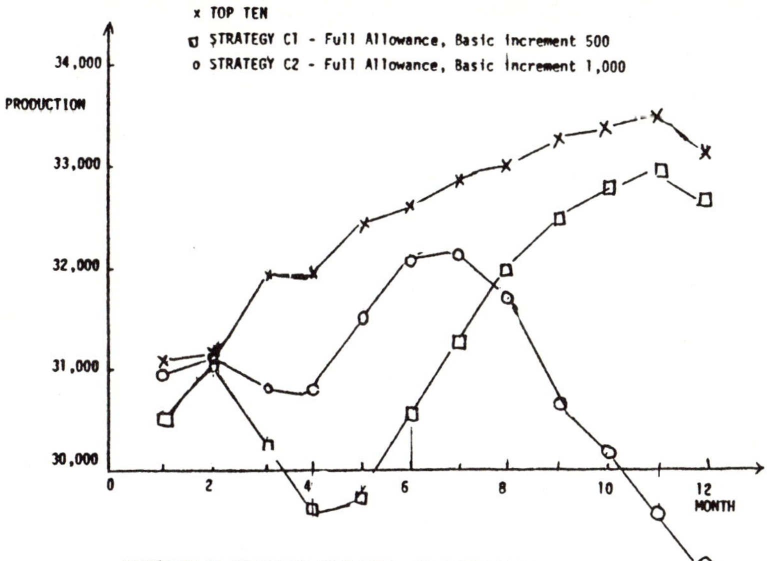

VARIATION OF PRODUCTION WITH TIME - NO TARGET LIMITS

Fig. 5(a)

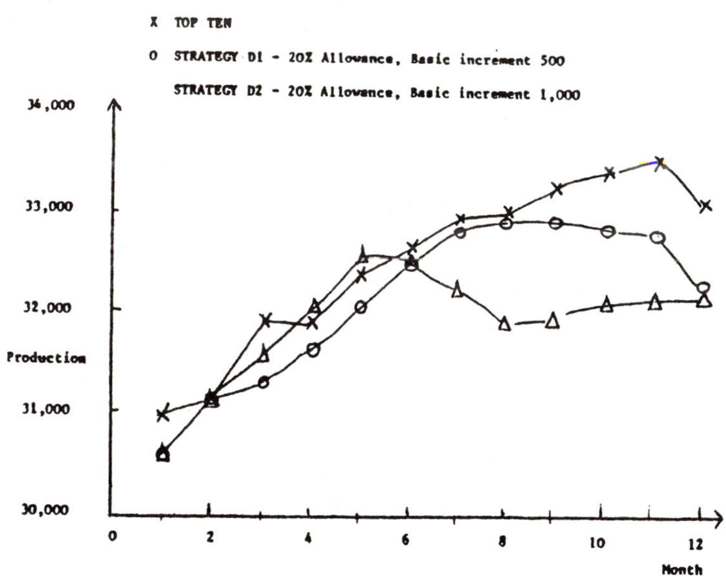

VARIATION OF PRODUCTION WITH TIME - NO TARGET LIMITS

Fig.5(b)

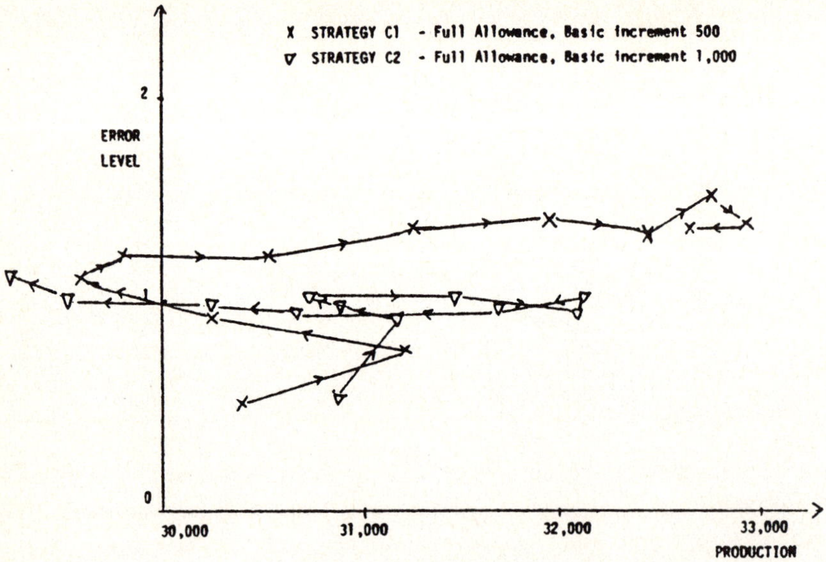

VARIATION OF ERROR LEVEL WITH PRODUCTION - NO TARGET LIMITS

Fig. 6(a)

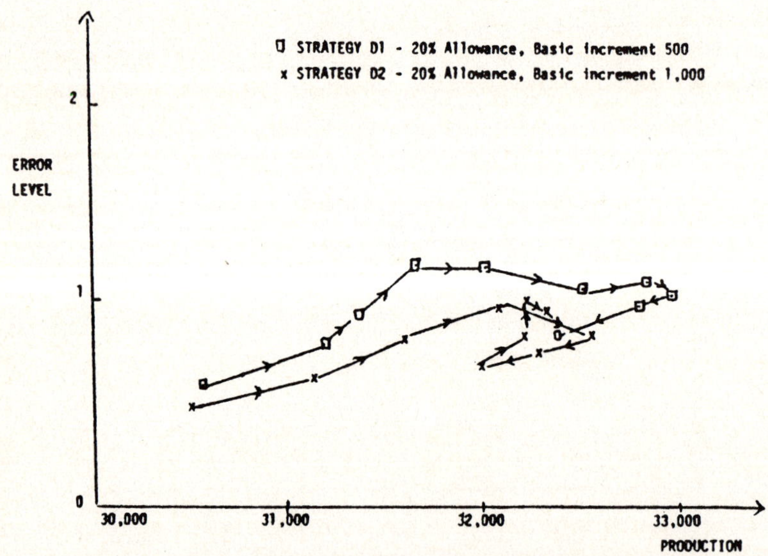

VARIATION OF ERROR LEVEL WITH PRODUCTION - NO TARGET LIMITS

Fig. 6(b)

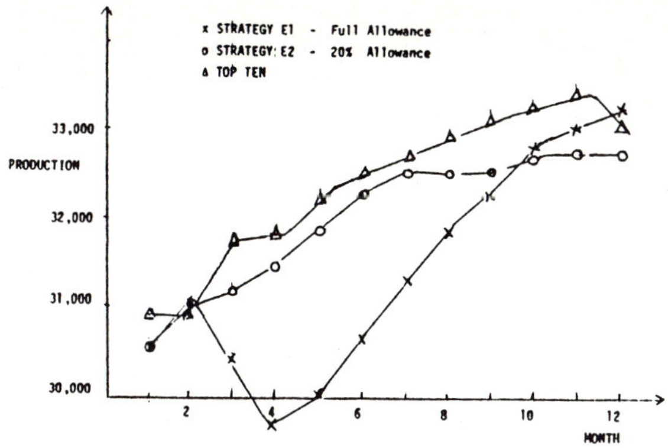

VARIATION OF PRODUCTION WITH TIME - NO LIMITS, REWARDED FOR INCREASED PRODUCTION

Fig. 7(a)

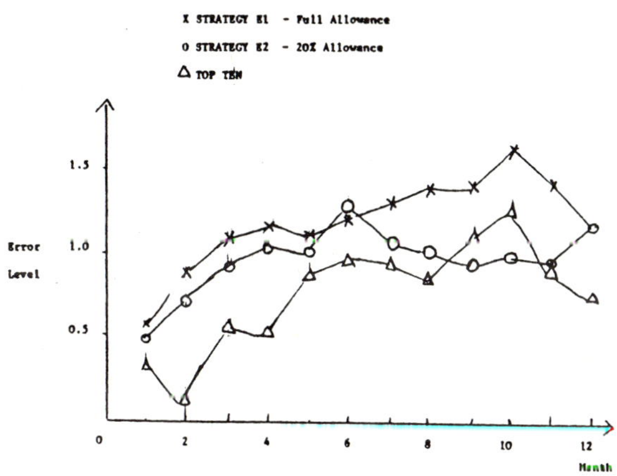

VARIATION OF THE ERROR LEVEL WITH TIME - NO LIMITS REWARDED FOR INCREASED PRODUCTION

Fig 7(b)

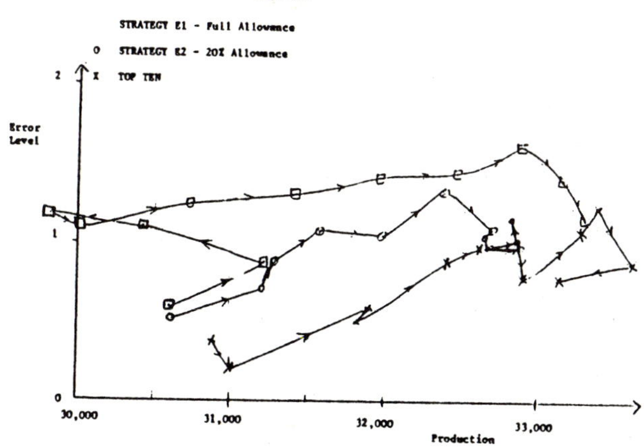

VARIATION OF ERROR LEVEL WITH PRODUCTION - NO LIMITS REWARDED FOR INCREASED PRODUCTION

Fig.7(c)

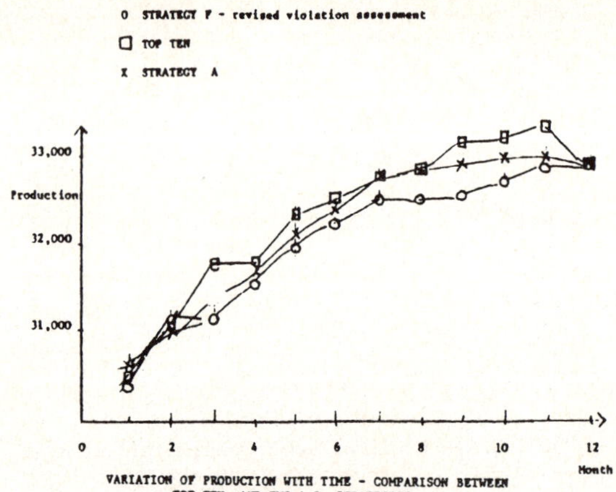

VARIATION OF PRODUCTION WITH TIME - COMPARISON BETWEEN TOP TEN AND TWO A.I. STRATEGIES

Fig.8(a)

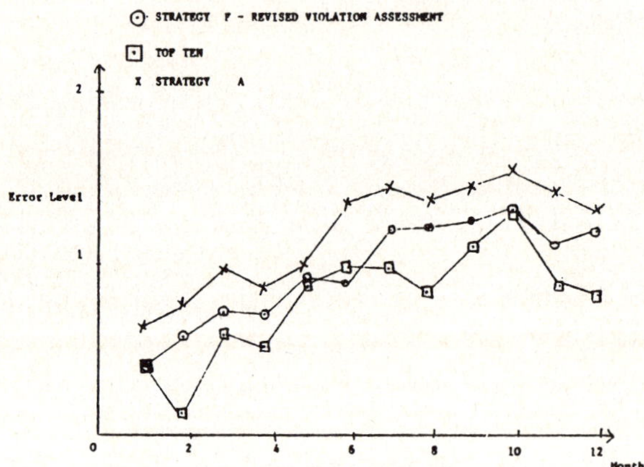

VARIATION OF ERROR LEVEL WITH TIME - COMPARISON BETWEEN TOP TEN AND TWO A.I. STRATEGIES

Fig.8(b)

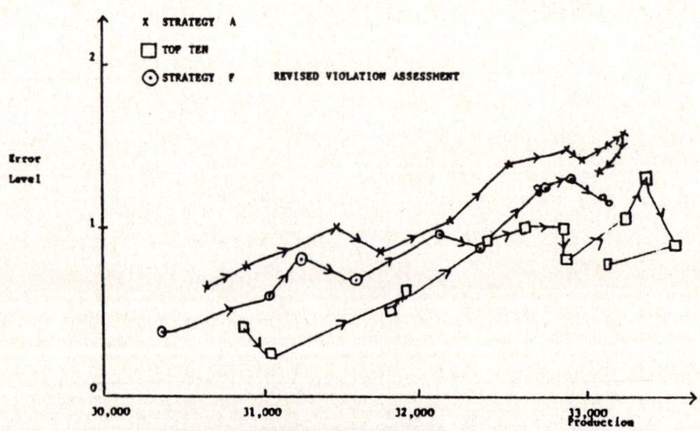

VARIATION OF ERROR LEVEL WITH PRODUCTION COMPARISON BETWEEN TOP TEN AND TWO A.I. STRATEGIES

Fig.8(c)

Artificial Intelligence in Economics and Management
L.F. Pau (Editor)

A.I. CONCEPTS FOR OFFICE AUTOMATION

G. Kappel[1] A M. Tjoa[1] R.R. WAGNER[2]

(1) Institut für Informatik
Universität Wien
A-1010 Wien
Austria

(2) Institut für Informatik
Universität Linz
A-4040 Linz
Austria

For the integration of office information systems with database systems coventional design tools (classical data models) are not adequate. Therefore, semantic data models developed by researchers of the area of artificial intelligence are investigated for automating office procedures. In this paper the RM/T model is extended for this purpose. Furthermore, the concept of a relationship-graph for representing complex objects (unformatted data) is proposed. This relationship-graph is sufficient for the representation of text objects and can be easily mapped to RM/T-relations.

1. INTRODUCTION

Recently in a number of papers the importance of semantic modelling for artificial intelligence research is investigated (/Greenspan 82/, /Kellog 84/,/King 80/,/Mylopoulos 81/,/Rowe 82/,/Tjoa 84/,/Vassilou 84/,/Wiederhold 83/,/Wong 77/). In the field of office automation it becomes apparent that for the integration of office information systems with database systems the classical data models (e.g. relational model, network models) are not adequate design tools. Therefore, it was investigated whether semantic data models are more sufficient for this purpose (/Tsichritzis 83/).

At the universities of Vienna and Linz a pilot project was started in which concepts of A.I. (especially semantic data modelling) are embedded in an office automation environment. Main efforts within this project are: a) Semantic modelling of office information systems
b) Modelling of complex objects.

At first several semantic data models were compared with regard to their relevance for office systems (/Schrefl 84/,/Tjoa 85/).

This comparison leads us to the opinion that the RM/T model is well suited for modelling office information systems. Nevertheless some extensions are necessary for using the RM/T model in the office environment (section 2).

Whereas in section 2 only single objects are considered (i.e. office information system based on the form flow concept) in section 3 the modelling of complex objects is regarded. In this section we restrict our objectives to the notion of text objects. Until now only few approaches are proposed in the literature for modelling complex objects (e.g. /Adiba 84/,/Lamersdorf 84/). In this paper we want to introduce the concept of the relationship-graph which is sufficient to describe the structure of a text. The relationship-graph can easily be transformed to RM/T-relations. (This transformation is not subject of this paper).

2. THE A.I. CONCEPTS OF SEMANTIC MODELLING FOR OFFICE INFORMATION SYSTEMS

The comparison of data models (/Kappel 85b/) results that the RM/T model suits very well the requirments needed for office modelling. However, some extensions are necessary:
- integration of time dimension
- description of events with their pre- and postconditions
- development of algorithms for the automatic generation of queries (at the user interface with A.I. methods).

2.1 APPLICATION OF THE TIME DIMENSION SOLUTION FOR FORM FLOW CONCEPTS

In office information systems the life-cycle of a form represents the dynamic flow of information in an office. The components of a form flow system are:

(1) Work stations as <u>active elements</u>.
Work stations are either <u>office workers</u> or <u>triggered processes</u>. Office workers deal with forms by receiving forms, filing forms, filling in forms, and sending forms to other work stations.

(2) Forms as <u>passive elements</u>.

In this section a method for representing a form flow in the RM/T database is introduced.

<u>Identification of a form (or document) in a form flow system</u>

Each document is represented by an association over the following objects:
- Form type
- <u>i</u>-type objects (which play the key role of the form)
- "Form"-status-object (which is unique for every station at the beginning and at the end of the processing at a work station, i.e. 'entity-time'-concept for a form type).

A form flow can be represented by:
1) The E-relation of the FORM-TYPE
2) The E-relation of the existing form-status-object-types
3) The association between the form-type and the form-status-object-types representing the state of a form type
4) A flow-graph-relation representing the allowed state transitions of form-types. In this relation the work stations where these transitions take place are defined by the attribute STATION.

<u>Example</u>: A form-flow can be represented by RM/T-relations in the following way:

1) E-relation FORM-TYPE

FORM-TYPE¢
:
α_1
α_2
:

FORM-TYPE¢	FORM-NAME
:	:
α_1	FORM 1
α_2	FORM 2
:	:

2) E-relation FORM-STATUS-OBJECT-TYPES

FORM-STATUS-1¢
β_1
β_2
β_3
:

FORM-STATUS-2¢
γ_1
γ_2
γ_3
:

P-relation

FORM-STATUS-1¢	STATE-DESCRIPTION
:	:
β_1	initial fill-in
:	:

3) Association between the form-types and form-status-object-types called STATE-FORM-STATUS

STATE¢	FORM-TYPE¢	FORM-STATUS¢
:	:	:
σ_1	α_1	β_1
σ_2	α_1	β_3
σ_3	α_1	β_3
:	:	:
σ_i	α_2	γ_1
σ_{i+1}	α_2	γ_2
:	:	:

Note: FORM-STATUS-1¢ and FORM-STATUS-2¢ are subtypes of FORM-STATUS¢

4) Flow-graph-relation

STATE-TO¢	STATE-FORM¢	STATION¢
σ_2	σ_1	π_1
σ_3	σ_2	π_2
σ_3	σ_i	π_2
:	:	:

Note: STATE-TO and STATE-FROM are subtyples of STATE¢.

This relation represents the following transitions: In station π_1 the form-type α_1 with status β_1 is handled and after the manipulation the form-type α_1 gets the status β_2 etc. In other words: the precondition of the status β_2 is the status β_1. With this concept complex preconditions of form flows can be expressed (e.g. the precondition to generate a form-type α_1 with status β_3 is the manipulation of form-type α_1 with status β_2 and the manipulation of form-type α_2 with status γ_1).

A form of a certain form-type is now represented by:
- its form type e.g. α_1 of the example above
- its i-type
- its form status object e.g. β_1 of the example above.

2.2 INTERPRETATION AND DERIVATION OF FORMS FROM AN RM/T-DATABASE

2.2.1 The automatic generation of form attribute values from an RM/T-database.

Given an RM/T data model with its relations a user or enterprise-administrator can define (new) form schemas. Therefore, it is necessary to generate with an algorithm the sequence of lossless joins which are necessary to derive data from the database. It is clear that in the form the attributes defined are solely attributes of P-relations and C-relations since surrogate attributes are hidden from the user. The generation of the lossless join sequence can be performed with the well-known tableau-mechanism. But the complexity of this method makes it unsuitable in practice. A more suitable algorithm for generating such a loss join sequence of third normal form relations is introduced in (/Tjoa 79/). This method is based on a corollary of the theorem of Delobel and Caisey /Delobel 73/ as it is introduced in /Schenk 77/.

2.2.2 An instrument for the support of the interpretation of defined form schemas

Although it is possible to create a lossless join sequence with the help of an algorithm for a defined form schema, the user or enterprise-administrator must verify whether the semantic interpretation of the form is correct. The RM/T model with its concepts of catalog relations and graph relations provides a powerful instrument for checking whether the identification objects specified by the user are sufficient to describe the other attributes of the form(schema).

The following steps are necessary for this:
Let $r_1, r_2, \ldots, r_n$ be user key attributes to identify a form, and let $A_1, A_2, \ldots, A_m$ be the attribute names in the form schema.

(1) Determine the relations in which the attribute names $A_1, \ldots, A_m$ appear with the help of the catalog relations:

$R_1 \leftarrow \text{CATA}[\text{ATTNAME}=A_1 \vee \ldots \vee \text{ATTNAME}=A_m]$

$R_2 \leftarrow (\text{CATRA}*R_1)[\text{R¢}]$

$R_3 \leftarrow (\text{CATR}*R_2)[\text{RELNAME}]$

Note: in R_3 we will only find P-relations since the attributes used in the forms are not surrogate attributes.

(2) Determine the object types which are described by the P-relations found in step (1):

$R_4 \leftarrow \text{PG}[\text{SUB}=\text{RELNAME}]R_3$

$R_5 \leftarrow R_4[\text{SUP}]$

(3) Determine the objects types which are derivable from the given key-object types $r_1, \ldots, r_n$:

$R_1' \leftarrow \text{CATA}[\text{ATTNAME}=r_1 \vee \ldots \vee \text{ATTNAME}=r_n]$

$R_2' \leftarrow (\text{CATRA}*R_1')[\text{R¢}]$

$R_3' \leftarrow (\text{CATR}*R_2')$

$R_4' \leftarrow \sigma_{\text{RELTYPE}=\text{E}}R_3'[\text{RELNAME}]$

$R_6 \leftarrow \text{CG}[\text{SUP}\varepsilon\ R_4'] \cup \text{UGI}[\text{SUP}\varepsilon R_4']$

$R_7 \leftarrow \text{CLOSE}'(R_6)[\text{SUP}]$

Note: CLOSE' has the same meaning as the function CLOSE defined in /Codd 79/. It generates the transitive closure of the relation R in the following way: CLOSE'(R) is the minimal superset of R such that if both (SUP:m,SUB:k) and (SUP:k,SUB:n) belongs to R, then (SUP:m,SUB:n) belongs to CLOSE'(R).

(4) Are the determined object types defined by $r_1, \ldots, r_n$?

$R_8 \leftarrow R_5 \setminus (R_7 \cup R_4')$

if $R_8 = \emptyset$ then "the form is identified by $r_1, \ldots, r_n$" else go to step (5).

(5) Determine object types which are interrelated with $r_1, \ldots, r_n$ into association types and which are not derivable from $r_1, \ldots, r_n$.

$R_9 \leftarrow$ CLOSE(AG)[SUB=SUP]R_8

$R_{10} \leftarrow R_9$[SUB]

Note: R_{10} contains the additional object types which determine the form schema.

After the specification of the form schema which includes the definition of the i-type attributes (the i-type attributes define the object types $r_1, \ldots, r_n$) the algorithm either confirms that the specification is correct or delivers additional object types. In the case that there are additional object types the user or enterprise-administrator can:

- define further i-type attributes (and start the algorithm again)
- if nothing is specified the system additionally takes the elements of R_8 (which are all attributes, not specified by the i-type-attributes).

3. COMPLEX OBJECTS

Of course, office systems do not deal only with formatted data, but it is also necessary to introduce text-, voice and image objects. Therefore, we define the notion of complex objects by restricting to text objects. In this paper we introduce a concept which is inspirated by Schank's conceptual dependency theory (/Schank 75/).

3.1 GENERAL STRUCTURE OF TEXT OBJECTS

The basic element of a text object is a word. A set of words is a text-line. A set of text-lines is a paragraph, etc. Of course, the set of words which build a text-line must be an ordered set, since the order of the words of a text-line is important. Therefore, a <u>text object</u> can be defined as follows:

a) The basic element of a text object is a word.
b) Every object of any tpye, which is not a word is a ordered set of objects of the directly subordered type.
c) Every object of a text is identified by an implicte property (object number 0_nr).

The object number is created by the system. Every object number must be unique.

Let C_i be the object number of the chapter i of a text, then by means of the object number C_i it can be determined which text belongs to this chapter. The same is valid for the following object types:

sub-chapter (SC_i)
paragraph (P_i)
sub-paragraph (SP_i)
text-line (TL_i)

Only for the object word this property cannot immediately be applied. The description of the object word will be given elsewhere.

3.2 THE RELATIONSHIP-GRAPH OF A TEXT

Every text can be described by a graph. By means of this graph the relations between the objects can be represented in a clear way. The nodes of the graph represent the objects, whereas the edges are the relations between the objects. For the so called <u>relationship-graph</u> of a test two different kinds of nodes are defined.

a) <u>Object-nodes:</u>
Object-nodes are represented by circles. The content of the object-node represents on the one hand the object type and on the other hand the object itself. The object types are written by capital letters and objects of the same type are distinguished by diffe-

rent indices. By means of this notion we can for example represent the chapter i of a text by the object-node C_i.

Every object is not only identified by an atomar attribute value (i.e. object number), but also by other objects (e.g. a chapter is identified by a chapter-title). If such an identifying object does not exist, an object-node with the content 'ω' is used. Such an object-node is also used for marking the end of a sequence of objects. Every object-node within a text must be unique.

b) Attribute-nodes:

An attribute-node is represented by a rectangle. The content of an attribute-node is an attribute-name. By means of attribute-nodes all explicite properties of a text are represented. These two different nodes are the basic elements of the relationship-graph for describing text objects. In the following four different kinds of edges are defined.

a) id (identified by)-edge:

By an id-edge every object is assigned an attribute or an object for the purpose of identification (see figure 1). It must hold, that identifying objects (titles) are objects of the type text line.

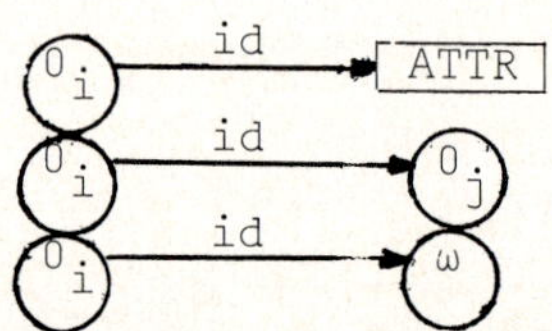

Fig.1: Usage of id-edges

b) dom (domain)-edge:

For every attribute-node there must be a dom-edge which assign the attribute an element x (x∈dom(ATTR)).

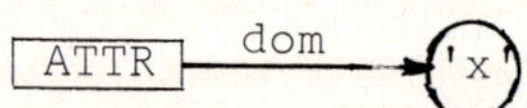

In every atomar domain an element with the value 'ω' (unknown) is contained. The two nodes and two edges of the relationship-graph are sufficient to describe the characteristics of a text.

Example:

For this example we assume that John Cash sends his friend Bud Spencer a message. John characterizes the text by the following input:
TITLE:='Message to Bud';DATE:='1985-03-24';RECEIVER.='Spencer'; KIND_OF_TEXT:='Message'

All other properties are computed by the system:

TEXT_NUMBER:=T*;TEXT_NAME:=ω;TEXT_AUTHOR:=ω;KEYWORD:=ω;TEXT_RECEIVED:=0 (if the text is received by Bud Spencer it will be set to 1);USER_NUMBER:=JC

To identify the message a text-line number TL* is assigned. The relationship-graph for this example is shown in figure 2.

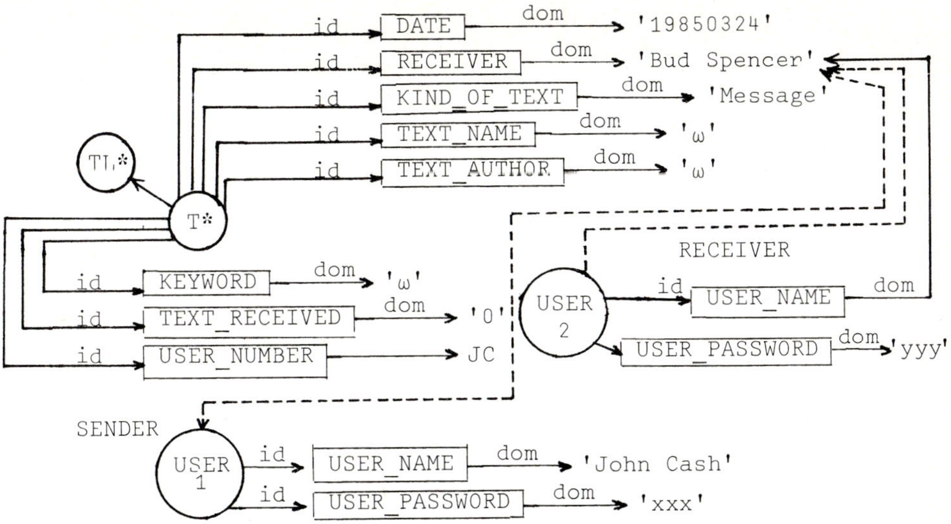

Fig.2: Relationship-graph of the example above

By the broken lines the implicite contained information that John Cash send a message to Bud Spencer is described.

Every text can be seen as a sequence of text objects (i.e.: every text consists of a sequence of chapters, a sequence of sub-chapters, a sequence of paragraphs, etc.). In the relationship-graph a sequence of objects if described by so called predecessor (pd)-edges.

c) pd-edges:
If an object 0_i is a predecessor of an object 0_j a pd-edges is used to describe such an situation.

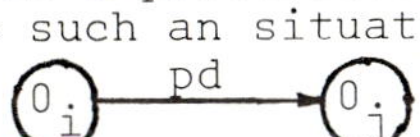

If the object 0_i='ω' then the object 0_j is the last element of a sequence of objects:

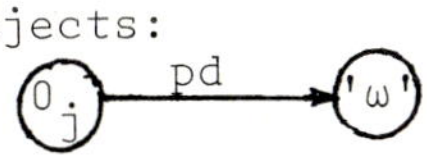

For the objects defined in section 3.2 a text consist of the following sequences of objects:

- SEQUENCE_OF_CHAPTERS: $C_1 \xrightarrow{pd} C_2 \xrightarrow{pd} \ldots \xrightarrow{pd} C_n \xrightarrow{pd} \omega$
- SEQUENCE_OF_SUBCHAPTERS: $SC_1 \xrightarrow{pd} SC_2 \xrightarrow{pd} \ldots \xrightarrow{pd} SC_n \xrightarrow{pd} \omega$
- SEQUENCE_OF_PARAGRAPHS: $P_1 \xrightarrow{pd} P_2 \xrightarrow{pd} \ldots \xrightarrow{pd} P_n \xrightarrow{pd} \omega$
- SEQUENCE_OF_SUBPARAGRAPHS: $SP_1 \xrightarrow{pd} SP_2 \xrightarrow{pd} \ldots \xrightarrow{pd} SP_n \xrightarrow{pd} \omega$
- SEQUENCE_OF_TEXT-LINES: $TL_1 \xrightarrow{pd} TL_2 \xrightarrow{pd} \ldots \xrightarrow{pd} TL_n \xrightarrow{pd} \omega$

For the sequences of objects the following rules are defined:
SR1: An element 'ω' specifies the end of a sequence of objects.
SR2: In the surrogate of an object the 'ω' element must not exist.
SR3: If an object never is a successor then it is the first object of a sequence of objects.
SR4: An object must not be a predecessor of itself.

d) First and last edges:

Until now the structural elements of a text are described isolated. But, between the sequences of objects hierarchical relationships consist (e.g. every chapter consists of a certain number of sub-chapters and therefore to every chapter of a text a section of the sub-chapter sequence of the text can be assigned). This hierarchical relations are represented in the relationship-graph by first and last edges:

$$O_i \xrightarrow{\text{first}} \bar{O}_j \qquad O_k \xrightarrow{\text{first}} \bar{O}_l$$

The cross-lines of O_j and O_l ($\bar{O}_j$,$\bar{O}_l$) means that first and last edges can only connect objects of higher level to objects of lower level. For the first and last edges the following rules are defined:

FL1: Every object of the relationship-graph is connected with other objects by at least one first and one last edge.

FL2: From $O_i \xrightarrow{\text{first}} \bar{O}_j$ and $O_i \xrightarrow{\text{last}} \bar{O}_j$ it follows that $\bar{O}_j$ is the only component object of O_i.

The relationship-graph consisting of the two nodes and four edges is sufficient to describe the structure of a text.

Example:

In the following we want to describe the example above by using the additional concept of first and last edges.

The content of the message should be:

Dear Bud,
I want to remember you that we will meet us tomorrow.
John

The relationship-graph of this text is shown in figure 3.

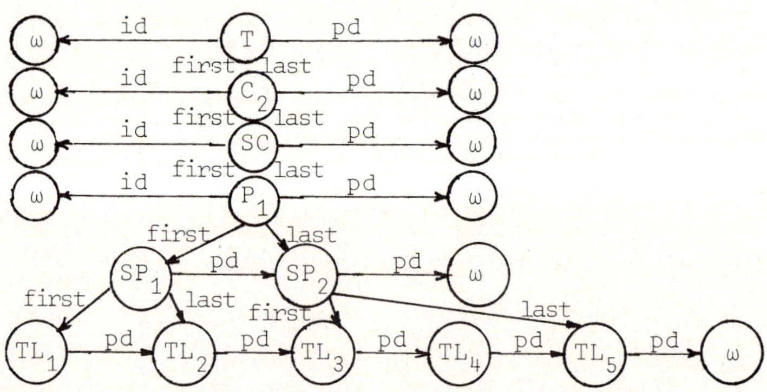

Fig.3: Relationship-graph of the example above.

Acknowledgement:

The authors are very indebted to P. Moser for the many discussions concerning the modelling of complex objects by using the concept of the relationship-graph. Thanks also to M. Hofer-Mozelt for typing this paper.

REFERENCES

[1] Adiba, M., Experiments of office automation and CAD-databases. Proc.IBM Europe Institute, Davos, (1984).

[2] Codd, E.F., A relational model for large shared data banks, CACM, Vol.13(6), (1970).

[3] Codd, E.F., Extending the database relational model to capture more meaning, ACM TODS, 4,4, (1979).

[4] Delobel, C., R.G. Casey, Decomposition of a database and the theory of boolean switching functions, IBM J. Research and Development 17, (1973).

[5] Greenspan, S., Mylopoulos, J., Computing more world knowledge in the requirements specification, Proc.Int.Conf.Software Engineering Tokyo, Japan, (1982).

[6] Kappel, G., Tjoa, A M., Wagner, R.R., Form flow systems based on NF2-relations, GI-Fachtagung, DBS für Büro, Technik, Wissenschaft Springer Verlag, Berlin-Heidelberg-New York, (eds. Blaser, Pistor) (1985a)

[7] Kappel, G., Tjoa A M., Wagner, R.R., Comparison of different extended relational models of form flow systems, Int.Conf.Applied Informatics, Grindelwald, (1985b).

[8] Kellog, G., Knowledge Management: A practical amalgam, Proc.AAAI, AAAI-82, (1982).

[9] King, J., Modelling concepts for reasoning about access to knowledge, ACM SIGPLAN notices, Vol.16(1), (1981).

[10] Lamersdorf, W., Müller, G., Schmidt, J.W., Language support for office modelling, Proc. 10th VLDB 1984, Singapore, (1984).

[11] Mylopoulos, J., An overview of knowledge representation, ACM SIGPLAN notices, Vol.16(1), 1981.

[12] Rowe, N., Three papers on rule-based estimation of statistics on databases, Computer Science Rep.Stanford Univ., 82-148, (1982).

[13] Schank, R., Conceptual Information Processing, North-Holland, (1975).

[14] Schenk, K.L., Pinkert, J.R., An algorithm for servicing multi-relational queries, Proc. ACM SIGMOD, (1977).

[15] Schrefl, M., Tjoa, A M., Wagner, R.R., Comparison Criteria for semantic data models, Proc. IEEE COMPDEC Conf., Los Angeles, (1984).

[16] Tjoa, A M., Wagner, R.R., Some more dependencies on the relational model and their relevance to queries on relational data bases, Euro IFIP 79, London, (1979).

[17] Tjoa, A M., Wagner, R.R., Comparison of dynamic aspects in semantic data modelling, Proc. Applied Informatics, Grindelwald,(1985).

[18] Tsichritzis, D., OFS An integrated form management system, Proc. Eight VLDB, (1982).

[19] Vassilou, Y., The combined role of A.I. and database management in information systems. IBM Europe Institut, Davos, (1984).

[20] Wiederhold, G., Milton, J., Sagalowicz, D., The knowledge-based management systems project, Stanford Univ., June (1983).

[21] Wong, H.K.T., Mylopoulos, J., Two view of data semantics: A survey of data models in artificial intelligence, INFOR 15(3), (1977).

Artificial Intelligence in Economics and Management
L.F. Pau (Editor)

Knowledge based retrieval in an office

H.-J. Appelrath, M. Ester, A. Ultsch
Swiss Federal Institute of Technology (ETH) Zürich
Department of Computer Science
ETH-Zentrum
CH-8092 Zürich

Abstract
In this paper we discuss a novel approach for the design of a personal information retrieval system. Since 1984 the project KOFIS (Knowledge based Office Information System) is conducted in our research group at the ETH Zürich. KOFIS is a knowledge based personal information retrieval (IR) system running on a personal workstation. The system can be viewed as an expert system for storing and retrieving documents and domain dependent knowledge in an office environment.

1. Characteristics of KOFIS

KOFIS is a single-user system for storing and retrieving full text documents as well as references to them. It offers the same capabilities as typical IR systems but differs from them in the following ways:

In conventional IR systems the type and number of relations among terms in the information structures used for retrieval, such as 'broader term' 'narrower term' or 'synonymous' for example, are limited and fixed in the number of arguments.
In KOFIS it is possible to define relations of arbitrary denotation and arity.

Classical thesaurus relations typically represent knowledge about the way words are used. But in addition general relations can be used to express knowledge about the area of work the user is in. When reading any document your knowledge increases: you learn some new facts.
In KOFIS we want to offer the user the chance to enter this information in such a form that it can subsequently be manipulated by the system. This means the system is able to answer questions about stored facts and use a deduction mechanism to come up with logical conclusions. For these purposes we employed the decarative language PROLOG.

Standard multiuser IR systems usually have built-in document retrieval algorithms.
In a personal system like KOFIS however, it is desirable to be able to formulate the retrieval strategies as an input to the system in order to tailor the system to one's information needs ([SEYD], [SHOV]).
In KOFIS PROLOG-rules are operating on facts (stored in a PROLOG database), yielding new facts. This makes it possible to formulate individual retrieval strategies. Rules are also used to express the user's domain specific knowledge and to enforce consistency constraints on the system.

The aim of the project is to implement a prototype of a small and efficient tool for annotating and searching documents and knowledge in a "scientific office".

2. The archtitecture of the KOFIS prototype

KOFIS is implemented in MODULA-2 ([WIR2]) and runs on the personal workstation Lilith ([WIR1]), developed at the ETH Zürich, with a bitmap display and a pointing device (mouse).

The following figure shows the software architecture of KOFIS.

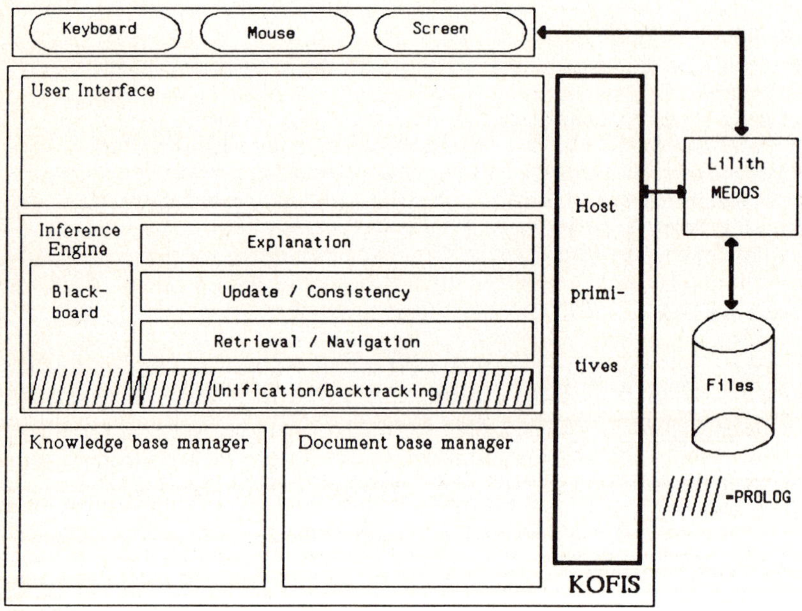

First we have designed and implemented an interface to make KOFIS portable to other hosts (f.e. UNIX-based systems at our Institute).
We locate this interface (Host primitives) between KOFIS and the host dependent parts such as storage devices, keyboard, mouse and screen. The component Host primitives contains elementary procedures for I/O and commandline processing, functions and conversions for string manipulation, procedures for window, buttons and scrollbar handling and finally the definition of implementation dependent constants and types.

In addition tothe host primitives there are four main components in KOFIS: User interface, Inference engine, Knowledge base manager and Document base manager. In the following we briefly describe the first three of these components.

User interface

which consists of a working environment handler, a window handler and modules for parsing input and editing texts.

Working environments are user-defined pre-compiled collections of windows representing objects of the types terms, facts and documents and so on and menus listing operations on these objects. Examples of operations provided by the corresponding windows are: insert or delete a document, a term, a fact or a rule, retrieve documents by and-or-expressions of facts (traditional document retrieval), retrieve facts by exact or partial match queries of the form '<factname> (<term$_1$>, ...,<term$_n$>)' (knowledge retrieval). Working environments allow the free exchange of data among windows.

Users are able to define their own working environments by defining the geometry, type, size and menu of the constituting windows in order to reflect his office work-style.

The definition is done in a standard textfile and therefore this user profile can be edited with a normal text editor, which offers a flexible way to customize your own working environments when using KOFIS. There are four different types of windows (terminal, list, structure and editor) with corresponding features. Attributes like name, resizable or non- resizable, scroll or noscroll, position, width and heigth, positions of tabulators, menu entries can be given by the user.

Inference engine

with modules

for the explanation of system answers (it is not implemented in the prototype),

to update the document and knowledge base including consistency checking (see chapter 4),

for retrieval of documents and knowledge

which are all based on

a common unification and backtracking mechanism provided by a Prolog interpreter and

a blackboard for temporal storage and to manage relevant terms, facts und rules.

Knowledge base manager

which contains modules for administration of terms, rules (both are internally stored) and facts which are stored externally in the symmetric multi-key access system GridFile ([NIEV]).

3. Necessary extensions to PROLOG

The KOFIS system relies on the language PROLOG: terms, facts, rules and some standard operations on these objects are translated into PROLOG. In its pure form however, a PROLOG system only incorporates a simple horn clause proof procedure with unification and backtracking.

Standard PROLOG does not provide mechanisms to supervise modifications to its database and uses as control strategies only backward chaining and backtracking ([APPE]). This strategy was not enough for the efficient implementation of retrieval mechanisms. The PROLOG interpreter of C. Muller ([MULL]), that we used has an interface to a procedural programming language (MODULA-2). We extended it in the following ways:

- type checking of arguments, control of the arity of defined predicates;

- recognition of typo-errors and flection form differences in arguments;

- implementation of a flexible meta-system to speed up the standard PROLOG control strategy; the basic concepts - but in the context of DB - are discussed in [APBE];

- incorporation of a blackboard to store actual knowledge and to control the activation of relevant knowledge;

- an extension to PROLOG which offers different integrity concepts like the proof of complex user defined integrity constraints concerning more than one predicate at a time ([APES]);

- action and transaction concepts for the time dependent test and flexible reaction in case of integrity violations ([APES]);

- an interface to the GridFile for external storage and retrieval of facts; concepts and realization of a cache to link the PROLOG database and an external access system are presented in ([APPE]).

4. Some remarks to modelling and consistency checking

We used an extension of the well known database description formalism called semantic data model SDM ([HAMC]) to describe all objects (terms, facts, rules and documents) and operations. In order to use this formalism to model knowledge representation, we had to extend both the SDM language and the known mechanisms for handling violations of integrity constraints.

The important step to model the KOFIS world in the proper formalism of an extended SDM is done in [JASP].
In DB applications the types of data are known in advance, however, they change dynamically in the environment of AI applications ([MYLO]).

SDM is a data model intended for DB and KOFIS shares the above features with other expert systems: the relevant types of facts and documents cannot be foreseen and the user should not be restricted to a fixed set of them.

Therefore we introduced an additional kind of abstraction to SDM: the metaclass construct to represent metaknowledge (metaknowledge is knowledge about knowledge representation not about the real world). It connects the class of types with the class of instances (of types).

A type or class in SDM can be described by the following parameters:

name of class,
number of attributes,
names of attributes,
types of attributes,
descriptions of attributes (MANDATORY, MULTIVALUED, . .).

Integrity constraints are classified in two ways to support a better understanding and adequate checking of integrity violations. With these extensions we were able to use DB technology for the design of a knowledge based office information system.

First we classify the integrity constraints according to their SDM formulation.

SDM inherent constraints

A conceptual schema, written in SDM, contains many integrity constraints implied by the relations between the objects. These constraints must be fulfilled by every schema written in SDM.

Schema inherent constraints

Some application dependent constraints for the data can be stated when knowing the schema and thus be built into the system by the programmer. These constraints, like those of the SDM inherent type, are not stated as explicit rules in the system and cannot be changed by the user.

User defined constraints

Another type of application dependent constraints cannot be built into a system but can be added by the user: constraints which do not refer to the schema but to its extensions.

Secondly the integrity constraints are classified according to the method of handling their violation. Violations of all kinds of integrity constraints can be treated in different ways. We propose the following classification which gives the user the chance to specify a more or less restrictive treatment of integrity violations.

Rejection

The system rejects the user update.

Acceptance with information

The system accepts the user update but informs him about bad consequences.

Acceptance with question for additional user updates

The system accepts the user update but asks for additional user updates to get or keep as much information as possible.

Acceptance with automatic system updates

The system makes the user update, automatically initiates consequent system updates to reach a consistent state and informs the user about these updates.

Because KOFIS is a single user system, every user can get his own integrity solution and determine which updates should be tested, which conditions must be fullfilled before the desired update is done and which reactions should be selected. The formulation of triggers to express the integrity constraints and the PROLOG realization of these concepts is described in [APES].

5. Conclusions

This paper characterizes a new approach to the design of personal information retrieval systems. We employed artificial intelligence technologies used for the construction of expert systems and theorem provers in order to implement a personal expert system for storing and retrieving documents and domain dependent knowledge.

The design and implementation of KOFIS is based on two solid concepts.
First the use of a formal model (SDM) stemming from database technology in order to formulate consistency constraints and their enforcement.
Second the usage of the declarative programming language PROLOG for a consistent implementation of the deduction mechanisms. These mechanisms are used for retrieval, inference of conclusions and enforcement of the consistency.

We have extended SDM to be able to describe a knowledge representation consistently and to be able to fomulate different classes of integrity constraints. The described extensions to PROLOG made it possible to implement an information retrieval system with a deductive language. This allows to incorporate customizable retrieval strategies in order to reflect one's information needs and makes it possible to implement the consistency mechanisms in a uniform way.

The KOFIS user-interface, using user-definable working environments, is highly adaptable and can reflect individual work-styles.

6. Literature

[APPE] Appelrath, H.-J.: "Von Datenbanken zu Expertensystemen", Informatik-Fachberichte Nr. 102, Springer-Verlag, Heidelberg, 1985.

[APBE] Appelrath, H.-J.; Bense, H.: "Zwei Schritte zur Verbesserung von PROLOG-Programmiersystemen: DB-Unterstützung und Meta-Interpreter", in: "DB-Systeme für Büro, Technik und Wissenschaft" (A. Blaser, P. Pistor. ed.), Informatik- Fachberichte, Nr. 94, Springer-Verlag, Heidelberg, 1985, pp. 160 - 176.

[APES] Appelrath, H.-J.; Ester, M.: "Integrity in a knowledge based office information system: modeling with extended SDM and implementation with Prolog", in: "Büro-Automation 85" (H. Wedekind, ed.), Teubner-Verlag, Stuutgart, 1985.

[HAMC] Hammer, M.; McLeod, D.: "Database Description with SDM: A Semantic Database Model", ACM TODS, Vol. 6, No.3, 1981, pp. 351 - 386.

[JASP] Jasper, H. "Die Modellierung eines wissensbasierten Büro-Informationssystems", Master thesis, ETH Zürich/ University of Dortmund, 1985.

[MULL] Muller, C.: "Modula-Prolog", Bericht Nr. 63, Institut für Informatik, ETH Zürich, 1985.

[MYLO] Mylopoulos, J.: "An Overview of Knowledge Representation", Proceedings of the Workshop on Data Abstraction, Databases and Conceptual Modelling, Pingree Park, 1980, SIGMOD record, Vol. 11, No. 2, pp. 5 - 12.

[NIEV] Nievergelt, J; Hinterberger, H.; Sevcik, K.C.: "The GridFile: An Adaptable, Symmetric Multikey File Structure", ACM TODS, Vol. 9, No. 1, 1984, pp. 38 - 71.

[SEYD] Seydel, D.: "Structure, Functions and Operations of an Integrated Information and Documentation System on Minicomputer", in: Keren, C., Perlmutter, L. (ed.) "The Application of Mini- and Microcomputers in Information, Documentation and Libraries", 1983.

[SHOV] Shoval, P.: "Knowledge representation in consultation systems for users of retrieval systems",in: Keren, C., Perlmutter, L. (ed.) "The Application of Mini- and Microcomputers in Information, Documentation and Libraries", 1983.

[WIR1] Wirth, N.: "Lilith: A Personal Computer for the Software Engineer", Proceedings of the 5th International Conference on Software Engineering, San Diego, 1981.

[WIR2] Wirth, N.: "Programming in Modula-2", Springer-Verlag, Heidelberg, 1982.

Artificial Intelligence in Economics and Management
L.F. Pau (Editor)

INTEGRATED PROBLEM SOLVING IN MANUFACTURING

Suranjan De

Department of Management Sciences
The University of Iowa
Iowa City, Iowa 52242
U.S.A.

A central tenet of this paper is that in addressing complex manufacturing problems, the major focus should be on key decisions and tasks, with the specific aim of improving the effectiveness of the manager's problem solving process. That entails modeling the decision-making process and integrating that with the rest of the problem solving process. A decision support system (DSS) framework that attempts to address these concerns in a unified manner is proposed. Possible applications are discussed.

1. INTRODUCTION

In manufacturing, planning and control decisions are required in order to achieve efficient, productive utilization of resources. The complexity of the underlying decision-making process in manufacturing results from the fact that the decisions involve comparisons of a large number of alternatives with complex interactions among system components. The exclusive use of conventional managerial wisdom, based largely on experience and intuition, may not be adequate for effective decision-making. On the other hand, in most of the operations research methodology, efforts have been focused on searching, finding and working with formal structures and models while the decision context in which they have been embedded have been taken for granted. The primary focus should be on key decisions and tasks, with the specific aim of improving the effectiveness of the manager's problem solving process.

Instead of viewing decision-making as a process of information grinding, one may view it as a process of tentative, arduous deliberation. In this view, the making of decisions is treated as complex tasks themselves. In a complex problem environment such as manufacturing, it is simply not possible to decide on circumstances, decide on goals, decide on means and then pick the appropriate solution--one simply does not have the information or the computing competence to do so. Rather, one ought to keep breaking large problems into smaller ones until one reaches decisions which can be handled correctly fairly easily. The smaller decisions are then combined into bigger ones. In doing so, however, one may have to take back or revise one decision because of information discovered, or conclusions drawn in making another decision. On the other hand, once the combined decisions grow large enough, it may be necessary to reassess earlier decisions and the processes by which they were arrived at, to make sure nothing is forgotten and errors have not been made.

The hierarchical planning notion of dividing large, complex problems in manufacturing into smaller, more manageable ones has been exploited before [1, 2]. This approach has been pursued because it could be extremely difficult, if not impossible, to deal with all the decisions that need to be made in such cases via a monolithic system. Even if that were possible, such an approach would probably be unresponsive to the needs of managers at each level of the organization because it would prevent interactions between the managers and the system. On the other hand, strategic, tactical and operational decisions in manufacturing cannot be made in isolation because they interact strongly with one another. Decisions made at the higher levels provide constraints for lower level decision-making; in turn, detailed decisions provide the necessary feedback to evaluate the quality of aggregate decision-making. Besides, aggregate decisions are typically made early on whereas detailed decisions are postponed as long as possible. This is important in view of the fact that much of the information needed at the detailed level is uncertain at the time aggregate decisions are made. Hence, in a monolithic system detailed decisions would be made earlier than necessary. It is, therefore, important to adopt an integrated view of the multilevel planning hierarchy.

2. DSS IN MANUFACTURING PLANNING AND CONTROL

Significant progress has been made in the last ten years in developing operations research techniques that address many of the issues in hierarchical planning. For a review of some of these efforts, see [2, 3, 4, 5]. In spite of the tremendous progress made as far as the modeling aspects are concerned, there are some serious drawbacks in the systems based on these methodology, at least from a decision-maker's point of view. It seems that the chief benefit of models should be its ability to deepen the decision-makers' insights into their system; the overriding importance given to developing effective algorithms has detracted from the ability of such systems to act as an effective decision-making aid.

Effectiveness of the decision-making process can be enhanced if the system provides DSS capabilities; in other words, the system should not only solve a problem but solve it in terms specific to the user. This implies that the system examine a problem in the particular context of the user; that entails knowing or inferring the user's goals and needs, what specific ramifications each alternative may have for the user, how a particular decision may affect the user's employees, owners, competitors, customers and suppliers and what priorities the user places on these possible effects. The importance of these considerations can hardly be overstated. Users, when asking questions of the system, expect their intentions to be recognized and responded to. They expect assistance from the system in order to interpret their answers, correct their misconceptions and choose an alternative means to fulfilling their goals when a dead end is reached. Besides, users do more than ask questions; they give commands, make comments, seek clarifications and provide descriptions of their desires. Through a process of dialogue and iterative problem solving, the man-machine system may be better able to characterize the problem at the detailed level. Language can, therefore, play a vital role in enhancing the hierarchical planning process. What we need, then, is a helpful, intelligent system that must share with the user knowledge of the domain of discourse, knowledge of some of the user's intentions and goals as well as knowledge of what the user thinks the system can do.

It is my contention that building an effective DSS in manufacturing (or other problem domains) requires the ability to model decision-making behavior over and above traditional problem solving concerns: large databases, efficient algorithms, etc. This means that one ought to address the issue of modeling the decision-making process and integrating that with the rest of the problem solving process. The following section presents a broad framework that attempts to address these concerns in a unified manner. Appropriate references are cited later for readers interested in the details of various aspects of the framework.

3. CONCEPTUAL FRAMEWORK FOR INTEGRATED PROBLEM SOLVING

The major features of this framework can be stated as follows. First, the focus is on developing techniques for understanding and solving in a uniform manner manufacturing problems that cut across various disciplines: long range planning, M.R.P., operations control, etc. Since our focus is on problems that could either be well-structured (e.g., job-shop scheduling) or ill-structured (e.g. new product management), the methodology developed for plan generation is appropriate not only for creating detailed plans or solutions but also for understanding plans, i.e., ascertaining goals and recognizing any acts that may have to be performed in attempting to realize that goal. Plan understanding involves very broad inferential knowledge of a large number of actions and goals, without as much depth of calculation on each single goal pursuit; it is particularly appropriate for ill-defined and difficult problems. Plan creation, on the other hand, means that, given a goal, one must link methods together in an admissible or optimal way to realize that goal. Plan creation is problem solving, and as usually studied, the problem domain is well-structured and limited to a small set of goals. Third, the issue of incorporating a natural language interface to the planning component of the system is addressed. Finally, it must be noted that in order for the system to be effective as a decision-making aid, merely being able to translate utterances of the managerial decision-maker into some internal form that the system can interpret and solve planning problems is not enough. The system's ability to understand (or infer) the user's plans and the user's goals from the natural language utterances and detect inconsistencies or incomplete information, if necessary, is an intrinsic part of the natural language understanding task. Note that inferring the user's intentions itself requires some planning capability beyond that of plan creation and is closely interwined with language understanding. This integrated view of problem solving in manufacturing is referred to here as integrated understanding. For a more detailed exposition of the above-mentioned linguistic concerns, see [6].

This approach would be an improvement over traditional operations research approaches in several ways. First, in order to solve manufacturing problems effectively, one must allow the formal description of distinct problems belonging to a rather large area. In the framework proposed here, the user can state the problem in a natural language or some subset thereof. This implies that given the statement of the user, the system ought to be able to infer the assumptions, the constraints and the goals (or objective functions) that characterize the manufacturing problem to be solved as well as fetch the input (numerical) data from either the database or the user. Second, in order to avoid the continual interpretation of the problem statement in the course of problem solving, it is important to have an internal representation scheme whereby the problem (including its assumptions, constraints and objective functions) can be represented. Typical internal representation schemes include AND/OR graphs, algebraic inequalities, etc. What is required is a mechanism whereby the system, in reading the statement of a problem, will translate as much information as possible into an internal form. As discussed in the following section, the internal representation scheme proposed here is much richer than the traditional knowledge representation schemes used in many manufacturing problems (e.g., in traditional mathematical programming models, knowledge about the problem domains is typically represented by some rather straight-forward constraints stated as algebraic inequalities). Finally, the problem solving strategies themselves will benefit immensely from effective knowledge representation schemes. In particular, the use of domain-specific information to enhance the problem solving process is considered.

The overall strategy for integrated understanding can be stated briefly as follows. The user poses a query in a natural language such as English. This natural language input has to be translated into an input in a target language which the system can process. In the course of processing the input sentences, the system may have to carry out computations, perform deductions, determine plans and eventually generate a response for the decision-maker. From the point of view of the user, though, the system is merely trying to understand what the user is interested in and tries to generate appropriate responses. Therefore, although the primary interest here lies in solving problems in manufacturing, the focus of an integrated understanding system lies in trying explicitly natural language processing to the plan generation process.

This model of integrated understanding makes the following assumptions. First, the users of the system are rational agents who are capable of forming and executing plans to achieve them. Both the user and the system are assumed to be goal-directed reasoning systems that can perform actions including linguistic communication and mental actions such as inference. Second, linguistic concerns arise in an attempt to achieve some goal (e.g., obtain information, request to perform some task). Third, the system is capable of inferring the user's plans (intended plan recognition) by observing him/her perform some action. The system attempts to understand the user's utterances by recognizing the goals that motivated the user. Finally, the system is capable of detecting obstacles or conflicts in the user's plans. Plan inferencing concerns the attempted reconstruction of the user's plans based on actions that the user was observed performing. This process depends both on the system's knowledge of how plans are constructed and on his original beliefs about what goals the other agent (the user) is likely to have.

The proposed integrated understanding system functions as follows. The system has three functional components, each of which performs some form of goal-directed reasoning: linguistic level reasoner, communicative level reasoner, and task level reasoner. First, the system receives as input an utterance of the user (or the managerial decision-maker) through the natural language interface which it translates into an internal form which the system can process. This process of translation of the input from a source language into a target language based on the lexical, syntactic and semantic knowledge of the language is carried out by the linguistic level reasoner. This aspect of natural language was developed earlier and is discussed in detail in [7, 8].

The utterance in an internal form as obtained above is then examined by the system. Based on the mood of the sentence, the effect of the communicative act is attributed by the system to be a goal of the user. The next task is to infer, if possible, using intended plan recognition and shared beliefs, how the actions of the user fit into a plan achieving a goal the user is expected to have. If a plan cannot be uniquely specified, a system goal to discover the user's goal is created. Then more detailed system goals need to be created to achieve the intended goals of the user. Given these detailed system goals, the system can use its own beliefs about the problem domain to determine conflicts or obstacles at which the user's plans might fail, or that the user might need help. Then the system could adopt the negation of these goals as goals for the system. The system could now construct a plan that achieves the system's goals, especially goals to overcome the user's obstacles. Depending on this goal, this plan may include communication actions, such as response to the user's query or utterance, or perhaps questions to clarify the user's goals. Now the resulting sequence of the actions could be executed. A schematic diagram of the integrated understanding system just described is given in Figure 1.

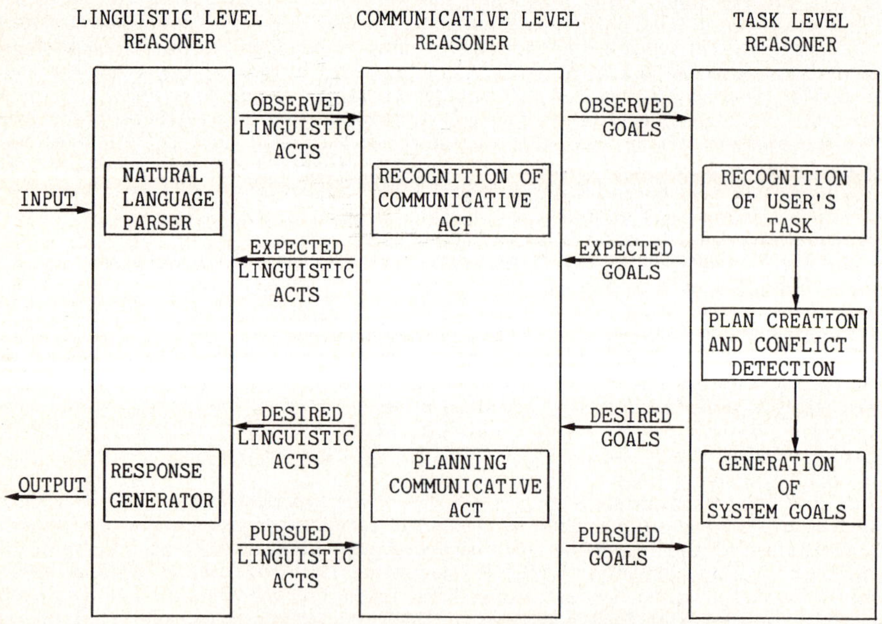

Figure 1. Integrated Understanding System

The issues that arise in the linguistic level reasoner are traditional natural language processing issues and can be addressed using techniques outlined in detail in [7, 8]. Beyond that, there are two levels of analysis that must be considered. The first is the communication level, which includes such goals as introducing a topic, clarifying or elaborating on a previous request, modifying the current topic, etc. The topics generally concern some task in the manufacturing domain that the user needs assistance in performing. Some of the interesting aspects of the communicative level reasoner from a language point of view include the generation of responses that provide more information than required but not something that is not useful to the user, the generation of responses to sentence fragments and, of course, the analysis of indirect speech acts. These aspects are discussed in detail in [6].

The next level of analysis is the task level where the goals pertain to specific manufacturing problems that must be solved. Those include goals such determining the bill of materials or available machine capacity, the number, size and locations of facilities, scheduling of activities at an aggregate or detailed level, etc. What is interesting about the basis of this framework is that the problems at both the levels (communicative & task) are reducible to that of plan inferencing and plan creation.

4. POSSIBLE APPLICATIONS

The broad framework outlined earlier can be used to support the overall production management decisions by identifying ways in which the decision process can be partitioned, by selecting adequate models to deal with individual decisions at each hierarchical level, by designing linking mechanisms for the page for Figure 1 transferring of higher level results to the lower hierarchical levels which include means to disaggregate information, and to provide interface mechanisms with the user whereby the results can be evaluated and plans revised, if necessary.

At the strategic level, the most important decisions have to do with the design of production facilities, involving major capital investment decisions for the development of new capacity and the expansion of new capacity. The problem essentially is to determine the number, sizes and locations of facilities that a firm needs in order to serve its markets. Decision support systems can be very useful in providing information in an aggregated form to allow for all the dimensions of the problem and to prevent top level managers from being distracted by unnecessary operational details.

At the tactical level, a major problem is that of aggregate production planning. Once the physical facilities have been decided upon, the basic problem to be resolved is the effective allocation of resources to satisfy demand and technological requirements, taking into account the costs and revenues associated with the production and distribution process. Again the process of flexible interaction that the DSS framework discussed here provides will go a long way to enhance the decision-making process.

Finally, after making an aggregated allocation of capacity among product families, it is necessary to deal with the day-to-day operational and scheduling decisions which require the complete disaggregation of the information generated at higher levels into details consistent with managerial procedures followed in daily activities.

It is my contention that the framework proposed here can be used not only to provide sophisticated problem solving strategies but sophisticated knowledge representation schemes as well that allow the system to explain the derivation of results to the user, to effectively respond to 'what-if' type questions so crucial to managers. The natural language interface, apart from allowing the user to ask a wide variety of queries, provides the user with a rich specification language for the description of the manufacturing environment. Finally, the problem solving process is oriented towards answering the user's queries or responding to other needs of the user.

References

[1] Hax, Arnoldo C. and Dan Candea, Production and Inventory Management, Prentice-Hall, Inc., Englewood Cliffs, New Jersey, 1984.

[2] Bitran, Gabriel R. and Arnoldo C. Has, "On the Design of Hierarchical Production Planning Systems," Decision Sciences, Vol. 8, No. 1, January 1977, pp. 28-54.

[3] Bitran, Gabriel R., Elizabeth A. Haas and Arnoldo C. Hax, Hierarchical Production Planning: A Single Stage System," Operations Research, Vol. 29, No. 4, July-August 1981, pp. 717-743.

[4] Bitran, Gabriel R., Elizabeth A. Haas and Arnoldo C. Hax, Hierarchical Production Planning: A Two-Stage System," Operations Research, Vol. 30, No. 2, March-April 1982, pp. 232-251.

[5] Dempster, M. A. H., M. L. Fisher, L. Jansen, B. J. Lagewig, J. K. Lenstra and A. H. G. Rinnooy Kan, "Analytical Evaluation of Hierarchical Planning Systems," Operations Research, Vol. 29, No. 4, July-August 1981, pp. 707-716.

[6] De, Suranjan and Andrew B. Whinston, "Some Language Issues in Manufacturing Decision Support Systems," to be published in Proceedings of the 16th Annual Pittsburgh Conference on Modeling and Simulation, April 25 - April 26, 1985.

[7] De, Suranjan, Shuh-Shen Pan and Andrew B. Whinston, "Natural Language Query Processing in a Temporal Database," forthcoming in Data and Knowledge Engineering.

[8] De, Suranjan, Shuh-Shen Pan and Andrew B. Whinston, "Temporal Semantics and Natural Language Processing in a Decision Support System," working paper, Purdue University, May 1984.

Artificial Intelligence in Economics and Management
L.F. Pau (Editor)

INTELLIGENT KNOWLEDGE-BASED SYSTEMS: A TOOL FOR MANUFACTURING PLANNING & SCHEDULING

Philippe Rixhon

Philippe Rixhon Ltd.
Friedensgasse 35
CH-4056 Basel

The careful integration of intelligent knowledge-based systems (IKBS) can help to solve the problem of growing planning and scheduling complexity. Based on the project we are conducting for a medium-sized high-tech manufacturing company, this article presents the first lessons we learned and the first results we got investigating practical applications of knowledge engineering. The following issues are considered: when did we find the knowledge engineering approach justified to solve planning and scheduling problems; what did we do to support a typical manufacturing decision like: "Do I make or do I buy a part"; how do we organize our projects and which tools are we using.

MANUFACTURING MANAGEMENT

1. Complexity

Manufacturing is very difficult to manage and for the manufacturing industry that is the place where money is won or lost. Once a company strategy is defined, two different processes are started: the product-directed process and the market-directed process. Both are crossing on the very action of manufacturing and predefine it.

Manufacturing planning is on the product side. Answering the question "how", the manager defines the quality parameters. He plans the use of the different resources of the company: manpower, machines, materials, utilities and facilities. Becoming more and more expensive all those resources require an accurate management to avoid any costly waste. Manufacturing scheduling is on the market side. Answering the questions "what" and "when", the manager defines quantity parameters like batch sizes or stock levels. The market and its demand patterns are evolving nowadays so rapidly that the complexity of this management is also growing at a tremendous pace.

2. Planning

Following robotics, planning is the domain of manufacturing which has been most explored by AI researchers. Very interesting studies are already made but remain far from a daily practical use. The main reasons are: the very dynamic environment in which manufacturing is planned and the very difficult integration of three levels of management: the strategic level: what to do, the tactical level: how and where to do it and the operational level where decisions are converted into action. Those are two of the multiple reasons why we postponed the investigation of such a difficult topic as routing sheets generation. We restrained ourselves to the first question of manufacturing planning: "Do I make or do I buy a particular component?".

Typically a planning manager receives from the design department the drawings of a product and its parts list and has to decide for each of those parts whether or not the company will produce them. Besides his experience about the technologies the company masters, he will consider the point-of-view of the technical direction for strategical reasons, the buying department about the availability of suppliers and the scheduling department for capacity reasons. The acquisition and storage of the required data and knowledge are not concentrated in one department. To take a decision, a meeting of several specialists is organized or a sheet of paper collects the information from one department to the other. The two systems are very costly and slow. They have another big disadvantage: they are very sensible to noise. If that week a supplier did not respect a due date and a production line stood, it will over-proportionally influence the decision.

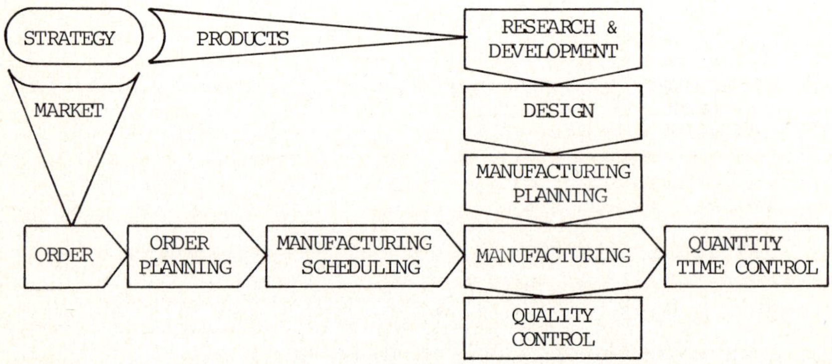

Figure 1
Product-directed and Market-directed Processes

3. Scheduling

Manufacturing scheduling has been the subject of many theses of operations research. Various mathematical models tried to solve this intricate problem. Most of them failed, at least in Europe where manufacturing is generally more customer-directed than product-directed. Once again we postponed what seemed to us more difficult like a complete job-shop scheduling system and concentrated ourselves to the solution of three questions: how to assign the right priority to a specific job, which size should a batch have and how high is the required stock level.

Today there are interesting tools to help the manager to schedule batches or to control inventories. But the only thing they do is to crunch numbers, they won't fix parameters like priorities, batch sizes or stock levels. Compared with the planning problem scheduling presents several differences. The knowledge is concentrated in one department and there is a direct access to the required data. The use of the knowledge is a typical database inferencing: short logical reasoning on a huge amount of data. With IKBS one can reinforce in those decisions speed and consistency.

4. Justification of IKBS

To resume the reasons why we want to introduce AI in manufacturing planning and scheduling, let us compare natural and artificial intelligences. Natural intelligence is perishable but artificial intelligence is permanent. Not only the expert can be sick or on holiday but just like many experts, he is not that young anymore and he will surely retire.

When natural intelligence is difficult to transfer and reproduce, artificial intelligence is easy to duplicate and document. It is a powerful training tool and the way to syndicate company's methods among different production units or plants. As we saw with the planning problem, the use of several experts to take decisions which follow a defined pattern is a very costly method and AI could replace it cheaply. AI is consistent and will be much less influenced by external noises like the last mistake of supplier X or by internal noises like expert's headaches. Obviously natural intelligence keeps a big advantage: creativity, and it will probably remains so for a long time.

THE MAKE-OR-BUY DECISION

In order to support the make-or-buy decision, we need the following outputs: a qualified advice like "make with certainty factor 80" and a hard-copy protocol telling why the advice was given. We divided the problem into two general constraints: a qualitative constraint and a quantitative constraint. Then we analysed those constraints and subdivided them again. As we are using a relatively small tool but also to keep an excellent transparency, we designed at a first level eight individual knowledge bases, each giving a qualified advice.

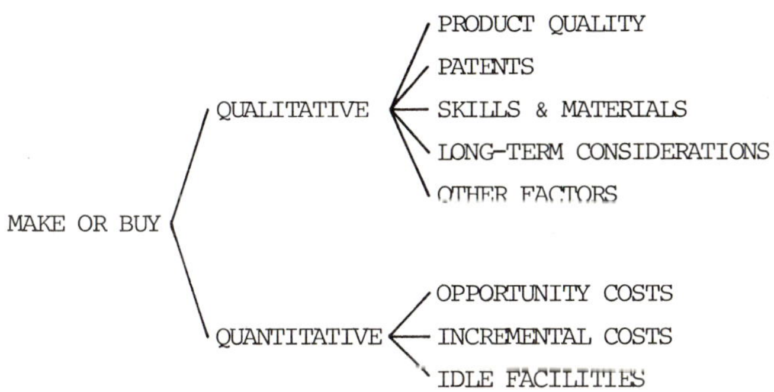

Figure 2
Hierarchical Structure of Knowledge Bases

On the medium level, we have what we call "sub-masters". Based on a very flexible overlay principle, they can control their individual knowledge bases. The weighted results of the individual knowledge bases induce the sub-master advice. The weighting coefficients are the result of an interview of the user by the system. That is the way to biase the advice according to the company changing environment.

On the top level, the weighted results of the two sub-masters induce the final advice. The weighting coefficients are like before the result of an interview. So we can now biase the advice according to the company strategy: some companies giving generally more importance to quality than to quantity parameters or vice-versa. The possibility to biase results will open the door to generic applications like a make-or-buy decision support system applicable to different companies.

Within an individual knowledge base we are using techniques like cycle control or what we call "supported data gathering". Our objective is always to mimic as much as possible the natural reasoning and to avoid a too mechanical consultation of the system. With a cyclic structure the system first gather some data, form an hypothesis and test it. As long as the user refuses the advice the system will gather more data, form new hypotheses and test them. For example knowing that the considered part is patented, the system will first recommend to buy it and not to make it. The user may refuse this advice. The system will then gather more data to define whether the potential supplier is a competitor, which could prohibit buying, or whether the part could be modified, which could similarly change its advice.

If the user is not familiar with the reasoning, he requires more support from the system. The questions are then documented to a maximum of one screen. When he becomes acquainted with the system, he can switch to a minimal support of one sentence pro question or even to no support at all. It should be noted that if we write many meta-rules to control the system and if the user asks the system why it took this or that decision, the system could explain why some meta-rule fired, which is not that meaningful for the user.

METHODOLOGY

1. Project Management

A typical project consists of three main steps: the problem assessment, the knowledge acquisition and the system integration.

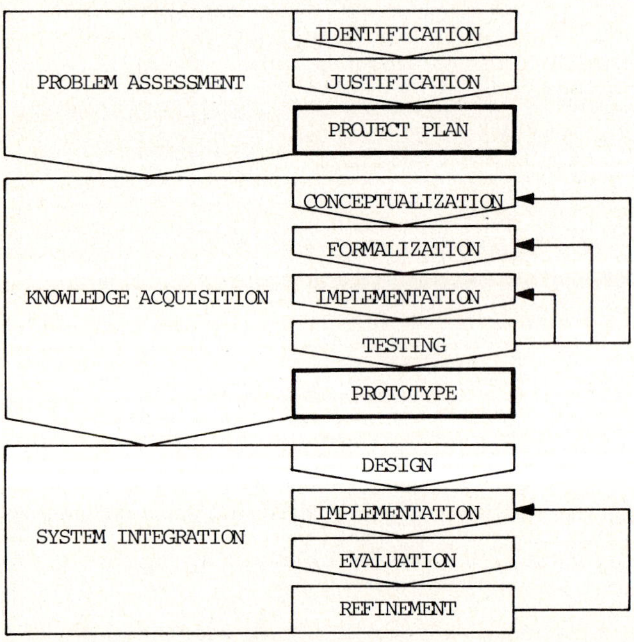

Figure 3
Project Management

During the problem assessment, we identify the problem and we have to justify the design of an IKBS to solve it. This justification covers two points: an economical point, which benefits does the knowledge system bring to the company, and a technical point, is the knowledge system feasible. The result of this assessment is a project plan defining how we will acquire the knowledge and realize a first implementation and what will it cost. If the first step lasts more than one week, we think this problem should not be considered as suitable for an investigation of knowledge engineering capabilities.

At the first stage of the knowledge acquisition, we have to find the concepts to represent the knowledge. At the second stage we design the structure to organize it, that is the so called formalization and at the third stage we formulate the rules to embody the knowledge. The expert tests then the knowledge base, which leads to reformulate some concepts or to redesign the knowledge structure or to refine the rules. At the end of this process we have a prototype. This step takes generally two to three months and the most difficult part of it is the structuration of the knowledge.

The main tasks of the design are to integrate the new system into the existing job organization and to build an appropriate user-interface. The first implementation is evaluated by the expert and the user and is then iteratively refined.

2. Knowledge Acquisition

To fill up the knowledge base we use currently two different methods. Essentially the expert interview and from time to time an induction engine. A few words on the expert. The real expert is the one who has no time to be interviewed. The expert has to be motivated and the best way we found is to show him as soon as possible a consultation, let him find the troubles and let the system becomes his "baby". The expert should not fear obsolescence, he should not be afraid to let the interviewer knows what makes him so valuable. The expert should not be influenced, the interviewer should not try to guess and tell the expert how he should proceed.

The induction engine method is still very immature. The possibilities of the system we use are so limited that we consider it only as a first investigating tool and as a cross-checking possibility. We can fill up the example-base with hundreds examples defined by up to 31 attributes. It has been useful in the manufacturing planning problem because this department keeps a protocol of every make-or-buy decision. For manufacturing scheduling we did not have such documentation. If you try then to define typical examples to induce the rules you know, not only it won't be a natural way but it will be a hard one.

3. Tools

The inference engine we use is M.1 a product of Tcknowledge sold in Europe by Framentec. The knowledge engineer writes the facts and rules with a standard text editor and saves them in a disk file. Starting a test he loads this file into the knowledge base. He can then debug the system, add and delete rules. The inference engine is memorizing its conclusions in the so called "cache". Starting a consultation, the user loads the file, consults the system and can at every moment ask the system to display a rule with the "list" command or to show him a conclusion with the "show" command.

This small shell based on the prolog language has many of the knowledge engineering and technical features of bigger tools. However two main improvements are required for a practical use in manufacturing planning and scheduling: hooks which would provide access to other languages and databases and upwards compatibilty to transplant the prototypes to the mainframes running the databases and main management systems of the company.

PERSPECTIVES

The progressive integration of simple IKBS produces today modest but unusual gains for resources planning and job-shop scheduling. The pay-off of those very modest systems is very short, a matter of a few months, when not of a few weeks.

But we personnally think that the main interest for a company is to learn, at relatively low-costs, the use of a new tool. This company will obviously reach a certain level of frustration due to the limitations of the available software and the not yet adequate hardware architecture. But then it will be able to define its own specifications for efficient and effective systems. This is very similar to what happened when we introduced in the factories computers to manage routing sheets, to control inventories or to plan capacities.

Within the world of knowledge engineering the time is come for the users, the tools suppliers and the computer scientists to sit together. More and more users should confront this new technique with the hard reality and come back to the suppliers and the scientists to complain about what is still missing. Only this iterative interaction will enhance the capability of knowledge engineering to solve real and practical problems and will prevent it to go back, a second time, to the academic museums.

We are convinced that the increased efficiency of knowledge engineering will allow us to integrate our first prototypes of manufacturing planning and scheduling in the existing m-nagement systems. Reinforced by this first success we would then be able to tackle more demanding problems like routing sheets generation and complete job-shop scheduling, two decisive steps towards the factory of the future.

REFERENCES

1. Hayes-Roth F., Waterman D.A., Lenat D.B.:
   Building Expert Systems
   Addison-Wesley, Reading/Massachussets, 1983.

2. N.N.:
   Conference on Knowledge Engineering and R & D
   Manchester Business School, Manchester, 1984.

3. Rembold U., Dillmann R.:
   Methods and Tools for Computer Integrated Manufacturing
   Springer, Berlin, 1984.

LIST OF AUTHORS

INDEX OF SUBJECTS

This is only a concise index, based on the paper titles and overall scope.